International Conference on Computer Graphics, Visualization, Computer Vision and Image Processing 2020; Big Data Analytics, Data Mining and Computational Intelligence 2020; and Theory and Practice in Modern Computing 2020

Held at MCCSIS 2020 (Held online due to COVID-19)

Lisbon, Portugal
21 - 25 July 2020

ISBN: 978-1-7138-2273-8

Printed from e-media with permission by:

Curran Associates, Inc.
57 Morehouse Lane
Red Hook, NY 12571

Some format issues inherent in the e-media version may also appear in this print version.

Printed with permission by Curran Associates, Inc. (2021)

For permission requests, please contact International Association for Development of the Information Society (IADIS) at the address below.

International Association for Development of the Information Society (IADIS)
Rua Sao Sebastiao Da Pedreira
No. 100, 30, 1050-209
Lisbon, Portugal

Phone: 351 21 3151373
Fax: 351 21 3151244

secretariat@iadis.org

Additional copies of this publication are available from:

Curran Associates, Inc.
57 Morehouse Lane
Red Hook, NY 12571 USA
Phone: 845-758-0400
Fax: 845-758-2633
Email: curran@proceedings.com
Web: www.proceedings.com

TABLE OF CONTENTS

DATA-DRIVEN APPROACH FOR GENERATING COLORMAPS OF SCIENTIFIC SIMULATION DATA

Yi Cao[1, 2], Xiaohua Wang[2], Huawei Wang[1, 2], Zhiwei Ai[1, 2] and Fang Xia[1, 2]
[1]*High Performance Computing Center, Institute of Applied Physics and Computational Mathematics, Beijing, China*
[2]*CAEP Software Center for High Performance Numerical Simulation, Beijing, China*

ABSTRACT

The colormap plays important roles in the exploration, analysis, and discovery of scientific data. Datasets generated by real-world simulation applications are becoming increasingly more complex: the distribution of the variable values within the data is often extremely uneven and accompanied by high levels of data noise. The heterogeneity of these data characteristics presents rich information about physical laws as well as technical challenges for colormap of visualization. Most default colormaps are defined by linearly interpolating dataset values and cannot be adapted to convey the physical meaning behind complicated data. In this paper, we introduce a data-driven approach for generating colormaps of scientific simulation data, that can overcome the visualization problems using noise-reduction-based parameter tuning of color control points and a wave-like colormap enhancement in brightness. Several real-world simulation data are used to verify the effectiveness of our proposed method, which means that our method could help domain scientists understand complicated data more clearly and quickly.

KEYWORDS

Colormaps, Color Perception, Information Theory, Scientific Visualization

1. INTRODUCTION

Color is a very important visual channel in visualization; Scientists use it to describe quantified patterns, perform category labeling, or make highlights. A colormap is a mapping from data values to colors that generates visual structures for the data (zhou, 2015). Colormaps play important roles in the exploration, analysis, and discovery of scientific data. A colormap is a great way to provide visual continuity, communicate information about data, give feedback in response to user actions, and help people visualize data. The most common plot rendering functions in data visualization rely on colormaps. For example, the ever-popular pseudocolor plot (VisIt, 2020) maps the values of a scalar variable to colors and uses these colors to paint values onto the variable's computational mesh.

However, it is difficult to choose a good colormap that intuitively represents a scientific dataset. The most commonly used color mapping model is defined by linearly interpolating data values within the range of the dataset (Thompson, 2013). Many visualization tools, such as VisIt (VisIt, 2020) and ParaView (Paraview, 2020), use the linear colormaps model by default. However, this model cannot be adapted to convey the physical meaning behind complicated data. Following the recent rapid growth of supercomputer performance, many real-world problems can now be solved using numerical simulation. Datasets generated by real-world simulation applications such as climate change, electromagnetic (EM) environments, and fusion energy, are becoming increasingly more complex: the variable values within the data are often extremely unevenly distributed and include high levels of data noise. Driven by need for high-fidelity in-situ visualization on supercomputers, it is necessary to study methods for the automatic generation of colormaps that can adapt to the complex scientific data.

To help domain scientists understand complicated data more clearly and quickly, this paper introduces a data-driven approach for generating colormaps of scientific simulation data. The main contributions of this paper comprise the following:

- An automatic parameter tuning method for colormap to generate the color control points suitable for the mapping from data values to colors that improves the adaptability to complicated scientific data.

- A wave-like enhancement method in brightness that could produce colormaps matching color perception to reveal more discernable details of complex scientific data in color space.

Experimental tests were performed using real-world applications such as EM environments and shock-wave propagation. It was shown that the colormap generation method presented in this paper can reveal many more details about the physical information than the default colormaps for complex scientific datasets. Moreover, our method can greatly simplify the complexity in parameter adjustment of colormaps. Scientists only need to input a few quantitative parameters as input to automatically obtain the data visualization results with more discernable details, which would greatly improve the efficiency of large data analysis for scientists.

2. RELATED WORK

Scientists often choose some classic colormaps such as the rainbow for exploring data. However, a rainbow colormap is usually not the best option for data representation. Borland list three aspects of how a rainbow colormap can be misleading (Borland, 2007), for instance, how it has no perceptual order and hides details. Visualization researchers have become aware of the choice of colormaps, and the visualization community has made significant improvements in how to carefully choose appropriate colormaps according to the data and tasks (Zhou, 2015). Brewer proposed a set of perceptual discrete colormaps that can be grouped into four categories: qualitative, binary, sequential, or diverging (Brewer, 1999). The colormaps were carefully designed in a perceptual color space, namely the HVC (Hue, Value, and Chroma) color space. To avoid the negative impact of the improper selection of colormaps, scientists use tools such as ColorMoves (Samsel, 2018) and ColorMeasures (Bujack, 2018) to interactively construct colormaps based on certain color scheme. By combining methods such as linear mapping and exponential mapping, the mapping relationship between data and color is established manually. The GenColormap tool (GenColormap, 2020) integrates a variety of perceptually driven colormaps, including those proposed by Wijffelaars (Wijffelaars, 2008), Green (Green, 2011), and Moreland (Moreland, 2009). It allows the custom adjustment of predefined colormaps.

There are many rules to guide users and there exist optimization methods to improve colormaps for data. Currently, several techniques (Bertini, 2007), (Eisemann, 2011), (Thompson, 2013) have been proposed to utilize automated methods that generate or optimize colormaps based on underlying data in scientific visualization. Eisemann et al. introduced a simple interpolation scheme for colormap design that emphasizes outliers on two-dimensional (2D) data visualizations (Eisemann, 2011). Histogram equalization has been proposed to better adapt colormaps to data. Thompson et al. propose a sampling-based method to generate colormaps that highlight important features (Thompson, 2013). Random sampling is used to determine the distribution of values observed in large-scale data while also avoiding possibly expensive pre-processing stages. Smart et al. (Smart, 2020] presented an approach for automatically generating designer-quality color ramps only using a single seed color. Schloss et al. investigated how inferred color-quantity mappings for colormap data visualizations were influenced by the background color (Schloss, 2019).

These methods typically require the user to have prior knowledge required to analyze the data, which can be a problem for scientists to explore the large-scale data with unknown laws. Therefore, it is desirable to provide an automatic approach to generate the appropriate colormap for given scientific data. Most previous work has been limited to the automatic visualization of complex data combined with high levels of noise.

3. DATA-DRIVEN APPROACH FOR GENERATING COLORMAPS

Consider a dataset as an expression about a distribution $\mathcal{D}$ of values. We reformulate the colormap generation of a dataset as an optimization problem based on data distribution $\mathcal{D}$. One of our contributions is an automatic colormap generation method that can be used to solve problem of adaptability to complicated scientific simulation data, which has typical characteristics such as non-uniform distributions of variable values and noise. The approach taken in this paper uses parameter tuning in distribution $\mathcal{D}$ to achieve it. The three fundamental tasks of the framework introduced in this paper are shown in Figure 1: data denoising, data normalization, and perceptual-driven color mapping. Among them, denoising and normalization are both performed consistently in the statistical space of three-dimensional data.

To generate a colormap, we first calculate the histogram of the relative frequencies of the values in the three-dimensional scientific dataset during a pre-processing stage. When the number of bins and Gaussian components for computation of a probability density function (PDF) is selected, and the influence factor of GMM for denoising is determined, our framework can automatically generate colormaps matching the target scientific data. Scientists only need to give the above quantitative parameters as input to obtain detail-enhanced images in this work. By automatically reducing noise intervals on the histogram and generating color control points matching the scientific data, the goal of automatically generating suitable colormaps can be achieved.

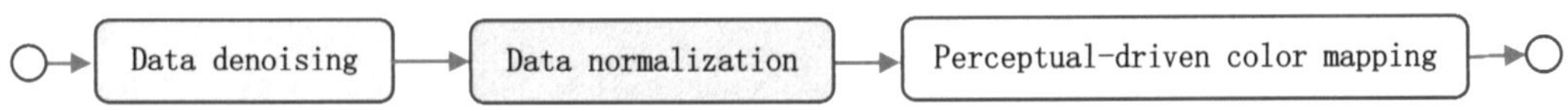

Figure 1. Framework overview

3.1 Normalization of Data Distribution

Scientific simulation data generated by real-world applications are usually characterized by a variable with data that tend to cluster around a particular value rather than being spread evenly across a range of values. It is necessary to adopt a transformation based on data normalization to guide the generation of a suitable colormap to help reveal the interesting structure in the data. The purpose of data normalization is to generate the color control points suitable for the mapping from data values to colors. Because we analyze and process data in the statistical space of three-dimensional data, we then use the histogram equalization method to normalize the data. Histogram equalization is a common method to enhance contrast in the field of digital image processing. The main idea is to change the gray histogram of an image from a relatively concentrated interval to an approximately uniform distribution over all gray values. This idea is extended to the generation of color control points of colormaps in our work. In this way, more space in the histogram will be reserved and used for frequently occurring values, so the entire range of possible values is utilized. Given a histogram distributed over the range of variable values in the dataset, we can then obtain the desired color control points of colormap.

3.2 Noise Reduction based on Data Distribution

Unlike quantized medical data with uniformly distributed values, there is a lot of noise information in the data of real-world applications. When the histogram equalization process is performed directly on these data, the noise will occupy meaningful parameter value ranges, which will reduce the effectiveness of the subsequent mapping of recognizable colors to the range of values. Therefore, before using the histogram equalization method to automatically generate the colormap, it is necessary to evaluate and reduce the noise intervals so that more recognizable colors could be distributed over the meaningful range of values. In scientific dataset, the noise intervals that do not have an actual physical meaning are often concentrated in a small range, and the relative frequencies of the noise values in this range are usually large. This phenomenon usually appears as a high spike-shaped distribution area on the histogram of three-dimensional data. We implement noise reduction scheme using two different ways including information theory and a Gaussian mixture model (GMM).

3.2.1 Entropy-Based Approach

Shannon's entropy is a measure of information richness. Applying entropy to the histogram statistics of the data, we can obtain the richness of the information in each histogram interval. From the perspective of information, a noise data interval often has the characteristics of high-frequency values and low information richness. In other words, the entropy value of the noise area is generally very low. In this paper, by computing the entropy of each histogram interval, the noise areas in the distribution can be identified and removed so that the noise can be eliminated in the color mapping process. The general entropy-based noise reduction is as follows:

1. Calculate the entropy of each histogram interval: $H(\mathrm{x}) = -\sum_{i=0}^{n} p(x_i) \log p(x_i)$.

2. Using the probability density of interval P_k, calculate the ratio of information quantity of each histogram interval: $R_k = H_k/P_k$. The interval with the smallest R_k becomes the interval with the minimum benefits.

3. If the interval with the minimum benefits also has the maximum probability density, the interval is considered to be a noise interval that interferes with the mapping results.

4. Reset the probability density P_k of the noise interval to 0, and then recalculate the histogram and cumulative distribution function S_k. The histogram equalization process is performed using the new histogram.

3.2.2 GMM-Based Approach

The GMM is a probabilistic model to describe the distribution of data with clusters in a parameter space, where each cluster is assumed to follow a Gaussian distribution. It can be used to automatically extract meaningful features in a distribution of values. When a limited number of Gaussian components are given, it is usually difficult to fit the high-frequency spike distributions with a narrow range of values. However, this is also representing a noise reduction result in distribution. In this paper, by computing the one-dimensional GMM of three-dimensional data, the noise intervals in the histogram can be removed. A GMM clustering based on the greedy EM algorithm is used to obtain a GMM distribution G (x) that fits the distribution of values in the dataset. In practice, we use the GMM result as an impact factor and superimpose it onto the histogram of the original data. The general steps of the latter approach are as follows:

1. Let the computational result of GMM be $F_i = G(i)^\alpha$, $i = 0,1,\dots,L-1$, where α is the impact factor, and its value range is [0,1].

2. During the histogram equalization, the F_i is added to the histogram interval to obtain a new histogram and probability density $P_k = \frac{n_k \times F_k}{\sum_{i=0}^{L-1} n_i \times F_i}$, $k = 0,1,\dots,L-1$.

3. The histogram equalization process is performed using the new histogram.

3.3 Perceptual-Driven Color Mapping

Using the noise-reduction based histogram equalization, we can obtain the color control points suitable for the mapping from data values to colors. The rest of the task is to generate color parameters for these control points. To obtain the visualization requirements of the complex scientific data, it is necessary to generate perception-based colormaps. The change of the brightness of a color produces a stronger discrimination result in color perception. Therefore, a color mapping with wave-like changes in brightness will usually yield data visualization results with more identifiable details. Given a pre-defined color scheme, while maintaining the hue and saturation of the color, we implement a wave-like brightness enhancement on the intervals with sparse values, and a colormap that is consistent with color perception can be obtained.

Given the number of intervals N, the algorithm extracts N+1 control points from the original colormap and uses them as the control points of the new wave-like colormap. The method of increasing or decreasing the brightness of the control point color in adjacent intervals can enhance the color contrast in each segment, thereby improving the overall recognizability of the colormaps. In practice, we first construct a Brewer-like colormap similar to the rainbow scheme as input by using the GenColormap tool (GenColormap, 2020), a wave-like new colormap with five intervals can then be generated. The changes in the discriminative powers (Eisemann, 2011) of the colormap are shown in Figure 2-3. Obviously, the discriminative powers of the new colormap have been substantially improved.

Figure 2. Perceptual-driven colormap enhencenment

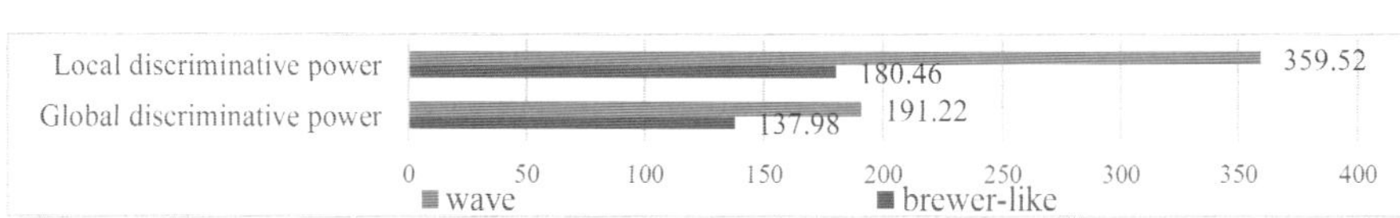

Figure 3. Discriminative power comparison of two colormaps

4. RESULTS AND DISCUSSION

The ultimate goal of this work is to help domain scientists understand complex data more clearly and quickly. In this section, we discuss the results of the application of our data-driven approach for generating colormaps in several real-world scientific simulation fields. The real-world simulation datasets used in this work were generated from EM environment and shock-wave propagation applications with float precision, as shown in Table 1. For the experiment, a Brewer-like colormap with five colors is used to replace the default rainbow as the default input. The colormap was applied to the automated color mapping framework introduced in this paper to obtain the final tuning colormap. The histograms for all representations used 256 bins and the GMM-based denoising used 4 Gaussian components by default. Scientists only need to give the above quantitative parameters as input to automatically obtain the detail-enhanced visualization images in this work. The experiment was performed on an Inspur server node with a 24-core Intel Xeon E5-2680v4 2.40 GHz.

Table 1. Real-world simulation data used in the experiments

Application	Shock-wave propagation	Radiation shielding of Unmanned Aerial Vehicle (UAV)	Radiation shielding of vehicles
Grid cell size	3.92 million	98.24 million	127.28 million

4.1 EM Environment

The EM environment refers to the overlapping of multiple EM signals that are distributed in the airspace and have some influence on both equipment and personnel. Currently, computational EM applications based on the JASMIN framework [Mo, 2010] generate data with complex characteristics, such as non-uniform distribution and noise. As a result, EM domain scientists need intuitive colormap data visualization to support the efficient analysis of these complex datasets.

4.1.1 Unmanned Aerial Vehicle Application

Figure 4 compares the results of an unmanned aerial vehicle (UAV) example of using the default rainbow colormap (Figure 4a), a perceptual-based Brewer-like colormap (Figure 4b), and a Brewer-like colormap based on logarithmic stretching and histogram equalization (Figure 4c). The top row of the figure uses the top view of the physical field based on volume rendering. The bottom row of the figure uses a side view of the cross section of the physical field. A comparison of the results shows that no matter whether the color perception-based colormap or histogram equalization is used, more abundant physical field information is obtained than when the default colormap is used.

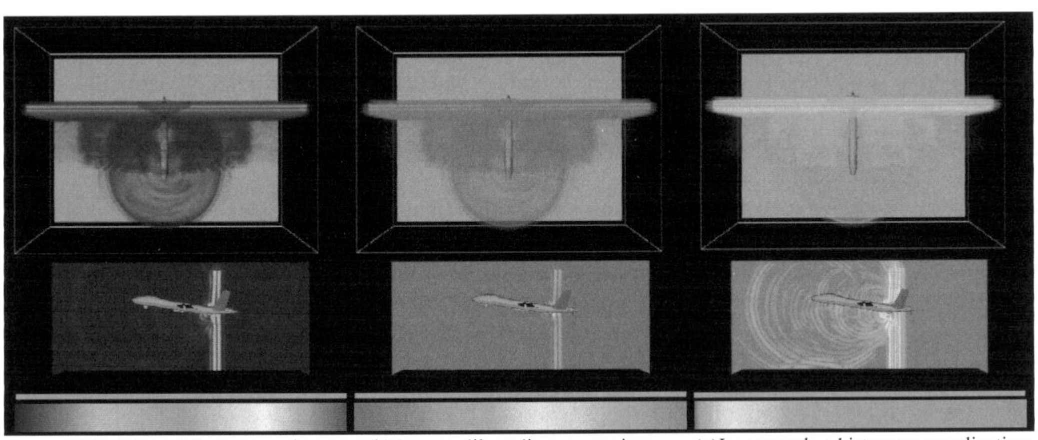

(a) Rainbow + linear mapping (b) Brewer-like + linear mapping (c)Log stretch + histogram equalization

Figure 4. Comparison of the results of linear mapping and histogram equalization

Figure 5 uses the perceptual-based Brewer-like colormap and specifically compares the results of entropy-based denoising (Figure 5a), GMM-based denoising (Figure 5b), and perception-driven color mapping enhancement (Figure 5c). It can be seen from the figure that regardless of whether entropy-based noise reduction or GMM-based noise reduction is used, a more detailed change in the physical quantities is obtained than when histogram equalization is used alone. The result of the colormap enhancement further visually highlights the subtle changes in the value range, and the enhancement results are remarkable.

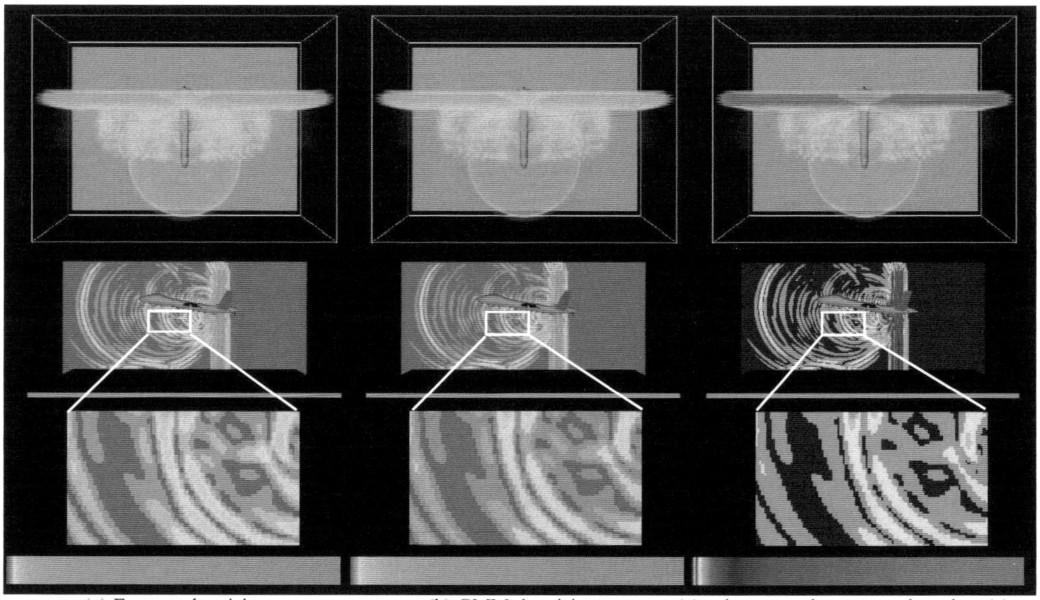

(a) Entropy denoising (b) GMM denoising (c) colormap enhancement based on (a)

Figure 5. Comparison of denoising results obtained using entropy and GMM

4.1.2 Vehicle Application

Figure 6 compares the results for a vehicle application of using the default rainbow colormap (Figure 6a), the perceptual-based Brewer-like colormap and histogram equalization (Figure 6b), and the result of entropy-based denoising and colormap enhancement (Figure 6c). The top row of the figure uses the side view of the physical field based on volume rendering. The bottom row of the figure uses a top view of the cross section of the physical field. It can be seen that the color perception-based colormap reveals more details of the physical field information than the default colormap. The result of the colormap enhancement further visually highlights the subtle changes in the value range, and the enhancement results are remarkable. As Figure 6c shows, the colormap enhancement method presented in this paper highlights and emphasizes the subtle transition changes in the variable values.

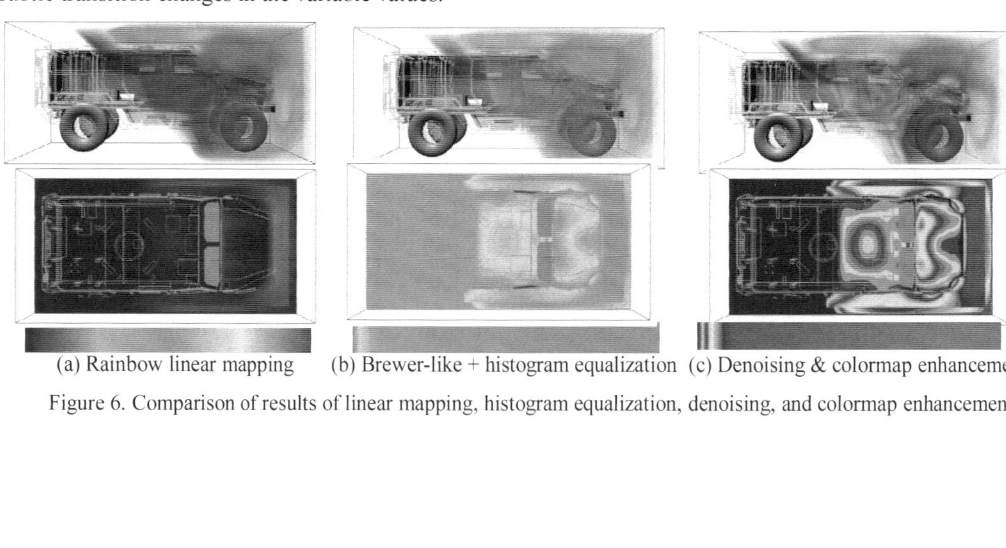

(a) Rainbow linear mapping (b) Brewer-like + histogram equalization (c) Denoising & colormap enhancement

Figure 6. Comparison of results of linear mapping, histogram equalization, denoising, and colormap enhancement

4.2 Shock-Wave Propagation

Shock waves are of fundamental importance in nearly all dynamic material systems, from cosmological phenomena such as interstellar dust cloud transport processes, star and galaxy formation, and the evolution of planets and other celestial bodies to everyday life experiences. Whenever material transport velocities exceed their respective acoustic wave propagation velocities, shock waves are the dominant energy dissipation process.

Increasing computer power in combination with the continuous development of numerical methods as well as input and verification data from experiments has led to elaborate numerical methods for the simulation of shock wave phenomena. Increasingly more complex real systems can be simulated with high accuracy. Currently, the simulation of shock waves based on the JASMIN framework [Mo, 2010] generate data with complex characteristics.

Figure 7 compares the results using the default rainbow colormap (Figure 7a), a perceptual-based Brewer-like colormap (Figure 7b), and a Brewer-like colormap based on logarithmic stretching and histogram equalization (Figure 7c). The cross-sectional side view of the physical field is used in the figure. A comparison of the result shows that no matter whether the color perception-based colormap or histogram equalization is used, more abundant physical field information is obtained than when the default colormap result is used.

Figure 8 uses the perceptual-based Brewer-like colormap and specifically compares the results of entropy-based denoising (Figure 8a), GMM-based denoising (Figure 8b), and perception-driven color mapping enhancement based on entropy-denoising (Figure 8c). It can be seen from the figure that regardless of whether entropy-based noise reduction or GMM-based noise reduction is used, the noise intervals found in the original dataset are successfully removed. These figures show that our approach can effectively filter out the noise intervals so that more discernible colors are distributed in the physically meaningful areas of the distribution. The result of the colormap enhancement further visually highlights the subtle changes in the value range, and the enhancement results are particularly remarkable.

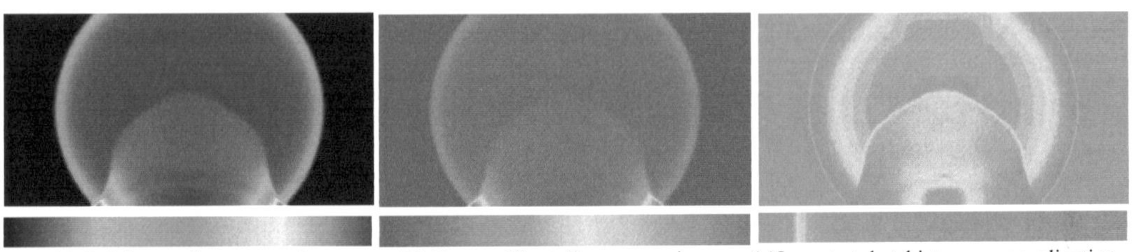

(a) Rainbow + linear mapping (b) Brewer-like + linear mapping (c)Log stretch + histogram equalization

Figure 7. Comparison of results of linear mapping, histogram equalization, and denoising

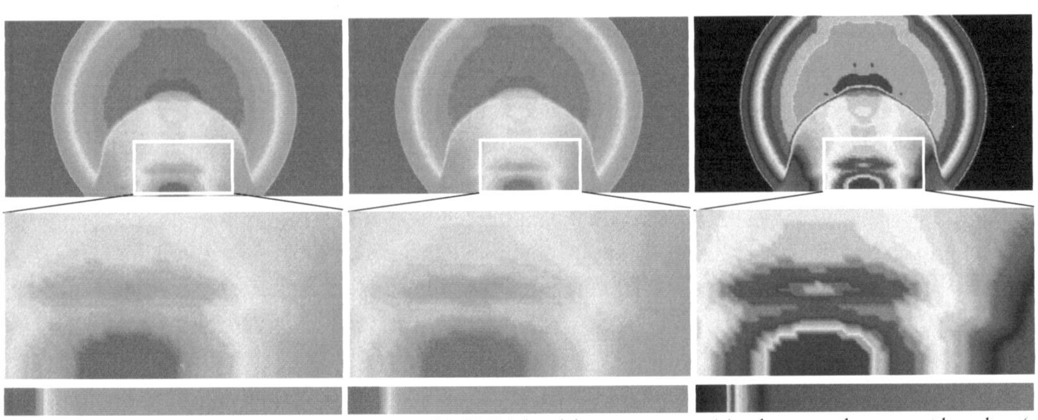

(a) Entropy denoising (b) GMM denoising (c) colormap enhancement based on (a)

Figure 8. Comparison of denoising results obtained using entropy and GMM

5. CONCLUSIONS

In this paper, we proposed a data-driven approach for generating colormaps of scientific simulation data. This approach can overcome visualization problems that occur when the distribution of the variable values within the data are extremely uneven and accompanied by high levels of data noise. An automatic colormap generation method was presented to solve the problem of adapting colormaps to the complex scientific simulation data. A perceptually driven parameter tuning method for colormaps was proposed to enable correct color perception for scientists that enhances the discernibility of complicated data in color space. The automatic colormap generation method was applied in several real-world simulation applications, e.g., EM environments and shock-wave propagation. Compared with the traditional rainbow colormap with a linear color mapping, the visualization images obtained by our method can be adapted to convey a more detailed physical meaning behind complex scientific data. The experimental test shows the effectiveness of our proposed method, and the results indicate that our method could help domain scientists understand complex data more clearly and quickly.

ACKNOWLEDGEMENT

This work was supported by the National Key R&D Program of China under grant NO.2017YFB0202203.

REFERENCES

Bertini, E. et al, 2007. See what you know: Analyzing data distribution to improve density map visualization. *Proceedings of the 9th Joint Eurographics / IEEE VGTC Conference on Visualization, ser. EUROVIS'07.* Aire-la-Ville, Switzerland, Switzerland: Eurographics Association, pp. 163–170

Borland, D. et al,2007. Taylor M R. Rainbow Color Map (Still) Considered Harmful. I*EEE Computer Graphics and Applications*, 27(2), pp. 14-17.

Brewer, C. A. et al, 1999. Color use guidelines for data representation. *Proceedings of the Section on Statistical Graphics,* American Statistics Association,pp. 55–60.

Eisemann, M. et al, 2011. Data Driven Color Mapping. *EuroVA 2011: International Workshop on Visual Analytics*, The Eurographics Association.

GenColormap, 2020. https://marlam.de/gencolormap/

Green, D. A., 2011. A colour scheme for the display of astronomical intensity images. *Bulletin of the Astronomical Society of India*, 39(2):289-295.

Mo, Z. Y., et al, 2010. JASMIN: a parallel software infrastructure for scientific computing, Front. Comput. Sci. China, 4(4): 480-488.

Moreland, K., 2009. Diverging Color Maps for Scientific Visualization. *Advances in Visual Computing, 5th International Symposium, ISVC 2009*, Las Vegas, NV, USA, November 30 - December 2.

Nee. et al, 2004. More than meets the eye. *Nature*. 429. 804-5. 10.1038/429804a.

Paraview, 2020. https://www.paraview.org/

Samsel, F. et al, 2018. ColorMoves: Real-time Interactive Colormap Construction for Scientific Visualization. *IEEE Computer Graphics and Applications*, 38(1):20-29.

Schloss, K. B. et al, 2019. Mapping Color to Meaning in Colormap Data Visualizations. *IEEE Transactions on Visualization and Computer Graphics*, vol. 25, no. 1, pp. 810-819.

Smart, S. et al, 2020. Color Crafting: Automating the Construction of Designer Quality Color Ramps. *IEEE Transactions on Visualization and Computer Graphics,* 26.1: 1215–1225.

Thompson, D. et al, 2013. A provably-robust sampling method for generating colormaps of large data. *IEEE Symposium on Large-Scale Data Analysis and Visualization (LDAV)*, pp. 77–84

VisIt, 2020. https://wci.llnl.gov/simulation/computer-codes/visit

Wijffelaars, M. et al, 2008. Generating Color Palettes using Intuitive Parameters. *Computer Graphics Forum*, 27(3): 743-750.

Zhou, L. et al, 2016. A Survey of Colormaps in Visualization. *IEEE Transactions on Visualization and Computer Graphics*, vol. 22, pp. 2051–2069. 2.

A 3D-SHOCKWAVE VOLUME RENDERING ALGORITHM BASED ON FEATURE BOUNDARY DETECTION

Huawei Wang[1, 2], Liu He[1], Zhiwei Ai[1, 2] and Yi Cao[1, 2]
[1] *Laboratory of Computational Physics, Institute of Applied Physics and Computational Mathematics, Beijing 100088, China*
[2] *CAEP Software Center for High Performance Numerical Simulation, Beijing 100088, China*

ABSTRACT

The mechanism of shockwave propagation in complex environments plays an important role in the damage and protection assessment. At present, domain experts are realizing shockwave propagation numerical simulations with high scientific confidence on thousands of processing cores, and thus large-scale three-dimensional (3D) data fields containing fine physical features are output. It is desired to effectively reveal complex spatial structures of shockwaves in the data fields so as to facilitate domain experts to make in-depth observation and analysis. In this paper, a volume rendering algorithm based on feature boundary detection is proposed to visualize 3D shockwave data fields. In the algorithm, a two-dimensional (2D) boundary detection technique is generalized to the 3D case and further used to extract feature data containing the wavefronts, and then, the feature data are resampled and composited in the ray-casting manner. The algorithm has been preliminarily applied to 3D shock fields, and the results show that the algorithm can effectively analyze the shockwave features and clearly show the 3D spatial structures of the wavefronts.

KEYWORDS

Shockwave, Volume Rendering, Boundary Detection, Wavefront, Visualization

1. INTRODUCTION

Relevant researches show that the destructive effect of an explosion is mainly caused by shock wave. As one of the main killing factors, shock wave can kill or destroy the target at a long distance. The mechanism of shockwave propagation in complex environments plays an important role in the damage and protection assessment. With the development of high performance computing, domain experts are using thousands of processing cores to realize high-confidence numerical simulations for the shockwave propagation mechanism. By means of numerical simulation, they carefully explore the propagation, diffraction and reflection laws of the shock wave under diverse conditions, and as a result large-scale 3D shockwave data fields with fine features are output. It is desired to effectively show complex shockwave features in these 3D data fields so that domain experts can perform in-depth observation and analysis.

To visualize 3D shockwave data fields, we can use direct volume rendering so as to see their internal structures. The direct volume rendering method transforms the discrete data in the 3D space directly into a 2D image without generating intermediate geometric primitives. Compared with the surface rendering method, the direct volume rendering method has stronger expressiveness of the data, so it has been widely used in the field of scientific visualization. Based on direct volume rendering, the visualization results of 3D shockwave data fields may provide domain experts with intuitive and high-quality references for analysis.

By assigning optical attributes to the sampling points of the volume data with a transfer function, the volume rendering method relies on translucent fusion to simulate the real observation effect of the material structure. It can increase/decrease the opacity of a matter via the transfer function so as to highlight/weaken its internal structure; however, it is usually difficult to reveal complex structural features via the transfer function in volume rendering. In order to get good rendering effect, one has to take much time and effort to design a complex transfer function, which is often high-dimensional and thus has an enormous parameter space.

In the propagation process of shock wave, the physical properties such as pressure and density have numerical mutations on and behind the wave front, thus the shockwave visualization belongs to a kind of drawing problem of 3D boundary surfaces with complex structures. However, because the data field across/along the wave front has a trans-scale change, it is difficult to describe the wave front by one or more scalars, e.g. the pressure and the magnitude of its gradient. Therefore, traditional volume rendering methods for simple material boundary are difficult to be applied to the rendering of shock wave.

In this paper, boundary detection is introduced to extract feature data instead of transfer function in volume rendering, so a volume rendering algorithm based on feature boundary detection is proposed to effectively render wavefront structures in shockwave data fields. In the algorithm, we use the boundary detection method to analyze the data fields and extract the data layer containing the wave fronts. Taking the 2D slices of the 3D data fields as the processing granularity, we transform the feature detection problem into the 2D case and thus realize the generalization of 2D boundary detection to 3D. Coupling boundary detection with volume rendering, we can then render a clear visual effect of shock wave fronts.

2. RELATED WORK

In order to effectively show internal features in data fields, a variety of volume rendering algorithms are proposed, including ray casting (Palmer et al., 1997; Ma, 1999), cell projection (Ma and Crockett, 1997), shear warp (Sano et al., 1997) and splatting (Li et al., 1997). Because the main calculation of volume rendering is focused on two stages: sampling and compositing, the typical parallel implementation mode includes the two steps of data parallel and image parallel, and the I/O strategy, data organization and load balance are the important factors affecting the parallel performance. In the distributed-parallel visualization software VisIt (Childs et al., 2010), Childs et al. (2005) proposed a contract-based visualization pipeline, which can perform some optimization strategies according to the rendering parameters, such as I/O pre-filtering and load balance, thus the execution efficiency of the pipeline is improved. They further proposed another load balancing optimization named by the hybrid parallel mode (Childs et al., 2006). Later, Moloney et al. (2007) proposed a dynamic load balancing strategy, which can estimate the rendering cost per pixel and distribute the computing tasks balancedly. Although the sort-last mode is widely used in parallel volume rendering, Moloney et al. (2011) found that several parallel volume rendering algorithms can have better performance in the sort-first mode. On large-scale parallel computers, Howison et al. (2012) proposed a MPI+OpenMP hybrid parallel volume rendering algorithm, which makes full use of the shared memory on multi-core nodes to reduce memory consumption and data traffic and thus scales successfully to 216000 processing cores.

In order to enhance the display effect of volume rendering, one of the most effective ways is to highlight the structural details in the volume data, such as boundaries, contours and so on. There have been some methods to enhance the effect of boundary display, for example, Lum and Ma (2004) proposed lighting transfer functions using gradient aligned sampling to highlight the boundary interfaces between substances. Tenginakai et al. (2001) proposed a statistical method to locate the salient iso-surfaces at material boundaries based on central moments of data. Roettger et al. (2005) proposed to classify material boundaries by grouping the spatial connected regions in the two-dimensional histogram. Huang et al. (2003) extended the transfer function to 3D by adding spatial information and then used a region growing algorithm based on cost function to accurately reveal material boundaries. Wang et al. (2010) used the Gaussian mixture model and the elliptical transfer function in the 2D feature space so as to improve the accuracy of the boundary interface and the design efficiency of the transfer function. Caban and Rheingans (2008) proposed texture-based transfer functions for direct volume rendering in order to effectively distinguish some structures and features with the same intensity and gradient values. Tzeng et al. (2005) proposed a volume classification approach coupling machine learning and painting metaphor, which enables the user to better extract materials of interest in a much higher dimensional space.

Edge detection is a basic problem in image processing and computer vision. The purpose of edge detection is to identify the points with obvious brightness changes in digital images. The classical edge detection algorithms include first-derivative detectors (such as Roberts detector, Sobel detector and Prewitt detector), second-derivative detectors (e.g. Laplacian detector) and nonlinear detectors (e.g. Kirsch detector). Generally speaking, with the increase of the sensitivity to edge, the sensitivity to noise increases at the same time for an edge detector; however, if removing the noise by image smoothing, the edge detector will have bigger uncertainty in edge location. Canny (1986) analyzed the edge quality for the existing detectors and then proposed Canny detector, which uses the optimal edge detection factors to suppress the noise and produce relatively complete edges. Later, some scholars extended and improved Canny detector from different aspects, including (Bergholm, 1987) and (Rothwell et al., 1995). Jin (2011) also proposed an improved Canny algorithm based on median filtering, which has a higher signal-to-noise ratio and can extract the edges more accurately. Recently, Yagüe-Fabra et al. (2013) proposed an edge detection method based on a 3D Canny algorithm for extracting the surfaces of industrial parts with homogeneous materials.

3. FEATURE DETECTION OF SHOCK WAVEFRONT

For a 3D shockwave data field, we first take its 2D slices as the basic processing granularity. Here, the input data field is represented as a multi-block rectilinear mesh. Slicing the data field perpendicular to the three axes, we obtain a series of 2D rectilinear meshes, which can be regarded as images in a sense. Figure 1 (Left) shows a slice of the shockwave pressure field. We then use the Canny algorithm to detect the boundaries of wave fronts on these slices.

In detail, the detection steps of the Canny algorithm are as follows:

1) Firstly, as a preprocessing step, smooth the image by a Gaussian filter to remove the noise. In this paper, the 5×5 Gaussian filter core is used.

2) Calculate the gradients of the image intensity. In order to detect the edges in different directions, the Canny algorithm uses two directional filters to detect horizontal and vertical edges in the smoothed image.

3) In order to make the detection results cleaner, use non-maximum suppression to eliminate false edges and re-process the noise. Non-maximum suppression is to suppress the elements that are not the maximum, and it is also a form of local maximum search.

4) In order to eliminate the remaining false edges, filter out the edges with small gradient values while retaining the edges with high gradient values, which can be achieved by using double thresholds: high threshold and low threshold. However, high and low thresholds usually need to be determined by continuous attempts.

After the above four steps, strong edge pixels will be retained in the final result. However, it is difficult to distinguish weak edge pixels. We use the connection method of edge tracking to determine which weak edges can be added to the final result. In order to track the edge connection, we need to observe the weak edge pixels and their 8 neighborhood pixels. As long as its eight neighbors contain a strong edge pixel, the weak edge pixel can be identified as a preserved point and then connected to the final result. As a result, we complete the connection of the edge lines, which forms the final detection results.

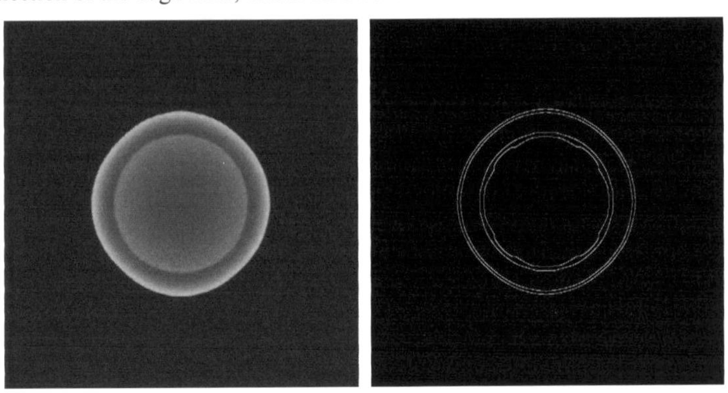

Figure 1. A shockwave data slice (Left) and the boundaries detected (Right)

Since the shockwave pressure takes a floating point value and varies violently in space, we need to carefully choose the parameters in the Canny algorithm. For example, in order to eliminate some unexpected boundaries in the wavefront detection, it is necessary to select appropriate high and low thresholds. In this paper, the low threshold is 0.016, and the high threshold is 0.058. Figure 1 (Right) shows the final detection results. The extracted boundaries have relatively good continuity, which proves the effectiveness of the Canny detection algorithm. However, there are two boundaries corresponding to each wave front, as shown in Figure 1 (Right).

To analyze the problem, we draw the variation chart of the underlying variable, as shown in Figure 2. Obviously, the variable value has a violent variation through each wave front. It is known in image processing that the image edge refers to the place where the pixel value of the image changes suddenly. In the variation chart in Figure 2, point 2 is the actual wavefront position; however, there is a mutation between point 1 and point 2 (namely front mutation), and there is also a mutation between point 2 and point 3 (namely back mutation), so two-layer boundaries appear for a wave front based on image edge detection.

One can see from Figure 2 that the front mutation is just a sudden pulse, which is much more violent than the back mutation, so the outer boundary corresponding to the front mutation is almost right on the wavefront while the inner one deviates from the wavefront obviously. We can observe the situation in Figure 3. In Figure 3, we overlap the results of Canny boundary detection with the actual data slice, and it is shown that the outer boundary almost coincides with the actual shock wavefront. Therefore, for boundary detection results for each wave front, we keep only the outer ring and ignore the inner one so as to obtain a clearer resulting boundary.

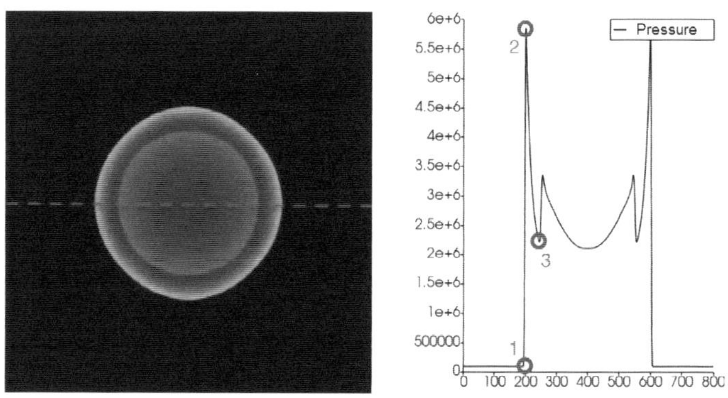

Figure 2. On a line (Left) the variation chart of the pressure is drawn (Right)

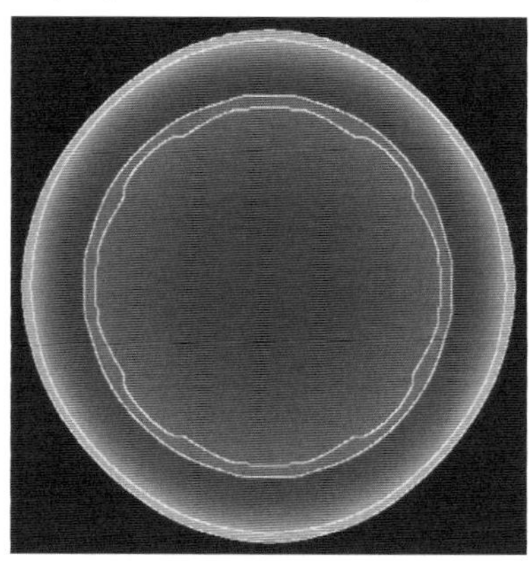

Figure 3. A shockwave slice overlapping the boundaries resulted by the Canny algorithm (amplified locally)

Suppose that the input 3D data field is based on an $m \times n \times k$ mesh. If slicing the data field perpendicular to an axis, e.g. the Z axis, we will have k data slices, i.e. k storeys of mesh cells. We then conduct the boundary detection on these slices using the Canny algorithm, where we will run into some different situations. For example, the boundary detection results may be as shown in Figure 4; at this time, we can also take the outer boundary and ignore the remaining ones for each wave front, similar to the situation in Figure 3. For more special cases that are not easy to process, for example, some slices passing through the upper/bottom part of a shockwave sphere, we will then continue to perform the boundary detection perpendicular to X axis or further Y axis, until all boundaries of wave fronts are determined in the whole data field.

Figure 4. Some detection results on data slices using the Canny algorithm

After the wavefront boundary detection is performed for the whole data field, the cells around the boundaries will be taken as the feature data, and the rest areas are marked invalid. In detail, we take a little box surrounding each boundary point into the feature data, and the half width of the box is d in three directions, e.g. $d = 3$ in our experiments. That is to say, we thicken the boundaries, or give the feature data a thickness, so that they can be resampled along any rays without cracks during the process of volume rendering. Note that the wavefront feature data need to be extracted only once, and they will stay the same when the view angle changes interactively and accordingly the volume rendering pipeline is executed again.

4. VOLUME RENDERING OF SHOCK WAVE

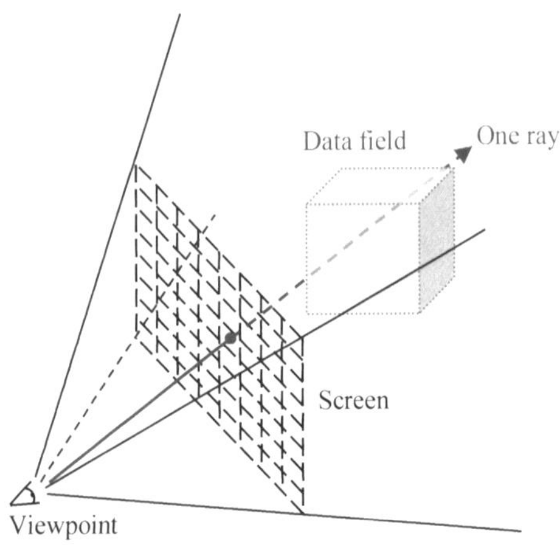

Figure 5. Ray-casting volume rendering

A simple description of ray-casting volume rendering is shown in Figure 5. A ray is cast from the viewpoint to each pixel in the screen, along which the data field is resampled. All sampling points will be mapped to color and opacity values from transfer functions. Compositing all sampling points on each ray according to the depth order, we then obtain the color for the pixel corresponding to the ray.

Coupling feature detection with ray casting, we then have our volume rendering algorithm for shockwave data fields as follows:

1) From a shockwave data field, extract wavefront feature data using the boundary detection method proposed in the previous section, and accordingly set the ghost zone tag to the original data field: 0 for all cells corresponding to the feature data and 1 otherwise;

2) In the rendering pipeline, neglecting the ghost zones, i.e. all cells whose ghost zone tags are equal to 1, resample the original data field along each ray and meanwhile interpolate variable values for all sampling points;

3) Composite the sampling points on each ray in the front-to-back order, and obtain the volume rendering image of wave front finally.

We have implemented the proposed volume rendering algorithm in the distributed-parallel visualization software VisIt. Because the wavefront detection method is a little complicated, its implementation is still serialized currently; we temporarily use an operator to merge the data field into one large block prior to wavefront detection. We will parallelize the whole algorithm in the next step to deal with large-scale data fields efficiently.

5. EXPERIMENTAL RESULTS

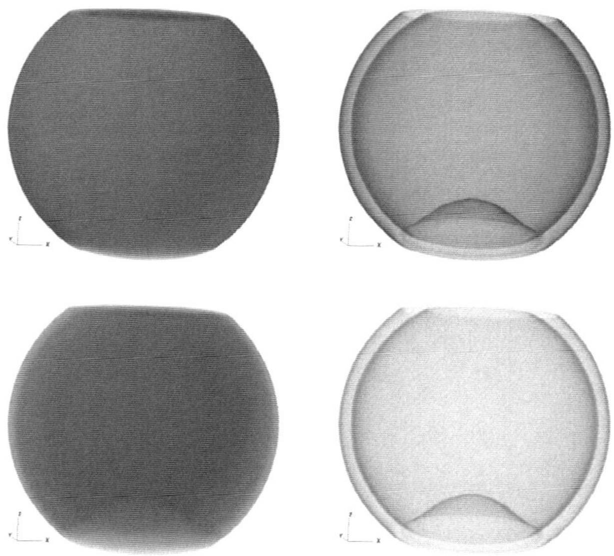

Figure 6. Comparisons of volume rendering results: The left column is for the traditional algorithm and the right column for the proposed algorithm; the opacity for the first row equals to 0.126 while the second row decreases to 0.042

For a test shockwave data field, we will check whether the proposed algorithm can clearly reveal the structure of shock wave front. The rendering results of shock wave using our algorithm are shown in Figure 6 (right). For comparison, we also render the data with the same parameters using the traditional ray-casting volume rendering algorithm, and the results are shown on the left of Figure 6.

At first, we set a small constant opacity of 0.126 (The maximum opacity is 1.0 in our program), as shown in the first row of Figure 6. For our algorithm, we can clearly see the structures behind and inside the front wavefront; but the internal structures are almost invisible for the traditional algorithm, although the opacity has been very small and the background field has been especially filtered out for the traditional algorithm. And then, further reducing the opacity to one third (i.e., the opacity becomes 0.042), we obtain the rendering results, as shown in the second row of Figure 6. The rendering effect for the traditional algorithm is still not ideal, and the internal wave fronts are only faintly seen.

In order to check the applicability, we further apply the algorithm to the time-varying process of shockwave propagation. The rendering results of wave fronts for the time-varying process are shown in Figure 7, where four typical time steps are listed, i.e. 0300, 0600, 0900 and 1200. The rendering results clearly show the evolution law of shockwave propagation: gradual expansion, obstacle reflection and further expansion. The results also show that the proposed algorithm can extract and render multi-wavefronts, even if they become irregular.

Therefore, the algorithm proposed in this paper can be used to deal with 3D complex wavefront structures. The algorithm clearly shows the internal structures of wave fronts by extracting the wavefront feature data out of the data field and then rendering the feature data only. Because the rendering of wave front mainly relies on feature detection, there is no need to spend much time to interactively design a suitable opacity transfer function.

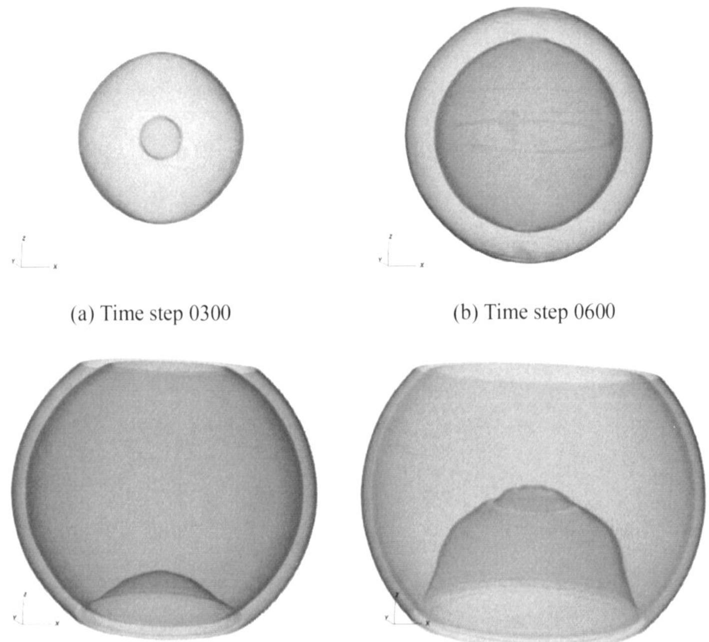

(a) Time step 0300 (b) Time step 0600

(c) Time step 0900 (d) Time step 1200

Figure 7 Time-varying wavefront evolutions in shockwave propagation

6. CONCLUSION

Aiming at numerical simulations of 3D shockwave, this paper presents a volume rendering algorithm based on feature boundary detection for extracting and exhibiting wavefront spatial structures from violently-varying 3D shockwave data fields. In order to detect 3D wave fronts, the algorithm generalizes the boundary detection technique for 2D image to 3D volume data, and accordingly the feature data containing wave fronts are extracted from shockwave data fields. And then, the algorithm resamples and fuses the feature data according to the ray casting method, thus the clear visualization of complex wavefront structures is realized in the end. The algorithm characterizes the physical feature of wave front by the extracted feature data instead of a transfer function, thus there is no need to take much time and effort to design the transfer function. The algorithm has been initially applied to the visualization of 3D shockwave data fields, supporting domain experts to observe and analyze the evolution process of shock wave.

In the next step, we will continue to improve the proposed algorithm. Firstly, we will improve the 3D boundary detection technique to well adapt to complex wavefronts as well as general situations. And then, we will enhance the illumination effect on wave fronts to make them more prominent from the volume rendering image. In addition, we will further address the problem of efficiently-parallel implementation so as to deal with large-scale data fields. As a result, the high quality visualization of large-scale complex shockwave data fields will be achieved.

ACKNOWLEDGEMENT

This work was supported by National Key R&D Program of China (No. 2017YFB0202203) and Foundation of Laboratory of Computational Physics.

REFERENCES

Bergholm, F., 1987. Edge focusing. *In IEEE Transactions on Pattern Analysis and Machine Intelligence*, Vol. 9, No. 6, pp. 726-741.

Caban, J. and Rheingans, P., 2008. Texture-based Transfer Functions for Direct Volume Rendering. *In IEEE Transactions on Visualization and Computer Graphics*, Vol. 14, No. 6, pp. 1364-1371.

Canny, J., 1986. A computational approach to edge detection. *In IEEE Transactions on Pattern Analysis and Machine Intelligence*, Vol. 8, No. 6, pp. 679-698.

Childs, H. et al., 2005. A contract based system for large data visualization. *Proceedings of IEEE Visualization '05*. Minneapolis, MN USA, pp. 191-198.

Childs, H. et al., 2006. A scalable, hybrid scheme for volume rendering massive data sets. *Proceedings of EGPGV '06*. Braga, Portugal, DOI:10.2312/EGPGV/EGPGV06/153-161.

Childs, H. et al., 2010. Extreme scaling of production visualization software on diverse architectures. *In IEEE Computer Graphics and Applications*, Vol. 30, No. 3, pp. 22-31.

Howison, M. et al., 2012. Hybrid parallelism for volume rendering on large, multi- and many-core systems. *In IEEE Transactions on Visualization and Computer Graphics*, Vol. 18, No. 1, pp. 17-29.

Huang, R. et al., 2003. Visualizing industrial CT volume data for nondestructive testing applications. *Proceedings of IEEE Visualization '03*. Seattle, WA USA, DOI:10.1109/VISUAL.2003.1250418.

Jin, Y., 2011. *Research on an Improved Canny Algorithm for Image Edge Detection*. Master's thesis, Chongqing Normal University. [In Chinese]

Li, P. et al., 1997. ParVox-a parallel volume rendering system for distributed visualization. *Proceedings of Symposium on Parallel Rendering '97*. Phoenix, AZ USA, pp. 7-14.

Lum, E. and Ma, K., 2004. Lighting transfer functions using gradient aligned sampling. *Proceedings of IEEE Visualization '04*. Austin, TX USA, pp. 289-296.

Ma, K. and Crockett, T., 1997. A scalable parallel cell-projection volume rendering algorithm for three dimensional unstructured data. *Proceedings of Symposium on Parallel Rendering '97*. Phoenix, AZ USA, pp. 95-104.

Ma, K., 1999. Parallel rendering of 3D AMR data on the SGI/Cray T3E. *Proceedings of the 7th Symposium on the Frontiers of Massively Parallel Computation*. Annapolis, MD USA, pp. 138-145.

Moloney, B. et al., 2007. Scalable sort-first parallel direct volume rendering with dynamic load balancing. *Proceedings of EGPGV '07*. Lugano, Switzerland, DOI:10.2312/EGPGV/EGPGV07/045-052.

Moloney, B. et al., 2011. Sort-first parallel volume rendering. *In IEEE Transactions on Visualization and Computer Graphics*, Vol. 17, No. 8, pp. 1164-1177.

Palmer, M. et al., 1997. Exploiting deep parallel memory hierarchies for ray casting volume rendering. *Proceedings of Symposium on Parallel Rendering '97*. Phoenix, AZ USA, pp. 15-22.

Roettger, S. et al., 2005. Spatialized transfer functions. *Proceedings of EuroVis05 Joint Eurographics - IEEE VGTC Symposium on Visualization*. Leeds, United Kingdom, DOI:10.2312/VisSym/EuroVis05/271-278.

Rothwell, C. et al., 1995. Driving vision by topology. *Proceedings of IEEE International Symposium on Computer Vision (ISCV '95)*. Coral Gables, FL USA, pp. 395-400.

Sano, K. et al., 1997. Parallel processing of the shear-warp factorization with the binary-swap method on a distributed-memory multiprocessor system. *Proceedings of Symposium on Parallel Rendering '97*. Phoenix, AZ USA, pp. 87-94.

Tenginakai, S. et al., 2001. Salient iso-surface detection with model-independent statistical signatures. *Proceedings of IEEE Visualization '2001*. San Diego, CA, USA, DOI:10.1109/VISUAL.2001.964516.

Tzeng, F. et al., 2005. An intelligent system approach to higher-dimensional classification of volume data. *In IEEE Transactions on Visualization and Computer Graphics*, Vol. 11, No. 3, pp. 273-284.

Wang, Y. et al., 2010. Volume exploration using ellipsoidal Gaussian transfer functions. *Proceedings of 2010 IEEE Pacific Visualization Symposium (PacificVis)*. DOI:10.1109/PACIFICVIS.2010.5429612.

Yagüe-Fabra, J. et al., 2013. A 3D edge detection technique for surface extraction in computed tomography for dimensional metrology applications. *In CIRP Annals - Manufacturing Technology*, Vol. 62, No. 1, pp. 531-534.

USING REORDERABLE MATRICES TO COMPARE RISK CURVES OF REPRESENTATIVE MODELS IN OIL RESERVOIR DEVELOPMENT AND MANAGEMENT ACTIVITIES

Celmar Guimarães da Silva[1], Luis Augusto Angelotti Meira[1], Antonio Alberto S. Santos[2] and Denis José Schiozer[3]

[1]*School of Technology, University of Campinas, Limeira, SP, Brazil*
[2]*Center for Petroleum Studies, University of Campinas, Campinas, SP, Brazil*
[3]*School of Mechanical Engineering, University of Campinas, Campinas, SP, Brazil*

ABSTRACT

Methodologies of oil reservoir development and management demand the creation of a set of reservoir models that represents the uncertainties of a reservoir. This set of uncertainties is often simplified by the use of Representative Models (RMs), i.e., models that represent the full set. Comparison of risk curves (a.k.a. complementary cumulative distribution functions) of reservoir variables is an approach used for helping oil engineers to select a set of RMs. A typical comparison chart of a given variable of interest superposes two risk curves: one of the entire model set, and another from the set of RMs. The level of similarity between the curves in this chart indicates the representativeness of the set of RMs regarding the entire model set. A visualization with some of these charts may help to compare the representativeness of the set of RMs regarding more variables (reservoir properties, production data etc.) or distinct sets of RMs. However, this kind of chart is not enough to provide an overview of these comparisons if the number of variables or sets of RMs increase. This paper shows how the use of reorderable matrices, depicted as heatmaps, can provide an overview of this dataset that can be helpful to engineers to make decisions. We propose to represent the dissimilarity of pairs of risk curves instead of the curves themselves. This solution enables our visualization to increase the number of sets of RMs and the number of variables to represent. We show the usefulness of our proposal in three case studies of oil reservoir benchmarks, and discuss the pattern we found in these cases.

KEYWORDS

Reorderable Matrix, Heatmaps, Oil Reservoir Model, Cumulative Distribution Functions, Risk Curves, Representative Models

1. INTRODUCTION

Oil reservoir development and management activities include, among others, a set of tasks related to reservoir characterization, uncertainties reduction, production forecast, and risk analysis. A reservoir structure is often modeled as a set of tridimensional grid blocks. Petrophysical properties like porosity and permeability of a given reservoir grid block, and the initial amount of oil, gas, and water inside this block are some of the other data that the model tries to estimate. The uncertain behavior of the reservoir along the time is also modeled, according to a set of possible exploitation strategies. The overall optimization process is guided by the analysis of production and economic data (output variables), such as the net production value and the volume of oil and gas produced along time. Examples of decision analysis to be taken by oil enterprises are where and when to place, open and close wells, in order to maximize their profit. All these variables have associated uncertainties, and therefore many models and strategies must be created, simulated, and analyzed before taking a decision (Schiozer et al., 2019).

An interactive selection of representative models (Schiozer et al., 2019) may help to reduce the overall computational time spend when selecting production strategies. A representative model (RM) represents a subset of the entire set of models created for a reservoir (Mahjour et al., 2020). A good set of RMs (also referred as *solution* in this paper) must faithfully represent the entire set of models.

The software RMFinder (Meira et al., 2016, Meira et al., 2020) uses optimization and visualization procedures to help decision makers to find good solutions. Part of these solutions is a set of *risk curve charts*, one for each variable. A *risk curve chart* contains two *risk curves* (a.k.a. complementary cumulative distribution functions or CCDFs) of a variable: one for the entire set of models, and other for the RMs only (see Section 3 for details). RMFinder returns a set $\boldsymbol{S}$ of best solutions to be visually analyzed by decision makers.

A problem arises when the set of variables or the number of solutions increases. To compare $|\boldsymbol{S}|$ best solutions with $|\boldsymbol{V}|$ variables each one, the decision maker must analyze $|\boldsymbol{S}|*|\boldsymbol{V}|$ risk curve charts. If the decision makers want to analyze all $|\boldsymbol{V}|$ variables and not only a subset of them, this number of charts makes unfeasible to do a reliable visual analysis of the results to find the best solution among the ones selected by RMFinder.

This paper tries to overcome this difficulty regarding risk curve charts by providing an overview of their data. Given that the main information of each of these charts is the difference of its pair of risk curves, we calculate the area $a(s,v)$ between both curves of a chart as an error, and use this measure as an indicator of the quality of the solution s_i for the variable v_j. We construct a *reorderable matrix* with $|\boldsymbol{S}|\times|\boldsymbol{V}|$ *cells,* where each cell has the value of $a(s_i,v_j)$, and depict this matrix as a *heatmap*. Matrix reordering algorithms help to identify patterns in the set of solutions, and the behavior of these solutions for each variable. The novelty of our approach is the visual data summarization that we provide to analysts as an overview of the error measures of many pairs of risk curves.

We applied our approach to RMs from three synthetic oil reservoirs. In our analysis, the reordering algorithm unveiled an interesting order of the variables. For each solution, variables at the end of this order have tendentiously more error in a given solution than the variables at the start of the order, regardless of the reservoir analyzed.

This paper is organized as follows. Section 2 briefly introduces theoretical background related to reservoir modeling, representative models, and reorderable matrices. Section 3 summarizes visualization strategies to compare risk curves. Our visualization proposal is defined at Section 4. Section 5 shows how our reorderable matrices present data from synthetic oil reservoir benchmarks. Section 6 concludes our paper and points out future work.

2. THEORETICAL BACKGROUND

In this section we briefly introduce concepts about reservoir modeling in oil engineering research. Besides, we present concepts related to reorderable matrices, which we use in our approach.

2.1 Reservoir Modeling Concepts

In the context of this work, a *reservoir model* can be defined as a tridimensional grid, in which each cell (grid block) has values of a set of attributes such as oil, gas and water saturation, porosity, and permeability, among others. In other words, a model m can be defined as a set of tuples in the format $[i, j, k, iv, val]$, where i, j and k correspond to the axes X, Y, and Z; iv is an input variable, and val is the value of this variable in the given cell (Aziz, 1993). This is a simplified way to model a reservoir; other approaches add spatial distortion to the cubic cells of this model to better represent reservoirs in the space (Correia et al., 2015; Mahjour et al., 2019).

A production strategy add wells to a reservoir model. There are two types of wells: *producer wells*, which extracts fluid; and *injector wells*, which insert fluid into the reservoir to help oil and gas extraction by increasing the internal pressure inside the reservoir (Dake, 1983).

Given a model and a production strategy, a reservoir can be simulated in a specialized software. This kind of simulation generates two types of output variables: *field variables*, such as water production (Wp), net production (Np), net present value (NPV), oil recovery factor (ORF), oil in place (OIP), water in place

(WIP), and water injection (Winj). It also outputs *well variables*, such as well economic index (WEI), among others.

As presented in the introduction, the selection of RMs is a relevant step that makes it feasible to run simulations based on models. Choosing the best RMs for a given set of models is not straightforward. This task may be accomplished by methodologies based on ranking, clustering or optimization (Meira et al., 2020). In this paper, we focus on RMFinder's interactive optimization methodology (Meira et al., 2020).

Given a set of M reservoir models, RMFinder tries to choose a subset R with k models of a set M of models such that the representativeness of this subset is optimal. Three aspects drive this optimization process. The first aspect is to find well-distributed models in M, according to all possible 2D projections of pairs of the field variables under consideration. A second aspect is that the models in R should have a distribution similar to those in M for each field variable, according to classes of values predefined for each variable (a.k.a. attribute-levels). In this paper, we are particularly focused on the third optimization aspect: to find R that provides similar CCDFs than M for each field variable.

Regarding user interaction in this methodology, decision makers can predefine models before optimization starts. After optimization, RMFinder shows cross-plots, risk curve charts, and bar charts that help decision makers to analyze the optimization results. If the optimization results are not satisfactory, the decision makers can change weights in each of three aspects of the optimization process according to their interests and run it again.

2.2 Reorderable Matrices

Reorderable matrices (Bertin, 2010) are data structures that store values of a function $c(x,y)$, where x and y are nominal variables, and c is often a quantitative function. They are frequently depicted as *heatmaps*, where x and y are mapped to X and Y axes, and c is mapped to colors according to a color map. Given that x and y are nominal, the rows and columns of the heatmap may be reordered to reveal patterns that are hidden due to unsuitable row and column permutations.

Wilkinson (2005) and Behrisch et al. (2016) indicate a set of patterns that a heatmap may present. We highlight the *Simplex pattern* (Wilkinson, 2005), which we observed in the context of this work. Wilkinson (2005) defines a Simplex pattern as a matrix $X_{n\times p}$ whose cell values are $x_{ij} = e^t / (1 - e^t) + u_{ij}$, where $i = 1, \ldots, n$; $j = 1, \ldots, p$; $t = (s_j - r_i)$; $s_j = j/p$; $r_i = i/n$; and u_{ij} is a random error. In other words, when a matrix has a Simplex pattern, its values tend to decrease from northeast to southwest, as depicted in Figure 1. A *pre-Simplex matrix* is a matrix that has at least one permutation in which it shows a Simplex pattern.

Matrix reordering algorithms permute matrices in order to unveil information. Some of them focus on revealing Wilkinson's patterns. We highlight FVS (Silva et al., 2017), a simple and fast algorithm (O(mn) for $m \times n$ matrices) for revealing Simplex patterns in pre-Simplex matrices. FVS sorts the matrix rows (columns) according to the order of the average values of each row (column). A state-of-the-art reordering method called Hybrid Sort (Silva, 2020) uses FVS to reorder a (possibly scrambled) matrix that was classified as pre-Simplex.

Figure 1. Illustrative example of matrix with the Simplex pattern. Values from 0 to 1 are colored according to a blue-white-red scale

3. VISUALIZATIONS OF SETS OF RISK CURVES

This section presents some strategies used by oil engineering works to represent data sets related to risk curves. First of all, we must compare the concept of risk curve against *cumulative distribution functions* (CDFs) or *complementary cumulative distribution functions* (CCDFs).

Suppose a random variable X that has a probability measure Q. A CDF $F(X,v)$ or $F(Q,v)$ returns the probability that X is less than or equal to v (Gentle, 2009). A CCDF (a.k.a. tail distribution function) F^C is defined as $F^C(X,v) = 1 - F(X,v)$ (Gass & Fu, 2016). Some works use the term *risk curve* (Kaplan & Garrick, 1981) as a synonym to CCDF (e.g. Schiozer et al., 2017, Schiozer et al., 2019, Meira et al., 2016).

A risk curve is commonly plotted in a line chart, whose X and Y axes represent, respectively, the variable X and the values of $F(X,v)$ (for CDF) or $F^C(X,v)$ (for CCDF). Figure 2(a,b) has a synthetic example of a probability function for NPV and two related risk curves (for 500 and 10 models).

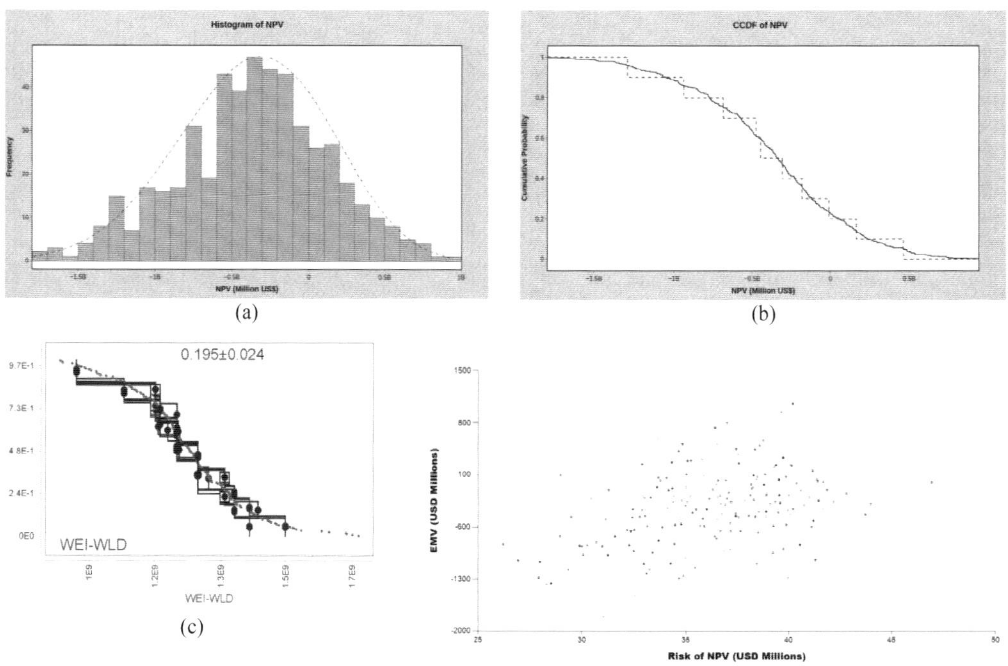

(d)

Figure 2. (a) Frequency values for a single field variable (NPV). (b) Two CCDFs of NPV, one for 500 models (solid line) and other for 10 models (dotted line). (c) Chart with 10 merged (superposed) risk curves for Well Economic Index (WEI) of a single well WLD. (d) Risk-return plot of oil production strategies

We identified four visual mapping approaches to overview and compare many risk curves in a single chart: superposition, summarization, juxtaposition, and hybrid approaches.

It is possible to do **line superposition** in the line chart, as in the "merged risk curves" chart (Meira et al., 2020) (Figure 2(c)). It superposes a set of 10 risk curves for a given variable in the best solutions found in a single execution of RMFinder. Despite its cluttered lines, this chart overviews the risk curves, and enables analysts to compare their similarities.

A **summarization** approach may use a scatterplot in which each mark represents a risk curve. The axes of this chart represent risk and return measures. Santos et al. (2020) map "Risk of NPV" to X axis, "Estimated Monetary Value (EMV)" to Y axis, and marks to production strategies, where each strategy has a risk curve for NPV. In Figure 2(d) we exemplify the same visual mapping with synthetic data for 199 strategies.

A **juxtaposition** approach places risk curve charts side-by-side in a matrix layout. As an example, Meira et al. (2020) presents a chart with 25 small risk curve charts in a 6 × 5 matrix layout. Each of these small charts shows 2 superposed risk curves: one for the entire set of models, and other for the nine representative models. The full chart does not define if the order of its risk charts is meaningful or not. Some similarity criteria could be used for this layout, such as the association between clustering and a Peano-Hilbert curve used by Silva et al. (2019) for drawing multiple reservoir models. Figure 3 exemplifies five juxtaposed risk curve charts created by RMFinder. Purple and black lines refer to the RMs and the entire set of models, respectively.

A **hybrid** approach is proposed also by Meira et al. (2020). They use juxtaposition and superposition of many risk curves in 20 risk charts for showing the best 10 solutions for a given oil field. We adopted the same approach in the Figure 4. The charts refer to 11 field variables (NPV, ORF etc.) and to productivity indexes of 9 wells (WEI-IN1, WEI-IN2 etc.). Purple and black lines are similar to those in Figure 3, except that there are 10 superposed black lines per chart, one for each solution.

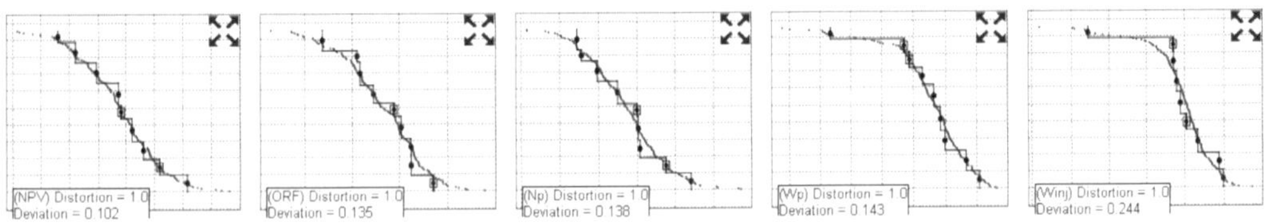

Figure 3. Juxtaposed risk curve charts of five variables (generated by RMFinder). The RMs and the entire set of models are depicted as purple and black lines, respectively

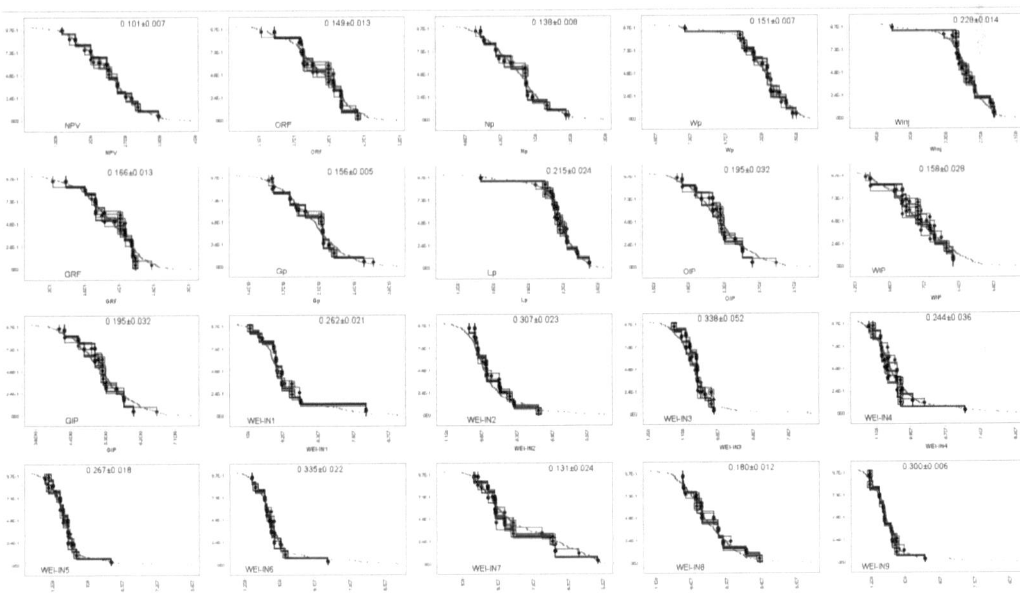

Figure 4. Juxtaposed risk curve charts with superposed risk curves (generated by RMFinder). The RMs and the 10 solutions are depicted as 1 purple line and 10 black lines, respectively

4. ERROR COMPARISON HEATMAPS

The previous section presented some approaches for visualizing sets of risk curves. In this paper, we propose to use heatmaps as a summarization approach for comparison of pairs of risk curves. As we presented before, given two risk curves of a same variable – one for representative models and other for the entire set of models – the sum of the areas between them can be considered as a error value (Figure 5). The smaller the sum, the more representative the RMs are. We aim to show these error values as the cells of our heatmap.

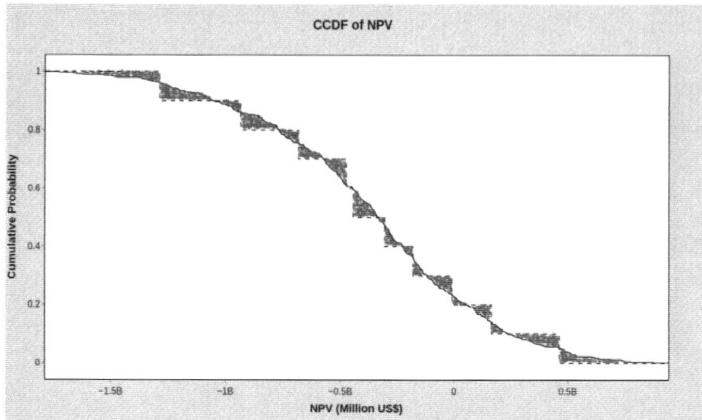

Figure 5. Error (red areas) between the risk curve of the entire model set (regarding variable NPV) and the risk curve of a set of RMs

In the visual mapping proposed for our *error comparison heatmaps*, the Y axis shows solutions defined as best choices of RMs by a software (in our case, the RMFinder software). The X axis shows field or well variables. The color of each cell represents the error value related to the solution and variable to which the cell refers. The color map has a green-white-purple scale, where green is the absence of error and purple the greatest error in the dataset. The white color was configured according to the need of the analysts during the analysis process. We selected these colors in order to avoid conflict with other colors already used in the analysis of oil variables. Besides, given that variables and solutions are categorical variables, they may be permuted if necessary. Therefore, matrix reordering algorithms can be used to unveil patterns in this matrix to the users.

This matrix may be useful at least in the following tasks:

a) *Comparing solutions with the same number of RMs to choose one of the solutions.* Figure 6 exemplifies this use. It shows field and well variables for 10 solutions, each one with nine RMs. The matrix was sorted by FVS (Silva et al., 2017). The white value in the color map was empirically defined as 0.2. Columns with purple cells at the right of the matrix indicate that most of the solutions under analysis do not appropriately represent the variables WEIPR6 and WEIPR4 (Well Economic Indexes of producer wells PR6 and PR4).

b) *Comparing solutions with distinct number of RMs to observe which variables produce more or less error.* This comparison can also help to define criteria to choose an ideal number of RMs to be used. The section Results will present some matrices related to this task.

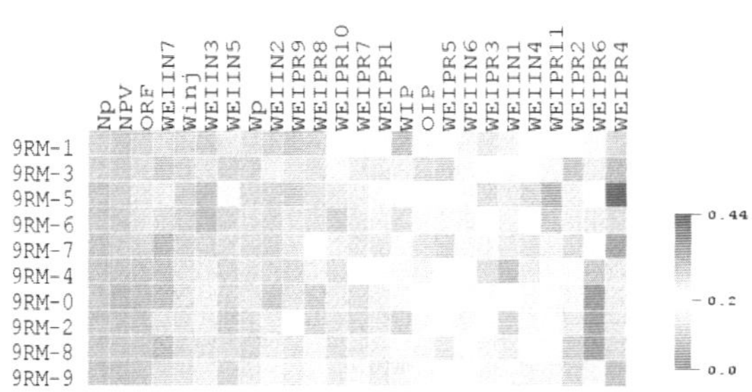

Figure 6. Error comparison matrix with 10 solutions (Y axis) and 25 variables (X axis). All solutions have 9 RMs. Cell colors may vary from green (absence of error) to purple (maximum error in the dataset)

5. RESULTS

We generated risk comparison matrices to represent error in the solutions created by RMFinder for three synthetic reservoir benchmarks freely available: *UNISIM-I-D* and *UNISIM-II-D*, available at UNISIM's website (http://www.unisim.cepetro.unicamp.br/benchmarks); and *Olympus*, available at ISAPP website (https://www.isapp2.com/optimization-challenge/timeline.html). The solutions vary according to the number of RMs in each solution. In addition, some matrices have 10 solutions for each possible size of the set of RMs. Our matrices may have field and well variables, according to the needs of the analysts.

Figure 7(a) shows the error comparison matrix of solutions for UNISIM-I-D. The names of the solutions have the format "*n*RM-0", where *n* indicates the number of RMs in the solution. The value 0.2 is shown as the white color in the matrix. The dominant green region of this matrix indicates that solutions with 16 or more RMs may satisfy the analysts. It is worth noting that both axis of this matrix were sorted by FVS. Therefore, the average error of each solution have a strong correlation with the number of RMs in each solution – note that only solutions 22RM-0 and 23RM-0 are out of their natural order.

Variables OIPHB, WEII19, WEIP21, and WEIP08 have the worst average values in these solutions. The first one is an oil in place (OIP) variable of a part of the reservoir called "high block" (HB), which is at the east of the reservoir. The other variables are related to well economic indexes (WEI) of injector well I19 and producer wells P21 and P08, which are also at the same region. The results indicate that the solutions found could not completely capture some important petrophysical property uncertainties of their regions.

Figure 7(b) also shows similar matrices for UNISIM-II-D reservoirs, but with distinct ordering of variables (when compared to UNISIM-I-D). The green region of the matrix seems to be smaller than the one of UNISIM-I-D data, suggesting that only solutions with 17 or more RMs are acceptable. As in the UNISIM-I-D matrix, the rightmost variables of each of UNISIM-I-D's matrices present the worst average values for the solutions in their respective matrices. The results for Olympus were very similar to those of UNISIM-II-D and were omitted in this paper.

In both matrices of Figure 7, the reordering algorithm FVS revealed a Simplex pattern. This pattern seems to match the information in the three cases, given that the order of the Y axis after reordering was almost the ascending order of the number of RMs. This makes sense in the context of RMs, because the more RMs, the best the representation of the entire model. However, we could not find until this moment a clear explanation about why the variables were ordered in such ways in each figure. It suggests that the order may be related to greater uncertainty in the regions of the wells with greater error, but only further investigation can confirm this hypothesis.

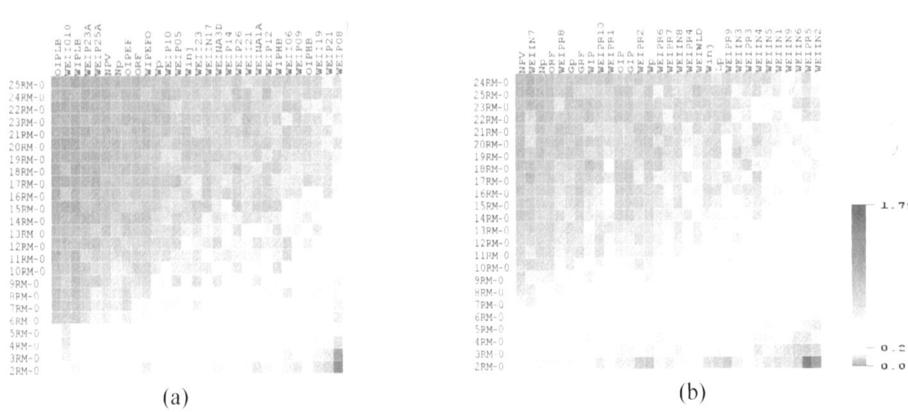

(a) (b)

Figure 7. Error comparison matrix of solutions calculated for the following reservoirs: (a) UNISIM-I-D and (b) UNISIM-II-D. The number of RMs per solution varies from 2 to 25. Cell colors may vary from green (absence of error) to purple (maximum error in the dataset)

6. CONCLUSION

This work presented a new approach for visualizing differences between pairs of risk curves. Our proposal uses reorderable matrices to show the error of each set of RMs when compared to the entire set of models of a given reservoir, regarding probabilities of a set of field and well variables. When solutions with distinct numbers of RMs are compared, our proposal has the potential to show which variables have errors that are harder to reduce; in other words, which variables need more RMs to be correctly represented.

Future works include a better definition of what is an acceptable error, and the implementation of this proposal as an interactive software with easy access to risk curve charts related to each variable and solution presented in the error comparison matrix.

ACKNOWLEDGEMENT

We gratefully acknowledge the support of EPIC – Energy Production Innovation Center, hosted by the University of Campinas (UNICAMP) and sponsored by Equinor Brazil and by FAPESP – São Paulo Research Foundation (grant number 2017/15736-3). We also thank the support of FAEPEX/PRP/UNICAMP (grant #2224/20) We acknowledge the support of ANP (Brazil's National Agency of Oil, Natural Gas and Biofuels) through the R&D levy regulation. Acknowledgments are extended to the School of Technology (FT), Center for Petroleum Studies (CEPETRO), and School of Mechanical Engineering (FEM) at UNICAMP. We also acknowledge the funding from Energi Simulation and thank the Computer Modelling Group Ltd. (CMG) for software licenses and technical support.

REFERENCES

Aziz, K. 1993. Reservoir Simulation Grids: Opportunities and Problems. Journal of Petroleum Technology 45 (7), pp. 658-663.

Behrisch, M. et al., 2016. Matrix reordering methods for table and network visualization. Computer Graphics Forum 35(3), pp. 693–716.

Bertin J., 2010. Semiology of graphics: Diagrams, networks, maps. USA: Esri Press, 2010.

Correia, M.G. et al. 2015. UNISIM-II-D: benchmark case proposal based on a carbonate reservoir. In: SPE Latin American and Caribbean Petroleum Engineering Conference, Quito, Ecuador. SPE-177140-MS, pp. 18–20.

Dake, L.P., 1983. Fundamentals of Reservoir Engineering, Volume 8, 1st Edition. Elsevier Science.

Gass, S.I., Fu, M.C. (eds.), 2013, Encyclopedia of Operations Research and Management Science. Springer, Boston, MA.

Gentle, J.E., 2009, Computational Statistics, Statistics and Computing, Springer Science + Business Media, LLC.

Mahjour, S.K. et al., 2020. Developing a Workflow to Select Representative Reservoir Models Combining Distance Based Clustering and Data Assimilation for Decision Making Process. Journal of Petroleum Science and Engineering 190, pp. 1-20.

Mahjour, S.K. et al., 2019. Developing a Workflow to Represent Fractured Carbonate Reservoirs for Simulation Models Under Uncertainties Based on Flow Unit Concept. Oil & Gas Science and Technology 74, pp 1-16.

Meira, L.A.A. et al., 2016. Selection of Representative Models for Decision Analysis Under Uncertainty. Computers & Geosciences 88, pp. 67-82.

Meira, L.A.A. et al., 2020. Improving representativeness in a scenario reduction process to aid decision making in petroleum fields. Journal of Petroleum Science and Engineering 184, 106398.

Santos, S.M.G. et al. 2017. Risk management in petroleum development projects: Technical and economic indicators to define a robust production strategy. Journal of Petroleum Science and Engineering 151, pp. 116–127.

Schiozer, D.J. et al., 2017. Risk quantification combining geostatistical realizations and discretized Latin Hypercube. J Braz. Soc. Mech. Sci. Eng. 39, pp. 575–587.

Schiozer, D.J. et al., 2019. Model-based decision analysis applied to petroleum field development and management. Rev. IFP Energies nouvelles 74, 46.

Silva, C.G. et al., 2017. A fast feature vector approach for revealing simplex and equi-correlation data patterns in reorderable matrices. Information Visualization 16(4), pp. 261–274.

Silva, C.G. et al., 2019. Visualization of Ensembles of Oil Reservoir Models Based on Pixelization, Small Multiples and Reservoir Similarities. In: Offshore Technology Conference Brasil, 2019, Rio de Janeiro.

Silva, C.G. et al., 2020. Hybrid Sort – A pattern-focused matrix reordering approach based on classification. Proceedings of CGVCVIP 2020 (accepted full paper, to appear).

Wilkinson, L., 2005. The Grammar of Graphics. Springer Science & Business Media. New York, USA.

LASER SPOT DETECTION AND CHARACTERISTIC ANALYSIS IN PLASMA INTERACTION SIMULATION

Zhiwei Ai, Yi Cao, Huawei Wang and Li Xiao
Institute of Applied Physics and Computational Mathematics, Beijing 100094, China
CAEP Software Center for High Performance Numerical Simulation, Beijing 100088, China

ABSTRACT

The analysis of beam divergence mechanism during laser plasma propagation is one of the hot topics research. Among them, laser spot detection and characteristic analysis is one of the important indicators to evaluate the energy distribution of the exit surface of the propagation system. The channel environmental factors during the plasma laser transmission are complex and changeable. This scene will cause distortion of the laser spot, making it difficult to achieve spot detection and precise analysis of characteristics. This paper presents a novel visual analysis method to study the beam divergence mechanism. First, the dynamic threshold segmentation method is used to analyze the numerical simulation data to generate a laser spot image. Second, the use of image edge detection technology to achieve spot contour drawing based on image pixels. The above two key technologies have been applied to the accurately positioning of the spot contour and the analysis of the spatial distribution characteristics of the spot. Experiments show that this technique is helpful to verify the correctness of the physical model of the laser plasma interaction simulation program, and is also effective.

KEYWORDS

Laser Profile, Image Processing, Circle Fitting

1. INTRODUCTION

The important of the spatial characteristic distribution and characteristic analysis of the laser spot is reflected in the correct recognition of the physical model and data modeling. Diagnosing data quickly is one of the difficulties faced by data analysis in laser-plasma interaction simulation. In the analysis of the beam divergence mechanism when the bundled light propagates in the plasma, the visual analysis of the spatial distribution of the laser spot profile is a hot spot of concern. The channel transmission environment during plasma laser propagation has diversity and complexity. In the process of plasma laser propagation, laser spot drift, intensity flicker, dispersion, distortion and other phenomena may cause the energy of the laser receiving end to diverge. In severe cases, the laser energy propagation is interrupted. Various factors cause distortion of the laser spot, making it difficult to accurately locate the spot profile. In the process of space laser propagation, the precise positioning of the spot profile will greatly affect the power of the laser transmission exit surface, which restricts the analysis of the beam divergence mechanism when the beam is propagated in the plasma.

According to the different positioning principles of traditional laser spot contour positioning, the algorithm can be divided into two types, including direct positioning method and indirect positioning method. Direct positioning method is to use discrete numerical calculation method to directly detect the spot contour on the laser spot image, such as threshold segmentation method (Shen et al., 2012) and edge detection method (Orujov et al., 2020). The indirect positioning rule is to calculate the centroid and beam waist parameters of the laser spot, and indirectly calculate the spot profile quickly. Common centroid algorithms include gray center of gravity method (Jeppe et al., 2017), ellipse fitting method (Kurt el al., 2012), Gaussian fitting method (Wu et al., 2017), etc. Figure 1a shows the energy distribution provided by the spatial distribution of the flat-top beam. Among them, the traditional technology only calculates the spot light centroid, beam width and other characteristic parameters to analyze the spot profile change, but it cannot calculate the fitted circle radius of the spot profile. The accuracy of the centroid calculation of this method will greatly affect the detection error of the spot contour. The paper proposes a novel solution. This method adopts a laser spot radius solving algorithm based on circle fitting and an image-based precise positioning and drawing algorithm for spot contours, to realize the visual analysis of the beam divergence mechanism during the propagation of concentrated light in plasma. As shown in Figure 1b, this method uses a physical field-based threshold segmentation method to describe the characteristic spatial distribution of the light spot. The white dotted line describes the outline of the laser spot, and calculates the energy deposition equivalent area of the spot to obtain the fitted circle radius of the spot. Experiments show that the algorithm can accurately locate the spot contour. At the same time, this method is suitable for the spot fitting circle radius of the batch mode of time series data. Therefore, this method is helpful to verify the correctness of the physical model of the laser plasma interaction simulation program. This method is helpful to verify the correctness of the physical model of the laser plasma interaction simulation program, and is also effective.

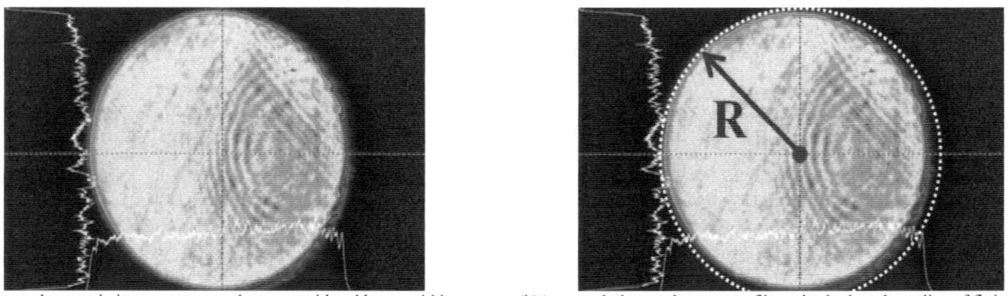

(a) The spot characteristic parameters such as centroid and beam width (b)Accurately locate the spot profile and calculate the radius of fitting circle

Figure 1. Laser spot contour positioning algorithm based on threshold segmentation

The remainder of this paper is structured as follows. Chapter 2 introduces commonly used detection techniques for laser spots. Chapter 3 introduces the two key technologies used to achieve laser spot detection. First, use dynamic threshold segmentation to detect and identify laser spots. Second, the image-based edge detection technology is used to realize the spot contour positioning and drawing algorithm, and the spot contour is drawn. Chapter 4 introduces the analysis of the spot characteristics in the laser plasma interaction simulation program.

2. RELATED WORK

At present, whether it is from the hardware or software, many have spent a lot of energy on the positioning research of the laser spot contour. Lambert et al. (1995) analyzed the factors that caused the laser beam distortion caused by atmospheric laser communication in detail from the aspects of space channels, transceiver devices and laser carrier. Jason et al. (2008) in the American Aerospace Corporation built a laser communication hardware and software test platform, and have always insisted on combining hardware and software to seek to design the best algorithm. From a morphological point of view, Singh et al. (2008) used Gaussian fitting curves to locate the spot centroid at the accuracy of sub-pixels. Yu (2006) proposed a spot center correction method for aberration data calculated by Zernike polynomials. Liu (2014) used Houng transform to improve the algorithm of laser spot center positioning accuracy. Wang et al. (2011) and Liu et al. (2011) introduced a curve-fitting sub-pixel positioning algorithm for the center of gravity. Tang et al. (2009) used Gaussian cumulative distribution fitting method 5 and Li et al. (2013), Wang et al. (2013), Zhao et al. (2014) and Qin et al. (2006) designed and implemented the least squares circle fitting in parallel to determine the spot center position and radius. Wang et al. (2007) started from the modulation method, modulating the communication light into circularly polarized light, reducing the introduction of noise in communication, and then using dynamic threshold segmentation to detect the spot profile. Mu et al. (2011) used the information distribution between time series data to control the error to a very small range, and determine the spot profile according to the ellipse fitting method.

With the continuous improvement of parallel computing power, the scale of computing grid of simulation program is also increasing. Taking the laser plasma interaction simulation program as an example, the grid size is close to 10 billion grid cells. Laser plasma interaction involves coupling multiple temporal- and spatial-scale nonlinear processes with very important physical phenomena. To study the generation and development of laser filament instability in the black cavity, a propagation model of the spatial beam uniform beam was established. The Lap3D simulation program was used to simulate large-scale filament formation under the physical conditions of the black cavity (Hu et al., 2015). The simulation program provide the results corresponding to the laser, initial intensity $A_0 = 2 \times 10^{15}$ W cm^{-2}, wavelength $\lambda = 1.05$ μm, and irradiated neutral plasma with uniform initial electron density and temperature. The electric field amplitude of a light beam is considered a Gaussian function with z = 0. Volume rendering with laser intensity of 56.6 ps (Figure 2) reveals significant filamentation. In this example, simulating a physical time of 56.6 ps requires 16,384 CPUs with 1024 × 1024 × 2048 cells (approximately 21 billion cells). The total time-varying data of the analog output of the entire process of 104 steps is 1.74 TB, and the parallel visualization is completed by using 128 CPU cores.

Figure 2. The volume plot of the laser intensity in 3D

Spot detection and characteristic analysis during laser transmission in plasma are challenging. Most of the traditional methods are image data processing, which cannot guarantee the spot analysis of the complete physical field. This paper proposes a method of spot detection and characteristic analysis based on numerical and image data, which can realize spot data analysis of any laser propagation surface. Therefore, this method can ensure the completeness and correctness of data analysis.

3. KEY TECHNOLOGY

This paper presents a novel visual analysis method to study the beam divergence mechanism. Firstly, the threshold-based segmentation method is used to describe the spatial distribution of the laser spot, and the laser spot image is generated. Secondly, the use of image edge detection technology to achieve point contour drawing based on image pixels.

3.1 Description of Spot Spatial Distribution Based on Threshold Segmentation

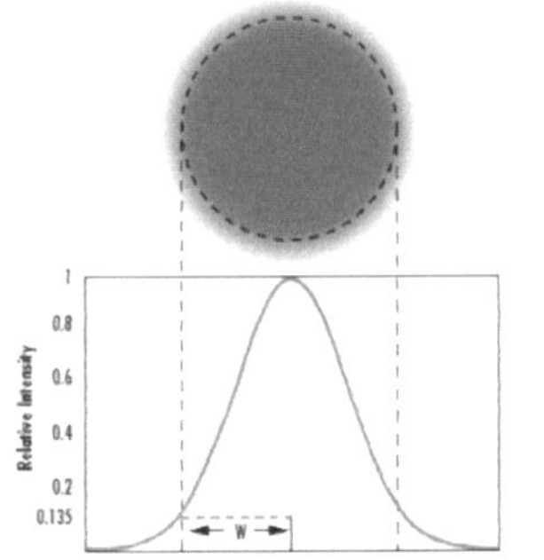

Figure 3. A Gaussian beam's waist is defined as the position where irradiance is its maximum of $1/e^2$ (13.5%)

Many laser optics applications assume that the laser beam is a Gaussian beam, and its irradiance distribution conforms to the ideal Gaussian distribution (Lu, 2003). In fact, all actual laser beams will deviate from the ideal Gaussian behavior. The M factor (also known as the beam quality factor) compares the performance of a real laser beam and a diffraction-limited Gaussian beam. The Gaussian irradiance distribution is symmetrical about the center of the beam, and decreases as the distance between the center of the beam along the direction of beam spread increases, as shown in Figure 3.

This distribution is described by Equation 1. I_0 is the peak irradiance at the center of the beam, r is the radial distance from the axis, $w(z)$ is the radius of the laser beam, z is the wave front, and P is the total power of the beam.

$$I(r) = I_0 \exp(\frac{-2r^2}{w(z)^2}) = \frac{2P}{\pi w(z)^2} \exp(\frac{-2r^2}{w(z)^2}) \quad (1)$$

For Gaussian mode TEM (Transverse Electromagnetic Modes), the beam width defined by the second-order moment is consistent with the beam width defined by the intensity reduction to $1/e^2$. The beam width defined by this method is very sensitive to the interference of high spatial frequencies, and there is always some base noise in the actual measurement process. Therefore, in this paper, another method is used to select appropriate isobaric lines to divide the power density distribution surface. The cutting plane should be selected so that the cut beam area contains 86.5% of the total power. At this time, the definition equation for calculating the cutting plane is Equation 2. In the formula, P_{rc} is the power within the beam radius, and P is the total power.

$$P_{rc} = (1 - e^{-2})P = 0.865P \quad (2)$$

In the laser-plasma interaction simulation program, the incident laser beam is mostly Gaussian beam. Based on the Gaussian spatial distribution characteristics, the algorithm proposes a threshold method based on accumulated energy deposition to describe the spatial distribution characteristics of light spots. Specifically, a weight-based histogram of physics field value distribution is used to count the occupancy of the physics field segment field value and total energy value one by one. Discrete the range of the physical field value into 1024 uniform eigenvalue intervals, and calculate the energy corresponding to each eigenvalue interval (energy = eigenvalue value * the number of cells in this eigenvalue). Starting from the smallest feature interval, the energy of each feature interval is accumulated in sequence, and the energy accumulation of the segmented feature interval is calculated. When the ratio of the energy accumulation of the segmented feature interval to the total energy value approaches 86.5%, it is determined that the maximum physical field value in the segmented feature interval is the laser contour segmentation threshold. The segmentation threshold is used as the screening criterion to distinguish the spot range of the physical field data and calculate the spot area. The laser beam also exhibits a normal distribution characteristic at the exit surface, so the fitting circle calculation is used to derive the fitting circle radius of the laser in the plasma propagation process. Figure 4a shows the spatial distribution of laser energy on the exit surface of a calculation model when the number of iterations is 49680; through the histogram of field value distribution based on the laser energy weight, the separation threshold of the laser profile is calculated to be 1.319. Figure 4b shows the grid cells with energy value higher than 1.319 are retained, and the spatial distribution of laser spot is drawn.

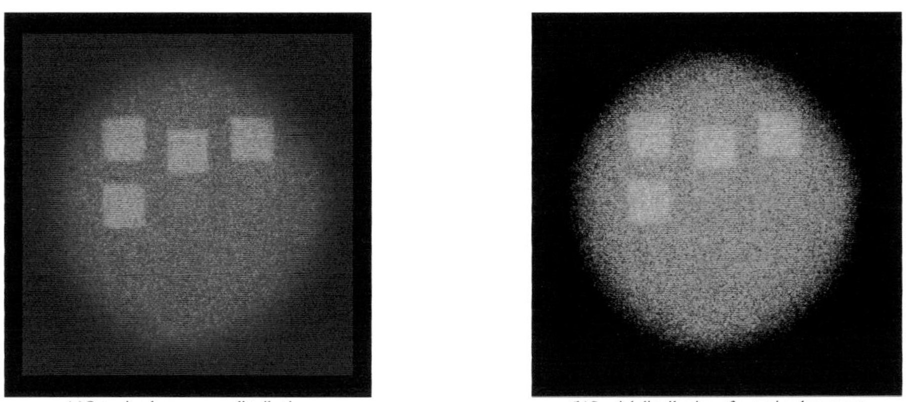

(a)Outgoing laser energy distribution (b)Spatial distribution of outgoing laser spot

Figure 4. A model calculates the spatial distribution of laser spot energy when the number of iterations is 49680

3.2 Algorithm for Spot Contour Positioning and Drawing Based on Image Pixels

The spot profile is a curve connected by continuous points (connected to the boundary), with the same variable value, color value or gray scale. As shown in Figure 5, the contour of the laser spot is obtained by directly using the contour drawing method of the threshold. Since the laser spot is the result of energy deposition, the contour drawing method based on physical values is simply adopted, and the outline of the laser spot cannot be depicted, as shown in the left figure. It can be observed by zooming in on the red local area, the contour distribution presents a locally closed space, and the edge of the laser spot cannot be continuous, as shown in the right part of Figure 5. Therefore, the contour drawing based on physical values cannot describe the outline of the laser spot and cannot meet the needs of data analysis.

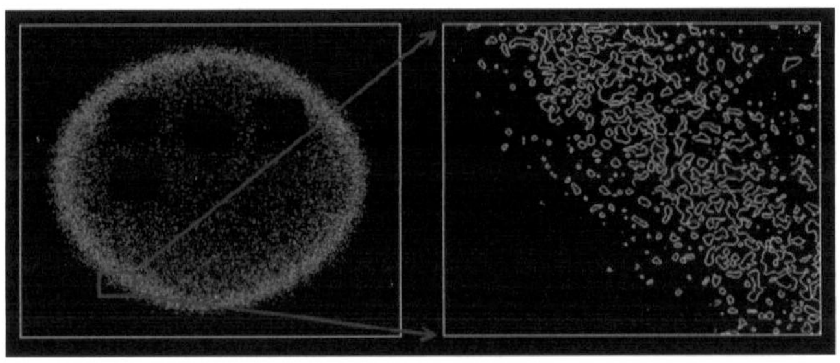

Figure 5. Drawing of threshold contours based on physical quantities

The image-based spot contour drawing method is an algorithm that directly separates the target from the background of the laser spot image. The essence is to find a certain separation value through a series of calculations. With this value as the boundary point, all pixels larger than the separation value are divided into one area, which is generally called the target; all pixels smaller than the separation value are divided into one area, which is generally called the background. In this process, the separation value is called the threshold, and the accuracy of the threshold will determine whether the target can be correctly separated, that is, the spot contour. The input object of the spot pixel positioning and drawing algorithm based on image pixels is the image pixel data of the laser spot. The algorithm flow includes: data filtering; threshold value processing, binary image; laser profile positioning, that is, on a black background, the edge of a white object is the spot contour. The work flow chart is shown in Figure 6. In the first step, read the color fill map of the spatial distribution of the laser spot, the image is a color map with RGBA signal channels. In the second step, the pixel values in the color fill map are subjected to median smoothing filtering to eliminate the influence of interference noise signals. In the steps 3, the image pixels are normalized to a single pixel value according to RGBA, to achieve the grayscale of the color image. In the step 4, based on the weighted image gray value histogram probability statistics, calculates the image segmentation threshold, according to the image segmentation threshold, and generates a black-and-white binary image of the laser spot. In the step 5, according to the binary black-and-white image, extracts continuous white points and connects them into a line to form a spot contour edge. The last step draws a color fill map of the field amount distribution and the spot contour edge by coupling to obtain the final laser spot profile.

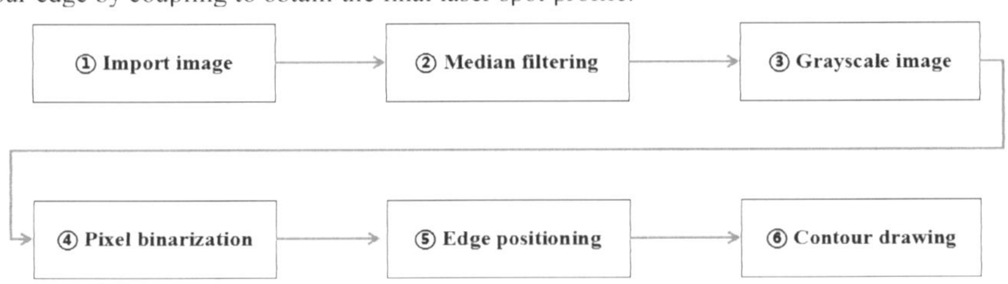

Figure 6. Flowchart of Algorithm for Drawing and Locating Spot Contour Based on Image Pixels

As shown in Figure 7, a schematic diagram of image processing at various stages of the image-based spot contour drawing method is introduced. Figure 7a shows the spatial distribution of spot energy based on circle fitting; Figure 7b shows the gray map of spot energy distribution; Figure 7c shows the gray map after the median filter processing, through the median filter; Figure 7d shows the binary image of the smoothed image, and the spatial area of the light spot is distinguished by black and white; Figure 7e shows the outline of the white spot area; Figure 7f shows the effect drawing of the coupling of the spatial distribution of the original light spot energy and the light spot contour.

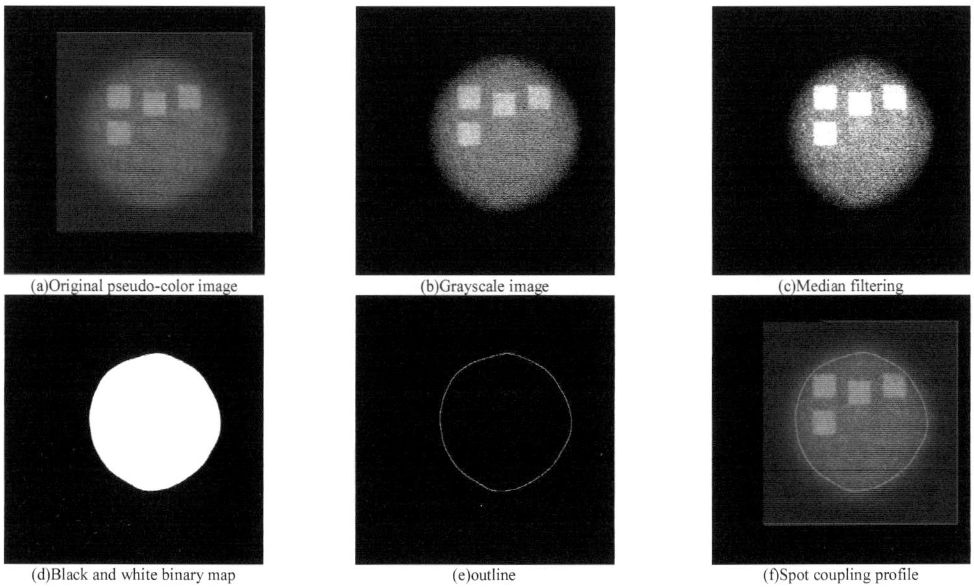

(a)Original pseudo-color image (b)Grayscale image (c)Median filtering

(d)Black and white binary map (e)outline (f)Spot coupling profile

Figure 7. Schematic diagram of image processing in various stages of image-based spot contour drawing method

4. SPOT CHARACTERISTIC ANALYSIS

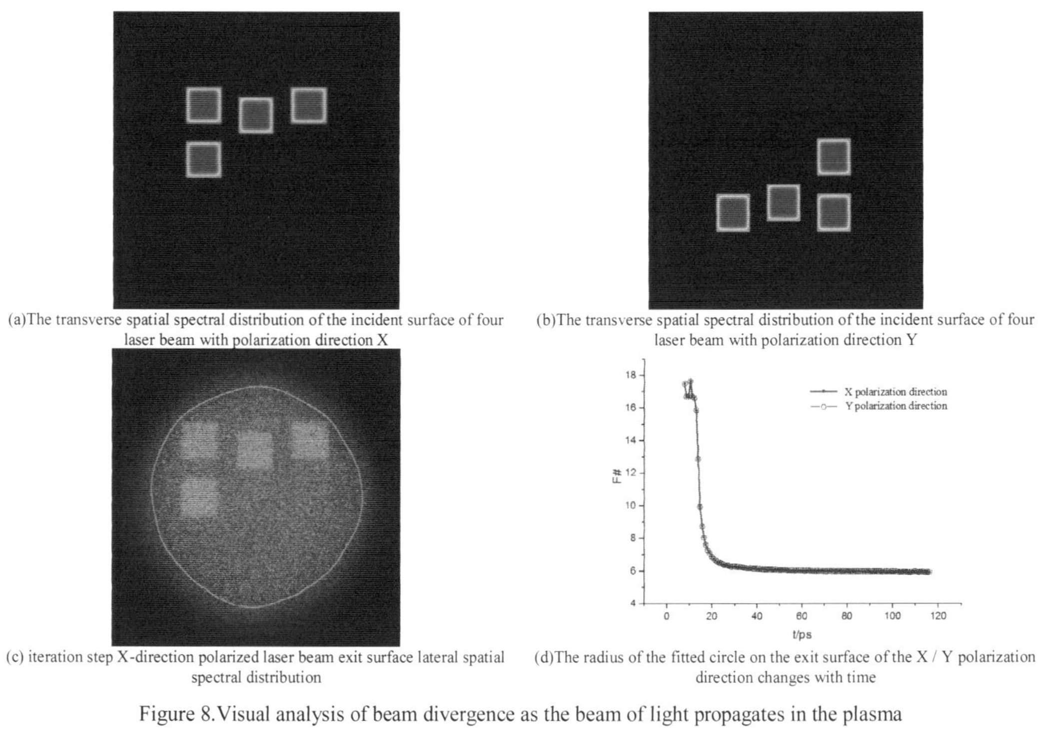

(a)The transverse spatial spectral distribution of the incident surface of four laser beam with polarization direction X

(b)The transverse spatial spectral distribution of the incident surface of four laser beam with polarization direction Y

(c) iteration step X-direction polarized laser beam exit surface lateral spatial spectral distribution

(d)The radius of the fitted circle on the exit surface of the X / Y polarization direction changes with time

Figure 8.Visual analysis of beam divergence as the beam of light propagates in the plasma

Spot characteristic analysis is a mean to verify the correctness of the simulation results of the laser-plasma interaction program and to discover important physical phenomena, and has very important practical application value. As shown in Figure 8, when the 8 laser beams are divided into two polarization directions and enter the plasma, the variation law of the circle radius of the beam divergence fit with time when the beam propagates in the plasma is studied. Figure 8a and Figure 8b are the transverse spatial spectral distribution of the incident surface of the four laser beams with polarization directions in the X and Y directions incident on the plasma. The red square area is the spatial distribution of the incident light; Figure 8c shows the spatial distribution of the X-direction polarized laser exit surface when the iteration step number of the simulation program is 46000, where the green outline is the spatial range of the laser power deposition distribution energy of 86.5%; Figure 8d shows the variation of the fitted circle radius on the exit surface with time. The X direction coordinate is the simulated physical time, and the Y direction coordinate F is the derivative of the fitted circle radius. When the four laser beams propagate in the plasma, the beam diverges and reduces the radius of the fitted circle. The experimental results are in line with physical expectations.

Figure 9 shows a time sequence diagram of the lateral spatial spot profile of the X-direction polarized laser beam exit surface at different iteration steps of a calculation model. It can be seen that in the initial stage of laser propagation, the spot profile distribution is irregular. With the evolution of time, the outline of the spot is gradually regular, and the radius of the spot remains basically unchanged.

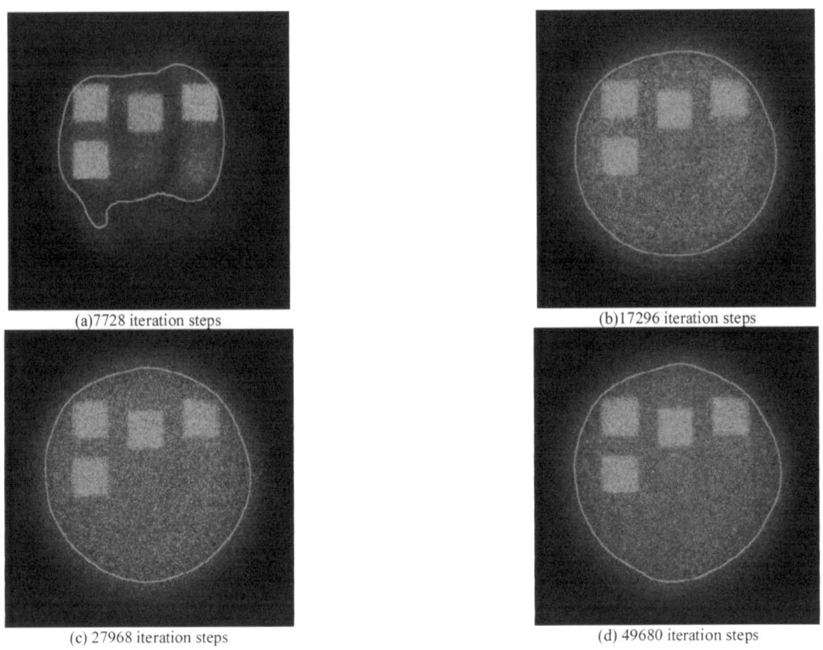

Figure 9. Time evolution chart of the transverse spatial spot profile of the X-direction polarized laser beam with different iteration steps

5. CONCLUSION

In order to support the three-dimensional laser-plasma interaction program, the laser-plasma interaction 3D simulation studies the large-scale filament formation phenomenon under the physical conditions of the black cavity, and analyzes the beam divergence phenomenon and spectral spatial light intensity distribution characteristics after filament formation. Threshold segmentation method for the description of the spatial distribution characteristics of the light spot and the image pixel-based spot contour drawing algorithm realize the visual analysis of the beam divergence mechanism during the propagation of the beam light in the plasma. According to the spot imaging characteristics and random noise characteristics, the outline of the spot propagated by the plasma laser is described. Experimental results show that the algorithm can achieve accurate positioning of the spot profile, assist scientific researchers in insight and understanding of key physical issues, improve the accuracy and efficiency of data analysis.This method can realize the precise location of laser spot outline of simple physical model. The disadvantage is that the influence of random disturbance factors on the laser profile is ignored. It is hoped that a laser spot contour algorithm with high robustness and practicability can be designed in combination with practical needs and considering all aspects of random factors.

ACKNOWLEDGEMENT

This work was supported by National Key R&D Program of China (No. 2017YFB0202203).

REFERENCES

Cardema, J. et al., 2008. Performance and characterization results of a lasercom testbed for the pointing, acquisition, and tracking subsystem of a satellite-to-satellite laser communications link. *SPIE.*

Casey, L. et al., 1995. Laser Communications in Space, *Artech House.*

Jeppe, F. et al., 2017. On the 'centre of gravity' method for measuring the composition of magnetite/maghemite mixtures, or the stoichiometry of magnetite-maghemite solid solutions, via 57Fe Mössbauer spectroscopy. *Journal of Physics D: Applied Physics.*

Kurt, O. and Arslan, O., 2012. Geometric interpretation and precision analysis of algebraic ellipse fitting using least squares method. *Acta Geodaetica Et Geophysica Hungarica*, Vol. 47, No. 4, pp. 430-440.

Li, P. Y., 2013. Research on the center of the sun's position detection algorithm based on image processing. *Taiyuan: Taiyuan University of Science and Technology.*

Liu, H. L. et al, 2014. An improved laser spot center location algorithm. *Computer Measurement and Control*, Vol. 22, No. 1, pp. 139-140.

Lu, B. D., 2003. *Laser optics: beam description, propagation transformation and cavity technical physics.* Higher Education Press, China.

Orujov, F. et al., 2020. Fuzzy based image edge detection algorithm for blood vessel detection in retinal images. *Applied Soft Computing Journal.*

Qin, Y. et al., 2006. Research on laser spot location of multi circle fitting method. *Journal of Xi'an University of Science And Technology*,Vol. 26, No. 4, pp. 519-522.

Shen, Y. and Li, G. Y., 2012. Image Threshold Segmentation Method Design. *Mechanical Engineering and Automation*, Vol. 0, No. 5, pp. 45-46.

Singh, R. et al., 2008. Analysis of accuracy of laser spot centroid estimation. *Proceedings of SPIE - The International Society for Optical Engineering.*

Tang, G. Q., 2009. Comparison of several laser spot center location algorithm. *Journal of Beijing Institute of Mechanical Industry*, Vol. 24, No. 1, pp. 62-64.

Wang, Y. L. et al., 2007. Laser spot detection and characteristic analysis in space optical communication, *Infrared and Laser Engineering*, Vol. 36, No. s1, pp. 434-438.

Wang, Z. Q. et al., 2011. Precise positioning algorithm of laser spot center in deformation measurement system. *Electronic Measurement and Instrument*, Vol. 25, No. 6, pp. 485-486.

Wang, Z. Z. et al., 2013. Center detection algorithm of non full circle laser spot center based on circle fitting. *Laser & Infrared*, Vol. 43, No. 6, pp. 709-711.

Wu, D. et al., 2017. Spot center extraction based on cross correlation and improved gaussian fitting. *Journal of Optoelectronics Laser*, Vol. 28, No. 2, pp. 202-210.

Wu, Y. N. et al., 2011. Investigation on a Scheme for Trajectory Filtering Based on Process Noise Control. *Journal of Air Force Engineering University (Natural Science Edition).*

Yu, W. L., 2006. Research on the method of calculating the center position of the laser spot. *Changchun: Changchun University of Science and Technology.*

Zhao, Y. H. el al., 2014. The method of calculating the center of the light spot based on morphology and optical flow equation. *Laser & Infrared*, Vol. 44, No. 2, pp. 214-216.

HYBRID SORT – A PATTERN-FOCUSED MATRIX REORDERING APPROACH BASED ON CLASSIFICATION

Celmar Guimarães da Silva
School of Technology – University of Campinas, Brazil

ABSTRACT

Matrix reordering algorithms permute rows and columns of an input matrix for unveiling patterns that are hidden due to inappropriate permutations. Most reordering algorithms are not pattern-focused and provide low-quality results for revealing some particular patterns. On the other side, few algorithms focus on revealing specific patterns with high-quality results, but they must know a priori that one of these patterns is hidden in the matrix. In this work, we define a matrix reordering algorithm that focuses on revealing a pattern from a pattern set while providing high-quality results. Based on permutation-invariant features of matrices, the algorithm Hybrid Sort uses an empirically-created classifier to classify an input matrix into a canonical data pattern. After that, the algorithm uses this classification to select a pattern-focused reordering algorithm to reorder the input matrix. Therefore, Hybrid Sort inherits the good output quality of the selected reordering algorithms. We report that the classifier reached F2-measures greater or equal to 85% to all patterns in our tests. Besides, we present some examples of this new method applied to synthetic and real-world matrices.

KEYWORDS

Reorderable Matrix, Heatmaps, Pattern Detection

1. INTRODUCTION

Visualization techniques aim to help users to amplify cognition (Card et al. 1999) to better understand datasets. Laying out marks appropriately is a way of reaching this goal, given that proper layout may unveil patterns, tendencies, and outliers in the dataset. Providing a good layout in matrix visualizations (such as heatmaps) means to find row and column permutations that show patterns (if they exist) in the matrix to the user. These permutations can help to perform tasks such as: defining the relative chronological order among a set of artifacts in archaeology according to their similarities, better presenting the results of sociometric tests and other social network data, displaying clusters or gradual changes in the composition of species (Liiv, 2010), and analyzing similarities between students and subjects in undergraduate courses (Barros et al., 2019).

The visualization literature presents a set of patterns that may be found in matrices and that are useful to enhance user understanding about the underlying dataset (Behrisch et al. 2016, Wilkinson 2005). Despite the existence of these patterns, most matrix reordering algorithms, such as the ones surveyed by Behrisch et al. (2016) and Liiv (2010), do not focus on discovering particular patterns in the input matrix. We found only a few pattern-focused reordering algorithms. Most of them try to discover only one or two particular patterns in a matrix (Rocha et al. 2017, Santos et al. 2016, Silva 2019, Silva et al. 2017). Also, we did not find any algorithm that combines reordering algorithms to focus on a particular set of patterns. As an exception, the SMB method (Medina et al. 2016) tries to unveil four patterns, but it does not combine a set of reordering algorithms.

In this paper, we demonstrate that it is possible to construct a hybrid reordering algorithm. Given an $n \times m$ input matrix whose cells have real values, our reordering algorithm (*Hybrid Sort*) combines a matrix classifier and some pattern-focused reordering algorithms to reveal canonical data patterns that may be hidden in this input matrix. Inspired on Medina et al. (2016), we created our own empirical classifier and selected three pattern-focused algorithms that are able to unveil all canonical data patterns. We connected properly the classifier and the selected algorithms. In this paper, we show that our classifier surpass SMB's one and also works with one more pattern. We also present how Hybrid Sort reorders some synthetic and real-world matrices.

This paper is organized as follows. Section 2 briefly presents some concepts regarding matrix patterns. Section 3 discusses works related to pattern-focused reordering algorithms. Section 4 details our hybrid algorithm, with focus on the construction of the matrix classifier. Section 5 exemplifies how our algorithm reorders synthetic and real-world matrices. Besides, it presents a complexity analysis of the algorithm and briefly discusses limitations of this research. Section 6 concludes the paper and points out future work.

2. THEORETICAL BACKGROUND

Behrisch et al. (2016) and Wilkinson (2005) defined nine relevant patterns that may be present in some permutation of a matrix. In a broad analysis, these patterns help users to overview a dataset, its topology, its partitioning and grouping, and the existence of connections among groups. They also aid to inspect adjacencies and connectivity in graphs. This work considered five patterns, known as *canonical data patterns* (Wilkinson 2005): Simplex, Equi, Band, Circumplex, and Block (Figure 1(a-e)). A *Simplex* pattern happens if cell values tend to increase from a matrix corner to its opposite corner. An *Equi-correlation* (a.k.a. *Equi*) pattern happens if cell values tend to increase in bottom-up or top-down directions. The *Band* pattern has its highest values in the main diagonal, and the values decrease from this diagonal to the corners of the secondary diagonal. The *Circumplex* pattern is similar to a Band pattern, but the matrix is taken as a torus, and the band has no start or end. The layout of a *Block* pattern is similar to a heatmap of a sequence of binary numbers with k digits, where each digit defines the values of a rectangular part of the matrix. The literature indicates other patterns that are more related to matrix-based representations of graphs (*Blocks*, *Off-diagonal block*, *Line/Star*, and *Bands*) (Figure 1(f-i)), or anti-patterns (*Bandwidth* and *Noise*) – matrices from which users cannot extract useful information (Behrisch et al. 2016, 2020).

A useful terminology about patterns is the "pre-pattern" terminology. As far as we know, its first use is in the work of Wilkinson (2005). Given a pattern P, a "pre-P" matrix is a matrix that can be permuted to reveal the pattern P. E.g., a pre-Band matrix can be properly permuted to show a Band pattern.

a) Simplex b) Band c) Equi d) Circumplex e) Block f) Bands g) Blocks h) Line/Star i) Off-diagonal blocks

Figure 1. Examples of matrix patterns. (a) to (e): Wilkinson's canonical data patterns; red, white and blue cells stand for high, intermediate and low values, respectively. (f) to (i): Binary patterns by Behrisch et al. (2017); black and white stand for 1 and 0, respectively. Source of the binary patterns: http://magnostics.dbvis.de/#/benchmark

3. RELATED WORK

In this section, we highlight a set of reordering algorithms that may be classified as *pattern-focused* algorithms. Each of them tries to find permutations of rows and columns to reveal a particular set of matrix patterns.

FVS (Silva et al. 2017) reorders the rows (and columns) of a matrix according to their mean values. This simple but useful approach can reveal Simplex and Equi patterns with time complexity $O(n^2)$ (for an $n \times n$ matrix). *Circumplex Sort* (Rocha et al. 2017) sorts the rows of a pre-Circumplex matrix according to index-weighted means of the values of each column. After that, the algorithm creates two stacks of rows. At each iteration, a row r is added to the stack whose top row is most similar to r. At the end, the algorithm concatenates both stacks. This process is repeated for columns. The method unveils a Circumplex pattern with time complexity $O(n^2)$. For pre-Band and pre-Circumplex input matrices, *Polar Sort* (Silva 2019) calculates two multidimensional projections – one for rows, and other for columns. In each projection, a barycenter of the projected points (representing rows or columns) is used to define a circular ordering of these points. This ordering is then replicated into the matrix, unveiling Band and Circumplex patterns with time complexity O(n^3). The *Block Reordering* method (Santos et al. 2016) receives a pre-Block matrix as input and returns a matrix with a Block pattern. The general strategy of this algorithm is (a) to choose iteratively a pivot column (i.e., a column with the lowest noise level of the set of columns considered in a single iteration), (b) to group columns that are similar to it, and (c) to order this groups. The order of the rows is defined by sorting each column of a set of representative columns of each group. The time complexity of the method is O(kn^2), where k is a configuration parameter of the Block pattern.

SMB and MAGNOSTICS are the most similar works to our proposal. SMB (Medina et al. 2016) uses multiple binarized versions of an input matrix to calculate an appropriate permutation of rows and columns. It defines binarization thresholds according to the matrix pattern that underlies the input matrix. Finding what is this pattern is a relevant point of this algorithm. It calculates linear regressions of sorted vectors with maximum and minimum values of rows and columns of the input matrix. The linear coefficients of these regressions form feature vectors that are used to classify the underlying canonical data pattern of the matrix (except Block pattern). Our classifier and feature vectors are inspired by SMB's ones. Our feature vectors have other coefficients than SMB, which enhanced our classification results. Besides, our classifier can detect the Block pattern, which was not the focus of SMB.

The authors of MAGNOSTICS (Behrisch et al. 2017) selected six feature vectors/descriptors (from a set of 31 ones) that can help to classify a given input matrix into one of the following matrix patterns/anti-patterns: Blocks, Off-Diagonal Blocks, Star/Lines, and Bands patterns; and Bandwidth and Noise anti-patterns (Behrisch et al., 2016). However, their classifier was not used to choose an algorithm to reorder a matrix, as we propose in the current paper. Besides, it does not deal with canonical data patterns.

4. HYBRID SORT

Hybrid Sort is based on pattern-focused reordering methods and a matrix classifier. It has three main steps: (1) classify the input matrix M into a pattern p; (2) select a reordering algorithm r according to p; (3) use r to reorder M. The following subsections discuss the construction of the classifier of Step 1 and the algorithm selector of Step 2.

4.1 Permutation-Invariant Features of Matrices

The proposed matrix classifier aims to classify a matrix into one of the canonical data patterns. More specifically, we defined our pattern set as: pre-Band, pre-Simplex, pre-Circumplex, pre-Equi, and pre-Block. The prefix "pre-" in the pattern names reinforces that the input matrix probably does not show the pattern in its current permutation. Therefore, a classifier must be based in permutation-invariant features, i.e. matrix properties that do not depend on positions of columns and rows.

Based on the work of Medina et al. (2016), we observed that we could define four vectors for each matrix $M_{m \times n}$: *minRows[1...m]* and *maxRows[1...m]* have, respectively, the minimum and maximum value of each row of M; and *minColumns[1...n]* and *maxColumns[1...n]* have, respectively, the minimum and maximum value of each column of M. Given that these vectors are dependent of the permutation order of rows and columns, we removed this dependence by sorting these vectors in ascending order.

Figure 2 exemplifies four of the five patterns of our pattern set. (The pre-Block pattern is not shown because it needs a separate treatment.) At the right and below each pattern, linear heatmaps represent the four vectors of that pattern, before and after sorting. Note that the set of sorted vectors of one pattern has not the same behavior in the other patterns. Therefore, these vectors are of interest to our classification approach.

Another problem to overcome is the dependence of the matrix dimension. Matrices with different sizes would return vectors with distinct sizes, which would hamper the classification. For that reason, we opted by replacing each vector by a linear equation of its values, generated by linear regression. This approach generated a list of four equations (and eight coefficients) that summarizes these vectors and, by extension, the input matrix. The equations have the format $y_\phi = a_\phi x + b_\phi$, where ϕ should be replaced with *minRows*, *maxRows*, *minColumns*, or *maxColumns*. The linear regression also helps to deal with noise in the input matrix. Low noise ratios tend to cause little changes in the equation coefficients.

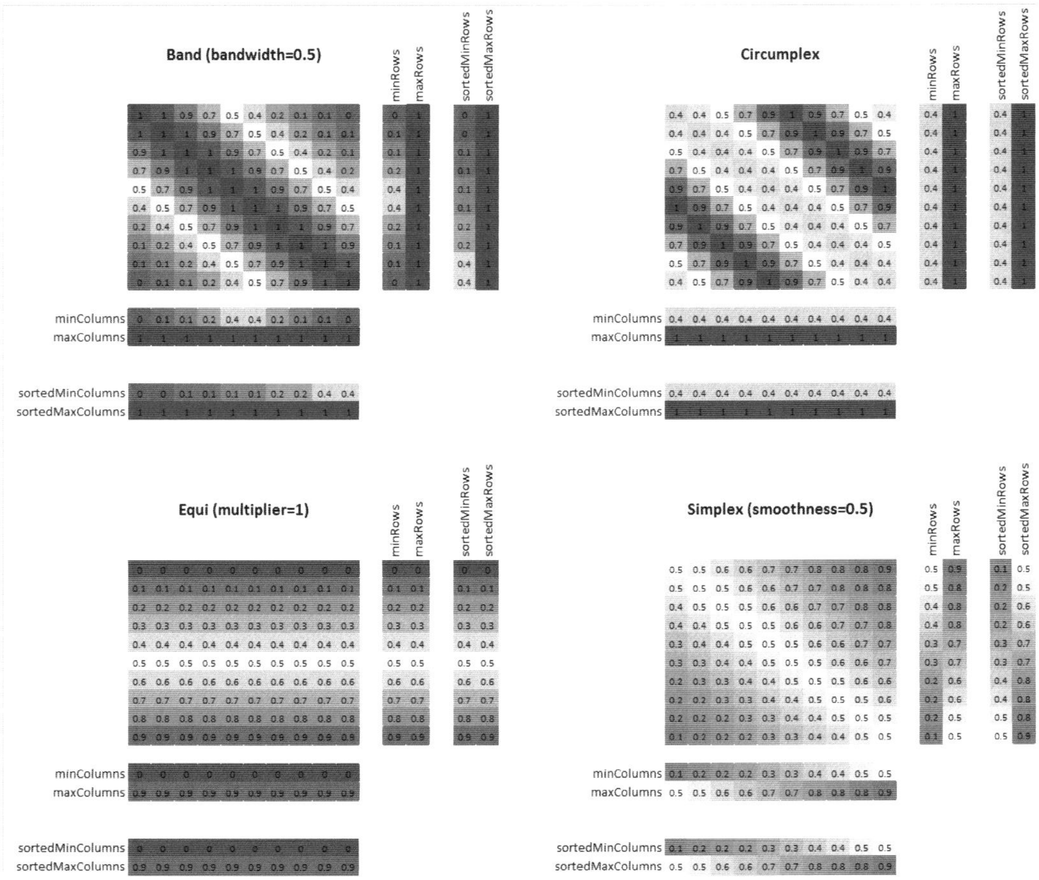

Figure 2. Examples of Band, Circumplex, Equi, and Simplex patterns in 10 × 10 matrices, and their respective vectors with minimum and maximum values per row and per column

Medina et al. (2016) opted by using only the angular coefficients of these equations for classifying an input matrix into one of the four patterns. In our current work we initially used all coefficients to try to produce a more reliable classification. During the work, we reduced this set as necessary.

We also noted that these coefficients do not help to identify the pre-Block pattern. However, we defined two other permutation-invariant boolean coefficients that aid in the identification of this pattern:

- *BalancedColumns*. Given a matrix normalized in values from 0 to 1, we call "high values" the values greater or equal to 0.5, and "low values" the ones lower than 0.5. Pre-Block and pre-Equi matrices have "balanced columns", i.e., columns whose proportion of high (and low) values is about 50%. Noise may increase or decrease this proportion, so we consider a column as balanced if it has a proportion of high values between 40 and 60%. If a matrix has at least 80% of balanced columns, then *BalcancedColumns* is *true*, which is quite indicative that the matrix is pre-Block or pre-Equi.
- *FewIntermediaryValues*. In a matrix normalized in values from 0 to 1, a Block pattern has only cells with value 0 or 1. Therefore, the occurrence of other values would reveal a tendency that the matrix is not pre-Block. However, noise can change this characteristic, and this verification must accept some other values closer to 0 or to 1. We define that values in the intervals [0, 0.2],]0.2, 0.8[, and [0.8, 1] are "low", "intermediary", and "high values", respectively. We count the number of rows with at least 70% of their cells having only low or high values. If the matrix has 70% or more rows that have this characteristic, then *FewIntermediaryValues* is *true*, and this suggests that the matrix has a pre-Block pattern.

It is worth noting that the definitions of both coefficients are empirical. Nonetheless, they worked well in the experiments that we will present later on this paper.

In summary, we have ten coefficients that form a vector of permutation-invariant features of a matrix: $[a_{minRows}, b_{minRows}, a_{maxRows}, b_{maxRows}, a_{minColumns}, b_{minColumns}, a_{maxColumns}, b_{maxColumns}, BalancedColumns, FewIntermediaryValues]$. This feature vector is the basis for our classifier.

4.2 A Matrix Classifier Based on an Empirical Decision Tree

Based on the presented feature vector definition, we constructed a matrix classifier algorithm. We follow the assumption that our input matrices must contain one of the following patterns: pre-Band, pre-Equi, pre-Simplex, pre-Circumplex, or pre-Block.

First, we studied if our feature vectors would provide enough separability between the first four matrix patterns. We considered in this study a set of feature vectors derived from an ensemble of 1,026 matrices configured with distinct patterns, parameters and sizes. Our ensemble is divided into 342 groups of 3 matrices with the same configuration per group. The configurations were:

- A size from the set {100×100, 150×150, 300×300};
- A noise ratio from the set {0%, 1%, 5%, 10%, 30%, 50%};
- A pattern from the set: Band with bandwidth values {0.1, 0.25, 0.5, 0.75, 1, 1.5}; Circumplex; Equi with multiplier values {0.5, 1, 2}; Simplex with smoothness values {0.1, 0.25, 0.5, 0.75, 1, 1.5}; and Block with values of parameter *k* belonging to the set {3, 5, 7};

We used the software Tableau to study visually the relationship between feature vectors and matrix patterns. We used no statistical tool to help in this process. In our analysis, we concluded that we need only three coefficients of the defined feature vector to classify a matrix into one of the four patterns: $a_{minRows}$, $a_{maxRows}$, and $b_{minColumns}$. Figure 3 (top) shows a scatterplot of $a_{minRows}$ values per matrix pattern. We identified four data intervals by numbers from 1 to 4. These intervals indicate situations in which we have only Circumplex (1 and 3) or Band (2 and 4) patterns. Figure 3 (bottom) helps to analyze the remaining feature vectors, i.e., those with $a_{minRows} > 0.015$. We identified other five data intervals that are strongly related to a pattern: region 5 for Band pattern, regions 6 and 9 for Simplex, and regions 7 and 8 for Equi.

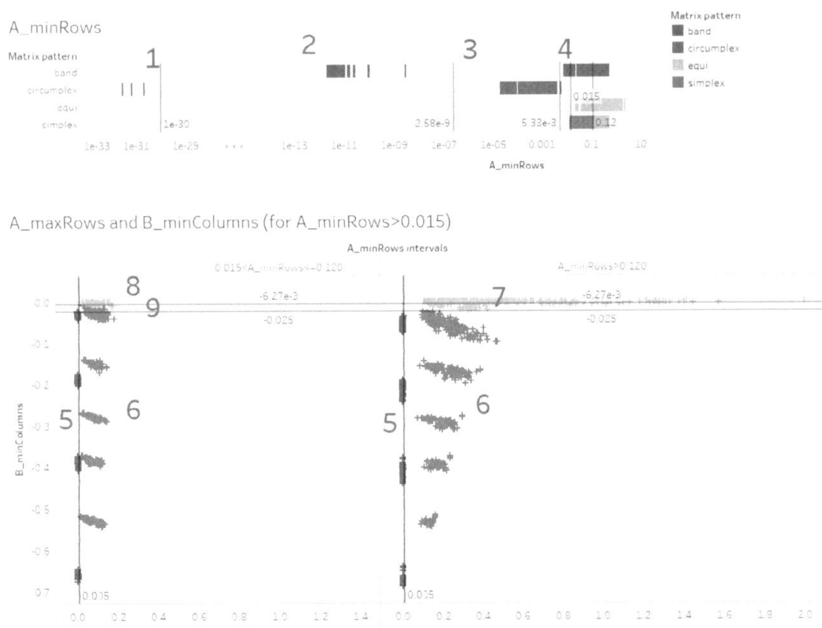

Figure 3. Values of feature vectors' variables per matrix pattern. Top: variable aminRows (A_minRows); bottom: variables amaxRows (A_maxRows) and bminColumns (B_minColumns). Blue numbers indicate regions of interest in each graphic

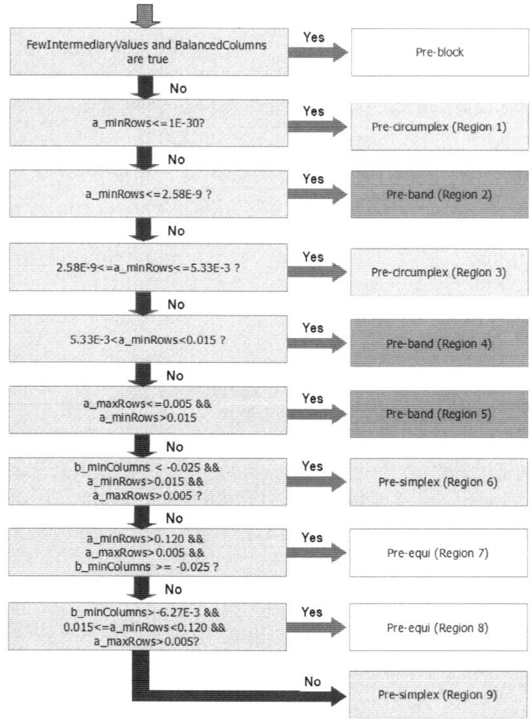

Figure 4. Empirical decision tree of the matrix classifier

We defined most of the decision tree in Figure 4 based on this previous analysis. This decision tree is the heart of the algorithm because a wrong classification would lead to choosing an inappropriate reordering algorithm.

Regarding pre-Block pattern, we noted that matrices whose properties BalancedColumns and FewIntermediaryValues are true could be classified as pre-Block. Consequently, this decision was added to the root of the decision tree in Figure 4. Section 5 will discuss the quality of the proposed classifier.

4.3 Selection of Pattern-Focused Algorithms

The Step 2 must select an algorithm that is good at unveiling the pattern informed by Step 1. According to the works presented at Section 3, we defined the following algorithms to be selected for each pattern: FVS (Silva et al. 2017) for pre-Equi or pre-Simplex, Block Reordering (Santos et al. 2016) for pre-Block, and Polar Sort (Silva 2019) for pre-Circumplex or pre-Band. These choices considered the high-quality of the output of these reordering algorithms and their fast running time in comparison to other algorithms, as presented in their respective papers.

5. RESULTS AND DISCUSSION

In this section, we first discuss the quality of our classifier. Next, we present how Hybrid Sort reorders some synthetic and real-world matrices. We also analyze the time complexity of this reordering method.

We tested our classifier with a set of 45,600 matrices. This set was divided into 50-matrices groups, and matrices of the same group have the same configuration. The set of matrix sizes was: $\{25 \times 25, 50 \times 50, 75 \times 75, 100 \times 100, 150 \times 150, 200 \times 200, 300 \times 300, 500 \times 500\}$. We considered the same noise ratios, patterns and pattern configurations used to construct the classifier. The test compared the actual patterns of each matrix with the patterns assigned by the classifier. We opted by creating matrices that have the data patterns in its current permutation, instead of scrambling its rows and columns. This decision makes sense because sorting the vectors of Section 4.1 makes the classifier immune to the ordering of rows and columns of the input matrix. Thus, we saved experiment time that would be lost with unnecessary permutations.

Figure 5(a) presents the results of this analysis as a confusion matrix. Its diagonal values are higher than 91% for most patterns. The exception is for pre-Block matrices, with 82.9% of correct classification, and with 13.7% of the input matrices incorrectly classified as pre-Circumplex. Nevertheless, we believe that these values are considerably good for an empirically-defined classifier. Besides, the F2-measure has good scores for all patterns: 95%, 93%, 92%, 86%, and 85% for Band, Simplex, Equi, Circumplex, and Block, respectively.

For comparison, Figure 5(b) shows a confusion matrix for the SMB's classifier. This matrix does not have a "block" column or a "block" row because this classifier does not deal with pre-Block matrices. However, it was created by the same process that create the Hybrid Sort confusion matrix, except by the absence of pre-Block matrices. We noted that SMB's classifier did many errors when it classified pre-Band, pre-Cirumplex or pre-Equi matrices as pre-Simplex ones (fifth column). Besides, the main diagonal of this confusion matrix has many values lower than 50%, which indicates that the classifier has low precision. The high number of matrices classified as "other" is also a concern. Therefore, we perceived that the results of Hybrid Sort's classifier are better than SMB's one.

In summary, we observed that it was possible to construct a classifier whose classification results surpass SMB's ones. Also, we noted that it is possible to improve our classifier.

Actual Class	Assigned Class				
	band	block	circumplex	equi	simplex
band	96,1%	0,0%	1,0%	0,7%	2,2%
block	2,5%	82,9%	13,7%	1,0%	0,0%
circumplex	6,4%	0,0%	92,3%	0,0%	1,3%
equi	3,3%	0,0%	0,0%	91,8%	4,9%
simplex	6,4%	0,0%	0,4%	1,2%	92,0%

a) Hybrid Sort

Actual Class	Assigned Class				
	band	circumplex	equi	simplex	(other)
band	11,8%	4,9%	0,0%	47,1%	36,2%
circumplex	11,0%	43,9%	0,0%	36,7%	8,4%
equi	0,0%	0,0%	19,8%	73,7%	6,5%
simplex	0,0%	0,0%	0,0%	100,0%	0,0%

b) SMB

Figure 5. Confusion matrices of (a) Hybrid Sort (b) and SMB's classifiers

Table 1 exemplifies the output of Hybrid Sort for five synthetic input matrices with distinct patterns. Its first row indicates pattern names and configurations, and the second one ("Original") shows an instance of these patterns. All instances have noise ratio 0.1 and size 200 × 200. The third row presents randomly permuted versions of these instances. The last row shows these shuffled matrices after being reordered by Hybrid Sort. In all patterns, there is a high visual similarity between matrices in the second and fourth rows.

As a first real-world example, we present a matrix that compares pairwise similarity of 12 mood-related adjectives (Browne 1992). This matrix has the same adjectives in both columns, and each cell shows how 472 persons correlate two adjectives. Figure 6(a) shows this table in its original order. Figure 6(b) shows how a scrambled version of this table is ordered by Hybrid Sort. Note that the rows and columns of (a) and (b) are in the same circular ordering. Both versions unveil a Circumplex pattern that shows similarities of groups of adjectives, such as "relaxed" and "calm", or "drowsy" and "dull".

A second real-world example is a matrix that correlates crimes and offenses (Thurstone 1927). For each pair of elements in a set of 15 crimes and offenses, 266 persons informed which of these elements they consider more serious. These answers were summarized as a set of triples [e1, e2, p], where p indicates the proportion of answers "e2 is more serious than e1". In the resulting table, row labels have values of e1, and column labels have values of e2. Each cell (r, c) has the proportion in which the crime (or offense) in column label c is more serious than the one in the row label r. Figure 6(c,d) shows this table in alphabetical order, and the same table after being reordered by Hybrid Sort. In Figure 6(c), homicide and rape have red columns that make evident the seriousness of these crimes for the interviewed individuals. When Hybrid Sort received this table as input, the algorithm classified the table as a pre-Simplex matrix, and consequently, it ordered the matrix with FVS. In the resulting heatmap in Figure 6(d), the Simplex-like pattern highlights an overall ordering of the people's opinions about the seriousness of the analyzed crimes and offenses. The ordering provided by Hybrid Sort also evidences that rape, homicide, abortion, seduction, and kidnapping were considered as the most serious crimes.

Table 1. Examples of Hybrid Sort's output when reordering matrices with canonical data patterns

Pattern configuration	Band (bandwidth =0.5)	Block (k=0.5)	Circumplex	Equi (multiplier =1.0)	Simplex (smoothness =0.5)
Original	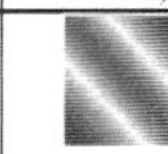	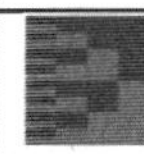	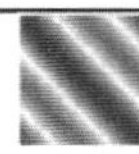		
Shuffled		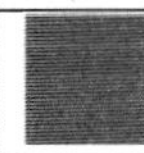			
Reordered	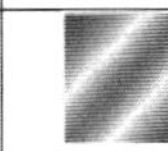		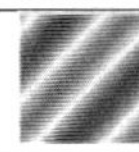		

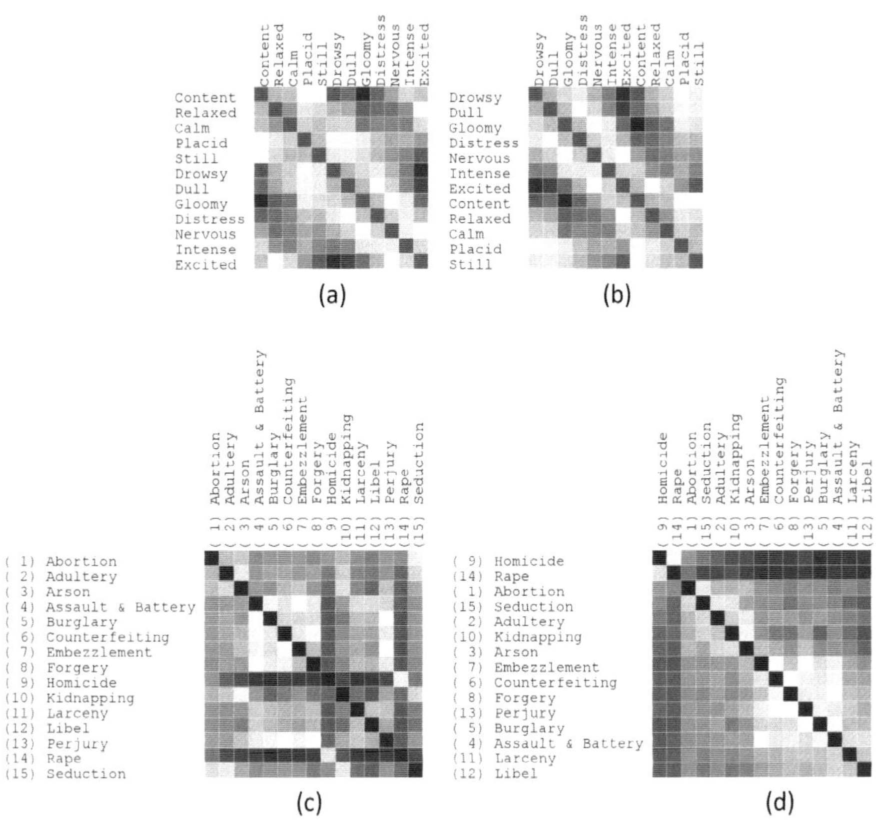

Figure 6. (a) Original and (b) Hybrid Sort's ordering of the "mood adjectives" matrix; (c) original and (d) Hybrid Sort's ordering of the "Crimes" matrix

The asymptotic time complexity of Hybrid Sort is as follows. The classification step is dominated by activities that browse the entire matrix, so it has time complexity $O(n^2)$. The algorithm selection is straightforward and has time complexity O(1). The reordering step depends on the selected algorithm, and the one with the worst time complexity is Polar Sort ($O(n^3)$). Therefore, we conclude that Hybrid Sort has time complexity $O(n^3)$. This complexity could be improved if we replace Polar Sort by a faster algorithm with output quality as good as it has for pre-Band and pre-Circumplex matrices.

The main limitation of this research is that the decision tree used by the matrix classifier supposes that every input matrix is pre-Band, pre-Circumplex, pre-Simplex, pre-Equi or pre-Block. Therefore, attempts to use Hybrid Sort to reorder matrices that do not have one of the five patterns considered by the decision tree will possibly result in not appropriate orderings of these matrices.

It is worth noting that we do not present in this paper experiments with synthetic matrices that could justify the quality of the output matrices reordered by Hybrid Sort. We opted by doing this because the output quality of the reordering methods used by Hybrid Sort was already analyzed and attested in their respective papers.

6. CONCLUSION

We presented in this work a matrix reordering method – Hybrid Sort – based on three steps: input classification, selection of a reordering algorithm, and execution of this algorithm. Its classifier uses a decision tree based on feature vectors extracted from the input matrix. It classifies the input matrix into one of the five canonical data patterns. The algorithm selector uses the inferred class of the matrix to choose FVS, Polar Sort or Block Reordering algorithms for the third step. The last step uses the selected algorithm to reorder the input matrix. The classifier reached good precision measures that overcome the SMB's classifier. The overall solution has time complexity O(n3). Future work includes: replacing Polar Sort by a faster multidimensional projection algorithm, aiming to reduce Hybrid Sort's time complexity; improving the classifier by using machine learning strategies for pattern detection; and expanding the algorithm to consider other patterns.

ACKNOWLEDGEMENT

We thank the grant #2224/20 from FAEPEX/PRP/Unicamp.

REFERENCES

Barros, R.T.C. et al., 2019. Use of reorderable matrices and heatmaps to support data analysis of students transcripts. Companion Proceedings of the 32nd SIBGRAPI – Conference on Graphics, Patterns and Images. Rio de Janeiro, Brazil, pp. 219-222.

Behrisch, M. et al., 2016. Matrix reordering methods for table and network visualization. Computer Graphics Forum 35(3), pp. 693–716.

Behrisch, M. et al., 2017. MAGNOSTICS: Image-based search of interesting matrix views for guided network exploration. IEEE Transactions on Visualization and Computer Graphics 23(1), pp. 31–40.

Behrisch, M. et al., 2020, GUIRO: User-guided matrix reordering, IEEE Transactions on Visualization and Computer Graphics 26(1), pp. 184–194.

Browne, M. W. 1992. Circumplex models for correlation matrices. Psychometrika 57(4), pp. 469–497.

Card, S. K. et al. 1999. Readings in Information Visualization: Using Vision to Think, Morgan Kaufmann Publishers Inc., San Francisco, CA, USA.

Liiv, I., 2010. Seriation and matrix reordering methods: An historical overview, Statistical Analysis and Data Mining 3(2), pp. 70–91.

Medina, B. F. et al., 2016, Smoothed Multiple Binarization – Using PQR tree, smoothing, feature vectors and thresholding for matrix reordering. Proc. of 20th Int. Conf. Information Visualisation (IV). Lisbon, Portugal, pp. 88–93.

Rocha, M. M. N. et al., 2017. Circumplex Sort: a two-phase method for revealing circumplex data patterns in reorderable matrices. Proc. Int. Conf. Computer Graphics, Visualization, Computer Vision and Image Processing 2017 and Big Data Analytics, Data Mining and Computational Intelligence 2017. Lisbon, Portugal, pp. 181–188.

Santos, A. M. et al., 2016, Block Reordering: Um algoritmo para evidenciar padrão Block em matrizes reordenáveis. Workshop of Undergraduate Works (WUW) in the 29th Conference on Graphics, Patterns and Images (SIBGRAPI'16), São José dos Campos, Brazil.

Silva, C. G. et al., 2017. A fast feature vector approach for revealing simplex and equi-correlation data patterns in reorderable matrices. Information Visualization 16(4), pp. 261–274.

Silva, C. G., 2019. Polar Sort: combining multidimensional scaling and polar coordinates for matrix reordering. Proc. Int. Conf. Interfaces and Human Computer Interaction 2019; Game and Entertainment Technologies 2019; and Computer Graphics, Visualization, Computer Vision and Image Processing 2019, Porto, Portugal, pp. 239–243.

Thurstone, L. L., 1927. The method of paired comparisons for social values. The Journal of Abnormal and Social Psychology 21, pp. 384–400.

Wilkinson, L., 2005. The Grammar of Graphics. Springer Science & Business Media. New York, USA.

INTELLIGENT STYLE TRANSFER OF FILM IMAGE BASED ON CYCLEGAN

Da Liu[1,2], Huixin Wang[1] and Bin Wu[1]

[1]*College of Intelligence and Computing, Tianjin University, Tianjin 300350, PR China*

[2]*China Research Institute of Film Science & Technology, Beijing 100086, PR China*

ABSTRACT

With the development and application of deep learning, image style transfer has achieved an important breakthrough. It has been able to intelligently generate stylized natural, realistic and high-quality images, which can be applied to film screens to reduce the cost of artificial effects. This paper proposes an intelligent style transfer method of film image style based on CycleGAN. In view of the high spatial resolution, large size and rich details of high-tech format film images, we have modified the input layer of the network so that the network can better process film images, and replace the original GAN loss with WGAN loss to achieve a more stable training effect. As a result, style features can be better transformed between images, and at the same time, SSIM loss is added to the cycle consistency loss to enhance the recovery of images similarity to the original image and improve the quality of the generated image. Experiments show that this method is effective in processing the style transfer of film images, and can intelligently generate high-quality and natural realistic style transfer images.

KEYWORDS

High-tech Format Film, Image Style Transfer, Cycle-Consistent Generative Adversarial Networks (CycleGAN), Wasserstein GAN (WGAN), SSIM

1. INTRODUCTION

Film is the product of scientific and technological progress and an organic fusion of technology and art. High-tech is an important booster for the upgrading and high-quality development of the film industry. In recent years, artificial intelligence (AI), machine learning, deep learning, cloud computing, high performance computing (HPC), computer vision, computer graphics (CG/CGI), and other intelligence science & technology and the new generation of information communication technology (ICT) are more and more widely used in the cinema industry. The continuous deepening not only innovates the film production model, enriches the film production methods, significantly improves the level, ability and efficiency of film production, but also actively promotes the information construction and intelligent upgrade of the cinema industry to promote the transformation of the cinema industry into a high-tech industry upgrade. The cinema technology chain in all-digital era is shown in Figure 1.

Adapt to the developing needs of people in modern society for high-quality film content, based on 4K (4096×2160), 8K(8192×4320), giant screen, high frame rate (HFR), high dynamic range (HDR), wide color gamut (WCG), visual special effects (VFX), immersive audio and other emerging audio-visual technologies, high-tech format film has become the development focus and application hotspot of the modern film industry. It has played a vital role in improving the audio-visual quality of film, movie watching experience and industrial efficiency. Therefore, vigorously developing high-tech format film, and promoting the intelligent application of high-tech format film production throughout the industry chain has become an important measure to promote fine film production and the construction of a strong film country.

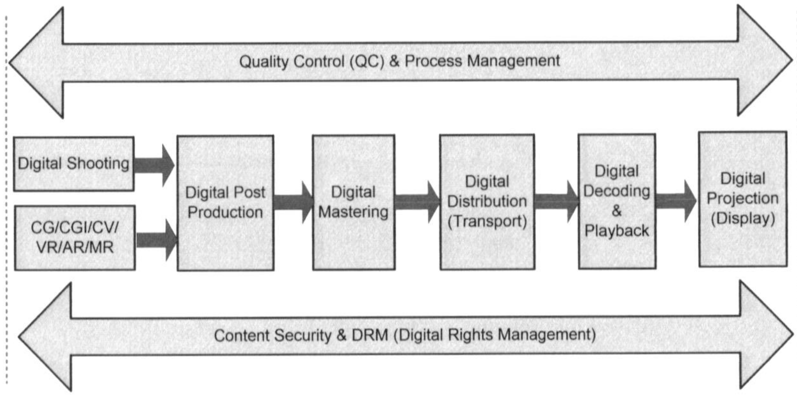

Figure 1. The cinema technology chain in all-digital era

Intelligentization is the basic trend and inevitable requirement for the development of modern film production. The intelligent transfer of styles for high-tech format film images is an effective means of modern film production, and has important application value for improving the level and efficiency of film production. Image style transfer refers to transferring the style of a reference image to another image while preserving the same structure and semantic information of the original image, which belongs to the research category of image translation, that is to realize cross-domain transformation of image. For example, a photo of a natural landscape is transform to the scene drawn by Van Gogh, as shown in Figure 2. Style transfer has a wide range of applications, and can be applied to film post production. Through image style transfer, the pictures taken by the camera can be transformed to other styles. The resulting picture will be more realistic and flexible.

Figure 2. The natural scene transformed to Van Gogh's scene

So far, most existing style transfer methods are based on deep learning methods, which can achieve transfer between different scenes and different styles, and can obtain realistic and natural style transfer images. Convolution Neural Networks (CNN), whose style transfer includes three main methods: single-model single-style, single-model multi-style, and single-model arbitrary style, but these methods will be limited and affected by the type and number of styles in the datasets. Generative Adversarial Networks (GAN), as a network trained by unsupervised learning small datasets, has great potential in the field of image style transfer, but training with only one GAN network may cause instability and result in poor final results. Cycle-Consistent Generative Adversarial Networks (CycleGAN) is composed of two symmetric GAN networks, especially for the field of style transfer to achieve better results. However, there is a clear difference between film images and general images. Most of the film images are high-resolution and large image sizes taken by the high-resolution professional film camera. The converted images need to take into account the artistry and true nature. The previous methods do not aim at this feature of film images, which will result in low quality of the generated results. The resulting image size is reduced, the resolution is also reduced, and it will be limited by storage and processing time, and the instability of network training will also be as a result, features cannot be transformed between images well.

In this paper, we propose a style transfer method of film images based on CycleGAN. According to the characteristics of film images, especially high-tech format film images, which based on emerging audio-visual technology, such as 4K, 8K, HFR, HDR, WCG, VFX, it can accurately transfer the style of reference images while saving the image content and details. Our method is based on CycleGAN's work on image style transfer. However, the image style transfer is directly performed by the CycleGAN method, for some parts of the source image, the original style cannot be transformed according to the reference image, and the resulting image quality is not high. Compared with general images, high-tech format film images has many technical performance advantages in the key technical indicators, such as spatial resolution, frame rate, quantization depth, dynamic range, color gamut. At the same time, the network of CycleGAN has some instability, which leads to bad final results. Our method has made some modifications to CycleGAN to make the model more suitable for film image style transfer. For the high-resolution, large-size and rich-detailed characteristics of film images, we have modified the input layer of the network on this basis so that the network can better process film images, while replacing the original GAN loss with WGAN loss to maintain the stability of training and adding structural similarity (SSIM) loss to the cycle consistency loss to improve the quality of the final generated image.

This paper proposes a method for film image style transfer based on the CycleGAN. On the one hand, this paper can realize the mapping of complex features to complex features, and change the style features of the source image according to the reference image. Meanwhile, the loss function used in this paper can ensure more stable results and high image quality results.

The main contributions of the paper are as follows:

(1) Propose a new high-tech format film image style transfer framework based on CycleGAN. For an input high-resolution, large-size and rich-detailed film image, the style can be transformed according to the reference image. The framework is end-to-end and requires no user interaction. We modify the input layer of the network so that the network can better process film images;

(2) Replace GAN loss with WGAN loss to ensure the stability of the model, so that the style features can be better transformed between the two images;

(3) The SSIM loss is added to the cycle consistency loss, and the quality of the generated image can be improved by adding the SSIM loss.

2. RELATED WORK

The problem of image style transfer is originally from the rendering of non-real images, which is closely related to the two fields of image texture modeling and image reconstruction. Texture is the key element of image style, texture characteristic is the characteristic that the image presents irregularity in the local area and regularity in the whole, and it mainly including roughness, directionality and contrast. The image texture transfer can be achieved by modeling the texture during image reconstruction. Texture modeling solves the problem of style features, mainly including parametric texture modeling methods based on statistical distribution and non-parametric texture modeling methods based on Markov random field (MRF); image reconstruction is to restore images based on features, mainly including online images optimized slow image reconstruction method and fast image reconstruction method based on offline model optimization. Gatys et al. (2016) proposed the first use of Convolution Neural Networks (CNN) for image style transfer. It is a pioneering work of image style transfer. The Gram matrix is used to model and extract the style of the image, and then use a slow image reconstruction algorithm. The Gram matrix is made close to the Gram matrix of the style graph, the high-level features of the VGG network are close to the features of the content graph, and the final reconstructed image contains both image content and image style. However, because the feature extraction is done in the high-level CNN feature space, some low-level information will be lost and some distortions will appear in the result. Li et al. (2017) proposed a MRF loss to replace the Gram loss, and split the style image and the reconstructed image into patches. For the patch of the reconstructed image to find the closest style patch, it can also work well when the style image is an image close to the content image retain structural information. The above method is based on the slow image reconstruction method for image style transfer, which is slow and consumes resources. There are still certain limitations in practical applications. The fast image style transfer algorithm uses the fast image reconstruction method optimized by the offline model to reconstruct the stylized results, and the forward network is pre-trained to solve the problem of large amount of calculation and slow speed. Li and Wand (2016) and Johnson et al. (2016) use the forward network to learn a style, and use the gram matrix for style modeling, but this single-model single-style algorithm requires training a model for each style, which is not particularly conducive to use. The work (Li & Wand, 2016 , October) on the basis of the trained style network, an affine transformation is performed on the Instance Normalization layer, namely Conditional Instance Normalization (CIN), which corresponds the parameters of the CIN layer to the style. For a new style, only the parameters need to be retrained to achieve a single multi-style effects of the model. In the CNN feature space, Zhang and Dana (2017) find the style patch that matches the content patch to exchange, and then use the fast image reconstruction algorithm to quickly rebuild according to the feature map after the exchange, but the time overhead is large. Inspired by the CIN layer, Ulyanov et al. (2017) proposed the Adaptive Instance Normalization (AdaIN). The input of AdaIN is the image style and content features extracted through VGG, which is trained on large-scale style images and content images, so that AdaIN can directly transfer the content image into different styles. The shortcomings of this method are also obvious. This data-driven approach leads to stylization effects that are very related to the type and number of styles in the training data set. Dosovitskiy and Brox (2016) have generated impressive results based on generative adversarial networks (GAN), but the training process is not very stable. However there have been some GAN-based works (Li et al., 2018; Verma & Smith, 2017) in the field of image style transfer that have achieved good results.

Completing image style transfer based on GAN is a promising direction. GAN and its derivative model have important application value for the intelligent post-production of movies, and have great significance for the intelligent upgrading of cinema industry. Generative Adversarial Networks (GAN), proposed by Goodfellow et al. (2014), is a novel unsupervised learning method, which based on Zero-Sum Game and Nash Equilibrium theories. The core parts of GAN are generator and discriminator, also known as generative model and discriminative model. GAN can solve the training problem of small data sets, and does not need to calibrate the data. It can be learned directly on the network. Radford et al. (2015) introduced a convolutional neural network, called deep convolution generative adversarial network (DCGAN). It changed the network architecture of GAN to make the network training more stable. Although the network has a good architecture, it does not really solve the GAN training stability problem. Wasserstein GAN (WGAN) proposed by Arjovsky et al. (2017) has made progress in GAN stability training. The generative model of the traditional GAN is to convert random noise into a picture, but in the image style transfer, we need to convert the image into a image, so this time we must use the image as the input of generative model, and generative model is to learn a mapping. However, training using only one GAN is unstable, which may cause all photos to be mapped to mode collapse of the same picture. At this time, CycleGAN (Zhu et al., 2017) was proposed to solve this problem. CycleGAN is a combination of two GANs, which can realize the conversion between unpaired images, especially suitable for image style transfer.

3. METHOD

The input of our network is mainly two images: one input image is a large-scale high-resolution film image, and the other input is a reference image with special style. Through the adversarial networks, the style of the input image is converted into the style of the reference image, while maintaining the realism and naturalness and high quality of the resulting style transfer image.

The network framework of this paper is shown in Figure 3. Our network is based on the CycleGAN network, which is composed of two unidirectional symmetric GAN models. These two networks form a ring network. It can be seen from the figure that the network is composed of two sets of generators and two sets of discriminators, and information is shared between them. Input a pair of source image X and reference image Y, the input image X is passed to the first generator G, and then the newly generated image fake_Y is passed to another generator F, the fake_Y is restored to get rec_X. Similarly, the training process of the source image Y can be obtained. The input image Y is passed to the generator F, and then the newly generated image fake_X is passed to another generator G to restore fake_X. The discriminator D is used to discriminate whether the image is the original image or the generated image, DX judges the authenticity of the source image X and fake_X, and DY judges the authenticity of the source image Y and fake_Y.

3.1 Network Architectures

Generator Network. For the generator network, the encoder mainly includes 3 convolution neural networks (CNN), the convolution kernel is 3×3, and the step size is 2; the converter includes 6 residual networks, which are composed of 2 convolution layers, and can guarantee that the previously entered information can be input into the following network. It can reduce the difference between the previous input information and the subsequent input information, to ensure that the details of the output image of the network remain intact; the decoder is mainly composed of 2 deconvolution layers and 1 convolution layer Composition, the convolution kernel of the deconvolution layer is 3×3, the step size is 2, and the convolution kernel of the convolution layer is 7×7. When inputting a 1024×1024×3 image, after convolving the image through 2 convolution layers, 1024 output features with a size of 256×256 can be obtained. After the residual network processing, the 256×256 output features of the previous step can be passed to the converter to obtain feature vectors of the same size.

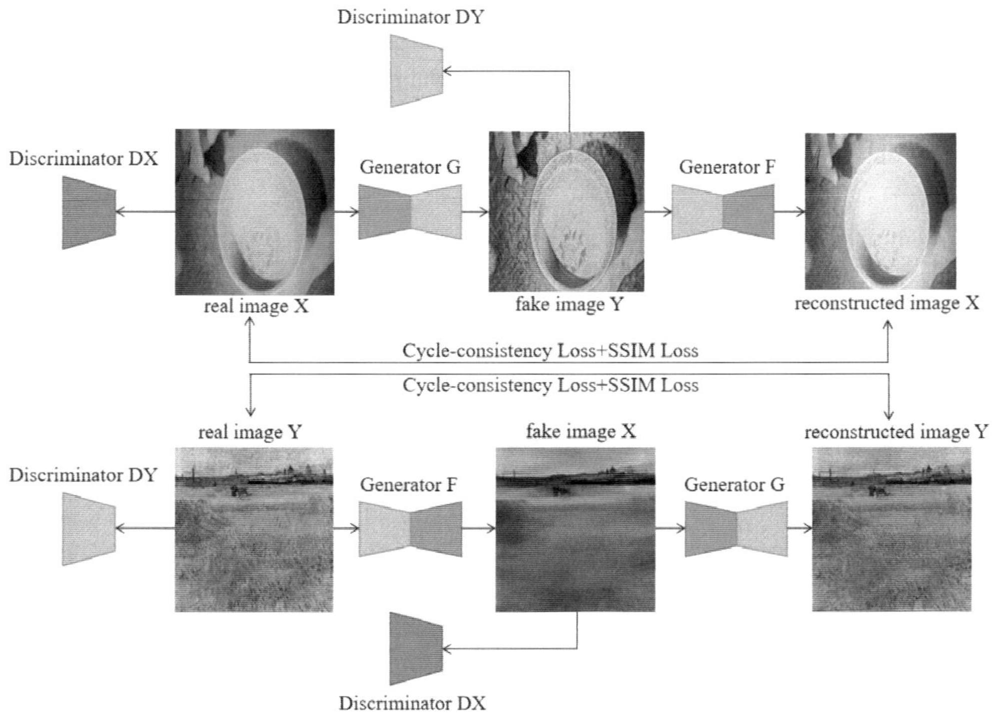

Figure 3. Our network framework

Discriminator Network. The discriminator network needs to identify the real image or the generated image by extracting image features. Therefore, this paper uses a convolution neural network (CNN) as a discriminator. For the discriminator network, we mainly use 4 fully convolutional layers and a 1D output convolution layer to implement the discrimination function. Use 70×70 PatchGAN to identify whether 70×70 overlapping image blocks are real or fake. This block-level discriminator structure has fewer parameters than the full-image discriminator, and can be applied to images of any size in a fully convolutional manner.

3.2 Loss

Avoid color images as the proceedings will be printed in black and white. The goal of this paper is to learn the mapping function between two domains X and Y given training samples, where $x_i \in X$ and $y_j \in Y$. For simplicity, we omit the subscripts i and j. DX and DY are two adversarial discriminators. DX is used to distinguish the image {x} from the transformed image {F(y)}, and DY is to distinguish {y} from {G(x)}. The objective function consists of three parts: the first is the WGAN loss, which is used to match the distribution of the generated image with the data distribution in the target domain to maintain the stability of training; the second is the loss of cycle consistency loss and structural similarity (SSIM) loss, cycle consistency loss can be used to prevent contradictions when learning G and F mapping relationships, SSIM loss is used to strengthen the similarity between the restored image and the original image and maintain the quality of the generated image; the third is a loss of identity that can maintain the color composition between input and output.

WGAN Loss. For the traditional GAN network, there are problems such as training difficulties, the loss of the generator and discriminator cannot indicate the training process, and the lack of diversity in the generated samples. Wasserstein GAN (WGAN) (Gulrajani et al., 2017) solves the problem of GAN training instability, no longer need to carefully balance the training level of the generator and discriminator, and basically solve the problem of mode collapse, ensuring the diversity of generated samples. From our test results, we can see that in some test results, the use of GAN loss will make some styles of the reference image unable to be transferred to the source image. This is because the standard discriminator loss uses cross-entropy loss, which causes the gradient to disappear. In order to solve this problem, we have improved according to WGAN: the loss of the generator and discriminator no longer takes the log function, the output of the discriminator is no longer a probability, so the last layer of the discriminator is removed sigmoid layer; after the discriminator is updated every time, the absolute value of the parameters is truncated to no more than a fixed constant c; use Root Mean Square Prop (RMSProp) or Stochastic Gradient Descent (SGD) instead of using momentum-based optimization algorithms (including momentum and Adam).

Cycle Consistency Loss and SSIM Loss. When lossy compression is performed on an image, or an image has noise, distortion, etc., Wang et al. (2004) proposed a metric to measure the similarity between the reconstructed image and the original image: Structural Similarity (SSIM) index. SSIM loss is a loss function driven by perception. The goal is to allow the network to learn to generate visually pleasing images, and SSIM loss has been shown to improve the quality of generated images. In order to improve the quality of the final generated image on the basis of SSIM loss, we chose MS-SSIM loss (Wang et al., 2003). MS-SSIM loss considers SSIM loss on the M scale as follows:

$$MS-SSIM(x,y)=[l_M(x,y)^{\alpha_M}\prod_{j=1}^{M}[c_j(x,y)]^{\beta_j}[s_j(x,y)]^{\gamma_j} \quad (1)$$

Where the luminance is l (x, y), the contrast is c (x, y), and the structure is s (x, y),

$$l(x,y)=\frac{2\mu_x\mu_y+c_1}{\mu_x^2+\mu_y^2+c_1} \quad (2)$$

$$c(x,y)=\frac{2\sigma_x\sigma_y+c_1}{\sigma_x^2+\sigma_y^2+c_1} \quad (3)$$

$$s(x,y)=\frac{\sigma_{xy}+c_3}{\sigma_x\sigma_y+c_3} \quad (4)$$

For convenience, we set α_M and β_j to 1, and the loss calculated at the center pixel can be approximated to estimate the loss of patch P:

$$L_{MS\text{-}SSIM}(P)=1-MS\text{-}SSIM(\tilde{p}) \quad (5)$$

We added SSIM loss to the cycle consistency loss to enhance the similarity between the reconstructed image and the original image.

Identity Loss. In the process of image generation, due to the influence of the generated image, the mapping of color features may be changed, and the color composition between the reconstruction image and the source image changes greatly, making people visually feel the difference between the source image and the reconstruction image larger. Therefore, the identity loss (Zhu et al., 2017) is added to make the color composition of the source image and the reconstruction image consistent. The loss of identity is as follows:

$$L_{identity}(G,F)=E_{y\sim P_{data}(y)}[\| G(y)-y\|_1]+E_{x\sim P_{data}(x)}[\| G(x)-x\|_1] \quad (6)$$

We integrate different loss functions:

$$L_{loss}=\lambda L_{WGAN}+\alpha L_{cyc+MS\text{-}SSIM}+\beta L_{identity} \quad (7)$$

4. EXPERIMENTS

Training. For all experiments, we set $\lambda = 10$, $\alpha = 1$, $\beta = 0.1$ in formula (7). All networks are trained from scratch, with a learning rate of 0.0002. One epoch means that all samples in the training set have been experienced once. We maintain the same learning rate in the first 100 epochs, and linearly decay the rate to zero in the next 100 epochs.

Implementation Details. The requirements of the experimental environment in this paper are as follows: The processor is Intel Xeon, the graphics card used is Quadro M4000, and it runs on Linux Ubuntu 16.4 operating system. This paper uses the PyTorch framework, programming in Python, the number of iterations is set to 100.

Dataset. For reference images, a total of 2076 images in four styles including Vangogh, Monet, Cezanne, and Ukiyoe were collected (see Figure 4). Considering that the film images are mostly images in natural scenes, as shown in Figure 5, we collected a total number of 6015 images with an image size of 1024×1024 for experiments.

(a) Vangogh Style

(b) Monet Style

(c) Cezanne Style

(d) Ukiyoe Style

Figure 4. Example of style images

Figure 5. Example of film images

Quantitative Results. We trained our model on four datasets, and transferred the style the source image to generate a new image, so that the generated images have the style of Vangogh, Cezanne, Ukiyoe and Monet. We show the results in Figure 6. For example, the generated Vangogh style image seems to be Vangogh's drawing of this picture in reality. Compared with the source image, it keeps the content and details of the source image. Compared with the style image, it inherits the style information of the style image, including texture and color. The image obtained by our method keeps a good balance in style and content.

We also compare our method with the methods of Gatys et al. and Johnson et al. in Figure 7. The methods of Gatys et al. and Johnson et al. transfer the image style information such as color and texture of the style image to the source image, but at this time, the content and details of the source image are kept less. Although the images generated by these two methods can generate images with corresponding styles, they will make people feel unnatural and unreal, and it can be clearly seen that they are generated artificial false images. But the image generated by our method keeps more details and contents of the source image after the style is transferred, and the generated image is just like the real image generated in this style. The methods of Gatys et al. and Johnson et al. will produce uneven color distribution. For example, the second image in Figure 7, the method of Gatys et al. has abrupt green areas and the method of Johnson et al. has sudden red areas, but our method will not produce this kind of unnatural color transfer error. And the results by Gatys et al. and Johnson et al. will lose some details of the source image, for example, for the first image, the results obtained by Johnson et al. lose the sky information of the source image. For the fourth image, the results obtained by Gatys et al. lose the exposed land distribution information of the source image, but our method can keep more details of the source image.

Especially for the style transfer of film images, in practical application, more attention is paid to the natural authenticity of the image after style transfer. The image after style transfer needs to make the audience feel real, which is different from the general style transfer. Compared with Gatys et al. and Johnson et al., our method keeps the content and details of the source image as much as possible while performing style transfer, and generates a more natural and realistic style transfer image. Our method is more suitable for style migration of film images.

5. CONCLUSION

We proposed a method for intelligent style transfer of film images based on CycleGAN. In view of the high-resolution and large size of high-tech format film images, as well as the instability of CycleGAN training and the low quality of the generated images, we modified the input layer of the network to train the network, and replaced the original GAN loss with the WGAN loss which makes the training process more stable, and the style features can better migrate between images. The SSIM loss is added to the cycle consistency loss to improve the quality of the generated image. The method in this paper can be based on the characteristics of film images, according to the reference image to transform the style of the source image to generate high-quality, natural and realistic images.

Figure 6. Qualitative results

(a)Source image (b)Style image (c)Gatys et al. (d)Johnson et al. (e)our results

Figure 7. Example style transfer results. Comparison with Gatys et al. and Johnson et al.

REFERENCES

Arjovsky, M., Chintala, S., & Bottou, L. (2017). Wasserstein gan. *arXiv preprint arXiv:1701.07875.*

Digital Cinema Initiatives (2018). Digital cimena system specification Version 1.3.

Digital Cinema Initiatives (2019). DCI statement on technology evolution in digital cinema.

Dosovitskiy, A., & Brox, T. (2016). Generating images with perceptual similarity metrics based on deep networks. In *Advances in neural information processing systems* (pp. 658-666).

Gatys, L. A., Ecker, A. S., & Bethge, M. (2016). Image style transfer using convolutional neural networks. In *Proceedings of the IEEE conference on computer vision and pattern recognition* (pp. 2414-2423).

Goodfellow, I., Pouget-Abadie, J., Mirza, M., Xu, B., Warde-Farley, D., Ozair, S., Courville, A., & Bengio, Y. (2014). Generative adversarial nets. *In Advances in neural information processing systems* (pp. 2672–2680).

Gulrajani, I., Ahmed, F., Arjovsky, M., Dumoulin, V., & Courville, A. C. (2017). Improved training of wasserstein gans. In *Advances in neural information processing systems* (pp. 5767-5777).

Johnson, J., Alahi, A., & Fei-Fei, L. (2016, October). Perceptual losses for real-time style transfer and super-resolution. In *European conference on computer vision* (pp. 694-711). Springer, Cham.

Li, C., & Wand, M. (2016). Combining markov random fields and convolutional neural networks for image synthesis. In *Proceedings of the IEEE Conference on Computer Vision and Pattern Recognition* (pp. 2479-2486).

Li, C., & Wand, M. (2016, October). Precomputed real-time texture synthesis with markovian generative adversarial networks. In *European conference on computer vision* (pp. 702-716). Springer, Cham.

Li, S., Xu, X., Nie, L., & Chua, T. S. (2017, October). Laplacian-steered neural style transfer. In *Proceedings of the 25th ACM international conference on Multimedia* (pp. 1716-1724).

Li, Y., Liu, M. Y., Li, X., Yang, M. H., & Kautz, J. (2018). A closed-form solution to photorealistic image stylization. In *Proceedings of the European Conference on Computer Vision (ECCV)* (pp. 453-468).

Radford, A., Metz, L., & Chintala, S. (2015). Unsupervised representation learning with deep convolutional generative adversarial networks. *arXiv preprint arXiv:1511.06434.*

Ulyanov, D., Vedaldi, A., & Lempitsky, V. (2017). Improved texture networks: Maximizing quality and diversity in feed-forward stylization and texture synthesis. In *Proceedings of the IEEE Conference on Computer Vision and Pattern Recognition* (pp. 6924-6932).

Verma, P., & Smith, J. O. (2018). Neural style transfer for audio spectograms. *arXiv preprint arXiv:1801.01589.*

Wang, Z., Bovik, A. C., Sheikh, H. R., & Simoncelli, E. P. (2004). Image quality assessment: from error visibility to structural similarity. *IEEE transactions on image processing*, *13*(4), 600-612.

Wang, Z., Simoncelli, E. P., & Bovik, A. C. (2003, November). Multiscale structural similarity for image quality assessment. In *The Thrity-Seventh Asilomar Conference on Signals, Systems & Computers, 2003* (Vol. 2, pp. 1398-1402). Ieee.

Zhang, H., & Dana, K. (2017). Multi-style generative network for real-time transfer. *arXiv preprint arXiv:1703.06953.*

Zhu, J. Y., Park, T., Isola, P., & Efros, A. A. (2017). Unpaired image-to-image translation using cycle-consistent adversarial networks. In *Proceedings of the IEEE international conference on computer vision* (pp. 2223-2232).

DATA INTERPOLATION BASED ON CONTEXTUAL ANALYSIS FOR GENERATING TOMOGRAPHIC IMAGES IN CONCRETE SPECIMEN

Roger Manuel Quispe Urure , Marco Antonio Garcia de Carvalho,
Marinara Andrade Nascimento Moura and Gisleiva Cristina dos Santos Ferreira
School of Technology, University of Campinas
Limeira - SP - Brazil

ABSTRACT

In the Construction area, inspections of concrete structure could be carried out using non-destructive tests, such as ultrasonic tomography. Usually, images generated by this technique are improved by means of spatial interpolation data. This research proposes the use of a new spatial interpolation technique in order to generating tomographic images of concrete. This approach was originally used on wood tomographic images and is based on contextual analysis according to the location of the point to be interpolated. Also, it is considered the influence zone of each route obtained in the concrete ultrasonic test. The ultrasonic tests were performed in cylindrical specimens with and without PVC tubes, simulating voids in concrete. The achieved result of our analysis are compared to the ground truth images and those obtained by Inverse Distance Weighting, using accuracy metric and image processing operations. The results indicated high accuracy values (greater than 90%), i.e, the spatial interpolation technique (method) is promising in identifying the presence of voids in concrete elements.

KEYWORDS

Concrete, Data interpolation, Ultrasonic Tomography, Thresholding

1. INTRODUCTION

The performance and safety of concrete constructions depend on periodic monitoring and inspections of the structural elements. The standards present at Brazilian Association of Technical Standards (ABNT, 2019) establish ultrasonic tests to evaluate the concrete used in building structural system. These kind of tests does not affect the integrity of the structures and allows identifying non-visible anomalies, for instance.

Ultrasonic test has been widely used in concrete inspection, to evaluate the quality and degradation state of these structures by the identification of heterogeneities, defects or cracks (Hola et al. 2015, Lluveras Núñez et al, 2017). The ultrasonic tomography images in particular, has shown great importance in the evaluation of cementitious materials by using different techniques for images generation (Haach and Ramirez 2016, Beniwal et al. 2016). Some author also presents the advantages of using interpolation for generation and reconstruction of images (Fan et al, 2017; Moura et al, 2020).

This paper describes a new spatial interpolation technique to generate tomographic images of concrete.

The proposed technique is based on a strategy adopted for wood inspection by ultrasound [Strobel 2017]. Considers an elliptical model for the propagation of the ultrasonic pulse and is based on contextual analysis of the point to be interpolated.

This article is organized as follows: Section 1 presents the introduction, objectives and organization of the text, in section 2, describing the related works, explaining the differential of the proposal in relation to existence, in section 3 explaining the steps of the methodology for contextual analysis, in section 4, describing a sample, explained or tried, and how the results will be applied and finally in section 5, highlighting the performance of the method and the final considerations of the work.

2. MAIN CONCEPTS AND RELATED WORKS

This section provides main concepts on ultrasonic tomography on concrete, as well as, presents the related research's. At the end of this section we highlight the main contributions of our work.

2.1 Fundamental Concept

Non-destructive tests are techniques used to inspect materials without damaging them. The ultrasonic test consists of determining the time that the ultrasonic wave takes to pass through a certain material. The equipment has a piezoelectric crystal that converts the signal into mechanical vibration. The electrical signal is emitted by the generator and is received by the receiver obtaining the TOF (Time of Flight) in microseconds as shown in Figure 1 adapted from Cavalcanti (2010)

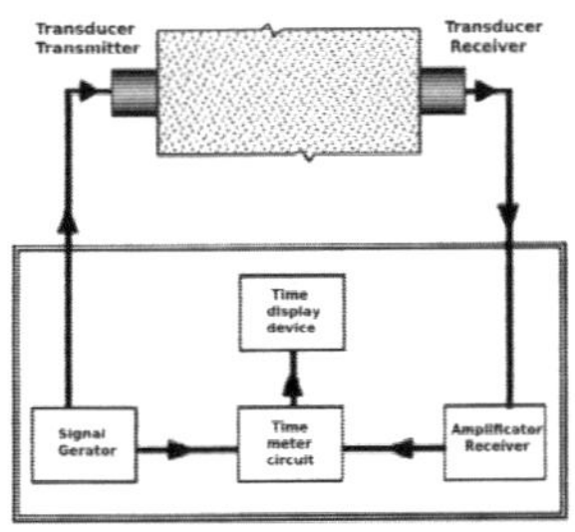

Figure 1. Ultrasound Equipment

In the ultrasonic reconstruction of a homogeneous material, the mechanical waves propagate in straight lines between the transducers. On the other hand, in a concrete specimen, the mechanical waves may deviate from an internal void, resulting in lower TOF [Perlin and de Andrade Pinto 2019].

These changes in TOF values are represented on the ultrasonic tomographic image. The tomographic ultrasonic technique provides methods of sampling a larger number of points, rather than a single point, with an automated way of data collection and processing [Koulountzios et al. 2019]. Thus, the voids are represented through an image.

2.2 Related Works

The interpolation method is widely used to predict data. A spatial interpolation can predict the values of the unknown points by processing the surrounding variables with meaningful values within the same region (Feng et al. 2014). This is often used when the measured data needs to be transformed from discrete points to a continuous data surface (Cheng & Kou ,2019).

Khairi et al (2019) reconstructed a tomographic image based on the integral values obtained by an image reconstruction algorithm. To optimize the tomographic image, an artificial neural network is used, mainly because it is considered as a tool that handles both uncertain and complex systems.

Feng et al (2014) used a proposed interpolation method to reconstruct a tomographic image from stress wave TOF data. They considered that every point in the cross section of a tree trunk was related to other points and the adjacent points were more closely related than distant points. Their results showed a good match between tomographic images and the true physical conditions of the samples.

Du et al. (2015) used the wave tomography method using interpolation to detect internal defects in wooden logs. Strobel (2017) implemented an improvement in the method of (Du et al, 2015) adding a speed compensation method and significantly improving the results.

Although the use of interpolation for generation and reconstruction of images is still not widely discussed, several studies presents the advantage of the method applied to concrete. (Fan et al, 2017), used the maximum likelihood expectation maximization algorithm and ultrasonic TOF data to reconstruct concrete images. TOF data interpolation and normalization were proposed and validated for image reconstruction system. In Moura et al (2020), the interpolation technique was used to estimate the acoustic velocity, of ultrasonic tests, at the unmeasured test points of a concrete beam. The Inverse Distance Weighting Algorithm was proposed to generate the tomographic images. The resulting images indicated the presence of internal flaws in concrete.

The methodology used in Du et al (2015) and Strobel (2017) was applied to wooden logs. In this work, we propose an adaptation of the methodology used by the authors, replacing the main material used. Thus, we intend to verify if the same methodology can be applied to concrete, using cylindrical specimens.

The key contributions of our work are the following:

- We conduct the whole process, from the generation of the concrete samples to the quantitative analysis of the images generated by the interpolation.
- In the interpolation process, we adapt and use a method originally applied in tomographic wood analysis.
- Our results and analysis are evaluated in a quantitative way, based on image processing and classification measures techniques.

3. PROPOSED APPROACH

In this section, we describe our approach employed to improve and analyze tomographic images generated by ultrasonic test. It consists of three main steps, illustrated in Figure 2 and described through the remainder of this section.

In order to organize the discussion, these steps are grouped in three major topics, i.e., (a) ultrasonic test; (b) Data interpolation using contextual analysis; (c) quantitative tomographic analysis.

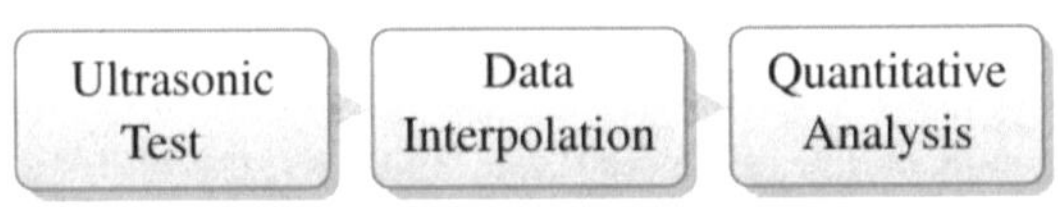

Figure 2. Proposed approach

3.1 Ultrasonic Test

The ultrasonic test was performed according to the Brazilian Standard NBR 8802 (ABNT, 2019) standard detailed in section 2.1. The samples used have the dimensions: 20x10*cm* and 30x15*cm*. Also, we generate 2 specimens with defect, simulating voids in concrete, and 2 without defect, illustrated in Figure 3. The dimensions of the PVC tubes that simulate the concreting voids are shown in Table 1.

Table 1. PVC pipes dimensions

Pipe	Diameter(mm)	Length(mm)
1	2.5 cm	5 cm
2	5 cm	15 cm

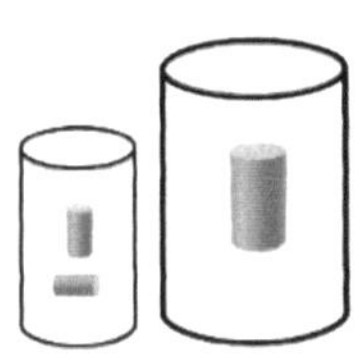

Figure 3. PVC pipes location

The arrangement adopted to compute the TOF was the direct measurement, according to the cross section of the sample, with eight points distributed equally on the surface of the specimen. This configuration produces an arrangement known as a diffraction grid.

3.2 Data Interpolation by Means of Contextual Analysis of Concrete Specimen

This work applies and adapts an existing technique in the area of wood inspection by ultrasonic test. We consider the concept of affected zones in the image interpolation step, where for each measurement route an elliptical zone is associated (Zeng et al, 2013). This is illustrated in Figure 4.

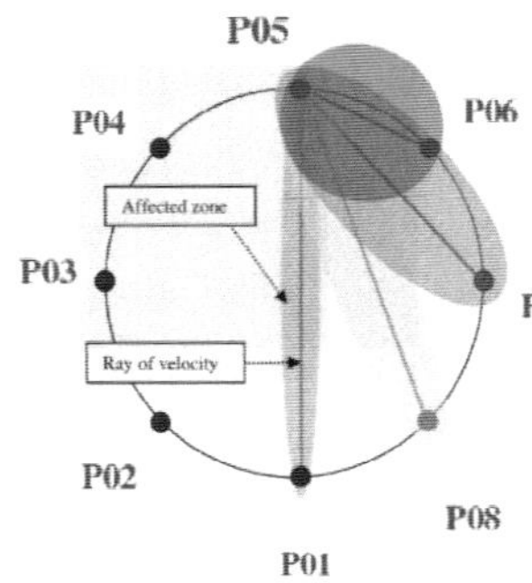

Figure 4. Routes and its elliptical influence zones

To define the types of measurement routes, we rely on work of Lin et al (2008). Four types of routes were defined for a diffraction grid with eight measurement points as shown in Figure 5. Finally, an ellipse of variable eccentricity is associated to each route, according its length.

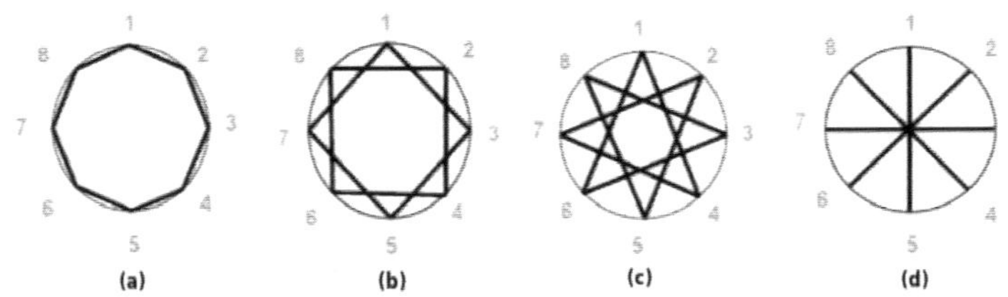

Figure 5. The four types of routes in a diffraction grid with 8 measured points: (a), (b):Analysis of the context near the concrete surface: (c), (d):Contextual analysis of the central region of concrete

The proposed approach consists on computing the interpolated points based on the contextual analysis of they locations, divided in two categories: *(i)* analysis of the context near represented by routes Figures 5(a), 5(b); *(ii)*, Contextual analysis of the central represented by Figures 5(c), 5(d).

In the first category, analyzing the context near to the concrete edge, the technique consider all possible routes and selects only the three ellipses whose center is closest to the point to be interpolated. These routes are considered the most representatives. In this way, only those routes that will emphasize a possible deterioration and discarding outliers. In the contextual analysis of the central region, it is considered different ellipse eccentricity in order to evaluate the influence of the route, and corresponding velocity of ultrasonic pulse, in the point to be interpolated.

3.3 Quantitative Evaluation

Usually, the efficiency of an interpolation technique is assessed by means of a visual comparative analysis of the images generated before and after the process. Additionally, the experts know-how are considered.

Strobel (2017) evaluates the results of an interpolation technique on wood logs using quantitative evaluation. The method consists on compare two images, a model and the segmented image, using a classification model, i.e., by means of a confusion matrix.

In this paper we propose a method of quantitative evaluation, where images are seen as a classification model evaluated by means of metrics, resulting in a confusing matrix.

According to each samples and its dimensions, with or without voids, we build a model image with three colors: white, black and gray, i.e., the ROI (Region of Interest), the background and the interpolated regions, respectively. The segmented image was obtained by means of threshold operation defined by Equation 1.

$$g(x,y) = \begin{cases} 0, & \text{if } f(x,y) \leq T \\ 1, & \text{otherwise} \end{cases} \quad (1)$$

Where *g(x,y)* and *f(x,y)* are the segmented and interpolated images and T is the value defined to divide two distinct regions into two levels of gray, white and black, respectively. Finally, the accuracy is computed according to Equation 2, where (TP, TN) is true positive and negative and (FN, FP) is false negative and positive.

$$A = \frac{TP + TN}{TP + FN + FP + TN} \quad (2)$$

4. EXPERIMENTS AND RESULTS

In this section we first introduce some specific aspects related to the experiments and then we present the results obtained the efficiency of the proposed approach. We compared our approach with the Inverse Distance Weighting (IDW) method, used in the same context (Moura et al, 2020).

Initially, the materials were selected, created and the samples characterized before the ultrasonic test. Such procedures follow standard recommendations and were made in Laboratory of the University of Campinas. In order to perform measurements during the ultrasonic test we divide and label each specimen in seven cross sections according to the illustrated in Figure 6. From each cross section is possible to obtain a model image, known as ground truth, and use them to compare with the segmented image. We work with 12 samples in total, where six are of type 20x10cm (with and without PVC tubes) and six of type 30x15cm (with and without PVC tubes).

In essence, the implemented experiments consisted on interpolating the concrete samples, after the ultrasonic tomography, using the proposed method. The results of TOF obtained by the ultrasonic equipment are in microseconds.

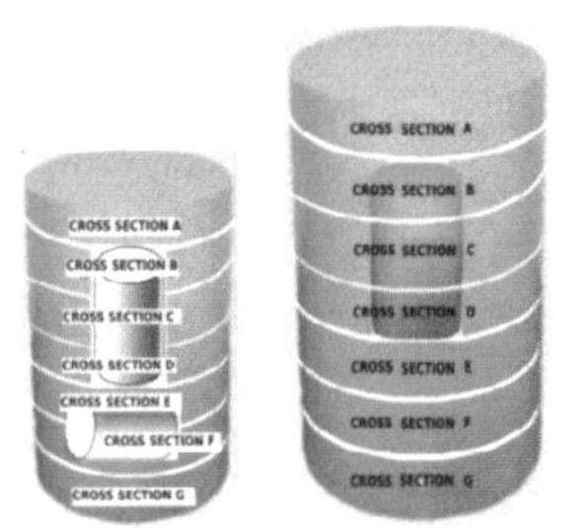

(a) (b)

Figure 6. Concrete voids: specimens used in this work and its seven cross sections: (a)20 x 10cm; (b)30 x 15cm

This procedure was repeated for all samples and the average accuracy was computed. In Figure 7 shows the resulting interpolated images obtained from the contextual analysis and IDW algorithms, respectively, for 20x10*cm* specimen. Each cross section is compared in sequential order as shown in the Figure 7. In this figure, the black regions indicate the presence of voids in concrete.

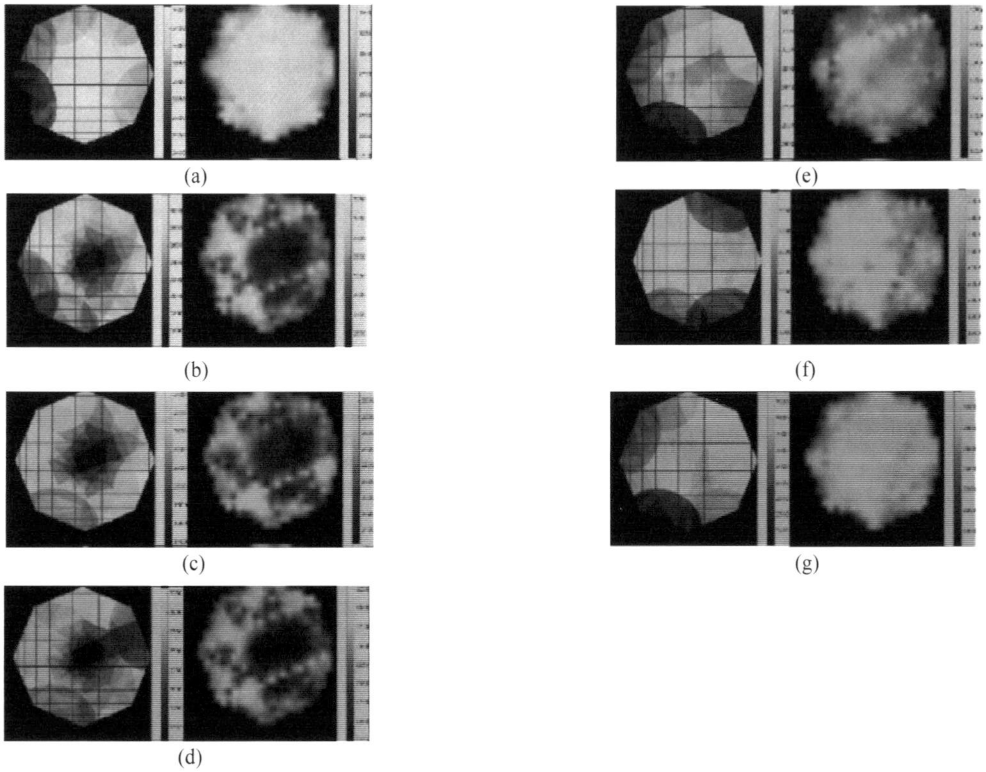

Figure 7. Interpolated resulting images of the 20x10cm specimen: (a),(b),...(g) cross-section, proposed method (left) and IDW technique (right)

The results obtained to the cross section B of samples 20x10*cm* and 30x15*cm* are shown in Figure 8. Note that the Thresholding operation is very dependent on the threshold that defines the void region on concrete, as we can see in Figure 8(f).

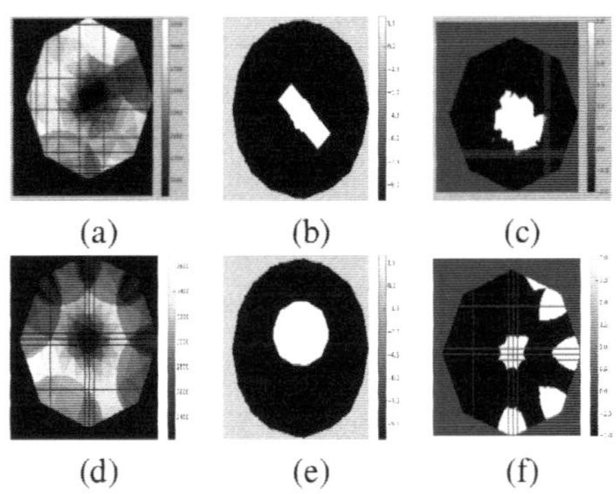

Figure 8. Resulting images of cross section B (a) Sample 20x10*cm* interpolated by the proposed method; (b) Sample 20x10*cm* model image; (c) Sample 20x10*cm* segmented image; (d) Sample 30x15*cm* interpolated by the proposed method; (e) Sample 30x15*cm* model image; (f) Sample 30x15*cm* segmented image

The Table 2 shows the analysis of the proposed method based on accuracy metric. This performance is computed using all cross sections of each specimen, compared to they corresponding *ground truth*. We compare our results with the IDW technique for both samples, 20x10*cm* and 30x15*cm*. The best performance for each cross section is highlighted in bold.

Table 2. Performance of the proposed method using accuracy metric for the sample 30x15*cm* and 20x10*cm*

	20x10cm		30x15cm	
Cross Section	Contextual Analysis	IDW	Contextual Analysis	IDW
A	**92.8**%	92.3%	**54.4**%	40.6%
B	**93.5**%	79.3%	71.5%	**74.0**%
C	**94.1**%	72.6%	70.4%	**73.6**%
D	**90.9**%	77.0%	71.5%	**73.5**%
E	**92.8**%	92.2%	**48.8**%	32.8%
F	**91.5**%	90.9%	**70.0**%	54.9%
G	**92.8**%	92.2%	**47.1**%	37.1%

As we can observe in Table 2, in the case of 20x10*cm* sample, our proposed approach generates better results when compared to IDW method. In the case of 30x15*cm* sample, our results are slightly lower than those obtained by the IDW method. The best IDW results correspond exactly to the regions where the PVC pipe is located, as illustrated in Figure 8(d). This may be associated with the segmentation method adopted and needs to be further investigated.

5. CONCLUSION

In this paper we presented a new approach to interpolate points in concrete tomographic images using ultrasonic test. The method uses contextual analysis, according to the point location to be interpolated and the relevant routes of the ultrasonic pulses that cross the concrete sample. We applied our method in 12 concrete samples, with two different sizes and configurations (with and without voids simulated by PVC tubes). The initial results indicated that our approach provides enough information and more suitable images to identify voids, when compared to ground truth images and evaluated by accuracy metric. Also, in most of cases, the contextual analysis interpolation was superior to the IDW technique.

Future work includes the use of a more accurate equipment to acquire data in ultrasonic tests, as well as to improve the variety and number of samples in dataset. In addition, we intend to generate a 3D tomographic image from the combination of all cross sections that make up the specimen.

ACKNOWLEDGEMENT

The authors would like to thank the Laboratories of Soils and Materials of the University of Campinas, Brazil. Part of this research was supported by São Paulo Research Foundation (FAPESP), grant 2018/185204.

REFERENCES

ABNT (2019). Nbr 8802: Test method for pulse velocity through Concrete. ABNT – Brazilian Association of Technical Standards. Rio de Janeiro, Brazil.

Beniwal, S., Ghosh, D., & Ganguli, A. (2016). Ultrasonic imaging of concrete using scattered elastic wave modes. *Ndt & E International*, *82*, pp 26-35.

Cavalcanti, R. S. (2010). Tests of ultrasonic waves and artificial neural networks in the evaluation of the compressive strength of concrete (in Portuguese). *Master thesis*, Universidade Católica de Pernambuco.

Cheng, D., & Kou, K. I. (2019). FFT multichannel interpolation and application to image super-resolution. *Signal Processing*, *162*, pp 21-34.

Du, X., Li, S., Li, G., Feng, H., & Chen, S. (2015). Stress wave tomography of wood internal defects using ellipse-based spatial interpolation and velocity compensation. *BioResources*, *10*(3), pp 3948-3962.

Fan, H., Zhu, H., Zhao, X., Zhang, J., Wu, D., & Han, Q. (2017). Ultrasonic image reconstruction based on maximum likelihood expectation maximization for concrete structural information. *Computers & Electrical Engineering*, *62*, pp 293-301.

Feng, H., Li, G., Fu, S., & Wang, X. (2014). Tomographic image reconstruction using an interpolation method for tree decay detection. *BioResources*, *9*(2), pp 3248-3263.

Haach, V. G., & Ramirez, F. C. (2016). Qualitative assessment of concrete by ultrasound tomography. *Construction and Building Materials*, *119*, pp 61-70.

Hola, J., Bień, J., & Schabowicz, K. (2015). Non-destructive and semi-destructive diagnostics of concrete structures in assessment of their durability. *Bulletin of the Polish Academy of Sciences Technical Sciences*, *63*(1), pp 87-96.

Khairi, M. T. M., Ibrahim, S., Yunus, M. A. M., Faramarzi, M., Sean, G. P., Pusppanathan, J., & Abid, A. (2019). Ultrasound computed tomography for material inspection: Principles, design and applications. *Measurement*, *146*, pp 490-523.

Koulountzios, P., Rymarczyk, T., & Soleimani, M. (2019). A Quantitative Ultrasonic Travel-Time Tomography to Investigate Liquid Elaborations in Industrial Processes. *Sensors*, *19*(23), pp 5117.

Lin, C. J., Kao, Y. C., Lin, T. T., Tsai, M. J., Wang, S. Y., Lin, L. D., ... & Chan, M. H. (2008). Application of an ultrasonic tomographic technique for detecting defects in standing trees. *International Biodeterioration & Biodegradation*, *62*(4), pp 434-441.

Lluveras Núñez, D., Molero-Armenta, M. Á., Izquierdo, M. Á. G., Hernández, M. G., & Anaya Velayos, J. J. (2017). Ultrasound transmission tomography for detecting and measuring cylindrical objects embedded in concrete. *Sensors*, *17*(5), pp 1085.

Moura, M. A. N., Carvalho, M. A. G., and Ferreira, G. C. S. (2020). Influence of measuring points in ultrasonic tests on th etomographic image quality of concrete. *In International Conference in Central Europe on Computer Graphics, Visualization and Computer Vision (WSCG)*. Plzeň, Czech Republic, pp. 1–8.

Perlin, L. P., & de Andrade Pinto, R. C. (2019). Use of network theory to improve the ultrasonic tomography in concrete. *Ultrasonics*, *96*, pp 185-195.

Strobel, J. R. A. (2017). Associated Ellipse Based Interpolation Method Contextual Analysis of Routes for Generation of Ultrasonic Tomography in Wood Logs, (in Portuguese). *Master thesis*, UNICAMP.

Zeng, L., Lin, J., Hua, J., & Shi, W. (2013). Interference resisting design for guided wave tomography. *Smart materials and structures*, *22*(5), 055017.

SEGMENTATION AND RECOGNITION OF CONNECTED HANDWRITTEN CHARACTERS

Shehan Panditharatne and Lochandaka Ranathunga[1]
Faculty of Information Technology, University of Moratuwa, Sri Lanka
[1]Dr.

ABSTRACT

Optical Character Recognition is still an open problem in computer science. This paper explores segmentation of connected (touching/overlapping) handwritten characters through implicit segmentation and explicit segmentation. Explicit segmentation is achieved through rules based on background thinning and analyzing the contour hierarchy. Implicit segmentation is achieved through generating a dataset of connected characters and training a CNN. This research was inspired by the need to recognize math documents containing algebraic equations. Recognition of 72 characters (alphanumeric and math symbols) are achieved through the proposed methods. The scope of the implemented OCR is limited to maximum of two connected characters.

KEYWORDS

Implicit, Explicit Segmentation, Connected, Touching Characters

1. INTRODUCTION

Handwritten text is still a widely used method of communication in today's world. Even with the advancements in digital text applications, handwritten text is still the medium for text in fields such as education. Thus, it's vital to make advancements in recognizing such texts. There exist many researches regarding handwritten text recognition. Even though many advancements have been made, handwritten character recognition is still considered an open problem.

This research paper was based on our final year thesis on recognizing handwritten documents containing algebraic equations. Given sufficient space between lines of the document, they can be easily segmented by smearing the text into blobs using morphological operations. In the segmented line, characters separated by spaces can be segmented through the peaks and throughs of the vertical projection. This leaves us with single characters or connected (touching/overlapping) characters. This paper focuses on recognition of these single or connected characters using implicit and explicit segmentation methods since the previous steps are of common knowledge. The scope of this research however is limited to two connected (touching/overlapping) characters. The source code and the sample images used for evaluating the system can be found at: (Panditharatne, 2020).

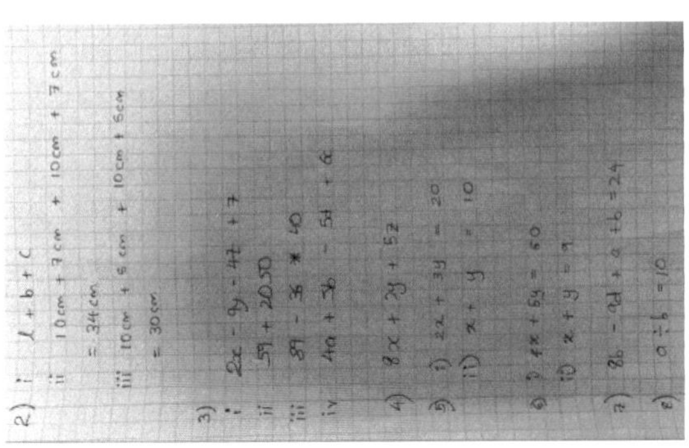

Figure 1. Sample document

2. RELATED WORK

Character segmentation is considered one of the most crucial steps in handwritten OCR (KAUR, BAGHLA, & KUMAR, 2015). Correct segmentation of characters is imperative for correct classification of characters in later stages.

Although characters that are separated by spaces can be easily segmented there are challenges in segmenting touched or overlapping characters. Touching, connected, overlapping, intersecting characters will all be referred as connected characters from here onwards for simplicity.

In research, character segmentation is broadly classified into two main techniques (Rehman, Mohamad , & Sulong , 2009).

2.1 Explicit Segmentation

A classical approach where an image of a word sequence is partitioned to several, individual character images using rules.

In (Casey & Eric, 1996) Casey et al. demonstrates a method of using vertical projection (vertical histogram) of a line to find separation of characters. Vertical projection is the count of foreground pixels in each column of the line. The minimums(valleys) of the projection serves as a detector for white space between successive letters thus the segmentation points. However, when touching or overlapping characters are introduced this method fails to correctly segment the characters. Thus, this method serves as a successful method for segmentation non-cursive handwriting.

In (Lu, Chi, Siu, & Shi, 1999) Lu et al. proposes an approach of segmenting hand-written two-digit strings by thinning the background of the image. After retrieving the skeleton of the background, the algorithm locates several feature points that can be used to segment the image. Possible segmentation paths are then constructed between the detected feature points of the upper background contour and the lower background contour. Since there can be multiple possible segmentation paths, they are ranked using fuzzy rules generated from a decision-tree approach. Then the segmentation paths with the highest ranks are tested according to an acceptance criterion.

2.2 Implicit Segmentation

Recognition based segmentation method where character recognition and segmentation are achieved simultaneously. Segmentation can be regarded as a byproduct of the recognition process (Rehman, Mohamad , & Sulong , 2009). Thus, the recognizer decides on the best segmentation hypothesis. In (Zhan, Lyu, & Lu, 2018) Zhan et al. proposes a new architecture based on a CNN to recognize handwritten digit strings. A Connectionist Temporal Classification (CTC) layer is used in the output layer to calculate the loss and decode the feature sequence.

In (Meany & Arola, 2018) Meany et al. trains a CNN on the IAM Handwriting word dataset. They have limited the length of the words to 1-6 characters to achieve best performance. They have trained the dataset on a 1-layer CNN and a 3-layer CNN. They have achieved accuracies of 71.6% and 76.9% respectively for the test set.

2.3 Character Classification

In (Meany & Arola, 2018), Meany et al. trains a CNN and a ResNet-50 on the EMNIST dataset to achieve character classification. They have trained the model on the EMNIST balanced dataset where there are 47 classes. The CNN reaches an accuracy of 84.8% and the ResNet reaches an accuracy of 88.5% on the test set.

3. METHODOLOGY

The methods proposed for implicit segmentation and explicit segmentation are discussed below. It's important to note that single character images or connected character images (segmented from vertical projection) are the inputs into the proposed methods. Connected characters are limited to two connected characters.

3.1 Implicit Segmentation

In implicit segmentation, character segmentation and character recognition are achieved simultaneously. This can be achieved using a Convolutional Neural Network. A dataset containing single characters and two connected characters will have to be generated as none such datasets were available online.

3.1.1 Generation of the Dataset

The dataset will be generated using merged EMNIST (Cohen, Afshar, Tapson, & Schaik, 2017) dataset (for 52 characters and 10 numbers) and the CROHME dataset (for 10 mathematical symbols). The CROHME dataset is a dataset of Online handwritten characters. However, through offline_CROHME (Huynh, 2018) tool it's possible to convert the online handwritten characters to offline character images. Only 10 mathematical symbols are chosen from the CROHME dataset as they are the most basic math symbols. The symbols are – (,), +, -, /, =, [,], division, *. The whole merged dataset is converted to binary colors because the pre-processing module of the OCR turns all images to binary colors using OTSU thresholding and the mathematical symbols of the CROHME dataset is in binary color. Thus, the grayscale color depth of EMNIST is sacrificed.

Images are generated by randomly taking a character from the merged dataset (EMNIST + CROHME) and combining it with a another randomly taken character from the merged dataset. The merged dataset should be balanced such that each character class (out of 72) has the equal number of images. Thus, will allow us to generate a dataset that is more balanced, as characters are taken from the merged dataset at random for combining.

Characters are combined by placing the second character where the first character ends. The characters are combined such that some images are touching characters and some images are overlapping characters. This variation between overlapping and touching characters can be achieved by randomly shifting left (by around 3 pixels) where the second character is placed.

Each generated image will have two labels. First label for the first character of the image and the second label for the second character in the image. For single character images the first label will contain the character in the image and the second label will contain a number to represent a blank character (72). The merged dataset has 72 (EMNIST+CROHME) types of characters and thus the generated dataset has 5256 (72x73) possible character combinations/classes. Each combination will have at least 600 images thus in total there are around 3 153 600 images (600x5256). The exact number of images in the generated dataset is 3 230 980. Each image in the dataset is sized at 28x56 (height x width) and is in binary colors. The following figure shows some samples of the generated images and their labels.

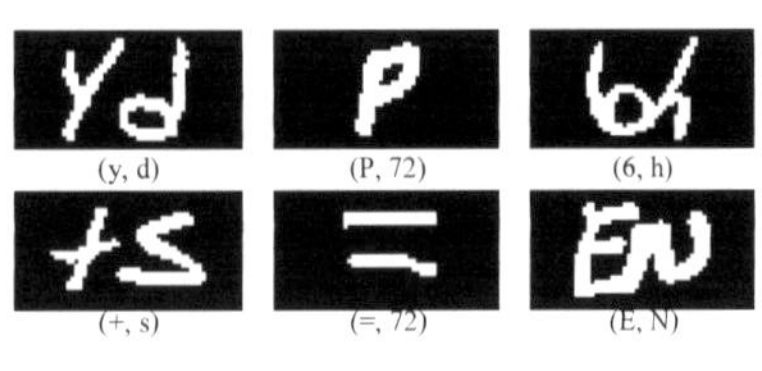

Figure 2. Samples of the generated dataset

3.1.2 Training the Model

The generated dataset will be trained on a 4-layer CNN, 6-layer CNN and on ResNet-50. The problem can be addressed as a multi label classification or a multi class classification. If the problem is addressed as a multi label classification, the output of the NN will have 145 (72+73) outputs and each image will have two labels (ex: - 0, 8 or 0, 72). If the problem is addressed as a multi class classification, the NN will have 5256 (72x73) outputs. Each class will denote one combination between two characters.

When training the model, it was observed that it's easier to address the problem as a multi class classification as the training images were too large to fit on memory and thus had to be loaded from the hard drive. Therefore, Keras flow from directory method was used to load the images from the hard drive.

For training the ResNet, images were resized to 56x112 and then was transformed into RGB. Train test split of 90/10 was used to train and evaluate the model.

3.2 Explicit Segmentation

First, a classification must be performed to recognize weather the image contains a single character or connected characters. The following approaches were implemented and tested.

- Through hierarchical clustering – First, the width and the white pixel count of each image is calculated. Through hierarchical clustering of these values, it is possible to classify characters as single characters and connected characters. The cluster of the image with the largest white pixel count will be chosen as the connected character cluster. The other cluster will be the single character cluster.
- Through a CNN - This classification can be addressed as a binary classification problem where a single character is classified as 0 and connected characters classified as 1. Since there are no such public datasets available for this purpose, a dataset was generated. This dataset was generated in similar fashion to the dataset generated in the implicit segmentation section. Instead of 5256 possible classes used in the implicit segmentation dataset, this dataset has two (binary) classes. The dataset contains 318 672 images where 50% of the images are single images and the rest are connected character images.

Figure 3. Samples of the generated dataset

A CNN with 8 Convolutional Layers will be used to perform the classification.

If the image is recognized as a single character, it can be directly sent to the character classifier to be classified. If the image is of connected characters, it will have to be further processed to segment into two characters.

3.2.1 Background Thinning Based Segmentation

The first step in segmenting the image is to perform background thinning of the input image. The following images are of input images and their respective background thinned images.

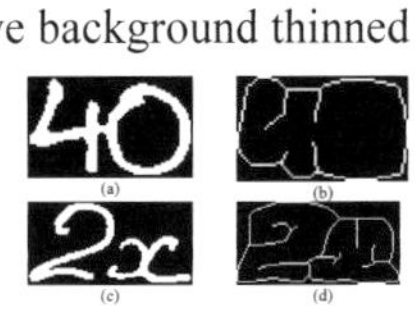

Figure 4. (a,c)Connected Character Image (b,d)Background thinned images

The next step is to separate overlapping characters from touching characters. This can be achieved by checking the contours of the background image. If there are two separable contours in the image, the image is recognized as two overlapping characters (d image above). Thus, they can be easily segmented by creating masks of the contours. Then the single character images are sent to the character classifier to be classified.

If the image doesn't contain two separable contours, it's taken as a touching character image (b image above). In such images, the background thinned image is divided into 3 sections along the x axis (width wise) and the middle section is chosen for further processing (red area in the c image below). It's assumed that, the candidate segmentation line between the characters is situated in this middle section. A kernel is applied to find candidate points in the upper part of the background skeleton (bounded by red in d,e image below). Another kernel is applied to find candidate points in the lower part of the background skeleton (bounded by green in d,e image below). These points are then connected to form a segmentation line (f image below).

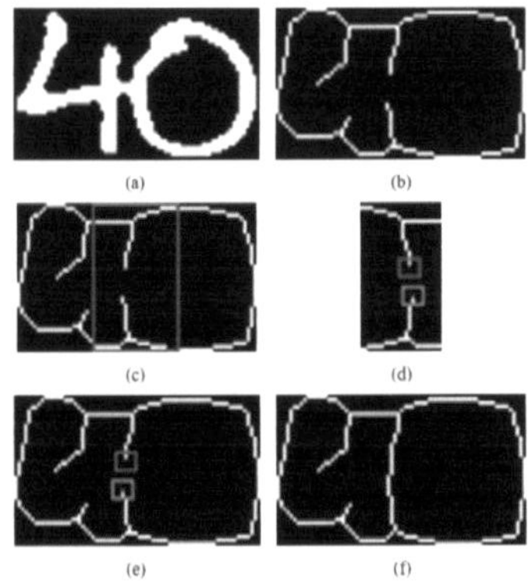

Figure 5. (a)Touching character image (b)Background thinned image (c)The middle section outlined in red (d) Candidate points found (Red- candidate point in upper part, Green- Candidate point in lower part) (e)Candidate points in the background image (f)Final image with connected candidate points

The above figure demonstrates how an input image (a) is processed to find the candidate points that are to be connected. Which in turn gives the segmentation line upon connecting the points (f).

In order to find the candidate point, in the upper part of the background thinned image, the following convolution kernel can be used.

2	2	2
-10	10	-10
-10	-10	-10

Figure 6. Convolution kernel to find candidate points in the upper part

Checking this convolution against a threshold of 3060 (255x10 + 255x2) allows us to find following types of candidate points.

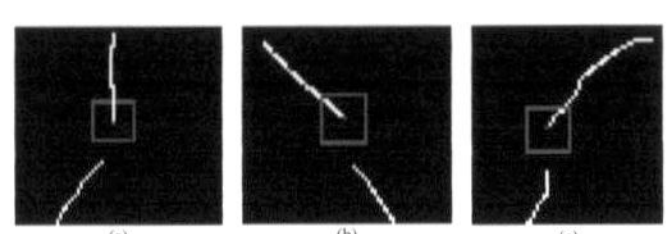

Figure 7. Types of candidate points found by the kernel

In order to find the candidate point in the lower part of the background thinned image, the above kernel can be applied after being rotated by 180 °.

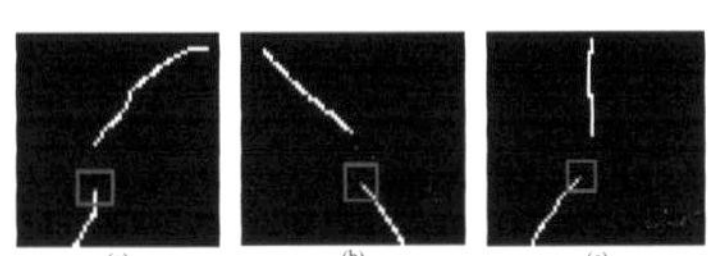

Figure 8. Types of candidate points found by the rotated kernel

If no candidate points can be found, then the image is not segmentable by the current algorithm.

The most trivial case is when there is only one candidate point each per upper and lower part of the skeleton is found. They can be directly connected to form the segmentation line. However, a choice must be made in case there are more than one point in each upper and lower parts of the skeleton. Points (x, y) found on the upper part of the skeleton will be referred to as top points and points (x, y) found on the lower part of the skeleton will be referred to as bottom points from here onwards.

If there are no top points and there is at least one bottom point, the bottom point's X value is chosen as the top point's X value and 0 will be chosen as the Y value.

If there are is least one top point and no bottom points, the top point's X value is chosen as the bottom points X value and the last row of the image is chosen as the bottom points Y value. In case there are multiple top points, the points are sorted such that the points whose Y values are the largest (closest to the bottom of the image) are at the start of the array and the first point is chosen as the top point.

If there are multiple top points and only one bottom point, the distances between the bottom point and the top points are calculated. The top point that gives the lowest distance to the bottom point is chosen as the top point.

Through connecting the candidate top point and the candidate bottom point, a segmentation line can be drawn and thus the image can be segmented to two characters using the contour hierarchy method.

3.2.2 Splitting Characters using Contour Hierarchy

If the background skeleton is separated clearly as follows (figure b, d), contour hierarchy can be used to split the image into two characters.

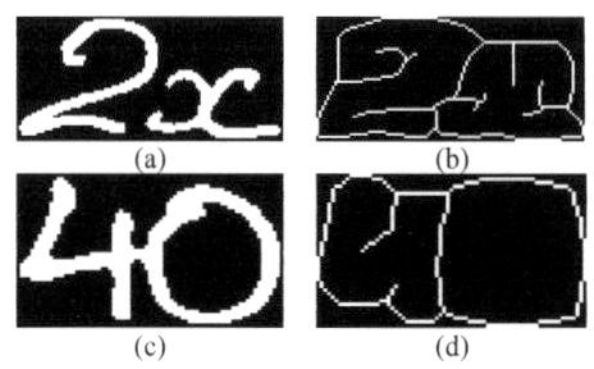

Figure 9. Images that can be split using contour hierarchy

The first step of the process is to find the contour hierarchies of the background skeleton as a tree. This retrieves the contours and creates a full family hierarchy list. The contour that encircles the whole region of interest is the contour at the top of the hierarchy (parent) and it will be assigned the value 0. The following figure shows the contour hierarchy where (a, e) images are of the background skeleton, (b, f) images are of the parent contour (rank 0) and (c, d, g, h) images are the child contours of the parent (rank 0) contour.

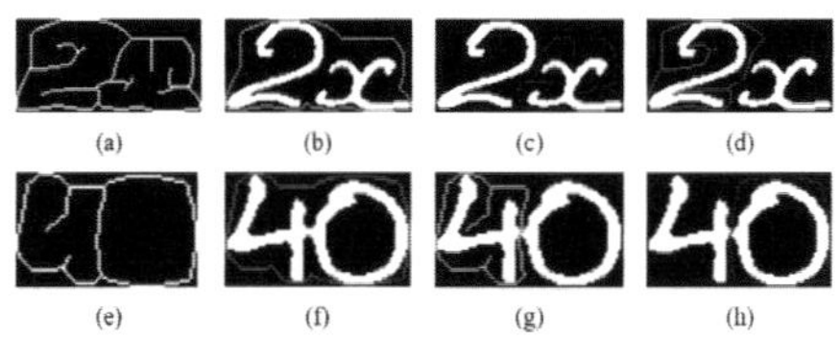

Figure 10. Contour hierarchy

If there are two child contours under the rank 0 parent contour, then the image can be segmented to two-character images. In case of overlapping characters (b), the image is segmented along the space between the characters. In case of touching characters (f), the background skeleton should be sent with the candidate segmentation line (image e).

If two child contours under the rank 0 contour can't be found, then this algorithm marks the image as being not segmentable.

3.3 Character Classification

In this module single characters are classified to their respective labels. The inputs are the single characters in the document or the segmented characters. The dataset will be a combination of the EMNIST dataset and the CROHME dataset with a total of 72 characters. These 72 characters are made up of the characters of the alphabet (A-Z and a-z), numbers (0-9) and mathematical symbols ((,), +, -, /, =, [,], division, *.). The CROHME dataset is a dataset of Online handwritten characters. However, through offline_CROHME [10] tool it's possible to convert the online handwritten characters to offline character images. The whole dataset will be pre-processed into binary colors because the pre-processing module of the OCR turns the document to binary colors using OTSU thresholding and the offline CROHME dataset is available only in binary color. The dataset will be trained on 4-layer CNN, 6-layer CNN and on ResNet50. The merged dataset has 880 709 training images and 140 862 test images.

4. EVALUATION

4.1 Module Wise Evaluation

4.1.1 Connected Character Recognition (Binary)

This is a sub module in the explicit segmentation module. This classifier is used to recognize weather an image is of a single character or connected characters (two connected characters). This module is tested on the dataset that is generated. There are 31 868 test images in the dataset.

Hierarchical clustering failed to correctly cluster the data in this dataset. Many irrelevant points were being recognized as clusters. Therefore, K-Means clustering with K=2 was used to cluster the data instead.

Table 1. Single or multiple character classification (binary)

	Test Accuracy
8-layer CNN	98.57%
K-Means clustering (K=2)	92.07%

4.1.2 Single Character Classifier

This is a sub module in the explicit segmentation module. Segmented and single characters are classified using this classifier. The test set has 140 862 (EMNIST+ offline CROHME) images belonging to 72 classes.

Table 2. Single character classifier accuracy

Model	Test Accuracy
4-layer CNN	87.73%
6-layer CNN	88.11%
ResNet-50	88.01%

4.1.3 Single or Connected Character Classification

Here the images of single characters or images of connected characters are classified. The segmentation and classification of characters are achieved simultaneously in the implicit segmentation module.

For explicit segmentation, 8-layer CNN was used to recognize connected characters followed by background thinning based segmentation. Finally, the segmented single characters are recognized using the single character 6-layer CNN model.

This evaluation is performed using the generated dataset mentioned in Implicit Segmentation section. Out of 3 230 980 images in the dataset 323 098 images are of the test set.

Table 3. Single or connected character classification

		Test Accuracy
Implicit segmentation	4-layer CNN	63.85%
	6-layer CNN	63.77%
	ResNet-50	96.01%
Explicit segmentation		31.61%

4.2 Evaluation on Real Data

The OCR as a whole was tested on 321 handwritten characters. These characters are spread over 4 documents containing characters, numbers and math symbols. These documents can be found at (Panditharatne, 2020). There are 215 single characters and 53 connected character pairs in the test set.

For testing implicit segmentation, ResNet-50 model was used.

For explicit segmentation, an 8-layer CNN was used to recognize connected characters followed by background thinning based segmentation. Finally, the segmented characters are recognized using the single character 6-layer CNN.

The documents were also tested with Google's Tesseract OCR (v5.0.0-alpha.20190623 with Leptonica). The backgrounds of the documents were removed through OTSU thresholding to improve accuracy.

Table 4. Accuracy on real data

	Accuracy on all characters	Single character Accuracy	Touch/overlapping character accuracy
Implicit Segmentation (ResNet-50)	190/321 = 59.19%	119/215 = 55.81%	70/106 = 66.03%
Explicit segmentation	188/321 = 58.56%	143/215 = 66.51%	45/106 = 42.45%
Google Tesseract OCR	160/321 = 49.84%	121/215 = 56.27%	39/106 = 36.79%

5. CONCLUSION

Looking at the evaluation accuracy for real data, it can be observed that the implicit segmentation module is less accurate on single characters. This is likely due to each character class in the generated dataset containing only around 600 images. Thus, adding all the single character images from EMNIST and offline CROHME to the generated dataset should improve the single character accuracy. However, this will make the dataset highly imbalanced. Therefore, more research should be done in this aspect.

The explicit segmentation module and the implicit segmentation module performs similarly on real documents. Although the implicit segmentation module has high accuracy on connected characters it performs a bit poorly on single characters compared to the explicit segmentation module.

The implicit segmentation module performs well on connected characters compared to the explicit segmentation model as expected. Convolutional Neural Networks perform better in image recognition problems compared to explicit rule-based methods. However, more accuracy can be gained through cleaning and expanding the dataset.

The proposed background thinning based segmentation algorithm fails to correctly segment characters in some instances. One instance is when the correct segmentation points lay outside of the middle part of the image. Another instance is when the convolution kernels fails to find any candidate points or finds the wrong candidate points. The following figure shows where segmentation line is drawn using incorrectly detected candidate points.

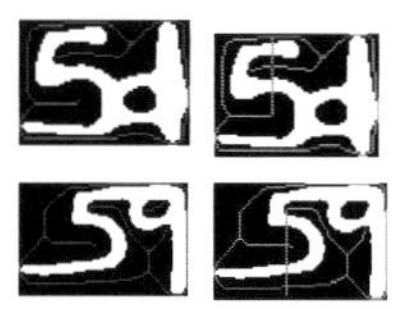

Figure 11. Incorrectly segmented images

The evaluation also shows that the proposed methods performs better on the tested documents than Google's Tesseract OCR.

The source code and sample images used for evaluating the system can be found at: (Panditharatne, 2020).

REFERENCES

Casey, G. R., & Eric, L. (1996). A Survey of Methods and Strategies in Character Segmentation. *IEEE TRANSACTIONS ON PATTERN ANALYSIS AND MACHINE INTELLIGENCE, 18*.

Cohen, G., Afshar, S., Tapson, J., & Schaik, A. (2017). *EMNIST: an extension of MNIST to handwritten letters.* The MARCS Institute for Brain, Behaviour and Development Western Sydney University Penrith, Australia.

Huynh, D. (2018, December 14). *Converting CROHME dataset for Online-handwritting recognition to Offline-handwritting recognition.* Retrieved September 8, 2019, from https://github.com/vndee/offline-crohme

KAUR, A., BAGHLA, S., & KUMAR, S. (2015). STUDY OF VARIOUS CHARACTER SEGMENTATION TECHNIQUES. *International Journal of Advances in Science Engineering and Technology, 3*(3).

Lu, Z., Chi, Z., Siu, W.-C., & Shi, P. (1999). A background-thinning-based approach for separating and recognizing connected handwritten digit strings. *Pattern Recognition, 32*, 921-933.

Meany, C., & Arola, M. (2018). Optical Character Recognition via Deep Learning. CA: Deep Learning, Stanford University.

Panditharatne, S. (2020, April 9). *xyz-ocr test images*. (GitHub) Retrieved April 9, 2020, from GitHub: https://github.com/shehan360/xyz-ocr/tree/master/TestImages

Rehman, A., Mohamad , D., & Sulong , G. (2009). Implicit Vs Explicit based Script Segmentation and Recognition: A Performance Comparison on Benchmark Database. *Int. J. Open Problems Compt. Math, 2*.

Zhan, H., Lyu, S., & Lu, Y. (2018). Handwritten Digit String Recognition using Convolutional Neural Network. *International Conference on Pattern Recognition.* Beijing.

GRAPHICAL USER INTERFACE PERSONALIZATION: USER STUDY OF IMAGE FREQUENCY PREFERENCES

Malwina Dziśko[1], Anna Lewandowska[1] and Anna Samborska – Owczarek[2]
[1]*West Pomeranian University of Technology, Żołnierska 52, 71-210 Szczecin, Poland*
[2]*FRIS - Thinking Styles, Wojska Polskiego 150/1, 71-324 Szczecin, Poland*

ABSTRACT

Recommending systems are undoubtedly a breakthrough in technology. Recommending systems are helpful to produce intelligent systems. These systems are becoming more and more popular and their main components are other embedded subsystems. The final result of intelligent system visible to the end-user is the graphical interface, which mainly consists of the graphical representation. It turns out, that wrongly chosen image frequency, to detail, chaotic and so, can affects the user's work efficiency. Thus, the image frequency is one of the components that should be investigated during graphical interfaces design. The main purpose of this work is to analyze the impact of the selection of the frequency level of images depending on the human thinking styles. The paper presents the selection of images with given frequency depending of one thinking style. To test the research hypothesis, we conducted perceptual experiments in which images with different intensity in different frequency bands were presented. Finally, we obtained statistical significance between the selection of images with different levels of frequency bands of images for the group of respondents with the thinking style based on the Ideas and the rest of the thinking groups.

KEYWORDS

Intelligent Graphical User Interface, Frequency Bands Images, Human Thinking Style, Perceptual Experiment - User Study

1. INTRODUCTION

Recommending systems become more and more popular. These systems make tight integrations of the calculation layer and physical processes. They are used more and more almost everywhere. They most often occur in the form of embedded systems (Lakshmi et al., 2019; Masayoshi et al., 1993). It controls physical processes that are further data sources for calculating the object control signal., They are considered as breakthrough not only in IT but also in other industries (Keenle et al., 2000). Thanks to these systems, it is possible to use the Internet of Things technology, where it is necessary to use even signals from various sensors and measuring devices (Field, 1989).

Intelligent systems are also important from the point of view of computer graphics interfaces and what follows of the final version of a graphic interfaces for the user - intelligent graphic interfaces preparation (Michael, 2000). Since physical Cyber systems occur in the form of a built-in embedded system in the final system, the graphic interface is finally visible as the output for the potential user (Kozhevnikov, 2007). It should be mentioned here, that one of the potential problem is preparing such an interface properly designed for a specific group of users, e.g. doctors, pilots, etc. Thus, incorrectly designed such an interface may affect the user's work efficiency with interface. It also turned out that the choice of user preferences is also influenced by the individual pattern of the user's perceptual, often called the thinking style (Field 1989; Zetzsche et al., 1989). Thus, it can be concluded that the design of graphic interfaces should take thinking style into account.

We distinguish many components by means of which we create an user interface. Among others the color of the objects displayed on the screen, the way objects are arranged on the screen, but also the complexity of the graphics used (Rossi et al., 2019).

As already stated, the contrast of image affects the user's choice of image. Thereby frequency of the images used in graphical interface could affect user's efficiency with this interface. In our paper, we decided to present the relationship between individual selection of images with different image frequency

(„Frequency determines the number of cycles of the periodic phenomenon occurring per unit of time. The frequency of 1 hertz corresponds to the occurrence of one cycle in 1 second. The Hz unit is not used when describing the image frequency. The image frequency is described in cycles per unit of distance" (Suchwałko et al., 2007)) – actually, the frequency bands of frequency and their thinking style. Finally, we show how this translates into creating graphic interfaces. We used perceptual psychometric model created by FRIS® in order to check thinking style of experiment respondent (Lewandowska et al., 2018; Dziśko et al., 2018).

To test the hypothesis - that the image frequency affects the selection of images by users, we conducted perceptual experiments using images with different content. The main goal of our work, is to analyze the impact of the level of image frequency and thinking style of a human observer. The problem was mentioned in the literature. However, in the literature, only the level of global contrasts of images is presented which does not present dependence of these contrasts on the thinking style of a human being. Therefore, this paper takes into account not only the global but also the local contrast of the displayed images and how it relates with the human thinking style (Lewandowska et al., 2018; Dziśko et al., 2018).

The obtained results were submitted to statistical analysis, which showed that there is a strong correlation between the selection of the image with a certain frequency and the human thinking style. Thus, the results confirmed that the human thinking style is strongly correlated with the individual choice of images with different frequency bands.

Conducted research are important from the computer graphics point of view, because they can further improve designing intelligent user interfaces, by taking on board one natural preferences. Since people differ one from another, their work efficiency with graphic interface may be varied. Some people reacts negatively when looking on images containing many intricate elements. For that reason, many graphical details in interfaces dedicated to totality of users should be avoided.

The research was carried out on images depicting natural, real life scenes to provide all users with the same level of knowledge in research. The experiments were deliberately not performed on the interfaces because some people could be familiar with them, thus they would not respond in a natural way, but learned.

Thanks to such kind of approach, it is possible to create a system that automatically selects interface complexity of graphics for user interface in relation to thinking style. This allows various social groups to use the intelligent interface, thereby improve their work with the system.

The concept of an experiment is described in Section 3. Section 5 explains in detail the subjective experimental procedure that we used. The results and analysis can be found in Section 6. Finally, Section 7 concludes the paper.

2. RELATED WORK

The popularity of recommending systems is recently growing up (Zetzsche et al., 1989). They are used in various industries ranging from used, ranging from building intelligent houses through in medicine (Stoppe et al., 2019; Zhang 2019). They are designed to facilitate the work of the human. The final kind of such system consist of large amount of embedded smaller sub-systems (Zetzsche et al., 1989; Zhang 2019). Final output visible to the end-user is a graphical interface which consists of among others displayed images.

It turns out, that an appropriate selection of frequency of images in graphic interface can improve the work of the human, while using interface(Zetzsche et al., 1989). The basis for such selection is not only the content of images, but also the level of their frequency. Literature indicates that the image frequency is the medium of visual information (Zetzsche et al., 1989; Rossi et al., 2019).

It is considered, that images with higher contrasts are more appealing to users, but they are less natural., So the higher the contrast, the more unnatural the picture. However, it should be taken into account that every person is an individuality, who can perceive and search the area of images in various ways (Zetzsche et al., 1989).

Graphical user interface. There are a lot of various user's interfaces that people are using day by day. As end-users we expect from them high effectiveness and intuitivness. However, it would be valuable when design of those interfaces would take into account scientific knowledge about human thinking styles. Stuart Card in his book (Card, 2017), argue that analysis of information processing will lead to new methods, which will be using thinking psychology in order to creating interfaces. He suggests that abovemnetioned analysis will lead to new ways to adapt psychology to our human needs. He also points out that in the studies of human-machine systems and engineering psychology for some time it has been common to include a flowchart of the entire human information processing system (Card, 2017). In the other hand, Aude Dufresne in (Dufresne et al., 1997) discusses the problem of the impact of human thinking styles on navigational strategies referring specifically to hypermedia. The author of this text draws attention to the knowledge of thinking styles of a human being, referring to the style of learning of users (Dufresne et al., 1997). However, in these papers, none of the authors specifies any human thinking styles.

Therefore, in this work, we decided to use an approach in which we used the human's thinking style for analysis. Thanks to this, it is possible to check the correlation between choosing a picture with the right level of frequency and the thinking style of a human being. Such kind of dependence will translate into creation of recommending graphical interfaces that could support automatic selection of graphic contrast usage in the user interface which is relative to the thinking styles.

Currently, it is difficult to find research that would check the impact of human thinking style on the creation of recommended user interfaces, while taking into account the selection of appropriate image frequency bands.

Therefore, we decided to carry out research taking into account human thinking style, including dependence on the field and independence from the field.

By dependence on the field, we understand the tendency to perceive holistic, in which the elements constitute the picture of the whole. By independence from the field, we mean the tendency to separate the components and make them and make them into parts - as if they are independent from the whole. Independence from the field means perceiving analytically, dependence from the field is perceiving globally (Dufresne et al., 1997).

3. CONCEPTION

The aim of the paper was to examine whether the human thinking style influences the human attention on the graphical components depending on their complexity (details level - high contrast in a particular frequency band). Therefore our research was divided into two parts. The first is a perceptual experiment that was conducted. In the second part the observers were asked to complete the FRIS® psychometric questionnaire. After that we obtained the complete data we carried out the analysis. The diagram of the work is presented in the figure below (see Figure 1.).

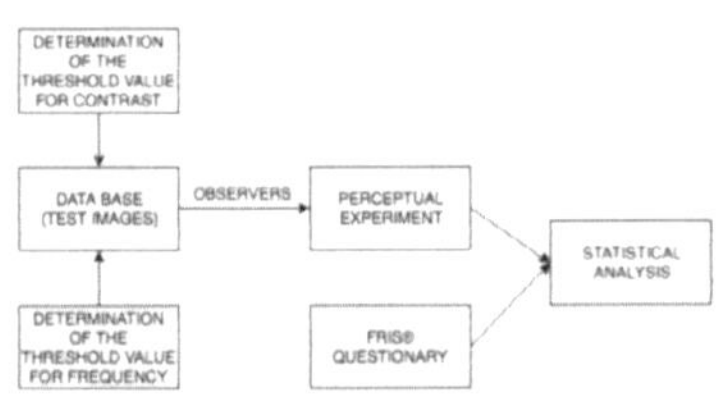

Figure 1. Preparation of the perceptual experiment and the process of gathering knowledge

4. HUMAN THINKING STYLES

The style of thinking is innate, and man acquires it from birth. Due to the fact that the style of thinking is innate, the preferences that a person acquires along with his style of thinking since birth are subconscious. Of course, people acquire subjective preferences with age, but these preferences correlate with the style of thinking that was already acquired at birth.

According to the literature, there are many approaches that aim to describe and determine the human thinking style (Kozhevnikov, 2007). Most of these approaches indicate bipolar scales. These are mostly: the reflection coefficient and impulsivity (Kozhevnikov, 2007). There are also thinking styles that are individual differences of every human being. These styles are measured using formal questionnaires or inventories. In our experiment, we used the FRIS® inventory to verify the thinking styles of the respondents. FRIS® is a psychometric questionnaire measuring the ranking of individual preferences. FRIS® defines 4 thinking perspectives:

- F: fact-based thinking (concrete, sequential, logical thinking)
- R: relation-based thinking (intuitive, field-dependent, relational thinking)
- I: Idea-based thinking (abstract, lateral, global thinking)
- S: structure-based thinking (field-independent, reflective, analytical thinking) (Samborska-Owczarek 2019A).

FRIS® is psychometrically reliable, valid, normalised and standardised. The 6 factors of the inventory are bipolar scales discriminating between pairs of thinking perspectives: F vs I, F vs R etc. with internal consistency 0.76 –0.82 Cronbach's α. The 4 superfactors 'internal consistency is 0, 82 (F), 0, 88(R) 0, 88(I) 0, 88(S) Cronbach's α. As a metrics in our experiment we used 1 nominal variable T S Thinking Style - the dominant (max-imal) thinking perspective of the subject (one from the set): T S = {F, R, I, S} (Samborska-Owczarek 2019; Samborska-Owczarek 2019A).

5. SUBJECTIVE EXPERIMENT

During the experiments, we checked whether the contrast level in a given frequency band and the human thinking style influences the selection of images by the user. Observers were asked to read the written instructions before the experiment.

Experimental procedure. We collected data through method called forced selection (Mantiuk et al., 2012). Observers were always forced to choose one of the pictures, even if they did not see the difference between them (Mantiuk et al., 2012). There was no time limit to do the experiment. In order to avoid observer fatigue the session was prepared in such a way that it took no longer than 30 minutes. The experiment was conducted using an eye-tracker that allows later to analyze the way the observers perceive displayed images.

Observers. In the experiment, we examined 201 respondents with normal or corrected for normal vision. The age of observers varied between 20 and 70. We ask observers to select the image visible in the image according to the given command.

Display conditions. Experiment was performed using the NEC monitor with a native resolution of 1680x1050 pixels. The display conditions were measured with a Minolta CS-200 colorimeter and Specbos 1201 spectroradiometer. The measurements were used to calibrate display and ensure that all images were reproduced in the sRGB color space. We also used an eye-tracker in order to follow the path of the respondents' eyes during experiment session.

Test images. The experiment was conducted on 15 images taken from Fotolia database (subset of an image set composed for FRIS® project (Samborska-Owczarek 2019A).) (see Figure. 2.) with different contrast levels (low, medium, high). To perform thresholding we used following procedure: first we calculate the contrasts for all images, then create a scale interval for each contrast range, and finally calculate the levels of the next 6 octaves of the global contrast. During single experiment session images were displayed in random order. To each of the images we attached one research task: "indicate the image, the most similar to the middle one" or "indicate the image that you like the most". Between each images presentation we displayed grey background without any images on it.

Figure 2. Test images taken to the experiments

Thereshold of frequency and contrast values. Frequency and contrast values were set to three thereshold levels: low, medium and high. In order to do this this we calculated the values of contrasts and values for individual frequency bands. Then we find the highest and the lowest value of frequency band of contrast. We separated domain ranking from highest and lowest contrast frequency into 3 parts. We assigned following labels for each part: Low, Medium, High. Finally, we match each contrast value from out data into one of three previously mentioned groups (see Figure. 3.).

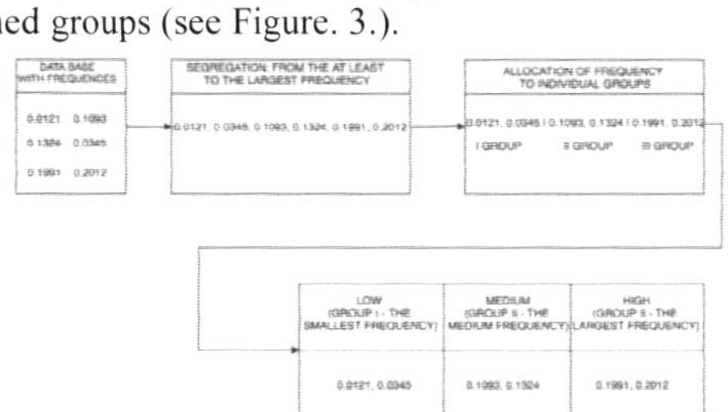

Figure 3. Example frequency distribution

6. RESULT AND ANALYSIS

After the experiment we carried out a statistical analysis. Statistical analyzes have shown that there is a statistical significance between the style of human thinking and the frequency of the image chosen by the respondent.

The obtained results suggest that differences in preferences between groups of respondents of various thinking styles are noticeable. Especially between the choice of respondents whose thinking style is based on Ideas and other groups of thinking styles (Fact, Relations and Structure).

Thanks to a large research group, we found that the difference between groups is statistically significant. The experiment was completed by 201 respondents. Numerosity of people based on different thinking thinking styles were following: Ideas (I) - 33, Facts (F) - 28, Relationships (R) - 40, Structures (S) - 100.

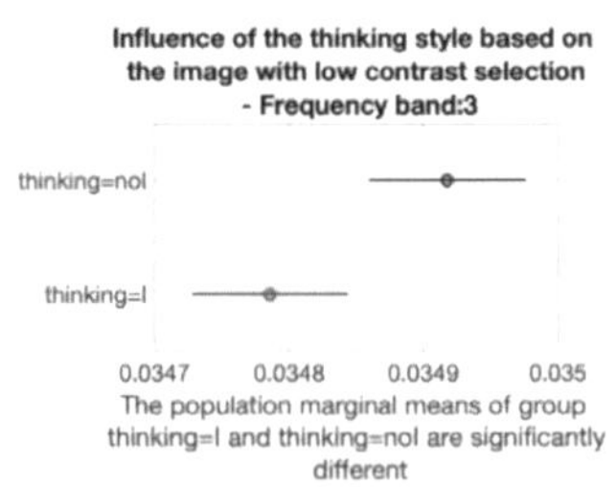

Figure 4. ANOVA comparison of observers preferences given for low frequency, for thinking style Idea-based thinking group and the rest of thinking groups. - Third band, where: I - Thinking style based on Idea, noI - other thinking styles than Idea

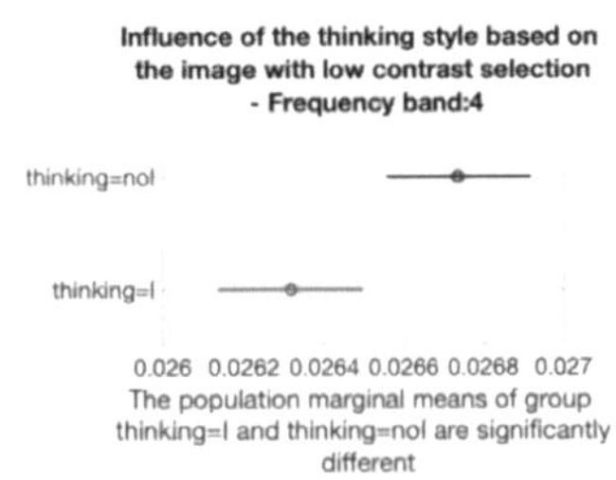

Figure 5. ANOVA comparison of observers preferences given for low frequency, for thinking style Idea-based thinking group and the rest of thinking groups. - Fourth band, where: I - Thinking style based on Idea, noI - other thinking styles than Idea

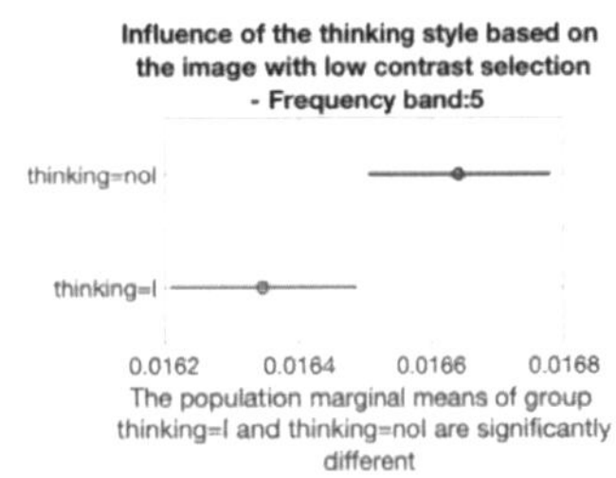

Figure 6. ANOVA comparison of observers prefeences given for low frequency, for thinking style Idea-based thinking group and the rest of thinking groups. - Fifth band, where: I - Thinking style based on Idea, noI - other thinking styles than Idea

Plots presenting achieve statistical significance are shown on Figure 4-6. Performed ANOVA analysis showed that, we obtained statistical significance between the groups of respondents based on the thinking style of the Ideas and the selection of images with low contrast. Particularly high correlation can be seen in low contrast images and low frequency bands(octaves): third, fourth and fifth. Statistical significance is changed as follows: for 3rd frequency band: $p = 0.0241$, 4th frequency band: $p = 0.0241$, 5th frequency band: $p = 0.0388$. Below in Table 1 also shows the results for thinking styles other than Ideas based. The table presents results only for low contrast, because for high and medium levels of contrast, we did not notice statistically significant data.

Table 1. Statistical significance for all cognitive styles - Low contrast

Thinking Styles	Level of statistical significance for low contrast for frequency band 3	Level of statistical significance for low contrast for frequency band 4	Level of statistical significance for low contrast for frequency band 5
Ideas	0.0241	0.0241	0.0388
Facts	0.1231	0.1427	0.1244
Structures	0.2332	0.1622	0.2103
Relations	0.0621	0.0556	0.0677

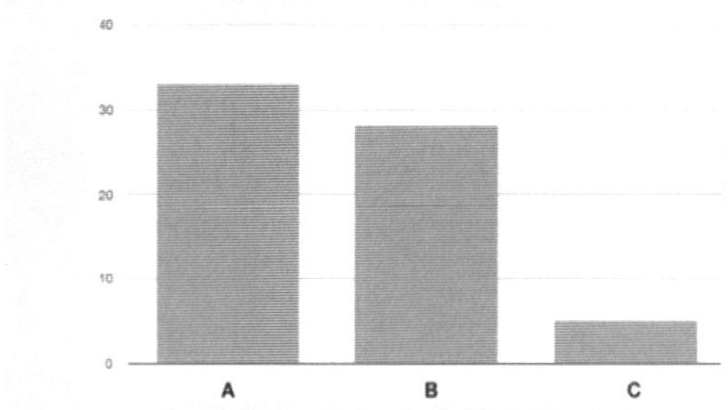

Figure 7. Quantitative analysis - groups based on thinking styles is Idea and other group. A - All respondents based on all group. B - All respondents based on Idea

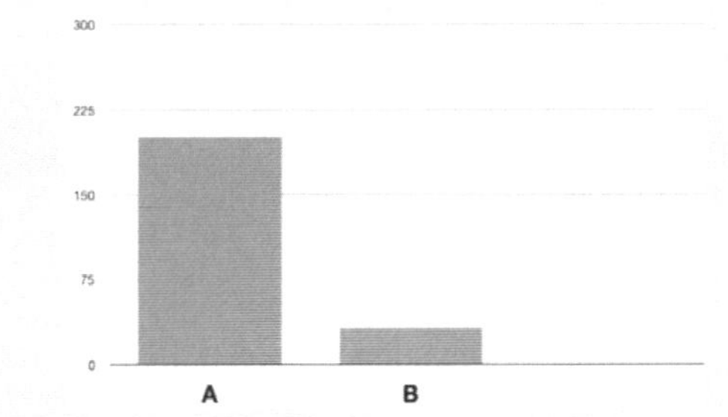

Figure 8. Quantitative analysis - groups based on Ideas. A - All respondents based on thinking styles is Idea. B - Respondents based on Ideas who chose low frequency bands. C - Respondents based on Ideas who chose other than low frequency bands

Subsequently, we conducted a quantitative analysis see Figure 7-8. It turned out that the greatest relationship is visible between groups based on Ideas and other groups. 33 respondents on the background of the whole group (see Figure. 7 A) are people based on a group of Ideas (see Figure. 7 B). It turns out that 28 respondents (see Figure. 8 B) from the group of 33 respondents based on a group of thinking styles is Ideas (see Figure. 8 A) chose images with low frequency bands see Figure 8. This is up to 85% of compatible choices. Thanks to data gathered from the eye-tracker, it turned out that users with an Idea- based thinking style focus on objects that are less detailed and less blackened. It is a visually confirmed by the ANOVA statistical analysis that respondents whose thinking style is based on relationships prefer low-frequency images (see Figure 9-10.).

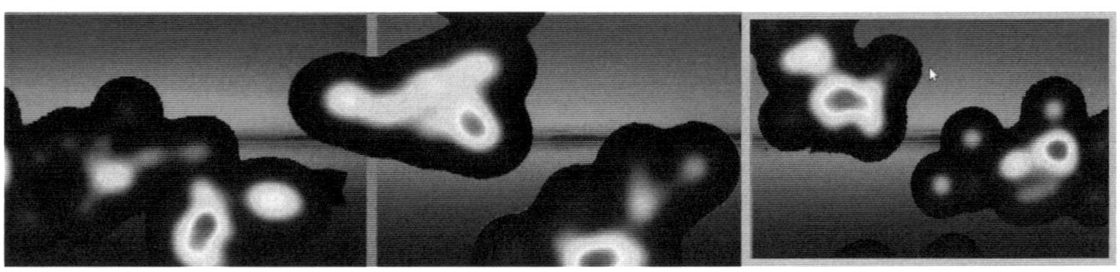

Figure 9. Heat map. Groups based on Ideas. Image with low frequencies. Green frame - the image chosen by the observer

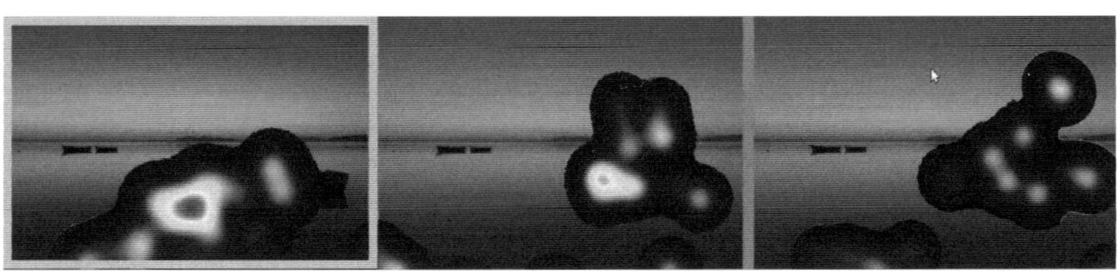

Figure 10. Heat map. Groups based on other thinking styles (Thinking styles: Relation, Fact and Structure). Image with low frequencies. Green frame - the image chosen by the observer (Observers which thinking styles was: Relation, Fact and Structure)

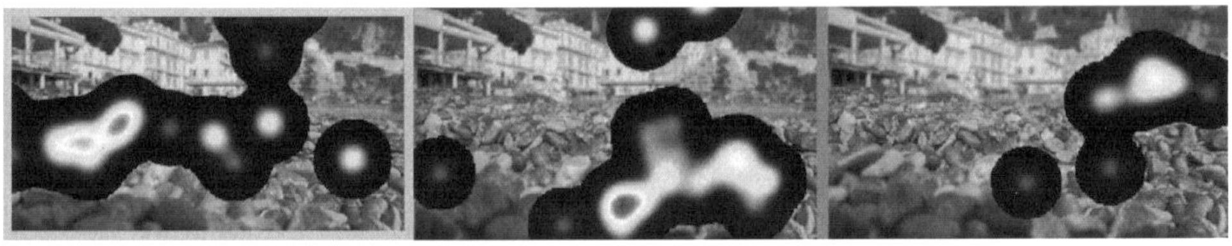

Figure 11. Heat map. Groups based on Idea thinking styles. Image with high frequencies. Green frame - the image chosen by the observer. (Observers which thinking styles was: Idea)

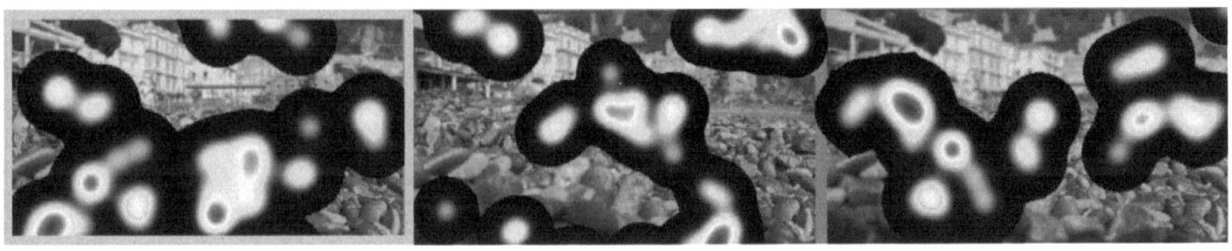

Figure 12. Heat map. Groups based on other thinking styles (Thinking styles: Relation, Fact and Structure). Image with high frequencies. Green frame - the image chosen by the observer (Observers which thinking styles was: Relation, Fact and Structure)

Visual analysis, thanks to using the eye-tracker, also showed that other thinking styles (based on relationships, structures and facts) focused on high or medium-frequency images (see Figure 10-12.). However, in this case we did not obtain statistically significant results.

Through the visual analysis, we also observed the time of focusing on images by observers. It turned out that Idea-based groups focus their attention on low- frequency images for an average of 9.2 seconds, while on high-frequency images the average focus time of these groups is 6.5 seconds. It is also noticable, that groups based on other styles than Ideas have focused their attention on high-frequency images longer - the average time is 8.4 seconds, with average focal length on low- frequency images of 6.1 seconds. It arise from the dependence on the fields based on Ideas (Lewandowska et al., 2018).

The most important result of this study, is the fact that there is a difference between the selection of low-contrast images and frequency bands for the group of respondents with the thinking style based on the Ideas and the rest of the thinking groups. That means, that respondents whose thinking style was based on Ideas choose much more often a picture with a low contrast and low frequency bands level than the rest of the respondents whose thinking style was based on the other FRIS® thinking styles. This indicates other groups prefer images with a low contrast level with a low frequency bands.

7. CONCLUSIONS

The main purpose of this work is to check whether human cognitive style affects human preferences related to the frequency of images. It turned out, that people with a thinking style based on Ideas choose images with low frequency in the third, fourth and fifth contrast bands.

Analysis show, that we should choose the images with high contrast in low frequency bands. Otherwise, it may turn out that the user who will work with the interface unsuitably prepared for his natural preferences will be less efficient and his frequency of errors will increase.

It is worth noting that many people are unaware of their thinking style, but the important thing is that thinking style is innate. Due to the fact that the style of thinking is innate, a person with a specific style of thinking acts subconsciously and in accordance with this style of thinking. Therefore, creating interfaces that will harmonize with the style of thinking is important because it will make the subconscious work easier with these interfaces.

Performed analysis confirmed the hypothesis. We have obtained statistically significant results, in particular between choices of a low contrast for its various octaves and a group of people, who according to the psychometric model of FRIS®, have the Ideas activated.

We obtained statistically significant results for a group of respondents with a thinking style based on Ideas.

The research included in this paper may refers into the creation of personal intelligent graphical interfaces that will automatically select the level of contrasts of images and frequency bands for people with a specific thinking style. By using the recommending system, which will automatically adjust the level of contrast to human thinking thinking style, it is possible to increase the efficiency of one work.

REFERENCES

Card, S., (2017), The psychology of human-computer interaction.

Dufresne, A., Turcotte, S., (1997), Thinking style and its implications for navigation strategies. Artificial intelligence in education knowledge and media learning system, 287-293.

Dziśko, M., Lewandowska, A., & Samborska-Owczarek, A., (2018), Does the Research Question Structure Impact the Attention Model? User Study Experiment. In *International Conference on Computer Vision and Graphics,* pp. 487-498.

Field, D., (1989), What the statistics of natural images tell us about visual coding. In: Proceedings of the SPIE, pp. 269–276.

Keeble, R., Macredie, R., (2000), Assistant agents for the world wide web intelligent interface design challenges. *Interacting with computers, pp.* 357-381.

Kozhevnikov, M., (2007), Thinking styles in the context of modern psychology: toward an integrated framework of thinking style, pp. 464– 481.

Lewandowska, A., Samborska-Owczarek, A., & Dziśko, M., (2018), Contrast Perception Across Human Thinking Style. In *International Conference Image Analysis and Recognition,* pp. 345-352

M. Lakshmi, et al., (2019), Navigation Through Eye-Tracking for Human–Computer Interface. In: *Information and Communication Technology for Intelligent Systems,* p. 575-586.

Mantiuk, R., Tomaszewska, A., Mantiuk, R., (2012), Comparison of four subjective methods for image quality assessment. In *Computer graphics forum,* pp. 2478-2491.

Masayoshi, M., et al., (1993), Interactive intelligent interface., pp. 5,201,034.

Michael F., (2000), Intelligent interface technology: from theory to reality?. *Interacting with computers*, pp. 323-336.

Rossi M., Sani S., Nibali M. Fornia L., Bello L., Byrne R., (2019), Mapping in Low-Grade Glioma Surgery. Low-and High-Frequency Stimulation, pp. 55-63.

Samborska-Owczarek, A., (2019), FRIS Thinking Styles Inventory, https://fris.pl

Samborska-Owczarek, A., (2019), FRIS Thinking Styles Inventory., https://fris.pl/ FRIS-validity-data.pdf

Stoppe, L., Husemann, C., (2019), U.S. Patent Application, pp. 175-468.

Suchwałko A., Wysocka-Król K., (2007), Politechnika Wrocławska, http://www.dydaktyka.ib.pwr.wroc.pl/materialy/ETP002901%20Diagnostyka%20obrazowa/Ćwiczenie_6.pdf

Zetzsche, C., Hauske, G., (1989), Multiple channel model for the prediction of subjective image quality. In: Proceedings of the SPIE, pp. 209–216.

ZHANG P., (2019), Objective method for assessing high contrast resolution of image based on Rayleigh criterion and testing operating method. U.S. Patent Application No 10/169,870.

AN ENHANCED INTERACTION AND FILTERING WIDGET

Yasmin Al-Zokari[1], Peter Dannenmann[2], Hans Hagen[3], Dirk Zeckzer[1]
[1]*Leipzig University, Augustusplatz 10, 04109 Leipzig*
[2]*RheinMain University of Applied Science, Rüsselsheim, Germany*
[3]*TU Kaiserslautern, Erwin-Schrödinger Straße, Kaiserslautern*

ABSTRACT

In information visualization, interaction mechanisms are an essential factor to the success of visualization. They should be easy to use and useful for filtering, exploring, and analyzing the data visualized. Usually, direct manipulation on the visualizations is the most important aspect that researches consider. However, users still tend to use controls (widgets) for some interaction, especially, when manipulating (e.g., filtering) the data. During our work with users on the visual representation of safety analysis results, we found limitations in the interaction capabilities of sliders. In order to overcome these limitations, we introduce our Range-Selection-and-Filtering RSF slider, which enables users to work more efficiently when selecting relevant data from large data sets compared to conventional slider designs by enhancing the ease of use and increasing its usefulness. Additionally, we applied this slider to different application domains and evaluated it.

KEYWORDS

Graphical User Interfaces, Interaction Styles, Interaction Techniques, User Interfaces

1. INTRODUCTION

In the "Safety Assessment and Risk Analysis" domain, there is a strong need to efficiently visualize analysis results. A safety-critical system could cause different levels of harm to users --i.e., injury, death, etc.-- or harm to the environment (Savive Pty Ltd, n.d.). The data is usually divided into several categories, e.g., unacceptable (high), tolerable (moderate), and negligible (low) risks (Bozzano & Villafiorita, 2010, p. 68). Safety analysis techniques and procedures are used to detect risks and hazards for removing, avoiding, or reducing the probability of the failure of a system (Bozzano & Villafiorita, 2010, p. xiii). Visualization enables engineers to efficiently analyze the resulting data. Usually, direct manipulations on the visualizations are the most important aspect that researches consider. Filtering is required by the tasks of safety analysts, because they search for the most safety critical events and prioritize them. Therefore, in this paper, we investigated and illustrated the strengths and weaknesses of different types of sliders and propose the Range-Selection-and-Filtering RSF slider for Minimal Cut Set (MCS) analysis. Sliders are an easy means to filter data and provide a sensitive mechanism for specifying values (Eick, 1994, pp. 119–120). Therefore, they are very well suited for supporting the analysts in their daily work.

Section 2 describes the requirements; Section 3 describes the state-of-the-art sliders. In Section 4, we describe our RSF slider. Section 5 provides the ease of use assessment. Section 6 shows two case studies for assessing usefulness and usability of our slider. Finally, Section 7 summarizes our findings and presents the future work.

2. REQUIREMENTS

In this paper, we present, describe, and discuss our RSF slider widget for interacting with numerical data. The assumptions and requirements are:

(a) Manipulation of multiple ranges: We assume that the numerical data should be categorized using n adjacent intervals

$I = \{I_i | i = 1...n\}$ (2.1)

$I_i = [l_i; r_i[; \quad i = 1...n-1$ (2.2)

$I_n = [l_n; r_n]$ (2.3)

$l_j = r_{j-1}; \quad j = 2... n$ (2.4)

(b) Provide the data distribution: We need to provide the distribution of the data.

(c) Support of color schemes for the categories: A distinct color is associated with each category (interval). This color can be used in coordinated views as representation of its category.

(d) Space efficiency: The widget should use a minimal amount of space.

(e) Easy to use: number of interaction steps to reach the required goal.

These requirements were derived from the applications described in Section 6. The color scheme (c) can be adapted to support people having color view deficiencies or color-blind visions (Ware, 2004, p.99). The selection of ranges according to (a) implies that the uncategorized data below l1 and above rn is not displayed. This means, the widget serves also as filtering widget. In this paper, we propose the RSF slider having the required properties (a) - (d).

3. RELATED WORK

Sliders were initially used by selecting a value for filtering the data (Section 3.1). Besides filtering according to single values, they can also be used to filter according to ranges (Section 3.2). The range sliders were then augmented with histograms to provide an overview over the distribution of the values (Section 3.3 and Section 3.4). In general, sliders consist of the following elements: one or more thumbs; a slider body, i.e., rectangle: the space between the thumbs; ticks, i.e., dividers: used for showing the values; and labels, i.e., text describing the values. These elements vary in number and shape. Some sliders also include additional elements.

3.1 Standard or Single-Thumb Sliders

Standard sliders are widely used in many applications, e.g., for showing the history of legal cases (Harris, et al., 1999), for finding accommodations (HomeFinder) (Williamson, et al., 1992), or selecting names (Ahlberg & Shneiderman, 1994a), and are provided by GUI libraries like Java Swing or the InfoVis toolkit (Fekete, 2004). This type generally consists of one thumb, a rectangular body, several ticks, and labels for the ticks. These sliders are mainly used for filtering by selecting a value. However, they can easily be combined to select ranges like in Figure 1. The main issues with these sliders (Al-Zokari, et al., 2011c) are: they use a large amount of screen space, which violates Requirement (d); they do not support colors in an obvious way (Requirement (c)); no information about the data or data distribution is provided (Requirement (b)); they are not easy to use which violates Requirement (e); and it is not easy to interact with them (Al-Zokari, et al., 2011a), because they are multiple (four in our case) and the user has to think while choosing the correct slider for the specific required range.

3.2 Range Sliders

Range slider (Ahlberg & Shneiderman, 1994b), (Tanin, et al., 1996) are also called dual-thumb, min-max, or dynamic-query sliders. Many approaches adopted this type of slider because of its powerful representation, such as Dyna-TreeMap (HCI Lab, U.S. Bureau of Census, n.d.), the dynamic queries of (Dang, et al., 2001), Ymap, Dotfire, or GRIDL (Shneiderman, et al., 2000), FilmFinder (Ahlberg & Shneiderman, 1994b), HomeFinder (Williamson, et al., 1992), Spotfire (Plaisant & Laboratory, 1993), (Ahlberg, 1996), (Card & Mackinlay, 1997), and the prefuse toolkit (Heer, et al., 2005)).

This slider has a second thumb allowing to select ranges instead of single values. However, thumbs can overlap (Figure 2). In this case, the user can only move the upper thumb. If the thumb movement is constrained, then this upper thumb can only be moved in one direction. For example, if the low thumb is over the high thumb then the user can only move towards the left, otherwise to the right. Therefore, the user cannot freely decide which way to move the thumbs and has no full control over the slider.

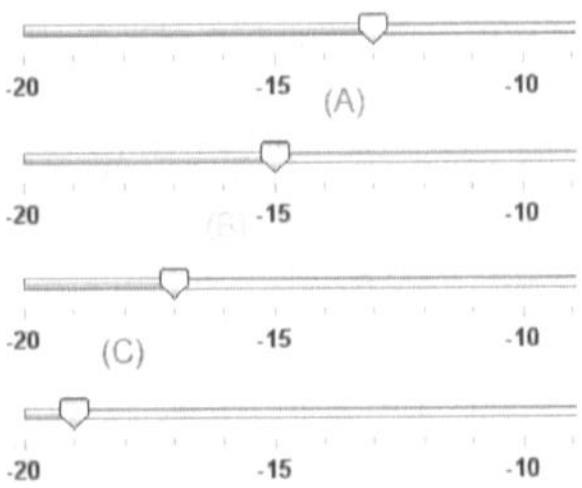

Figure 1. Four standard sliders defining the three ranges (A), (B), and (C)

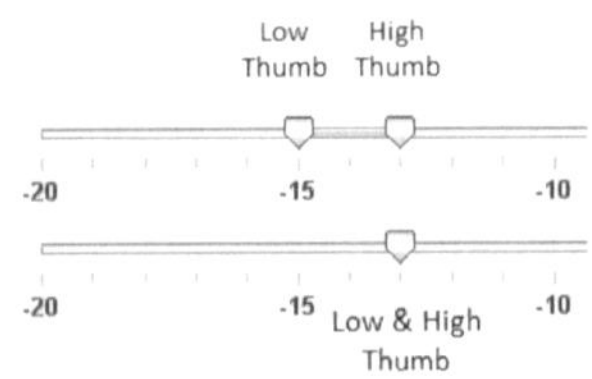

Figure 2. Thumbs overlap

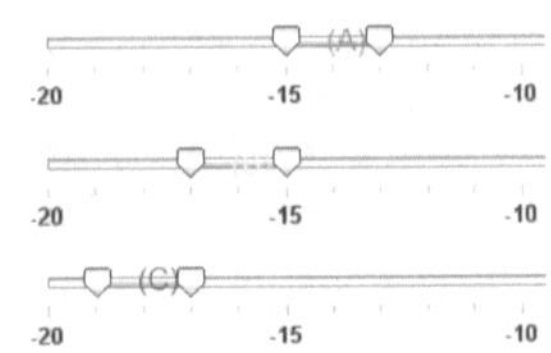

Figure 3. Three dual-thumb sliders defining three ranges (A), (B), and (C)

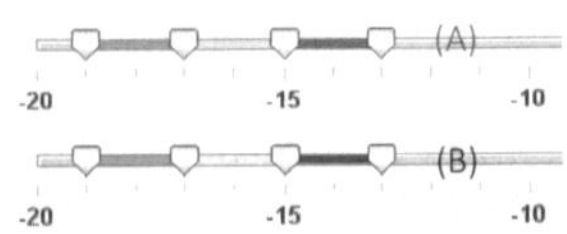

Figure 4. (A) Multi-Thumb slider with background colors. (B) As seen by users with total color blindness

This becomes challenging for more than two thumbs. As in the case of the single-thumb slider (Section 3.1), multiple range slider can be combined to select ranges like in Figure 3, where they are used to select the three ranges marked (A), (B), and (C). This combination fulfills the requirements (a) and (c). However, the solution still uses a large amount of screen space between the sliders, violating Requirement (d). Moreover, no information about the data or data distribution is provided violating Requirement (b). Solving the violation of Requirement (d), lead us to the colored multi-thumb slider shown in Figure 4 (A). This slider is implemented using and adapting the Swing library (Swing, n.d.). However, for users with color vision deficiencies, it is difficult to distinguish between the ranges and to map them to the main visualization (Figure 4 (B)). To enhance the flexibility of the slider, we have implemented it to be dynamic according to the needs of the users by being able to change the number and the colors of range. In addition of having the fixed coloring scheme for the full color vision and the deutranope and tritanope color deficiency visions (Figure 5).

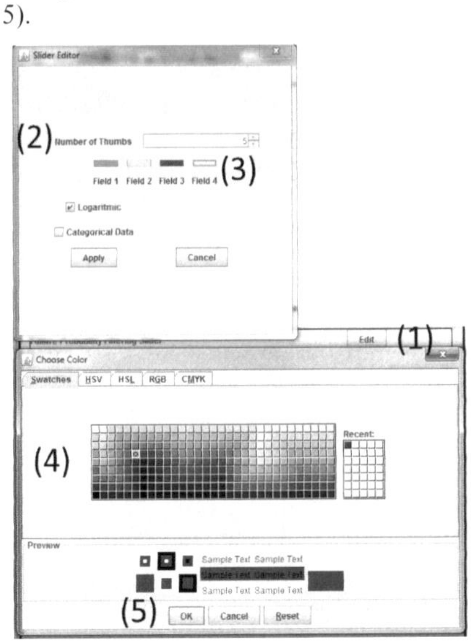

Figure 5. A) Adaptive coloring for the ranges and the number of thumbs

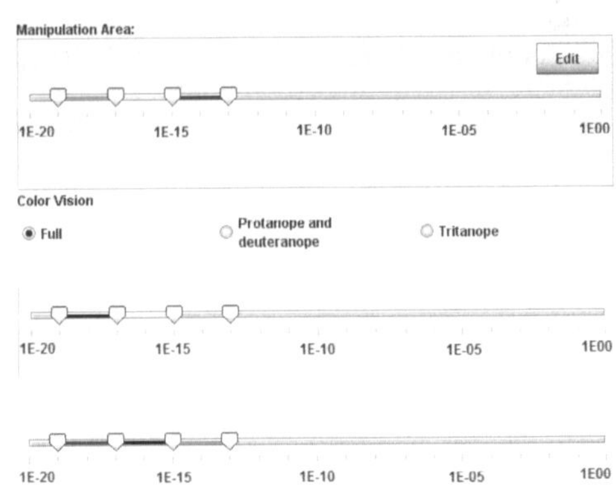

Figure 5. B) The fixed color schemes for different color visions

3.3 Interactive Legends

A special case of range sliders are the interactive legends by (Henry, et al., 2010) and (Tweedie, et al., 1996). This type provides information about the data visualized, i.e., size. However, the issues from the dual thumb slider are inherited (Section 3.2). The interactive legends with multiple handles improve the direct manipulation for interaction, especially selecting ranges. The additional improvements on the main elements of the slider were, that there are no restrictions on the number of thumbs, also called handles, and that the background is not rectangular. However, the handles still can overlap.

3.4 Histogram Sliders

(Li & North, 2003) added an internal histogram to the dynamic query slider and (Li, et al., 2003) compared these two approaches. It provides information about the distribution of the data being analyzed inside the slider's rectangle. The limitations of this type of sliders are: total overlapping of thumbs, the histogram is squeezed into the small slider's rectangle space, it is hard to distinguish the different levels, and the thumbs cover the histogram.

(Tweedie, et al., 1996) placed the histogram over the slider and show the relations within multi-attribute data sets. The limitations of this type of sliders are: total overlapping of thumbs, the information of the histogram outside the range is hidden when the thumbs move towards the middle (no overview information).

In general, the main elements of the histogram sliders are: two thumbs, a rectangular background (slider body), and a histogram placed inside or outside the rectangle. The histogram slider introduced by (Eick, S. G., 1994, pp. 119–120) used the rainbow color map. His slider has two more elements over the main ones: a barplot for discrete data and a density plot for continuous data. An interesting mechanism is, that the user can select/deselect arbitrary regions and get a thumb. Additionally, it shows the overview of the data being analyzed. The limitations of this type of sliders are: rainbow coloring for exploring data is "still considered to be harmful" (Borland & Taylor, 2007); the thumb is not recognizable; when the bar is gray and when it is over a light blue or orange color, it is difficult to recognize by the user (low contrast); and interaction for zooming is missing. The information is only visible when the mouse is over the bar, i.e., an overview is not available. However, if the total information was visible all the time, this slider would be very crowded. Another problem is that this type supports only one range. Therefore, it does not support the analysis with multiple ranges.

4. THE RANGE-SELECTION-AND-FILTERING (RSF) SLIDER

To fulfill all requirements stated in Section 2, we created the Range-Selection-and-Filtering (RSF) slider (Al-Zokari, et al., 2011b). This slider is a combination of previously available sliders (Section 3) with the following extensions: thumbs are not overlapping each other, thumbs do not overlap information.

We started with a multi-thumb slider as baseline (Figure 4). It consists of four thumbs on a rectangular body with ticks and labels. The thumbs were enumerated from 1 to 4 (left to right) and they were constrained such that if i< j then thumbi is left to or at the same position as thumbj. Each pair of thumbs (i; i+1) designates a range. In the given example, there are four thumbs defining three ranges. This slider has the following advantages: more space efficient as shown in Figure 1 and Figure 3, the categories can be mapped to the background colors of the ranges (area between two thumbs), the different color schemes can be used supporting users having color deficiency problems, and it is easy to understand.

However, the following issues needed to be resolved: overlapping thumbs cannot be recognized, overlapping thumbs can only be moved in the direction of the upper thumb (due to the range constraints). Allowing to move both thumbs does not solve the problem as then we need additional modifier keys to decide how many thumbs we want to move: only the upper one, separating it from the others, two, three, or more. To avoid the overlap of thumbs, we positioned them at different distances to the main axis (Figure 6): the position of the leftmost thumb (W) is lower than the position of thumb (X), and so on. Thus, the values V of the thumbs are always ordered: Vw <Vx <Vy <Vz. In addition, the thumbs are elastic in the sense of thumbs moving together. If, for example, thumb Z is moved to the left then eventually it will be at the same horizontal position as thumb Y and the range [VY ;VZ] will become empty. Moving the thumb Z further to the left will also move thumb Y keeping it vertically below the Z thumb (Equation 1). This holds for all movements of any thumb to the left and to the right.

Equation 1 $$Position(Y)_{Thumb(i)} = 12 - 8 * i$$ where i is the *i-th* thumb

Nevertheless, after applying this approach, to enhance the understandability of the thumbs position, we decided the following: the thumbs should point to the slider body, and the space between the leftmost/rightmost thumbs and the rectangle of the slider should be reduced (Requirement (d)).

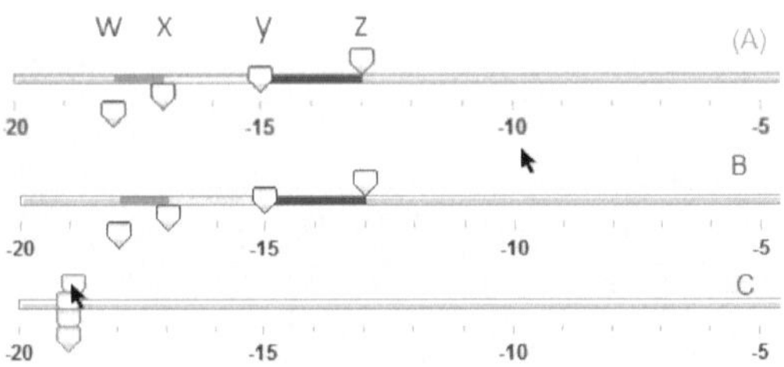

Figure 6. (A) The names of the thumbs of the RSF slider. (B) Clear importance even with total color blindness. (C) No overlapping thumbs problem

Figure 7. Slider icons. a) Java standard icon for the thumb. b) Our thumb design to point in two directions. c) Our thumb design to point in one direction with a pointer for both w and z thumbs. d) Our final thumb design

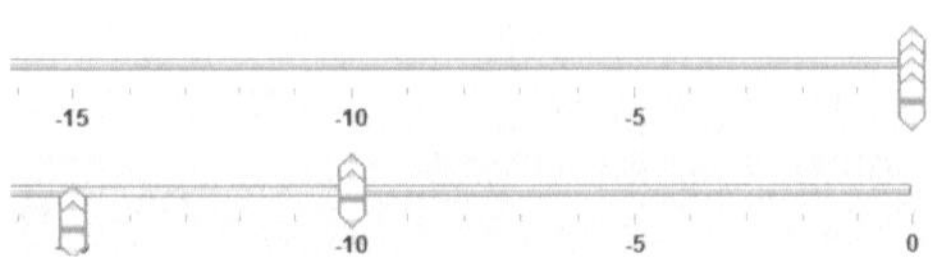

Figure 8. Double thumb slider problem (neither easy to use nor understand)

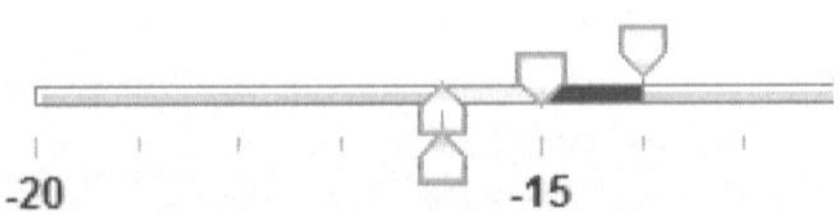

Figure 9. The problem when using the pointing thumbs

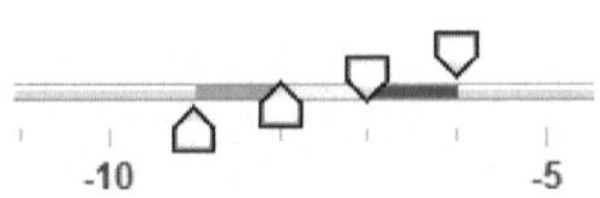

Figure 10. Final slider icon design (even number of thumbs)

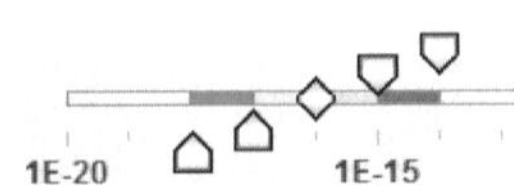

Figure 11. Final slider icon design (odd number of thumbs)

Therefore, we changed the thumb icons to the ones in Figure 7d. To let the thumbs always point to the slider body, the icon of the thumbs are changed depending on the value of the thumbs. This means, when the number of thumbs is odd, the shape of the middle thumb is that of a rhombus, the thumbs set for the higher values point downwards (towards the rectangle body of the slider), and the thumbs set for the smaller values point upwards. When the number of thumbs is even, half of the thumbs point downwards and the other half point upwards depending on their set values (Figure 10 and Figure 11). Alternative icon designs are shown in Figure 7b – Figure 7c. However, as can be seen from Figure 8 – Figure 9, the other icon designs were less suitable:

a) The standard Java icon: always pointing downwards 0a, in contrast to requirement 1.
b) The new double thumb icon: takes a lot of space and neither easy to use nor understand (Figure 7b and Figure 8).
c) The new thumb with a stick icon (pointing thumb): has a problem when overlapping (Figure 7c and Figure 9).
d) Our final design: easy to understand and use with no overlapping problems (Figure 7d and Figure 10).

To solve the movement restriction of the thumbs, lower thumb should not cross higher thumbs and vice versa, and make it easy to use, the thumbs are allowed to push each other. Thus, when arriving to the same position of thumb *y* moving thumb *z* to the left leads to moving thumb *y* to the left, and the range $[V_Y, V_Z]$ becomes empty. This has a *cascading effect*: the ability of adjusting successive thumbs (or interaction handles) in the movement direction by moving only one thumb. This means, moving thumb *z* further to the left will also move thumb *y* keeping it vertically below the *z* thumb, and when arriving to the same position as thumb *x*, thumb *x* is moved together with thumb *z* and thumb *y*, etc. This holds for all movements of any thumb to the left and to the right. Additionally, we added a histogram and the number of objects per label

(Figure 12). Since showing text horizontally leads to occlusions, we improved it by changing the orientation of the text to be vertical (Figure 13). Thus, this allows to get an overview over the data distribution and to support the user to choose the intervals.

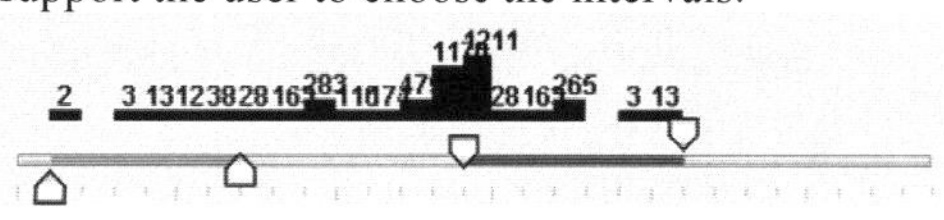

Figure 12. A data set of 4158 objects with horizontal text

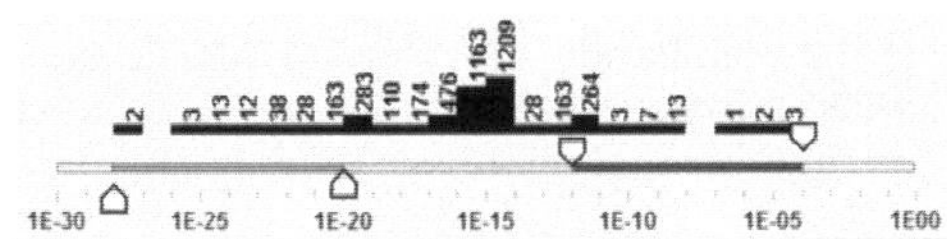

Figure 13. A data set of 4158 objects with vertical text (Final design)

Table 1. Relative Number of objects = objects in range / max{ objects in range}

Constant Number of objects	Relative Number of objects (height)	Histogram Height
] 0, 25[	] 0, 1/5[	5
[25, 50[	[1/5, 2/5[	10
[50, 75[	[2/5, 3/5[	15
[75, 100[	[3/5, 4/5[	20
[100, 125[	[4/5, 1[	25
[125, ∞[	[1]	30

The user is immediately aware, whether data is filtered, and which part of the data is currently assigned to which category. We use histograms with fixed height and with relative height (Table 1).

The RSF slider has the following parameters:

- Number of thumbs: number of ranges
- Color scheme: individual colors of the ranges
- Use of a logarithmic scale

This allows to adapt the slider to many application needs. The advantages of the RSF slider are:

- Space-efficient visualization of the ranges using multiple thumbs (Requirement d)
- Thumbs do not overlap each other (Requirement e)
- It is easy to adjust the thumbs and thus the ranges (Requirement e)
- Usable by users with color vision deficiencies because thumbs are at logically different levels (Requirement c)
- Total overview over the distribution of the data being analyzed (Requirement b)
- Detailed information for each range and sub-range (bucket) and the data that is currently filtered (Requirements b, e)
- Allow the users to determine how much of the data is currently being analyzed (Requirement e)
- The range selection can be small (Requirement e)
- No possibility to miss data outside the filtered range (Requirement e)

The RSF slider improves the analysis capabilities by reducing the time and effort for searching, manipulating, and navigating through the data. However, there are some limitations: it needs a bit more space than the multi-thumb sliders and it is not applicable if there are empty ranges, i.e., if there are values between the selected ranges that are filtered out. Finally, to provide a higher level for the provided information, the total number of objects in each range, a legend is provided next to the RSF Slider as shown in Figure 14 (Slider videos: Al-Zokari, Y, 2020).

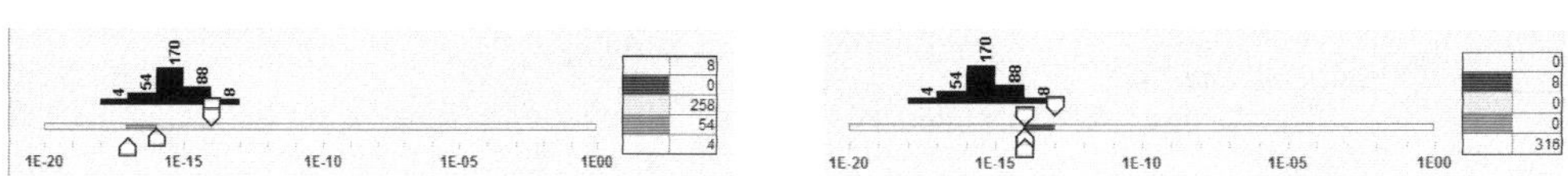

Figure 14. The dynamic legend showing the number of objects in each range

5. ASSESSMENT OF EASE OF USE

For assessing the ease of use of our RSF slider, we chose three adaptable ranges coded as *H*: high (in red), *M*: Medium (in yellow), and *L*: Low (in green). All movements for changing the ranges are shown in Figure 15. The *cascading effect* helps in reducing the movements of the thumbs. Thus, the "ease of use" of the RSF slider is higher than for the multi-thumb slider. The restriction for the multi-thumb slider is resolved by enabling the left thumb to move and push the right thumbs if they are at the same position. Similarly, the right thumb can move and push the left thumbs. The colored arrows show which thumb should be moved. The numbers show the minimum amount of movements that is needed to change the range. The different levels in light blue show the movements that cannot be performed at the same time. This means, if two movements are in the same level, i.e., the same light blue line that represents the body of the slider, any of the two movements can be performed, i.e., there is no restriction in the order of the movements. Thus, it is more flexible to choose the movement. However, if the movements are not in the same level, then if the movement order is different, the number of movements will increase. Therefore, the number of movements will not be the minimum any more for the same case.

From the root to the leaves of Figure 16, the total number of minimum thumb movements for both the multi-thumb and the RSF slider are counted. The reduction or increase *c* of the number of movements *n* is computed as shown in Equation 2.

$$\begin{aligned} n_{MTS} &:= \text{No. of movements of the multi} - \text{thumb slider} \\ n_{ES} &:= \text{No. of movements of the Dynamic Slider} \\ \text{Equation 2} \quad c &:= \frac{n_{MTS} - n_{ES}}{n_{MTS}} \\ ratio &:= \frac{n_{ES}}{n_{MTS}} \end{aligned}$$

LMH → H → M → L: 5/8 (a reduction of c = 37.5% movements)
LMH → H → LM: 4/5 (a reduction of c = 20% movements)
LMH → MH → L: 3/4 (a reduction of c = 25% movements)

Further, for other domains where the analysis steps do not have the same restriction sequence as in the one of the MCS analysis II context, and different sequences can be performed, such as the steps: L → LMH → L → H → M → MH, the reduction difference is even higher (Figure 15):

LM → LMH: 1/7 (a reduction of 85.71% movements)
LMH → L: 1/2 (a reduction of 50% movements)
L → H: 2/7 (a reduction of 71.42% movements)
H → M: (same as previous example): 3/4 (a reduction of 25% movements)
M → H: 2/7 (a reduction of 71.42% movements)

Additionally, an empirical evaluation was performed by (Al-Zokari, 2016) pp.386. It was not included in this paper due to the limited number of pages available.

6. APPLICATIONS

6.1 Software Visualization

In the area of software engineering, the static structure of a system is often represented using graphs. Considering object-oriented systems, nodes represent classes or interfaces. Edges can represent different relations of these classes and interfaces (Abuthawabeh & Zeckzer, 2013), Figure 17, proposed and (Abuthawabeh, et al., 2013) evaluated a matrix-based visualization of these graphs. The graphs and their visualizations are frequently used to solve software engineering tasks: reengineering of legacy systems, software understanding, debugging, and construction of systems, to name a few. For solving these tasks, not only the existence of links is important but also their strength. The latter becomes even more important when non-functional relationships are investigated. The strength of the relation is mapped to color saturation. To ease the recognition of differences, only three saturation levels are used. Hence, different strengths are combined into one strength level. The RSF slider is used in their work to determine, which intervals are mapped to which saturation.

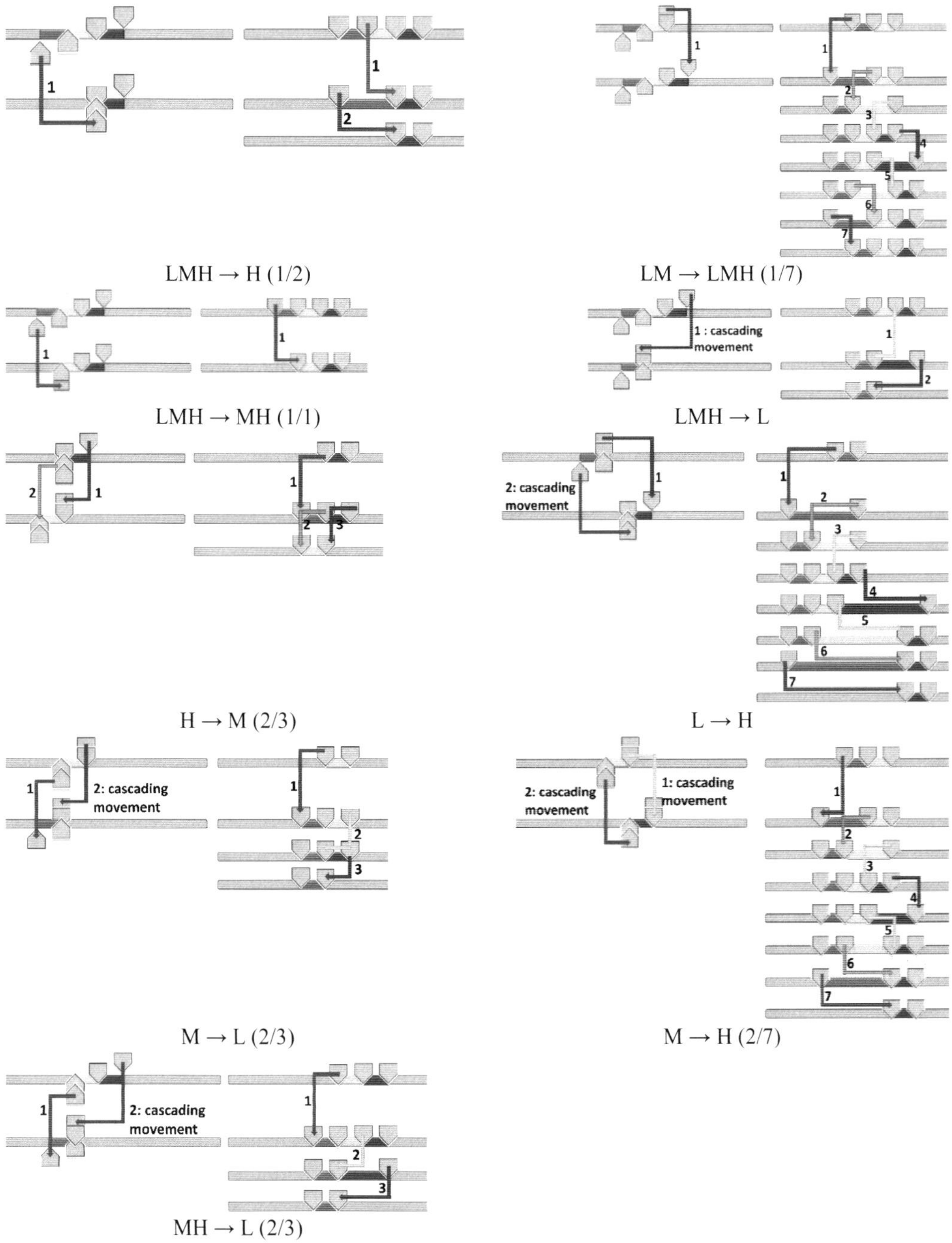

Figure 15. Minimum number of thumb movements for both multi-thumb and Dynamic Sliders. Format (# of movements for Dynamic Slider / # of movements for multi-thumb slider)

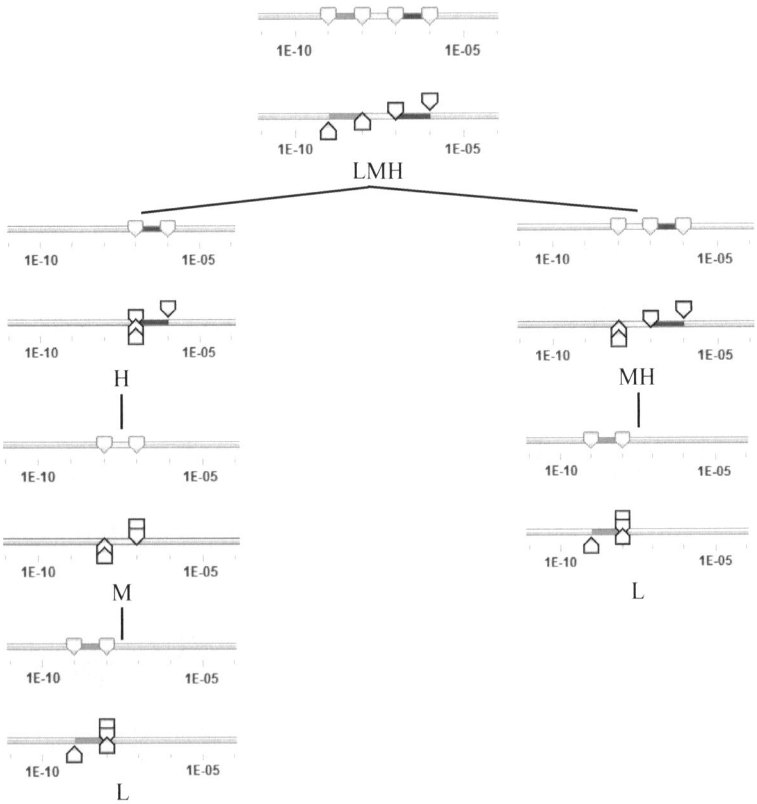

Figure 16. The representations of the multi-thumb (top) slider and the Dynamic Slider (bottom) for different analysis steps starting by user defined FP levels. H: high (red), M: medium (yellow), and L: low (green)

Regarding 'evolution' (evolutionary coupling, violet, fourth slider from top), a strength between 1 and 11 is considered to be low (least saturated), a strength between 12 and 22 is considered to be medium (medium saturation), and a strength between 22 and 32 is considered to be high (highest saturation). Here, the links having a strength below 11 are filtered out. In the matrix view (left) a large amount of evolution links is filtered out allowing to analyze links with medium and high strength. This helps the software engineer while analyzing a system. If parts (classes) of the system are commonly changed together, there is a semantic relationship. Therefore, this semantic relationship is important for software understanding and re-engineering and must be considered while implementing new functionality or fixing bugs.

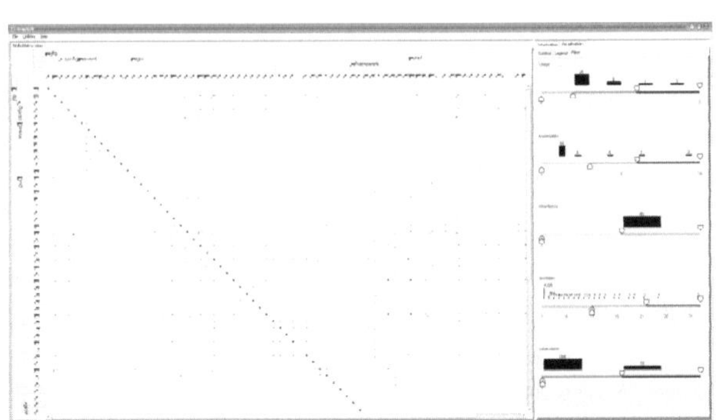

Figure 17. View of a software system. All edge types are visualized with saturations according to their strength. Low evolution scores are filtered out

6.2 Safety

In the area of (embedded) systems engineering, safety analysis is performed to avoid harm of the system to people or the environment (Bozzano & Villafiorita, 2010). Often, the individual values are of minor importance in this field. As they are based on estimations, their order of magnitude is the dominant factor. Moreover, for practical reasons, criticality is often determined by categorizing the numerical values assigned. One possible scheme called ALARP (Melchers, 2001) divides the complete range of failure probabilities into three categories: negligible, tolerable, and unacceptable. Commonly, the colors red (unacceptable), yellow (tolerable), and green (negligible) are used for these categories.

In (Al-Zokari, et al., 2011a), (Al-Zokari, et al., 2011c), and (Al-Zokari, et al., 2012d), a system was presented that displayed so called minimal cutsets (MCSs) based on the ALARP categorization of criticality. It supports to identify the system hazards with the highest failure probability based on MCS analysis. In (Al-Zokari, 2016) pp.497ff the following tasks where identified:

- T-1 Identify all MCSs according to the standard ranges.
- T-2 Identify MCSs with high FP (unacceptable). How many MCSs should be analyzed?
- T-3 Identify MCSs with small size (also called order).
- T-4 The combination of both T-2 and T-3, which is essential for finding unusual MCSs, e.g., those having a low FP and a small size.
- T-5 How safe is the hazard? Provide an overview over the safety of the hazard.
- T-6 How many MCSs should be analyzed when unacceptable MCSs are already solved (tolerable and/or negligible)? Identify them.
- T-7 Are there any MCS outside the system's standard analysis or the current investigation range (above unacceptable and/or below negligible)?
- T-8 How many MCSs with FPs lower than a certain value or in a certain range should be analyzed? Identify them.
- T-9 Identify the MCSs in the ranges below the high FP range (tolerable, negligible, and/or below negligible). How many should be analyzed?

Almost all safety analysts have little knowledge of visualization or interaction techniques. Therefore, if interaction (e.g., filtering) is required to achieve their tasks, the interaction technique should be easy to use, and helping to increase their productivity. The RSF slider presented in Section 4 is useful for this application. It supports to perform the safety tasks T-1 – T-2 and T-5 – T-9. Using the RSF slider, the user can easily use it for choosing those parts of the data range that she wants to filter (remove), as well as choosing which part of the data range is considered to be negligible (low), tolerable (medium), or unacceptable (high). As these ranges are supposed to be adjacent, no empty ranges can occur.

Figure 18 shows the two important parts of the system: the RSF slider and the visualization of the MCSs. The safety analyst sees that there are 6 MCSs in the high failure probability range that have to be analyzed first, 276 in the medium range, and 6 in the low range, so Tasks T-1 and T-2 are answered. This allows to answer the questions raised by Task T-7 (No) and Task T-6 (276). The answer to the question raised in Task T-5 is that the hazard is unsafe because there are 6 MCSs above the unacceptable range, but if these MCSs are solved the system will be tolerable. To accomplish Task T-8, e.g., for a failure probability lower than 10^{-18} would be 6 MCSs. For Task T-9, the answer depends on the amount of time and resources available. For example, if there is a short notice request for MCS analysis, e.g., 1 hour, the number of MCSs that have to be (can be) analyzed are 2 (the single points of failure). If there is a more time available (e.g., 3 hours), the number is 6 (the other 4 from the red range), etc.

7. SUMMARY AND FUTURE WORK

In this paper, we presented the Range-Selection-and-Filtering (RSF) slider that supports the users getting multiple levels of overview of the data being analyzed and filtering according to multiple ranges. We combined the features of multiple slider types, i.e., histogram, interactive legends, standard, and multi-thumb sliders. Moreover, we increased its usefulness and its ease of use by repositioning the thumbs to overcome the overlapping of thumbs and adapting the orientation of the thumbs' icons and introducing the cascading effect concept and applying it. This led to reducing the amount of interaction.

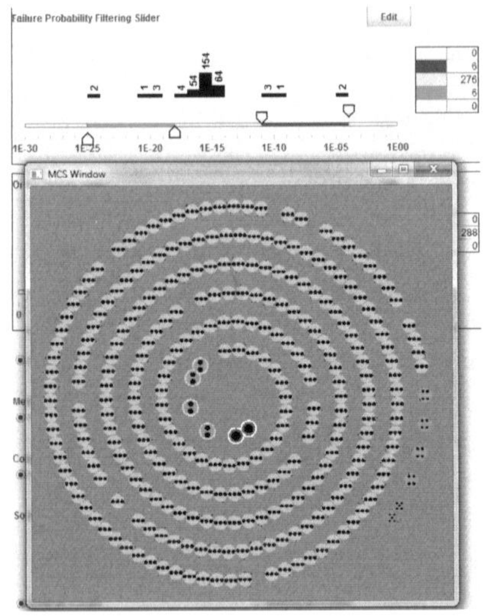

Figure 18. Slider with histogram and the data being analyzed (data size 288 MCSs)

We validated our design against the different slider types. From our case studies, we found that using the RSF slider is direct and no unnecessary thumb moves are required. Additionally, our design supports different color visions deficiencies by positioning the thumbs at a logical level that indicates the thumb's value. However, there are some limitations in this design, as it takes a little more space than the multi-thumb slider, and no empty ranges are possible. Nevertheless, this case is not a requirement in Minimal Cut Sets analyses, safety domain nor in Software Engineering. However, for future work having the possibility to enable empty ranges should be considered for other domains that require such a property. In the future, we need to perform an evaluation of our design to compare it to other sliders regarding usefulness and usability. Nevertheless, an empirical evaluation of our RSF slider was performed (Al-Zokari, 2016) pp.386, but we did mot include it in this paper due to the limited number of pages. The source code and executable files are available at (Al-Zokari, Y, 2020. Slider Source Code in GitLab).

ACKNOWLEDGEMENT

This work was supported partially by DAAD, IRTG 1131, and BMBF. We would like to thank our safety expert collaborator Mr Mohammed. Hibti from EDF "Electricite De France" for his time and collaboration.

REFERENCES

Abuthawabeh, A., Beck, F., Zeckzer, D. & Diehl, S., 2013. Finding Structures in Multi-Type Code Couplings with Node-Link and Matrix Visualizations. In1st IEEE Working Conference on Software Visualization 2013 (VISSOFT 2013).

Abuthawabeh, A. & Zeckzer, D., 2013. IMMV: An Interactive Multi-Matrix Visualization for Program Comprehension. In1st IEEE Working Conference on Software Visualization 2013 (VISSOFT 2013).

Ahlberg, C., 1996. Spotfire: an information exploration environment. SIGMOD Rec. 25.

Ahlberg, C. & Shneiderman, B., 1994. The alphaslider: a compact and rapid selector. In Proc. of the SIGCHI conference on Human factors in computing systems: celebrating interdependence (New York, NY, USA, 1994), CHI '94, ACM, p. 365–371.

Ahlberg, C. & Shneiderman, B., 1994. Visual information seeking using the FilmFinder. In Conference companion on Human factors in computing systems (New York, NY, USA, 1994), CHI '94, ACM, p. 433–434.

Ahlberg, C., Williamson, C. & Shneiderman, B., 1992. Dynamic queries for information exploration: an implementation and evaluation. In Proc. of the SIGCHI conference on Human factors in computing systems (1992), ACM, p. 619–626.

Al-Zokari, Y. I. et al., 2011. CakES: Cake Metaphor for Analyzing Safety Issues of Embedded Systems. In: H. Hagen, ed. Scientific Visualization: Interactions, Features, Metaphors. Dagstuhl(Germany): Schloss Dagstuhl–Leibniz-Zentrum fuer Informatik, p. 1–16.

Al-Zokari, Y. I., Schneider, D., Zeckzer, D. & Hagen, H., 2011. An Enhanced Slider for Safety Analysis. In IEEE VisWeek Poster (2011).

Al-Zokari, Y. I. et al., 2011. Enhanced CakES representing Safety Analysis results of Embedded Systems. In Federated Conference on Computer Science and Information Systems (FedCSIS) (2011).

Al-Zokari, Y. I. et al., 2012. Towards Advanced Visualization and Interaction Techniques for Fault Tree Analyses Comparing existing methods and tools. In PSAM11 & ESREL 2012 Conference (2012).

Al-Zokari, Y, 2020. Slider Videos. https://www.youtube.com/playlist?list=PLZ9SRRNo8TbbJa8cjqxdKuYjwshlH_IGI .

Al-Zokari, Y, 2020. Slider Source Code in GitLab. https://gitlab.com/yaso2com/rsf-slider .

Borland, D. & Taylor, R. M., 2007. Rainbow Color Map (Still) Considered Harmful. Computer Graphics and Applications, IEEE, 3, Volume 27, pp. 14-17.

Bozzano, M. & Villafiorita, A., 2010. Design and Safety Assessment of Critical Systems. CRC Press (Taylor and Francis), an Auerbach Book.

Card, S. K. & Mackinlay, J., 1997. The structure of the information visualization design space. In Proc. of the 1997 IEEE Symp. on Information Visualization (InfoVis '97) (Washington, DC, USA, 1997), IEEE Computer Society, p. 92–99.

Dang, G., North, C. & Shneiderman, B., 2001. Dynamic Queries and Brushing on Choropleth Maps. In Proceedings of the Fifth International Conference on Information Visualisation (2001), IEEE Computer Society, p. 757–764.

Eick, S. G., 1994. Data visualization sliders. In Proc. Of the 7th annual ACM symposium on User interface software and technology (1994), ACM, p. 119–120.

Fekete, J.-D., 2004. The InfoVis Toolkit. In Proc. of the IEEE Symposium on Information Visualization (Washington, DC, USA, 2004), IEEE Computer Society, p. 167–174.

Harris, C., Allen, R., Plaisant, C. & Shneiderman, B., 1999. Temporal Visualization for Legal Case Histories. Tech. Rep. Vol. 36, ASIS'99 Proceedings of the 62nd Annual Meeting of the American Society for Information Sciences, 1999.

HCI Lab, U.S. Bureau of Census, n.d. User Interfaces for the U.S. Bureau of Census Online Survey Interfaces and Data Visualization. http://www.cs.umd.edu/hcil/census/;Online; last access 29-Mar-2011.

Heer, J., Card, S. K. & Landay, J. A., 2005. Prefuse: a toolkit for interactive information visualization. In Proc. of the SIGCHI conference on Human factors in computing systems (2005), ACM, p. 421–430.

Henry, N. R., Lee, B. & Plaisant, C., 2010. Understanding Interactive Legends: a Comparative Evaluation with Standard Widgets. Computer Graphics Forum, Volume 29, p. 1193–1202.

Li, Q. et al., 2003. Dynamic query sliders vs. brushing histograms. In CHI'03 extended abstracts on Human factors in computing systems (New York, NY, USA, 2003), CHI EA '03, ACM, p. 834–835.

Melchers, R. E., 2001. On the ALARP approach to risk management. Reliability Engineering & System Safety, Volume 71, 2, pp. 201-208.

Plaisant, C. & Laboratory, H. C. I., 1993. Facilitating Data Exploration: Dynamic Queries On A Health Statistics Map. In Proc. of the Government Statistics Section, Annual Meeting of the American Statistical Assoc. (1993), p. 18–23.

Savive Pty Ltd, Safety-Critical. http://www.savive.com/inform/safetycritical.html; Online; accessed 31-Mar-2011.

Shneiderman, B., Feldman, D., Rose, A. & Grau, X. F., 2000. Visualizing digital library search results with categorical and hierarchical axes. In Proc. of the fifth ACM conference on Digital libraries (2000), ACM, p. 57–66.

Swing, Swing Examples. http://en.pudn.com/downloads3/sourcecode/java/detail6037_en.html; Online; last access 06-June-2011.

Tanin, E., Beigel, R. & Shneiderman, B., 1996. Incremental data structures and algorithms for dynamic query interfaces. SIGMOD Rec. 25, p. 21–24.

Tweedie, L., Spence, R., Dawkes, H. & Su, H., 1996. Externalising abstract mathematical models. In Proc. of the SIGCHI conference on Human factors in computing systems: common ground (1996), ACM, p. 406–ff.

Ware, C., 2004. Information Visualization: Perception for Design. Morgan Kaufmann Publishers Inc..

Williamson, C., Shneiderman, B. & Ablex, E., 1992. The dynamic HomeFinder: Evaluating dynamic queries in a real-estate information exploration system. In Proceedings of the 15th annual international ACM SIGIR conference on Research and development in information retrieval (1992), no. Vol. 36 in SIGIR '92, pp. 21-24,338-346.

EVALUATION OF COLOR SPACES FOR UNSUPERVISED AND DEEP LEARNING SKIN LESION SEGMENTATION

Michael Osadebey, Marius Pedersen and Dag Waaler
Norwegian University of Science and Technology, Norway

ABSTRACT

The reliability of skin cancer diagnosis is dependent on accurate lesion segmentation. The choice of a color space in most contributions on skin lesion segmentation for melanoma detection are based on qualitative rather than quantitative approaches. User experience and theoretical properties of the color space are the two major factors influencing the choice of the color space. For this reason, it may be difficult to optimize segmentation accuracy. This paper evaluates the discrimination power of 5 color spaces and 16 color channels for two unsupervised approaches and a deep learning approach on the segmentation of skin lesion in dermatoscopy images. 600 dermatoscopy images with different levels of cluttering and occluding objects from two different databases were utilized. This study suggests that no single color space or color channel is most suitable in real-world scenarios. Therefore, this study can be regarded as a general framework to select a single or combination of color channels that will enhance the segmentation accuracy of images with different level of scene complexities and illumination variations.

KEYWORDS

Skin Lesion, Color Space, Color Channel, Segmentation, Expectation Maximization, Deep Learning

1. INTRODUCTION

The primary goal of skin lesion segmentation is to identify and separate a lesion region from healthy skin, cluttering and occluding objects. Thus, the ease and difficulty of a segmentation task, as well as the accuracy and efficiency of a segmentation algorithm, is largely dependent on the clarity of the information expressed by color spaces (Lu et al., 2018). Color spaces are digital description of colors for human visual perception of images (Ibraheem et al., 2012).

A researcher's first choice in a segmentation task is a color space which can highlight only the pixels that describe the target object and suppress every pixel belonging to the background. Unfortunately, this ideal expectation may not always be realized. There is yet no color space that has universal application because they are designed with different attributes for different purposes. The discrimination power of a color space is the main reason researchers show preference for specific color space in some segmentation tasks (Yang et al., 2010). The Red, Green and Blue (RGB) color space is a popular color space for acquisition of dermatoscopy images because it is device dependent and particularly suitable for image display (Sanchez et al., 2013). Some contributions, such as (Silveira et al. 2009), prefer the blue channel of the RGB color space because it offers the good discrimination between the lesions and background pixels. However, other contributions such as (Ma et al., 2016) knocked down the use of any RGB channel for image segmentation, because the RGB color space is based solely on chrominance and does not contain separate information on intensity. Under varying illumination condition, it will be difficult to measure the difference between two colors in the RGB color space.

Some contributions advance the HSV (Hue, Saturation and Value) and CIELAB color spaces as having the potential to overcome the shortcomings of the RGB color space. The Hue channel refers to the purity of the color, the Saturation channel quantifies the amount of gray in the color, and Value is the intensity of the color. CIELAB is defined by the International Commission on Illumination (CIE) based on Luminance and the color channels A and B. The luminance channel measures the brightness of the colored image.

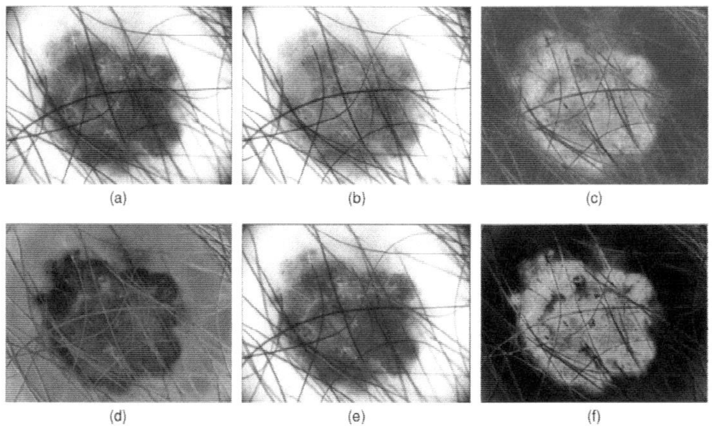

Figure 1. A dermatoscopy image in the (a) RGB color space, (b) Value channel of the HSV color space, (c) A channel of the CIELAB color space, (d) C_B component of the YCbCr color space, (e) X component of the CIEXYZ color spaces and (f) the Saturation channel of the HSV color space

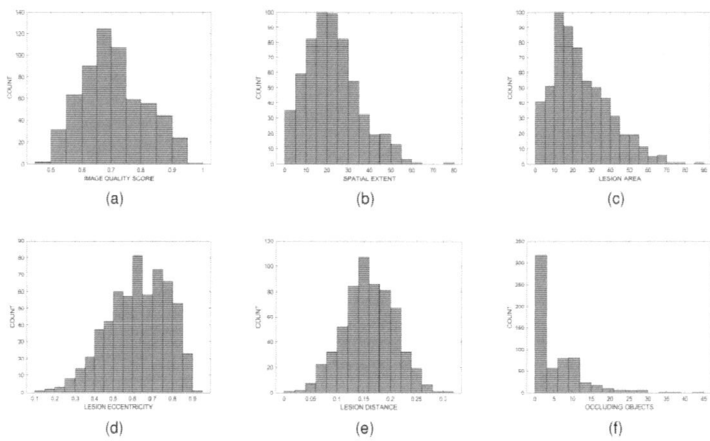

Figure 2. Histogram distribution of six attributes of the 600 test images. (a) Perceptual quality. (b) Spatial extent. (d) Eccentricity. (e) Lesion distance. (f) Level of cluttering and occlusion

The A and B color channels measures the green-red and the blue-yellow components of the colored image. CIELAB is regarded as a device-independent color space because its colors are independent of how they are created or displayed. The design of HSV and CIELAB color spaces conforms with human perception of colors (Abbas et al., 2013). The HSV and CIELAB color spaces, unlike RGB color space, can separate intensity from color information. This attribute is necessary for pre-processing tasks, such as histogram equalization, required to make correction for illumination variation and shadow attenuation required for skin segmentation. A variant and earlier version of the CIELAB is the CIEXYZ which was introduced in 1931. Figure 1 shows a dermatoscopy image in the RGB color space and color channels extracted from four different color spaces.

Although it is widely acknowledged that accurate and efficient skin lesion segmentation is dependent on the color space (Gomez et al., 2007), there is little or no contribution on how to quantitatively determine the optimal color channel or combination of color channels that will optimize skin lesion segmentation. Current contributions on selection of an optimal color channel can be broadly applied to human skin and face detection (Dang et al., 2017), (Shaik et al., 2015), but these are not application-specific to skin lesion segmentation. This has encouraged heuristics and user experience as the approaches adopted by current techniques on the choice of color space. For this reason, we propose a general framework to quantitatively evaluate the discrimination power of different color spaces and color channels and select the color channel or the combination of color channels that is optimal for a segmentation task that involves a large volume of dermatoscopy images.

2. MATERIALS AND METHODS

2.1 Sources of Data

The experiments for this study utilize 600 dermatoscopy images from two databases. 464 images are from the International Skin Imaging Collaboration (ISIC) archive (https://isic-archive.co). The other 136 images are from the Dermatology Service of Hospital Pedro Hispano, Matosinhos, Portugal (http://www.fc.up.pt/addi). Images from the two databases are single-lesion images acquired with different dimensions. The range of row M dimensions are $(665 \leq M \leq 6668)$. Corresponding column N dimensions are $(572 \leq M \leq 4439)$. Each image has ground truth provided by certified dermatologists.

2.2 Dataset Attributes

In order to evaluate the performance of the proposed method on images with different types of artefact, we classify the database images into five categories. The categories and number of images in each category are normal (233), dark corners (84), hair occlusion (93), clutter (57) and multiple artifacts (133). For each image in each category, six visual attributes that influence segmentation accuracy were identified and quantitatively evaluated. Visual attributes are labels that can be given to an image to describe its appearance (Kumar et al., 2011). The first visual attribute is perceptual quality $\boldsymbol{D_1}$ which was evaluated using BRISQUE, a no-reference image quality assessment method proposed by (Mittal et al., 2012). Metrics for quantifying the remaining visual attributes are defined in Eq. 1 - 5. Second visual attribute (Eq. 1) is spatial extent $\boldsymbol{D_2}$, where $\boldsymbol{A_s}$ is the total number of pixels that describe the region occupied by the lesion, cluttering and occluding objects in a test image. The metric was normalized using the area of the image. Third attribute (see Eq. 2) is area of lesion $\boldsymbol{D_3}$, where $\boldsymbol{A_g}$ is the number of pixels within lesion region in the ground truth image. Fourth attribute (see Eq. 3) is the lesion position $\boldsymbol{D_4}$, where $(\boldsymbol{x_s}, \boldsymbol{y_s})$ and $(\boldsymbol{X_g}, \boldsymbol{Y_g})$ are the pixel location of the lesion and image centroid, respectively. Fifth attribute (see Eq. 4) is the eccentricity of lesion $\boldsymbol{D_5}$, where $(\boldsymbol{a}, \boldsymbol{b})$ are the semi-major and semi-minor axes lengths of the lesion. Sixth attribute (see Eq. 5) is the level of cluttering and occlusion $\boldsymbol{D_6}$, where $\boldsymbol{A_{gs}}$ is the total number of pixels that do not belong to either lesion or healthy skin in the test image.

$$D_2 = 100\left(\frac{A_s}{MN}\right) \quad (1) \qquad D_3 = 100\left(\frac{A_g}{MN}\right) \quad (2)$$

$$D_4 = \left(\frac{\sqrt{(x_s - X_g)^2 + (y_s - Y_g)^2}}{\sqrt{X_g^2 + Y_g^2}}\right) \quad (3)$$

$$D_5 = \left(\sqrt{1 - \frac{b^2}{a^2}}\right) \quad (4) \qquad D_6 = 100\left(\frac{A_{gs}}{MN}\right) \quad (5)$$

2.3 Analysis of Dataset Attributes

The test images can be considered as having an acceptable level of perceptual quality. Figure 2a shows that the range of the perceptual quality scores is $(0.47 \leq D_1 \leq 0.96)$. The average perceptual quality score is 0.70. Figure 2b shows that the mean spatial extent is $D_2 = 23$ and more than half of the test images had spatial extent that lies in the range$(10 \leq D_2 \leq 30)$. The average area and eccentricity of the lesions, as shown in Figure 2c and Figure 2d, are $D_3 = 24$ and $D_4 = 0.62$, respectively. The area and eccentricity attributes are indication that a quarter of each image area belongs to the lesion region and the lesion region can be approximated by an ellipse or circle. Figure 2e shows that the mean and range of the lesions distance from the image center are 0.16 and $(0.01 \leq D_5 \leq 0.30)$, respectively. This implies that most of the lesions are located closer to the center of the image, which is common in these kinds of images. The histogram plot in Figure 2f show that about half of the test images can be considered as normal images. The remaining half of the test images contain different levels of cluttering and occluding objects.

2.4 Segmentation Algorithms

We utilize two unsupervised and one deep learning segmentation algorithms in this study. One of the unsupervised techniques is the expectation maximization (EM) algorithm (Dempster et al., 1977). The EM algorithm is an iterative procedure to model the parameters that most likely describe the observed data. Each iteration of EM algorithm alternates between the expectation and the maximization steps. The expectation step estimates the missing data given the observed data and current estimate of the model parameters. In the maximization step, the estimate of the missing data in the E-step are used in lieu of the actual missing data followed by maximization of the likelihood function. The likelihood increases at every iteration. The algorithm terminates when there is no significant change between the values at the E-step and the M-step. The other unsupervised segmentation technique is a three-stage segmentation algorithm proposed by (Guarracino et al., 2019), referred to as SD+. The first step is the conversion of an RGB image into the HSV color space where the saturation channel is extracted. Then detection of confounding factors such as shading and specular reflections. Further, there is an inpainting operation and preliminary segmentation which attenuates the confounding factors and create an initial binary mask. The final step executes morphological post-processing operation, refines the binary mask and extracts the lesion region. Deep learning was implemented using the U-net architecture, a fully convolutional neural network proposed by (Ronneberger et al., 2015) for biomedical image segmentation. A major advantage of the U-net architecture is that it can be trained with relatively few images with reasonable segmentation accuracy. The U-shaped architecture of the network is derived from its contracting and expanding path for implementing encoding and decoding of the input image, respectively. In this study, the encoding was implemented using two 3 x 3 convolutional layers consisting of 64 filters, ReLU and max pooling layer which downsamples the input by a factor of 2. The decoder was implemented using one 4 x 4 transposed convolutional layer consisting of 64 filters which upsamples the input by a factor of 2.

2.5 Implementation

Step 1. Categorization of Images
The data was categorized into 500 training and 100 test data I_t, where $t = \{1,2,\dots,100\}$. Images in both categories were selected to reflect overall attributes of the test data, that is, different types and levels of image artifacts such as dark corners, skin hairs, ruler markings, color chart, gel bubbles and ink marks.

Step 2. Color Space and Color Channel Extraction
Each image, originally acquired in the RGB color space, was transformed to $K_S = \{1,2,\dots,5\}$ color spaces and $K_C = \{1,2,\dots,16\}$ color channels. The color spaces are RGB, HSV, CIELAB, YCBCR and XYZ. Three color channels was extracted from each color space, except for the RGB with four color channels, namely red, green, blue and grayscale. The identification codes for each color space and color channel are displayed in Table 1.

Step 3. Lesion Segmentation
The U-net deep learning model was trained on the 500 training images using the stochastic gradient descent with momentum optimizer. The training parameter was set at learning rate 1×10^{-3}, 150 training epochs and batch size of 32. Skin lesions were extracted from each color space and color channel of the 100 test images using the EM and U-net. The SD+ algorithm, because it was designed or optimized for only a single channel, was utilized for only the saturation channel of the HSV color space. For both SD+ and U-net, the number of classes was set to 2 so the algorithms segment the image into the target object and background. Skin lesions, the target object, exhibit unique colors across different color channels. For example, the skin lesion is the darker pixels in the green channel of RGB and it is the brighter pixels in the saturation channel of HSV. This consistency property was exploited to accurately identify and extract the target object from each channel image. Furthermore, the output from EM and U-net were further processed to improve segmentation accuracy.

Step 4. Intra-Image Color Space and Channel Score
For each test image, the similarity between the target object extracted from each color space and each color channel image and the ground truth I_g is separately measured using the dice similarity index $d_{t,k}$:

$$d_{t,k}(I_{t,k}, I_g) = \frac{2|I_{t,k} \cap I_g|}{|I_{t,k}| + |I_g|} \quad (6)$$

Step 5. Intra-Image Optimal Color Space and Color Channel

For each test image, we collate the dice scores from all the K color space and color channel and form them into a set $\{d_{t,1,2,\ldots,K}\}$ as shown in Eq. (7). We apply the dice score as the parameter to determine the index of the color channel with highest discrimination power for each test image.

$$\bar{k} = \max_{k}\{d_{t,1,2,\cdots,K}\} \quad (7)$$

Table 1. Identification code assigned to each color space and color channel

CODE	COLOR SPACE	COLOR CHANNEL
1	RGB	Red
2	HSV	Green
3	CIELAB	Blue
4	YCBCR	Grayscale
5	CIEXYZ	Hue
6		Saturation
7		Value
8		Luminance
9		A
10		B
11		Y
12		CB
13		CR
14		X
15		Y
16		Z

Step 6. Inter-Image Mean Color Space and Channel Score

The dice score for each color space and color channel, computed in step 4, from all the test images are collated. The collated data are used to compute the mean dice score $\bar{d}_k$ for each color space and color channel

$$\bar{d}_k = \frac{1}{T}\sum_{t=1}^{T} d_{t,k} \quad (8)$$

The mean dice scores for each color space and each color channel:

$$\bar{d} = \{\bar{d}_k : \bar{d}_1, \bar{d}_2, \cdots, \bar{d}_K\} \quad (9)$$

The mean of all the mean dice scores $\hat{d}$ of each of all the color space and each color channels:

$$\hat{d} = \frac{1}{K}\sum_{k=1}^{K} \bar{d}_k \quad (10)$$

Step 7. Histogram of Optimal Color Space and Color Channel

The index $\bar{k}$ of the optimal color space and color channel, computed in step 5, are formed into an histogram. Let $f_{\bar{k}}$ be the number of times a color channel k becomes the optimal color channel across all the test images. The probability $p_{\bar{k}}$ that a color channel is the optimal color channel across the test images:

$$p_{\bar{k}} = \frac{f_{\bar{k}}}{T} \quad (11)$$

where $\sum p_{\bar{k}} = 1$

Step 8. Select the Optimal Color Space and Color Channel

We determine the optimal color channel image from the weighted sum of $p_{\bar{k}}$, the probability that a color channel is the optimal color channel across the test images and $d_{\bar{k}}$, the mean dice score with minimum distance relative to the mean dice score $\hat{d}$ of all the color channels:

$$\hat{I}_k = \max_{k}\{\lambda_1 p_{\bar{k}} + \lambda_2(1 - \|\bar{d}_k - \hat{d}\|)\} \quad (12)$$

where λ_1 and λ_2 are arbitrary weights.

3. RESULTS

Histogram distribution of dice score recorded by the SD+ algorithm is displayed in Figure 3. Figure 4a and Figure 4c shows, using the EM algorithm, the histogram distribution of the number of times a color space and color channel was determined to be the optimal color channel of a test image, respectively. For the same EM algorithm, the mean dice score for each color space (blue color) and the mean dice score (purple color) of all the dice scores are shown in Figure 4b and Figure 4d, respectively. For deep learning based on the U-net architecture, the histogram distribution of the number of times a color space and color channel was determined to be the optimal color channel of a test image are displayed in Figure 5a and Figure 5c, respectively. The mean dice score of each color space (blue color) and the mean dice score (purple color) of all the dice scores for the deep learning algorithm are shown in Figure 5b and Figure 5d, respectively.

4. DISCUSSION

The SD+ algorithm operates only in the saturation channel of the HSV color space. It recorded a dice score lower than 0.80 for 10 percent of the images. For about 30 percent of the images there was a dice score less than 0.9. This result suggests that SD+ is optimized using the saturation channel of the HSV color space. Although it can be considered as robust, there is room for improvement. The algorithm does not demonstrate the same level of robustness across all the test images. If other operating characteristics have not been optimized, there may be need to consider the combination of other channels to enhance segmentation accuracy.

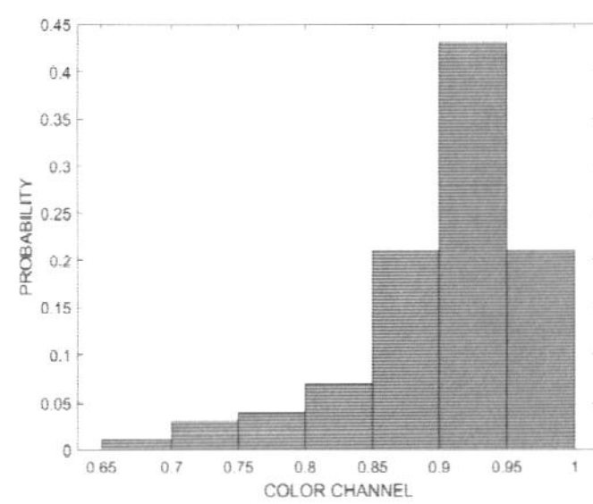

Figure 3. Histogram distribution of dice scores for unsupervised segmentation using SD+ (Guarracino et al., 2019)

Although the EM algorithm is powerful, its performance can be limited by presence of clutters and occluding objects. Unlike the SD+ algorithm, the EM algorithm does not incorporate a hair removal pre-processing step. For this reason, it will perform poorly in the presence of cluttering and occluding objects (Majtner et al., 2016), (Le et al., 2016). This is evident in Figure 4b where the average dice score for all the color spaces is $P < 0.6$. There is remarkable improvement in the performance of the EM algorithm when its operation changes from color space to other color channels (Figure 4c and Figure 4d). Color channels that demonstrated remarkable performance are the red, green, blue, grayscale, saturation, luminance and Y channels. As shown in Figure 4c, the blue channel can be considered the optimal color channel because it has a greater number of times $P \approx 0.3$ where it was determined as the optimal color channel of a test image. The fact that no color channel has $P = 0.5$ in Figure 4c suggests that no single color space can be considered as most suitable where images with different level of scene complexities and illumination variations are acquired for specific task.

Figure 5b shows that the deep learning algorithm demonstrated robust performance for all the color spaces except for the CIELAB and YCbCr color spaces. The HSV color spaces is the optimal color space because, as shown in Figure 5a, it has more number of times $P \approx 0.4$ than other color spaces, where it was deemed the optimal color channel. The deep learning algorithm did not repeat the same level of performance when it was operated using color channels, except for the Z color channel. Comparison of the results in Figure 5b and Figure 5d suggest that the deep learning algorithm performs better with more information provided by color spaces.

5. CONCLUSION

Skin lesion segmentation is an important image analysis task because the accuracy of subsequent steps leading to the diagnosis of skin cancer is dependent on accurate segmentation. This study proposes a general frameworkto evaluate how color spaces and color channels impact the segmentation of skin lesions.

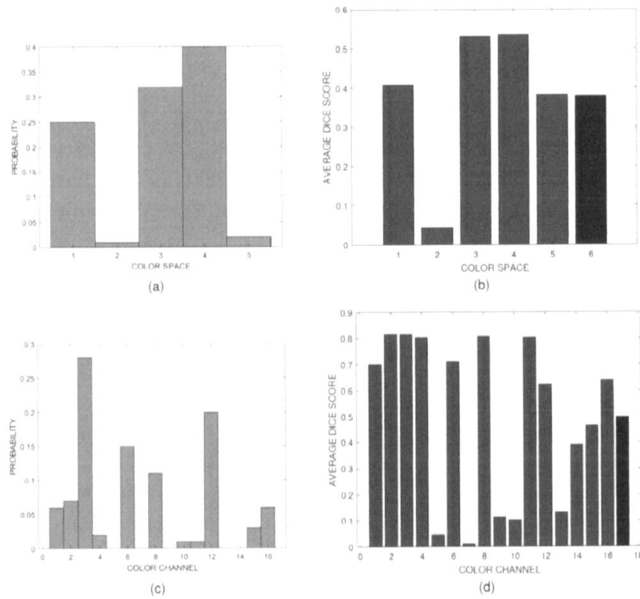

Figure 4. Expectation maximization algorithm (Dempster et al., 1977). (a) Histogram distribution of the number of times a color space was determined to be the optimal color channel of a test image. (b) The mean dice score of each color space (blue color) and the mean dice score (purple color) of all the maximum dice scores. (c) Histogram distribution of the number of times a color channel was determined to be the optimal color channel of a test image (d) The mean dice score of each color channel (blue color) and the mean dice score (purple color) of all the maximum dice scores in (c)

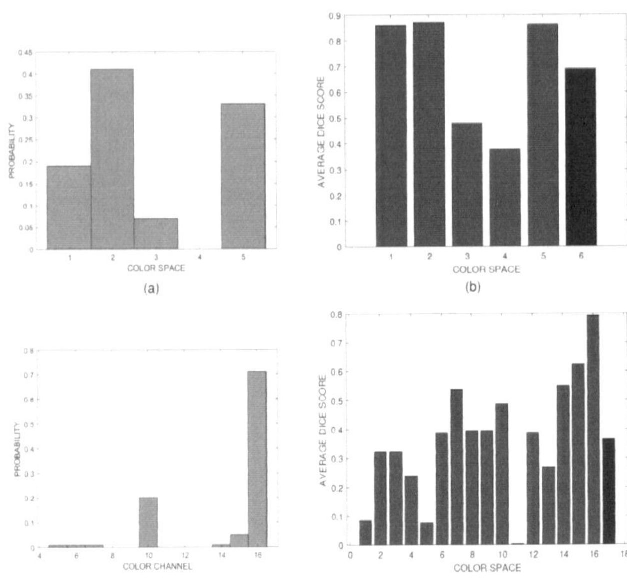

Figure 5. Deep learning segmentation using U-net architecture (Ronneberger et al., 2015): (a) Histogram distribution of the number of times a color space was determined to be the optimal color channel of a test image. (b) The mean dice score of each color space (blue color) and the mean dice score (purple color) of all the maximum dice scores. (c) Histogram distribution of the number of times a color channel was determined to be the optimal color channel of a test image (d) The mean dice score of each color channel (blue color) and the mean dice score (purple color) of all the maximum dice scores in (c)

The study suggests that (1) No single color space can be considered as most suitable where images with different level of scene complexities and illumination variations are acquired for specific task. (2) The discrimination power of a color channel is dependent on the level of clutters and occluding objects that are present alongside the target object. The outcome of this study can be applied in the design of a framework for automatic selection of optimal color channels to enhance the performance of segmentation algorithms on tasks that involves images with different level of scene complexities and illumination variations. Limitations of the study is that the training and testing data may not be reasonably large to optimize the segmentation and that the training parameters of the U-net may not result in optimal segmentation. Further, the simplified post-processing applied to the output of the EM and U-net may not optimize segmentation. Nevertheless, since same parameter was applied throughout the experiments, these limitations does not diminish the general concepts and potential applications of this study.

ACKNOWLEDGEMENT

M. Osadebey is supported by the European Research Consortium on Informatics and Mathematics (ERCIM).

REFERENCES

Abbas, Q., Celebi, M. E., Serrano, C., GarcíA, I. F., & Ma, G. (2013). Pattern classification of dermoscopy images: A perceptually uniform model. *Pattern Recognition*, *46*(1), 86-97.

Dang, T. D. (2017, July). The effect of Color space on discriminating power of Color local texture feature for Color face recognition. In *2017 International Conference on System Science and Engineering (ICSSE)* (pp. 249-252). IEEE.

Dempster, A. P., Laird, N. M., & Rubin, D. B. (1977). Maximum likelihood from incomplete data via the EM algorithm. *Journal of the Royal Statistical Society: Series B (Methodological)*, *39*(1), 1-22.

Gomez, D. D., Butakoff, C., Ersboll, B. K., & Stoecker, W. (2007). Independent histogram pursuit for segmentation of skin lesions. *IEEE transactions on biomedical engineering*, *55*(1), 157-161.

Guarracino, M. R., & Maddalena, L. (2018). SDI+: A novel algorithm for segmenting dermoscopic images. *IEEE journal of biomedical and health informatics*, *23*(2), 481-488.

Ibraheem, N. A., Hasan, M. M., Khan, R. Z., & Mishra, P. K. (2012). Understanding color models: a review. *ARPN Journal of science and technology*, *2*(3), 265-275.

Kumar, N., Berg, A., Belhumeur, P. N., & Nayar, S. (2011). Describable visual attributes for face verification and image search. *IEEE Transactions on Pattern Analysis and Machine Intelligence*, *33*(10), 1962-1977.

Le, T. H. N., & Savvides, M. (2016). A novel shape constrained feature-based active contour model for lips/mouth segmentation in the wild. *Pattern Recognition*, *54*, 23-3

Lu, Z., Jiang, X., & Kot, A. (2018). Color space construction by optimizing luminance and chrominance components for face recognition. *Pattern Recognition*, *83*, 456-468.

Ma, Z., & Tavares, J. M. R. (2015). A novel approach to segment skin lesions in dermoscopic images based on a deformable model. *IEEE journal of biomedical and health informatics*, *20*(2), 615-623.

Majtner, T., Lidayova, K., Yildirim-Yayilgan, S., & Hardeberg, J. Y. (2016). Improving skin lesion segmentation in dermoscopic images by thin artefacts removal methods. In *2016 6th European Workshop on Visual Information Processing (EUVIP)* (pp. 1-6). IEEE.

Mittal, A., Moorthy, A. K., & Bovik, A. C. (2012). No-reference image quality assessment in the spatial domain. *IEEE Transactions on image processing*, *21*(12), 4695-4708.

Ronneberger, O., Fischer, P., & Brox, T. (2015). U-net: Convolutional networks for biomedical image segmentation. In *International Conference on Medical image computing and computer-assisted intervention* (pp. 234-241). Springer,.

Sanchez-Cuevas, M. C., Aguilar-Ponce, R. M., & Tecpanecatl-Xihuitl, J. L. (2013). A comparison of color models for color face segmentation. *Procedia Technology*, *7*, 134-141.

Shaik, K. B., Ganesan, P., Kalist, V., Sathish, B. S., & Jenitha, J. M. M. (2015). Comparative study of skin color detection and segmentation in HSV and YCbCr color space. *Procedia Computer Science*, *57*(12), 41-48.

Silveira, M., Nascimento, J. C., Marques, J. S., Marçal, A. R., Mendonça, T., Yamauchi, S., ... & Rozeira, J. (2009). Comparison of segmentation methods for melanoma diagnosis in dermoscopy images. *IEEE Journal of Selected Topics in Signal Processing*, *3*(1), 35-45.

Yang, J., Liu, C., & Zhang, L. (2010). Color space normalization: Enhancing the discriminating power of color spaces for face recognition. *Pattern Recognition*, *43*(4), 1454-1466.

REPEATED PATTERN EXTRACTION WITH KNOWLEDGE-BASED ATTENTION AND SEMANTIC EMBEDDINGS

Hong Qu[1], Yanghong Zhou[1,2], K.P. Chau[1] and P.Y. Mok[1,2]
[1]*Institute of Textiles and Clothing, The Hong Kong Polytechnic University, Hunghom, Hong Kong*
[2]*The Hong Kong Polytechnic University Shenzhen Research Institute, Shenzhen, China*

ABSTRACT

Repeat pattern is a common structure in textile or graphic design, while scalable and reusable designs are required for production. We propose a new approach, based on Convolutional Neural Network (CNN), for automatic extraction of repeat patterns in this paper. CNNs are good at detecting repeat patterns through extracting multilevel features in the convolutional layers. In our method, we select filters quickly in single images by leveraging the combination of the learned filters from AlexNet's convolutional layers and boundary detection results from VGG16. Moreover, we use template matching to optimize final outputs in order to improve precision. We composed a dataset with 30 images, covering stripe, check and dot distributed patterns, each image with manual ground truth labels. The experimental results show that our method outperforms the state-of-the-art method in both precision and running speeds.

KEYWORDS

Repeated Pattern Extraction, Boundary Detection, CNN, Template Matching, Textile Design, AlexNet

1. INTRODUCTION

Repeat patterns are seen almost everywhere in our daily life, they are used in tiling, wallpaper, textiles, packaging, backdrops for text or illustrations in graphic media, jewelry, and architecture. Designers create them uses a wide range of media in both two and three dimensions. Most modern repeat pattern design is done on computers for guarantee speed and accuracy; electronic repeat patterns have a number of advantages since the artworks are scalable, reusable and can be easily adjusted to fit the screen sizes for production. It usually takes long time to turn a good idea into repeat patterns. Designing completely new patterns may be unrealistic, because the industry currently does not have an efficient mechanism of managing and searching numerous patterns to avoid developing similar products or to reuse existing patterns. Therefore, there is an emerging need for methods to extract repeat patterns automatically and efficiently. In addition, repeat pattern extraction is also required step in many tasks of computer vision and graphics, such as segmenting objects or reconstructing 3D appearance (Lettry *et al.*, 2017).

Automatic repetition detection in a single image is difficult as repeating elements are irregular in either or both their visual contents and spatial positions. Traditional repetition detection methods always first extract feature using handcrafted feature detectors (Liu *et al.*, 2004) and then retrieve similar features by clustering (Guo *et al.*, 2019) or patch correlation (Kuo *et al.*, 2017; Guo *et al.*, 2019) to identify the repeat contents. As the visual variance among semantically similar classes or context and the natural variations (e.g. lighting conditions), the handcrafted feature detector requires to be complex and robust. With the development of deep learning, Lettry *et al.* (2017) and Rodriguez-Pardo *et al.* (2019) proposed to use CNN to extract multilevel features and leverage activations of filters in the convolutional layers to detect repeated patterns on a grid, which shows the good capability of CNN on repetition detection task. However, the method of Lettry *et al.*(2017) have the drawback that the computational cost is expensive to use a large amount of the filters in CNN and use the activation peaks on all filters to seek the regular pattern. To address the problem, Rodriguez-Pardo *et al.* (2019) proposed to abandon the filters that are not significantly activated to reduce the computational cost, but this method made it difficult to evaluate the significance of the filters. They set an activation threshold and only kept the filters with the mean activation greater than the threshold. However, the most activated filters are not necessarily the filters with regular patterns.

In this paper, based on the pre-trained CNNs, we propose to use boundary as *a prior* knowledge to select the possible filters with regular repetitive patterns. As boundary prior is beneficial to screen out most of the background contents and focus on the foreground region, we apply the boundary prior on the filters and select the most activated ones with repetitive patterns to reduce computation. Next, a Hough-like voting method is used to compute the consistent displacement vector. Moreover, a template matching method is also used to optimize the computation of the consistent displacement vector to improve precision. Our main contributions are as follows:

- Combining boundary detection and pre-trained CNN for efficient repetitive pattern detection in a single image.
- Using template matching to optimize repeat pattern detection.
- Experimental results show that our proposed method outperforms Lettry's method (2017) in both precision and running speeds.

2. RELATED WORK

The detection for repeat patterns from a single image has been a challenge task in the field of computer vision. This task requires not only the understanding of image, but also find the regular mechanism automatically from various type of images without principled definition of that mechanism. To solve this problem, researchers have proposed methods in different ways. Liu *et al.* (2004) present a computational model for repeat pattern detection based on the theory of crystallographic groups, thus the repeat pattern classification and detection are based on their geometric structure rule. According to near regular textures, Cai *et al.* (2011) present a general method for detecting repetitive patterns by shape alignment and deformed template matching for the local patches of the texture.

Repeat pattern is of great value in image retrieval, Torii *et al.* (2013) achieve place recognition based on combination of robust detection of repeated image structures and a simple modification of weights in the bag-of-visual-word model. Doubek *et al.* (2010) make a difference is that they are not focusing on detecting repeat pattern on the same image, but on retrieving images of the same object. They implemented the retrieve of buildings on a small dataset.

In fashion industry, both Kuo (2017) and Tao *et al.* (2017) extract repeat pattern for dot distributed pattern. Kuo *et al.* (2017) extract pattern elements' shape information by edge detection firstly. Afterwards, the centroid positions of these identical pattern elements were used to extract the repeat pattern template using a vertical vector method. Tao *et al.* (2017) decompose repeat pattern into the repeat angle and the unit span. Then pattern sliced into pieces on various angles with various spans, and the similarity degree of slices on each angle with each span was calculated to constitute the similarity space in which the peak values suggested the potential repeat angles and unit spans. The similar method is also used in weave pattern repeat detection since fabric surface presents a periodic yarn structure. Zheng (2014) gets corner information by the Harris corner detector firstly, then searches for the adjacent corners in the horizontal or vertical direction to identify the repeat size of the weave pattern. But this method can only process fabric images with clear texture, horizontal weft and vertical wrap. In addition, Guo *et al.* (2019) propose seven local features to define weave pattern repeat, then use the recognition results to judge the fabric structure.

The above methods all define the repeat pattern by extracting different features manually. The experimental results will increase with the number of parameters considered. CNNs are utilized to detecting repeat pattern as it could extract as much information as possible from the available datasets automatically. Lettry *et al.* (2017) are the first to utilize CNN for repeat pattern detection in general situation. In order to make better use of the information captured by each layer in CNN, they sift activation peaks of each filter maps using a standard non-maxima suppression. Then extract the spatial regularities of activation peaks to detect the most consist repeat pattern. Rodriguez-Pardo *et al.* (2019) have made improvements base on Lettry's (2017) work, they add pre-processing part to align image. Besides, they ignore parts of filters which are not activated obviously to speed up. The algorithm suit to detect fronto-planar geometrically regular textures in fast speed. However, the whole paper pays more attention to the image synthesis of the extracted repeat patterns, so our experimental results are not compared with them.

3. METHOD

3.1 System Overview

CNN network has shown great capability of image representation learning in many tasks, such as image classification (Liu and Deng, 2015), object detection (Cai *et al.*, 2016), semantic segmentation (Kampffmeyer *et al.*, 2016). The CNN network consists of a set of layers, convolutional filter layer, pooling layer, fully connected layers, and so forth. The filters of different layers learn different semantic features at varied scale levels. Information learned from the higher layer contains more semantic information than the lower layers. Hence, when an image input to a CNN, the filters generate feature maps that respond to various semantic and scale levels, as well as region localization. When a repeated pattern exists in the input image, the feature maps that activate the repeated pattern are generated by CNN filters and the activated region follow a regular pattern. In this paper, we propose to fuse a boundary detection CNN and a classification CNN to select the most activated filters with repetitive patterns. Next, we compute the most activated peaks and consistent displacement vector using the selected filters. Finally, an optimization algorithm is proposed to refine the consistent displacement vector. The overall framework is shown in Figure 1.

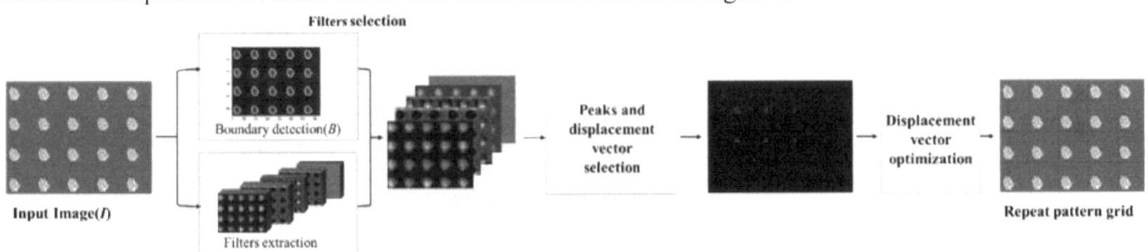

Figure 1. Illustration of our method: step (1) is filter selection; step (2) peaks and displacement vector selection; and step (3) optimization

3.2 Filter Selection

Given a classification CNN, we denote the filters in CNN as $F = \{F_n | n = 1,2 \dots, N\}$, $F_n = \{f_{l_n} | l \in L_n\}$ where L_n is the set of convolutional filters of the n-th layer. When the input image I containing a repeat pattern passes over the CNN network, CNN filters will generate characteristic regularly activation feature maps. The goal of the first step is to select filters with the possible regular activated feature maps. As boundary detection can greatly reduce the amount of image data and remove weakly related information while retaining important structural attributes, we use boundary detection as *a prior* to assist the filter selection. For boundary detection, we used the RCF network (Liu *et al.*, 2019), which could produce side outputs of each inside layers based on VGG16 (Simonyan and Zisserman, 2014). Due to that deeper networks hardly avoid problems such as vanishing/exploding gradients and training data shortage, RCF network uses the CNN features of all the conv layers directly to perform the pixel-wise prediction. Therefore RCF network could obtain accurate representations for objects or object parts in different scales.

Let us denote the detected boundary as B, we multiply B with the activated feature maps $f_{l_n}(I)$ of each layer and sum over all pixels：

$$f_{l_n}^B = \sum_{i,j} B \cdot f_{l_n}(I) \tag{1}$$

where (i, j) represent the pixel, the most possible filter with regular activated feature maps l_n^* of the n-th layer can be obtained by

$$l_n^* = \underset{l \in L^n}{\operatorname{argmax}}(f_{l_n}^B) \tag{2}$$

3.3 Peaks and Displacement Vector Selection

With the selected filters $\{f_{l_n^*}|n = 1,2,\dots,N\}$, we extract the activation peaks of feature maps and compute the probable size of repeated elements. For each filter $f_{l_n^*}$, we use the standard non-maxima suppression (NMS) algorithm to extract local maximum peaks $P_{f_n}^*$ in a region of certain distance. When the minimum neighborhood distance is $dist_{\min}$, $P_{f_n}^*$ can be computed in the region of $2dist_{\min} + 1$ using NMS algorithm. Due to different resolutions and strides of the filters, $dist_{\min}$ is determined by the number of local maximum peaks to guarantee enough extracted peaks on each filter map. We set the minimum number of extracted peaks as n, if the number of generated peaks is less than $n_{\min}$, then $\mathrm{dist}_{\min} = \mathrm{dist}_{\min} - 1$, loop recursively until the number of generated peaks is more than $n_{\min}$. The algorithm is shown below:

Input: the filter $f_{l_n^*}$, *the required number of extracted peaks* $n_{\min}$, *the initial minimum neighborhood distance* $dist_{\min}$.

$P_{f_n}^*$=NMS ($f_{l_n^*}$, $dist_{\min}$)
If length ($P_{f_n}^*$) >$n_{\min}$:
  Return $P_{f_n}^*$
Else:
  $dist_{\min} = dist_{\min} - 1$
  $P_{f_n}^*$=NMS ($f_{l_n^*}$, $dist_{\min}$)
  Return $P_{f_n}^*$
Output: $P_{f_n}^*$

For each selected filter $f_{l_n^*}$, we extract the activation peaks $P_{f_n}^*$ using the above algorithm. We then use the activation peaks of all the filters to compute the probable size of repeated pattern by the Hough-like voting algorithm for consistent displacement vector selection (Lettry *et al.*, 2017). We form a set $D_{f_{l_n}^*}$ of displacement vectors by computing a vector for each pair of peak activations in each filter $D_{f_{l_n}^*} = \{d^{i,j}: |p^i - p^j|, \forall p^i, p^j \in P_{f_n}^*, i \neq j\}$, where $|.|$ denotes the element-wise absolute value on vectors. Then displacement vectors for selected filters in each layer cast votes into the displacement vector Hough voting space $V: R^2 \to R$. We borrowed Lettry's (2017) method using:

$$V = \sum_{x \in R^2} \sum_{\substack{l \in L \\ f_{l_n^*} \in F_n}} \frac{1}{|D_{f_{l_n}^*}|} \sum_{d^{i,j} \in D_{f_{l_n}^*}} V_{f_{l_n}^*, i, j} \tag{3}$$

where V is smoothed using a 2-dimensional Gaussian filter with a kernel size of $\begin{pmatrix} \sigma_{L_n}^2 & 0 \\ 0 & \sigma_{L_n}^2 \end{pmatrix}$. The optimal displacement vector d^* , which has the dimensions of the minimal repeat pattern, is extracted as the maxima of voting space on the x and y axes :

$$d^* = (\operatorname*{argmax}_x V_{x,0}, \operatorname*{argmax}_y V_{o,y}) \tag{4}$$

3.4 Displacement Vector Optimization

When we know the size of the repeat pattern, repeat patterns of the same size can be found at any starting point in the same picture (see Figure 2). It is also important to note that when the starting point is known and the size of the repeat pattern d^* is accurate, the image region of all the grids are the same. However, d^* may be inaccurate, which will result in different grid regions. To refine the size of repeat pattern d^*, we use template matching.

Figure 2. Examples of repeat pattern: The left two images show repeat patterns of different scales. The first image and third image show repeat patterns of the same size can be found at any starting position

Let us denote the starting point of repeated pattern as $o = (0,0)$. Given an image I, we crop the region from the starting point o with size of d^* and use the region as a template of repeat pattern T. Given the template T, the matching process overplays the template on the searched image (W * H), moves it to all possible areas and computes a numerical index that indicates how well the template matches the image in that area. We denote the area on the searched image covered by the template as S_{hk}, where $1 \leq h \leq W - d_x^*$, $1 \leq k \leq H - d_y^*$. The correlation is used to measure the matching degree of template T and S_{hk}:

$$cor = \frac{\sum_{h,k}(T(h,k) \cdot S(h,k))}{\sqrt{\sum_{h,k} T(h,k)^2 \cdot \sum_{h,k} S(h,k)^2}} \quad (5)$$

The value of cor is between -1 and +1, with larger values representing a stronger relationship between the two images.

It should be noted that the template is not searched on the whole image, to reduce the computation time, but on the cropped images from the starting point o with size (d_x^*, H) and size (W, d_y^*) which are denoted as I_{ox} and I_{oy} respectively. To refine the d_x^*, the template moves on the cropped image I_{ox} and search the matched areas S_{h1} along y axis. From the starting point $(\frac{1}{3}d_x^*, 0)$, as long as the matched area S_{h^*1} can be found on the cropped image I_{ox}, d_x^{**} is refined to $h^* + \frac{1}{3}d_x^*$. Similarly, from the starting point $(0, \frac{1}{3}d_y^*)$, moving the template on the cropped image I_{oy} along the y axis, matched area S_{1k^*} can be founded on I_{oy} then d_y^{**} is refined to $k^* + \frac{1}{3}d_y^*$. Considering the pixel error that makes the templates of adjacent pixels similar, we also compute the distance Δd between then template S_{h1} and next template S_{h2}. If $\Delta d < 2$, then $d_x^{**} = d_x^{**} + \Delta d$. The same operation until the distance $\Delta d \geq 2$. This operation is not only useful to avoid the pixel error, but also is able to identify the stripe direction on the strip image. Because on the strip image, when searching template along the reverse direction of stripes, we can find the matched template on every pixel and obtain that $d_x^{**} = w - d_x^*$ or $d_y^{**} = h - d_y^*$.

Taking the refinement of d_x^* as an example, we crop input image I from the starting point (0,0) with size of (d_x^*, H) and search the matched areas with template T, which is shown in Figure 3(a). As existing the matched area S_{h^*1}so that $h^* > \frac{1}{2}d_x^*$, the $d_x^* = h^*$. The grid drawing using the refined d_x^* and the computed start point o^* is shown in Figure 3(b), which can be seen that the detected pattern is much more accurate than before.

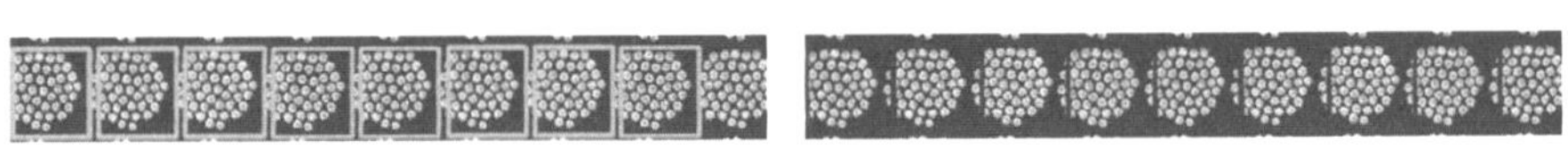

(a) (b)

Figure 3. The optimization effect of x-axis. (a): Effect before optimization. (b): Effect after optimization

4. EXPERIMENTAL RESULTS AND DISCUSSION

We present qualitative and quantitative results of our algorithm and compare to the state-of-the-art method in this section. To allow for quantitative evaluation, we first introduce our dataset with manual ground truth labels.

4.1 Dataset Preparation

Graphic patterns are basically classified into dot distributed patterns, check patterns and continuous stripe patterns (Kuo *et al.*, 2017; Tao *et al.*, 2017). There is no public dataset focusing on repeat patterns, and some downloadable images have either no ground truths (repeat pattern size) or the images have less than two complete repeat patterns, which would affect the analysis. Therefore, we created a new dataset based on some vector artwork downloaded from WGSN. We downloaded 30 self-created images covering three categories: stripe pattern, check pattern and dot distributed pattern. The image resolution is around 500*500pixel. There are 10 images for each type of pattern and more than two repeat patterns lying on a regular grid on the image. We manually defined the minimum repeat pattern size on the images as the ground truth.

4.2 Evaluation Metrics

As mentioned in Section 3.4, the position of a repeat pattern in an image is subjective. When an image composed of repeat patterns, a pattern of the repeat size selected from any position as the starting point could obtain the same density effect, as shown in Figure 2. Thus, we assume that each image starts draw grid from the same starting point (0,0) for unified evaluation. Intersection-over-Union (IoU) is used to evaluate the performance of repeated pattern detection. Since the repeat pattern has the same start point, d_x^* and d_y^* are the size of estimated repeat pattern in x-axis and y-axis respectively, g_x and g_y are the ground truth of minimal repeat pattern size, IoU accuracy is computed as follows:

$$IoU = \frac{\min(d_x^*, g_x) * \min(d_y^*, g_y)}{d_x^* * d_y^* + g_x * g_y - \min(d_x^*, g_x) * \min(d_y^*, g_y)} \tag{6}$$

In particular, when the image is stripe, the predicted and ground truth values of the reverse direction are equal to the corresponding image side length.

4.3 Qualitative Evaluation

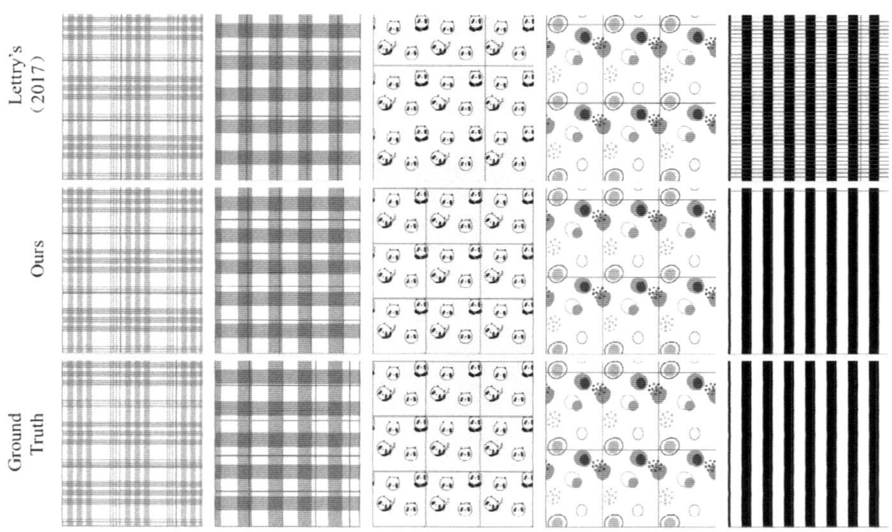

Figure 4. Qualitative comparison to related work: Lettry *et al.* (2017) and our ground truth. Our method performs better on all examples

We present the repeat patterns detected by our algorithm and Lettry's (2017) method on different types of images of the dataset in Figure 4. As shown, our method performs more precise on the detected size of repeat pattern than Lettry's (2017) method. Our method also performs well on complex patterns. As shown in the fourth column, Lettry's (2017) method corrupted due to the spatial non-regularity in the pattern combined with many pattern elements, but our method found the repeat pattern successfully. Moreover, for the repeat pattern detection on stripe image (column 5 in Figure 4), with the help of the optimization using template matching, our method can identify the strip direction. These results show that our method is very accurate on repeat pattern detection, performs well even on complex pattern images, and our method is able to identify the strip direction if stripe images.

4.4 Quantitative Evaluation

The dataset with ground truth was used for quantitative evaluation: we computed average IoU, the accuracy at different thresholds of IoU, and the time costs over the dataset. We compare our method with Lettry's (2017). Table 1 summarizes the quantitative evaluation of two methods over different types of our dataset: stripe, check, and dot distributed patterns.

Table 1. Experimental results

	Lettry's (2017)				Our Method			
	IoU Average	IoU ≥0.8 prec./(%)	IoU ≥0.9 prec./(%)	Time Costs/(s)	IoU Average	IoU ≥0.8 prec./(%)	IoU ≥0.9 prec./(%)	Time Costs/(s)
Check	0.88	80.00	60.00	4060	0.88	90.00	70.00	33
Dot	0.81	80.00	60.00	3989	0.94	90.00	90.00	19
Stripe	0.79	70.00	70.00	3380	0.95	90.00	90.00	127
All images	0.83	76.67	63.33	3810	0.93	90.00	83.33	60

Computer config: CPU Intel i7-6700x, GPU NVIDIA GTX 1080 Ti, Memory 32GB.

It can be seen from the table that average IoU for Lettry's (2017) and our method is 0.83 and 0.93, respectively, which demonstrates the benefits of our method. When the threshold of IoU is set to 0.8, the precision of our method is 90.00%; when the threshold is 0.9, our precision (83.33%) is 20% higher than theirs. Among the three types of pattern, the IoU precision of our method is higher than Lettry's (2017) especially in dot and stripe patterns under different thresholds. For stripe patterns, the precision for our method and theirs are 90% and 70%, respectively, when the threshold is 0.8; the precision is the same when the threshold was 0.9.

Comparing the time costs, our proposed method demonstrates the combination of boundary detection and learned filters could reduce computation and save time. For the same stripe pattern image, our method takes about 2 minutes, while Lettry's (2017) method takes about 1 hour. On the pattern of check and dot, the efficiency of our method is more obvious, which we need 100 times less computation time cost. Since the stripe pattern circulates in one direction, after filter selection it extracts more peaks in the reverse direction when extracting peaks of filter maps and costing more time at Hough-like voting process. It could explain the longer time costs of stripe patterns by our method, as shown in Table 1.

5. CONCLUSION

We presented a new method for repeat pattern detection through the boundary combination and template matching optimization. To reduce the computation, we use the detected boundary to select the most possible filters with repeat patterns on multi-level layers. Then, an optimized peak extraction algorithm and Hough voting algorithm are used to extract peaks on the selected filters and compute the repeat pattern size. After the repeat pattern size is obtained, a template matching method is used to optimize it over the whole image. Experimental results show that our proposed method obtain better results both in terms of precision and speed. In particular, our method increases computational speed by more than 60 times on average. In the future, we will explore using texture classification model and feature matching method to further improve the overall accuracy, efficiency and robustness of the method.

ACKNOWLEDGMENT

The work described in this paper was supported by grants from the Research Grants Council of the Hong Kong Special Administrative Region, China (Project No. 152161/17E and 152112/19E). The work was also partially supported by The Innovation and Technology Fund (Grant No. ITP/013/18TI) and Shenzhen Science and Technology Innovation Commission (Project No. JCYJ20170303160155330).

REFERENCES

Cai, Y. & Baciu, G., 2011. Detection of repetitive patterns in near regular texture images. *2011 IEEE 10th IVMSP Workshop: Perception and Visual Signal Analysis*, NY, USA, pp. 60-65.

Doubek, P. et al, 2010. Image matching and retrieval by repetitive patterns. *2010 20th International Conference on Pattern Recognition*, Istanbul, Turkey, pp. 3195-3198.

Guo, Y. et al, 2019. Automatic recognition method for the repeat size of a weave pattern on a woven fabric image. *Textile Research Journal,* Vol. 89, No.14, pp.2754-2775.

Kuo, C.-F. J. et al, 2017. Image database of printed fabric with repeating dot patterns part (I)–image archiving. *Textile Research Journal,* Vol. 87, No.17, pp. 2089-2105.

Lettry, L. et al, 2017. Repeated pattern detection using CNN activations. *2017 IEEE Winter Conference on Applications of Computer Vision (WACV)*, CA, USA, pp. 47-55.

Liu, Y. et al, 2004. A computational model for periodic pattern perception based on frieze and wallpaper groups. *IEEE Transactionas On Pattern Analysis And Matchine Intelligence,* Vol. 26, pp. 354-371.

Rodriguez-Pardo, C. et al, 2019. Automatic extraction and synthesis of regular repeatable patterns, *Computers & Graphic,* Vol.83, 33-41.

Simonyan, K. & Zisserman, A., 2015. Very deep convolutional networks for large-scale image recognition. *ICLR.*

Tao, C., Zhou, J. & YIN, M. J. T. R. J. 2017. Automatic identification of textile pattern consecutiveness based on similarity space. *Textile Research Journal,* Vol. 87, No.2, pp. 224-231.

Torii, A. et al, 2013. Visual place recognition with repetitive structures. *Proceedings of the IEEE conference on computer vision and pattern recognition,* Oregon, USA, pp.883-890.

Zheng, D., 2014. A new method for the detection and classification of weave pattern repeat. *Textile Research Journal,* Vol. 84, No.15, 1586-1599.

Liu, Y. et al, 2019. Richer convolutional features for edge detection. *IEEE Transactions On Pattern Analysis and Machine Intelligence,* Vol. 41, NO. 8. pp. 1939-1946.

Cai, Z. et al, 2016. A unified multi-scale deep convolutional neural network for fast object detection. *European conference on computer vision, Springer,* 354-370.

Kampffmeyer, M. et al, 2016. Semantic segmentation of small objects and modeling of uncertainty in urban remote sensing images using deep convolutional neural networks. *Proceedings of the IEEE conference on computer vision and pattern recognition workshops*, pp. 1-9.

Liu, S. & Deng, W., 2015.Very deep convolutional neural network based image classification using small training sample size. *2015 3rd IAPR Asian conference on pattern recognition (ACPR), IEEE*, pp. 730-734.

AUTOMATIC LABELING FOR FASHION DATASETS

Anissa Selmani, Houda Bakir and Hedi Zaher
Datavora. 45, Avenue of Japon, Monplaisir, Tunis, Tunisia

ABSTRACT

Creating image Datasets is a time-consuming step and a challenge for specific classification problems. The dilemma of this task concerns the manual annotation of training images. Thus, this paper presents an automatic labeling method without humans in the loop for Fashion datasets. First, we introduce a new descriptor for texture segmentation called LNLBP (Large Neighbourhood Local Binary Pattern) which is able to capture both micro-structure and macro-structure texture information. Then, using a Fuzzy logic system, the proposed method detects the change in texture, intensity and human pose in order to localize correctly the position of the fashion item. Finally, we generate the 'xml' files containing the coordinates and the labels in order to use them afterward for the training with the Google Tensorflow object detection API: for real-time clothes classification. The resulting dataset will be made publicly available for research.

KEYWORDS

Labelling, Segmentation, Human Pose, Fuzzy Logic

1. INTRODUCTION

In the last decade, extensive research and development efforts have been conducted in the field of computer vision, object detection and pattern recognition. Because of their potential values throughout science and industry, these advances are the product of Open image and video datasets available for researcher in order to localize and detect objects. However, creating labeled datasets is the most time-consuming and expensive part of applying machine learning due to requirements that labelers should be experts in the application domain. The great performance of supervised learning approaches that use such datasets resides in the data presented for the training and evaluation of the model. Numerous datasets are open to public and researchers. For instance, in Kaggle, in corporate or academic datasets or by using the new Google toolkit datasets research tool. However, the difficulty is to find the right dataset for a new specific problem. Collecting and preparing adequate datasets that offer excellent training and validation sets are time-consuming and meticulous tasks. These datasets present images containing one or many objects in single image. Datasets like CIFAR-10/100, ImageNet (Deng, et al. 2009), PASCAL VOC (Everingham, et al. 2015), COCO (Lin, et al. 2014) and ADE20K (Zhou, at al. 2017), were available for benchmarking classification algorithms and for the improvement of the original Convolutional Neural Network model by the Region-based Convolutional Network (R-CNN), Fast R-CNN, Faster R-CNN (Girshick, 2015), (. Girshick, et al. 2013), (Ren, et al. 2015) and Inception architecture (Szegedy, at al. 2015). Many papers in the literature had introduced some methodology and semi-automated tools (Russell, at al. 2008) to facilitate the labeling process. For example, in (Samiei, at al. 2018), a low-cost approach to plant phenotyping was proposed. This method uses gazes to detect weeds in dense culture (Qu et al. 2009) proposed to use the co-active learning for an automatic online images labeling. The idea of fashion classification is to build a system able to find and identify accurately clothing items in images. This field has many applications in social media, e-commerce and criminal law. Image classification refers to the labeling of images into one of a number of predefined categories. Thus, such a classification predicts classes of clothes using the knowledge learned over the training step. This process requires learning from a well-built labeled database. The performance of those algorithms strongly depends on the accuracy of the labeling. However, the labeled databases are usually limited since the annotation process is tedious, expensive, and depends upon human experts (Torralba et al, 2010). A study showed that the important factor in building a good model that performs adequately is to collect and label at least 90,000 reviews. For example, supposing that a single comment may take 30 seconds to be labeled, a worker needs to spend 750 hours or almost three months to complete the task. Considering that the median hourly rate for a data scientist in the US is $36.27, labeling this database will cost $27,202.5. In this paper we tackle some of these challenges and we take into consideration the complex dependencies between clothing and human pose. The contribution of our work is twofold: We present a novel texture descriptor to improve segmentation results. Then, we propose an automatic approach to detect, localise and label clothes in images using Openpose and the Fuzzy Logic. To the best of our knowledge, no single automatic method of clothing labeling has been reported in literature. However, there are the (Xiao, at al. 2017) Zalando fashion-mnist Dataset which is a collection of 70,000 examples (90 % training and 10 % for test) 28x28 gray-scale images of 10 categories and DeepFashion Datasets that contain over 800,000 images for 10 categories, 1,000 descriptive attributes, bounding box and clothing landmarks. In our work we used 75094 images of DeepFashion Dataset and we added 8175 images in order to validate our automatic labelling method in difficult and challenging human postures and with backgrounds. The rest of the work is organized as follows: Section 2 presents the methodology of the proposed technique. Section 3 describes our clothing labeling approach. Section 4 presents the experimental evaluation of the approach and finally the conclusion is drawn in section 5.

2. LABELING PIPELINE

Labeling is a fundamental stage of data pre-processing for machine learning. However, obtaining a hand-labeled dataset faces many challenges such as the insufficiency or unavailability of related external knowledge bases (Ratner, at al. 2016). Moreover, each wrong or inaccurate label affects negatively the quality and the performance of the used model. The proposed approach aims to reduce the cost of dataset creation. It consists of detecting automatically the bounding boxes that would contain distinct clothing articles worn by a person in given images. This process is based on the model of TensorFlow OpenPose that efficiently detects the 2D pose of persons in an image, combined with a reliable images segmentation algorithm.

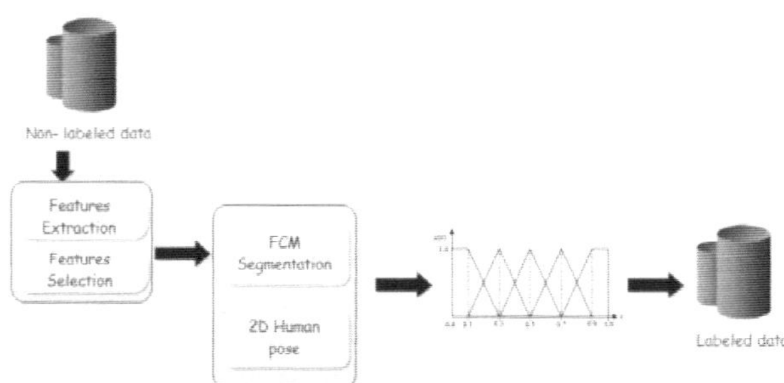

Figure 1. The chart flow of the proposed approach

There are two principal steps in our method and they are summarized in Figure 1. In the first stage, we extract features from each query image. Then we apply Fuzzy C-means (FCM), combined with teaching learning based optimization (TLBO) (Rao, at al. 2011), classifier over it. In the second stage, we use the OpenPose model in TensorFlow to perform human pose estimation. We used the 18 keypoints model trained on the COCO dataset in this work.

2.1 Data Collection

Collecting images is the first step in constructing a large clothing dataset, and the most common source is the shopping websites (Huang, et al. 2015), (Kiapour, et al. 2015). We crawled some well-known online shopping websites such as Collection of style, Mango and ZARA. Each clothing item has different images of varied poses and viewpoints without any background. The collected dataset offers a limited range of image variability because most of these images have an uniform size and orientation. Also, most persons are presented in a stereotypical pose and they don't contain any background clutter. To deal with this problem, we collect other clothing images from image search engines. The collected images come from users-generated contents such as blogs and forums which enrich the image set gathered from the shopping websites. We also added 75094 images from DeepFashion Dataset in order to compare and test our results. These images provide a greater variability of scale, pose and background clutter.

2.2 Image Segmentation

Considering the large number of classes where intra-class variability can be larger than inter-class variability and the inherent difference of pose and cloth appearances, the human semantic segmentation is becoming more complex (Simo-Serra, et al. 2014). Hence, the performance of a segmentation method depends highly on the quality of input features. Therefore, it is very important to use sufficient and significant image information to permit a proper segmentation. In this work, we propose a new segmentation method that proved its ability to perform well on a challenging clothing dataset.

2.2.1 Features Extraction and Selection Procedure

Taking into account the extensive variation of clothes in color, style, texture, and cutting, existing systems of clustering suffer from a serious confuse. Therefore, features extraction has an important influence on the segmentation task. In the case of simple image that does not contain textured regions, first-order statistics such as the local mean or variance will be sufficient. In the other hand, if an image displays textured regions with equal first-order statistics, higher-order statistics should be used. The local binary pattern (LBP) descriptor, proposed by (Ojala, et al. 1996), is widely used in texture analysis because of its computational simplicity and robustness to illumination changes. Clothing images often display important variations when they are taken under different scenery, such as illuminations and pose. Therefore, features must provide a higher-order description of the local image content to allow an appropriate segmentation. However, LBP cannot capture the full discriminative information in case of non-textured image and suffers from limited macro-textural structures detection. Thus, we propose a novel descriptor called LNLBP (Large Neighbourhood Local Binary Pattern) to improve the robustness and discriminative power of the basic LBP and its extensions (Guo, et al. 2010), (Liu, et al. 2012), (Qi, at al. 2012). Instead of trying to analyze texture formation on a pixel level, this descriptor forms a local pattern based on large neighbourhood. Thus, each LNLBP code can be regarded as a macro-structure texture. The new approach includes, for calculating the LNLBP texture descriptor, a four step process presented as follows: First, the original image sized (X, Y) is surrounded by (X + 2, Y + 2) eight zero matrices. Each matrix is oriented in a different direction presented by the Figure 2. Then, these extended matrices are thresholded to binary level (typically 0 and 1) based on a directional comparison with the original ones. Each resulting matrix is multiplied by 2 i−1, where i represents the matrix order. Finally, the sum of all the obtained matrices is computed to obtain the new pattern that characterizes the texture model, such as: $M = \sum_{i=1}^{8} \quad M_i$.

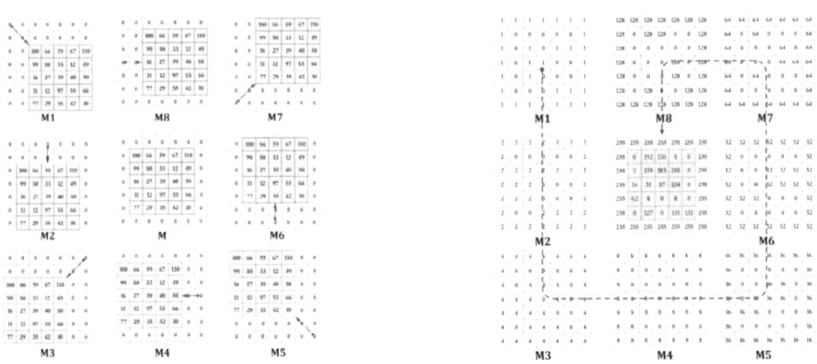

Figure 2. The LNLBP descriptor

However, high dimension data often contain a high degree of irrelevant and redundant information, which seriously degrade the performance of learning algorithms and require a large amount of memory and computation power. This kind of features is not involved in the distinction between data of different classes so it can be removed without having any effect on the classification performance. Thereby, features selection is the procedure frequently used to cope with these challenges by selecting significant and relevant features for each image. This process produces the best segmentation rate and the least computational effort while removing irrelevant and redundant features (Tu, et al. 2007). Fisher score is one of the most widely used supervised feature selection techniques (Gu, et al. 2012). High-quality features affect similar values to samples belonging to the same class and different values to samples from different classes. Thereby, the Fisher score of the i th feature is computed as below:

$$F(x_i) = \frac{\sum_{k=1}^{c} \eta_k(\mu_k^i - \mu^i)^2}{(\sigma^i)^2} \quad \text{where } (\sigma^i)^2 = \sum_{k=1}^{c} \eta_k(\sigma_k^i)^2$$

μ_k^i and σ_k^i are the mean and standard deviation of kth class corresponding to the ith feature.

μ^i and σ^i denote the mean and standard deviation of the whole dataset corresponding to the i^{th}feature.

2.2.2 Segmentation Algorithm (TLBO-FCM)

The FCM algorithm introduced by (Dunn, 1973) and improved by Bezdek (Bezdek, 1981), is an iterative method, based on minimizing the following objective function: $J = \sum_{j=1}^{N} \sum_{i=1}^{C} \mu_{ij}^m x_j - \vartheta_i^2$

where; μ_{ij}^m represents the degree of membership of the pixel $x_j$to the center i^{th} of the class ϑ_i .

x_j is the multidimensional attribute vector of the pixel and ϑ_i is the multidimensional center of the class.

Fuzzy c-means is a simple algorithm characterized by a fast convergence and an ability to handle large data sets. Despite these advantages, the initial cluster centers effected, largely, the FCM clustering results; through the gradient method for the extreme value that tend to receive local optimum not global optimum (Chu, et al, 2010). Therefore, we used Teaching learning based optimization (TLBO) (Rao, et al, 2011) to overcome this problem. TLBO is a population based meta- heuristic algorithm inspired by the teaching and learning procedure in a teaching environment. Combined with the FCM algorithm, TLBO is able to avoid the problem of local optima and to explore large solution spaces by exploiting different solutions (Paterlini, at al. 2006). TLBO-FCM algorithm consists of two steps. In the first step, TLBO algorithm explores the search space of the given dataset to find out the near-optimal cluster centers values. In the second step, those cluster centers with the best objective function values are used by FCM as initial cluster centers and then the final clustering is performed. This section deals with the performance comparison with the traditional algorithm FCM randomly initialized and the algorithm presented above TLBO-FCM. The fitness function presented by the equation (3) has been used for both methods. The main aim of this method is to improve the quality of clustering through the proposed TLBO-FCM algorithm. However, to correctly label an image, each part should be well partitioned to ensure dependency between labels. First, we extracted attributes such as Large Neighborhood Local Binary Patterns (LNLBP) and color information from each image. Then, the best ranked attributes have been selected for the segmentation operation based on TLBO-FCM algorithm. Figure 5 illustrates the result of segmentation algorithm. TLBO-FCM performs marginally better than the traditional FCM algorithm. Figure 6 shows the difference between the methods in point of view outputs stability. Clusters in (3b) are well separated than the clusters obtained by FCM method (3a).

Figure 3. (a) Image segmented with fuzzy logic (b) Image segmented with TLBO-FCM

2.2.3 Human Pose Estimation

Human pose estimation is among the most widely used method for clothing segmentation and recognition. For example, in (Dong, et al. 2014), (Yamaguchi, at al. 2012) researchers tries to utilize the human pose estimation in the context of regularization or supervision of part segmentation results. A successful detection of person in a given image provides a set of 18 points representing body parts. The body parts mapping order of COCO body model is obtained by using the method proposed by (Cao. et al, 2019) which predicts the principal key points or body parts such as head, shoulders, knees, etc. for each person in the image. Accordingly to OpenPose, the human body is a set of parts where each part contains its index and its relative coordinates that will later represent limits of clothing items in the image. In this work, we exploited these key points to assign a clothing label to each part in a reasonable way such as a tshirt is typically on the upper part of the body and not the feet. The parts from all detections are ordered in the same way, for example, the first part with number 0 refers to the person's nose.

3. CLOTHING LABELING

There is always some ambiguity related to the task of assigning clothing categories to images. For example, what is the length that makes the difference between a short dress and a tee-shirt? Which parts of a clothing item are significant enough that when visible, they make the item's identity clear? Since this information may not be reliable for every single image due to variations of pose and cloth appearances, as well as, the presence of self-occlusions. We opted to use fuzzy logic to allow model to merge uncertain information in a best way and incorporate heuristic control in the form of if-then rules. Once we obtain the segmented image and the coordinates of each human part, we can proceed to estimating the clothing labeling. The fuzzy logic controller receives the data related to the position of human body, and different classes resulting from the segmentation algorithm. The output of the fuzzy logic provides signals in the form of clothing labels. Based on these results, the system will thereafter, be able to precise the limits of the bounding boxes containing the clothing items, as well as, its nature. Figure 4 presents the membership functions of the inputs and outputs of the controller. The adopted membership functions for the fuzzy sets associated to the input and to the output were triangles, as shown in the previous figure. The values of the memberships function of the output are designed to separate the different categories of clothing items (T-shirt, trousers, short, etc) based on their textures and positions.

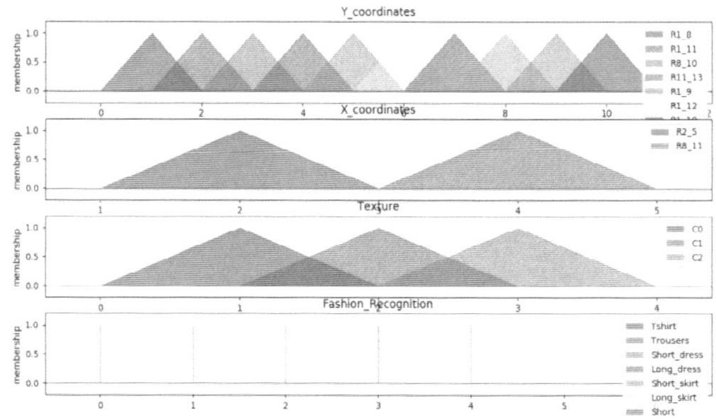

Figure 4. Fuzzy membership Functions

4. EXPERIMENTS

The proposed approach was implemented in python on a machine with 32 Gigabytes of RAM and intel i7-4790 processor at 3.6 GHz with 4 Cores and 8 threads and Nvidia Geforce GTX 1050 Ti. We used the Tensorflow library, scikit- fuzzy and OpenCV. We are intent on experimentally validating the two overarching objectives of our approach; the first objective is that our proposed system could achieve a proper segmentation based on the extracted features. The second one is that human position information could be successfully used in conjunction with the segmented image to produce an accurate annotation, whatever the position of the human model. We achieve clothing labeling performance similar to the hand-labeled dataset, while being faster. For example, a dataset composed of 83269 images, need about 7 days (6.987 days) to be labeled with our approach. The following table depicts the time analysis of the proposed clothing labeling method steps.

Table 1. Time analysis for the proposed approach

Pose estimation	Segmentation	Labeling	Total
3.2 sec	2.52 sec	1.53 sec	7.25 sec

We have run different experiments to evaluate the labeling precision of the created dataset. We sampled 2000 images from distinct clothing categories and label them manually using experts. In addition, we used labels from deepFashion dataset as a ground truth. We notice that the reached precision is around 91% but it varies from a category to another. The significant challenges facing our automatic labeling approach are missing information or erroneous poses estimation. Also,the misclassification for highly overlapping classes like large trousers and long skirt or long t-shirt and short dress, is evenly a principal cause of errors in our labels. In fact, our approach successfully classify and localise fashion items even in the case of complicated background and human poses. After performing the classification and the localization of the fashion items, we generated automatically the 'xml' files containing the coordinates of the labeled categories in the images. This work was compared with the user labeled dataset and the DeepFashion bounding boxes. Seen that the DeepFashion dataset only has one bounding box annotation per image although several clothing items are often present on the same image, the images could not be used in their raw state. They have to be cropped around the item of interest in the training and validation set. Besides, our dataset provides a complete annotation of the images. Each image could contain one or more bounding boxes depending on the number of clothing items present on it. In addition, the DeepFashion dataset has only three generic categories: "top", "bottom", "long", while our dataset is more precise in term of clothing items classification. We provide seven categories: "T-shirt", "trousers", "short dress", "long dress", "short skirt", "long skirt" and "short". Finally, the obtained results represent a relevant gain in time for a labeling process compared with the manual method. The created dataset is unlikely to be challenging enough to evaluate other huge datasets in term of collected images. But, in return, the proposed algorithm offers the possibility to create an unlimited number of annotated images according to user needs with a good accuracy rate.

5. CONCLUSION

The principal goal of our work is to provide, a faster way, to label images and to localise items for users without expertise in fashion field. It permits to produce an automatically labeled dataset, more precise than a hand-labeled example, without recourse to external data analysts or waste of time. We will offer the resulting dataset to download for research purposes. Despite these auspicious results, we believe much can still be done to improve. For example, by adding more categories of clothes and accessories and avoid the misclassification. In our future work we will use the resulted database to classify automatically clothes in real-time streaming.

REFERENCES

Alexander J Ratner, Christopher M De Sa, Sen Wu, Daniel Selsam, and Christopher Ré. (2016). Data programming: Creating large training sets, quickly. In D. D. Lee, M. Sugiyama, U. V. Luxburg, I. Guyon, and R. Garnett, editors, Advances in Neural Information Processing Systems 29, 3567–3575.

Bolei Zhou, Hang Zhao, Xavier Puig, Sanja Fidler, Adela Barriuso, and Antonio Torralba. (2017). Scene parsing through ade20k dataset. In Proceedings of the IEEE Conference on Computer Vision and Pattern Recognition.

Bryan C. Russell, Antonio Torralba, Kevin P. Murphy, and William T. Freeman. (2008). Labelme: A database and web-based tool for image annotation. Int. J. Comput. Vision, 77(1-3):157–173.

Cao, Z., Hidalgo Martinez, G., Simon, T., Wei, S., & Sheikh, Y. (2019). OpenPose: Realtime Multi-Person 2D Pose Estimation using Part Affinity Fields. *IEEE Transactions On Pattern Analysis and Machine Intelligence*, 1-1. doi: 10.1109/tpami.2019.2929257.

Christian Szegedy, Vincent Vanhoucke, Sergey Ioffe, Jonathon Shlens, and Zbigniew Wojna. (2015). Rethinking the inception architecture for computer vision. CoRR, abs/1512.00567.

Chung jui Tu, Li yeh Chuang, Jun yang Chang, and Cheng hong Yang. (2007). Feature selection using pso-svm. IAENG International Journal of Computer Science, 33:1, IJCS_33_1_18.

Edgar Simo-Serra, Sanja Fidler, Francesc Moreno-Noguer, and Raquel Urtasun. (2014). A high performance crf model for clothes parsing. In ACCV.

Han Xiao, Kashif Rasul, and Roland Vollgraf. (2017).Fashion-mnist: a novel image dataset for benchmarking machine learning algorithms. CoRR, abs/1708.07747.

J. C. Dunn. A fuzzy relative of the isodata process and its use in detecting compact well-separated clusters. (1973).Journal of Cybernetics, 3(3):32–57.

James C. Bezdek. (1981). Pattern Recognition with Fuzzy Objective Function Algorithms. Kluwer Academic Publishers, Norwell, MA, USA.

Jia Deng, Wei Dong, Richard Socher, Li jia Li, Kai Li, and Li Fei-fei.(2009). Imagenet: A large-scale hierarchical image database. In CVPR.

Jian Dong, Qiang Chen, Xiaohui Shen, Jianchao Yang, and Shuicheng Yan. (2014). Towards unified human parsing and pose estimation. 2014 IEEE Conference on Computer Vision and Pattern Recognition, 843– 850.

Junshi Huang, Rogério Schmidt Feris, Qiang Chen, and Shuicheng Yan. (2015). Cross-domain image retrieval with a dual attribute-aware ranking network. CoRR, abs/1505.07922.

Kota Yamaguchi, M. Hadi Kiapour, Luis E. Ortiz, and Tamara L. Berg. (2012). Parsing clothing in fashion photographs. 2012 IEEE Conference on Computer Vision and Pattern Recognition, pages 3570–3577.

L Liu, P Fieguth, L Zhao, Y Long, and G Kuang. (2012). Extended local binary patterns for texture classification. Image and Vision Computing, 30:86– 99.

M. Everingham, S. M. A. Eslami, L. Van Gool, C. K. I. Williams, J. Winn, and A. Zisserman. (2015). The pascal visual object classes challenge: A retrospective. International Journal of Computer Vision, 111(1):98–136.

M. Hadi Kiapour, Xufeng Han, Svetlana Lazebnik, Alexander C. Berg, and Tamara L. Berg. (2015). Where to buy it: Matching street clothing photos in online shops. In 2015 International Conference on Computer Vision, Proceedings of the IEEE International Conference on Computer Vision, 3343–3351.

Quanquan Gu, Zhenhui Li, and Jiawei Han. (2012).Generalized fisher score for feature selection. CoRR, abs/1202.3725.

R. V. Rao, V. J. Savsani, and D. P. Vakharia. (2011). Teaching-learning- based optimization: A novel method for constrained mechanical design optimization problems. Computer-Aided Design, 43:303–315.

Ross B. Girshick, Jeff Donahue, Trevor Darrell, and Jitendra Malik. (2013). Rich feature hierarchies for accurate object detection and semantic segmentation. CoRR, abs/1311.2524.

Ross B. Girshick. (2015). Fast R-CNN. CoRR, abs/1504.08083.

Salma Samiei, Ali Ahmad, Pejman Rasti, Etienne Belin, and David Rousseau. (2018). Low-cost image annotation for supervised machine learning. application to the detection of weeds in dense culture. In Computer Vision Problems in Plant Phenotyping (CVPPP 2018), NewcastlE.

Sandra Paterlini and Thiemo Krink. (2006). Differential evolution and particle swarm optimisation in partitional clustering. Comput. Stat. Data Anal., 50(5):1220–1247.

Shaoqing Ren, Kaiming He, Ross Girshick, and Jian Sun. (2015). Faster r-cnn: Towards real-time object detection with region proposal networks. In C. Cortes, N. D. Lawrence, D. D. Lee, M. Sugiyama, and R. Garnett, editors, Advances in Neural Information Processing Systems 28, pages 91–99.

Timo Ojala, Matti Pietikäinen, and David Harwood. (1996). A comparative study of texture measures with classification based on featured distributions. Pattern Recognition, 29:51–59.

Torralba, A., Russell, B., & Yuen, J. (2010). LabelMe: Online Image Annotation and Applications. *Proceedings of the IEEE*, *98*(8), 1467-1484. doi: 10.1109/jproc.2010.2050290

Tsung-Yi Lin, Michael Maire, Serge J. Belongie, Lubomir D. Bourdev, Ross B. Girshick, James Hays, Pietro Perona, Deva Ramanan, Piotr Dollár, and C. Lawrence Zitnick. (2014). Microsoft COCO: common objects in context. CoRR, abs/1405.0312.

Xianbiao Qi, Rong Xiao, Jun Guo, and Lei Zhang. (2012). Pairwise rotation invariant co-occurrence local binary pattern. IEEE Transactions on Pattern Analysis and Machine Intelligence, 36:2199–2213.

Xiaoli Chu, Ying Zhu, Juntao Shi, and JiQing Song. (2010). Method of image segmentation based on fuzzy c-means clustering algorithm and artificial fish swarm algorithm. International Conference on Intelligent Computing and Integrated Systems, 254–257.

Yanyun Qu, Lifeng Liu, Yuan Xie, and Zejian Yuan. (2009). Automatic online labeling images via co-active-learning. In Proceedings of the First International Conference on Internet Multimedia Computing and Service, ICIMCS '09, 145–150.

Zhenhua Guo, Lei Zhang, and David Zhang. (2010). A completed modeling of local binary pattern operator for texture classification. Trans. Img. Proc., 19(6):1657–1663.

SAMPLE SCENES FROM A DISTRIBUTION: A CONTENT CREATION PIPELINE FOR REALISTIC RENDERING FOR NEURAL NETWORKS TRAINING

Vadim Sanzharov[1], Vladimir Frolov[2], Alexey Voloboy[3] and Vladimir Galaktionov[3]
[1]Gubkin Russian State University of Oil and Gas, Russia
[2]Keldysh Institute of Applied Mathematics Russian Academy of Sciences, Moscow State University, Russia
[3]Keldysh Institute of Applied Mathematics Russian Academy of Sciences, Russia

ABSTRACT

In this paper we present our experience with development of a content creation pipeline targeted at generation of realistic image sequences with highly variable content. Our technique allows rendering of a single 3D object or a 3D scene in variety of appearances which includes changing of geometry, materials and lighting. In our work we were able to generate datasets for individual 3D objects and create procedural generator of interior scenes. Our solution is highly controllable and allows generating datasets with desired distribution of features in a reproducible manner. Using synthetic data in training, we have got increase of accuracy in CNN-based models comparing to usage of real-life data only. During our work we had to significantly improve the content creation pipeline for the existing open source GPU rendering system adapting it for our tasks. In this paper we suggest new approach for content creation which we call "sampling scenes from a distribution".

Figure 1. Examples of our applications. Road signs and cars were rendered as individual objects and then augmented to KITTI dataset for further CNN test; realistic rendering of the interior created as a consistent 3D scene randomizing of objects layout, material and lighting

KEYWORDS

Realistic Rendering, Procedural Pipeline, 3D Scene Generator, GPU Rendering, CNN Training Datasets

1. INTRODUCTION

Training of the modern artificial intelligence models faces two fundamental problems in practice: data quantity and data quality. *Data quantity* concerns availability of sufficient amounts of training and testing data. *Data quality* means how balanced is the data – are all the different classes, which the model must recognize, represented enough, do we have precise marking for it or not, how much noise (of any nature) is present in our dataset. Real-life data sets collected by people usually suffer from both insufficient quality and quantity. The real situation is even worse because during their research Compute Vision (CV) engineers need to change input datasets for testing of certain hypotheses. Due to inability to quickly obtain a new dataset the CV engineers have to consider subsets of the existing dataset which significantly limits their study.

Thus, synthetic (i.e. rendered with realistic image synthesis methods) datasets can be an option. The solution to data quantity problem can be achieved by using algorithms for procedurally setting of the optical properties of materials and surfaces. This way it is possible to quickly generate almost unlimited number of training examples with any distribution of objects (and therefore classes) present in generated images. *The quality problem is in fact more interesting*. On the one hand it is solved automatically: renderer produces precise per-pixel masks generating ground truth marking. On the other hand, it is actually not quite clear what a quality does actually mean for CV engineers. Some research papers on this topic (that we will describe in related work section) assume that quality is subjective realism for human eye. *This is important to some extent but wrong in general*. Realistic rendering in comparison to simple or real-time techniques could improve CNN performance (for example, classification precision). But in our opinion the main problem is different: in practice the CV engineers measure CNN performance on specific data sets and in such formulation of the problem *a quality means to look like other examples of target dataset*. This in itself significantly shifts priorities for the developed software.

2. RELATED WORK

There are a huge number of successful applications of realistic rendering for AI training. For us, first of all, *it is interesting how 3D content was obtained in these works*, how the full pipeline was built and what was the advantages and disadvantages of the selected ways.

2.1 Using Existing 3D Content

Firstly [Movshovitz et al] demonstrated importance of the realistic rendering usage in a problem of view point estimation. In their work authors took a database of the 91 3D CAD models obtained from doschdesign.com and turbosquid.com. These models were rendered with randomized direct lighting and random real photos as background image. We believe this work measured the influence of not realism itself, but rather the effect of increasing dataset variability, which to some extent has an effect with even simple lighting models. The reason is obvious: 3D models downloaded from the Internet resources in most cases are not ready for photorealistic rendering due to missing textures, unknown materials models (which were simply incorrectly exported to the current format or not supported by current rendering system) and, finally, just human errors that were made when preparing the 3D model for the aggregator site.

[Zhang et al] report about using 500K images from 45K scenes for training of semantic segmentation and normal/depth estimation problems. The 3D content was obtained from the SUNCG dataset [Song et al]. There are many problems with this approach, even apart of the well-known legal problems with the SUNCG dataset. Since originally the SUNCG 3D models were assembled in the Planner5D program (which is trivial in comparison to such content creation tools as Blender or 3ds Max) they don't contain realistic setup for materials or lighting. They are limited to just textures for Lambert reflection. *This content is not sufficient for photorealistic rendering*. No wonder that the other works where the SUNCG was used [Li and Snavely, 2018; Kirsanov et al, 2019; McCormac et al, 2017] were able to achieve basic level of realism only.

2.2 Augmented Reality

Preparation of 3D content is expensive and time-consuming task. Therefore, in practice it is worth to consider any possibility for reducing man-hours. Augmented reality is very advanced approach here. Even [Movshovitz et al, 2016] actually used it when randomizing backgrounds. [Alhaija et al, 2018] went further applying augmentation of rendered images to the KITTI dataset [Geiger et al, 2013]. Applying of the image-based lighting technique [Debevec, 2002] for individual car models in conjunction with augmenting real photos [Voloboi et al, 2006] gives cheap and quick result: both rendering computation complexity and content preparation is greatly simplified [Alhaija et al, 2018].

The main problem of image-based lighting methods is that they need the real high dynamic range (5-6 orders of magnitude) to be present in HDR image. Often it is not so [Voloboi et al, 2006]. Lighting prediction methods [like Valiev et al, 2008; Song and Funkhouser, 2019; Garon et al, 2019; Sorokin et al, 2020] can help here. They became a quite common task for mixed-reality systems. Other disadvantage of augmented reality is the task of automatic, correct placing of 3D models inside some reconstructed representation of scene. It can be easily supported in some cases (for example, [Alhaija et al, 2018] used segmentation methods to reconstruct the road plane) but is quite hard in general (for example, for interior photographs). Thus, the approximate geometry, lighting and camera parameters including tone mapping should be reconstructed in some way and this reconstruction itself is a significant problem. Nevertheless, the main advantage of augmented reality is that it can work directly in the image domain of CV researcher interest expanding existing datasets with new examples. *And thus, Domain Adaptation methods [Tremblay, et al, 2018] are not needed* which seems to be mandatory in practice for achieving high quality with other synthetic ways.

2.3 Procedural and Simulation Approaches

Procedural modeling is expensive, time-consuming and usually restricted to some specific task (for example, dirt or fire modeling) and sometimes to specific rendering algorithm. However, once created, procedural models are highly variable (infinite number of examples), give great quality for rendering (often with infinite-resolution details) and is traditionally used in many cinema content creation pipelines. [Tsirikoglou et al, 2017] used procedural modeling approach to generate cities and showed improvement for neural networks. Buildings, roads and city plan were procedural while other models (like cars, pedestrians, vegetation, bicycles) were sampled randomly from prepared data base. Also, some parameters were randomized for cars: type, count, placement, color.

Approaches based on the procedural modeling via machine learning look promising [Risi and Togelius, 2019; Spick et al, 2019] but there we meet the chicken and egg problem: we need to train these models first. Besides, these approaches are rather new and not proven for practice of general rendering tasks yet.

[Hodan et al, 2019] achieved high quality by using the existing cinema production content creation pipeline with Autodesk Maya and Arnold rendering system, high quality 3D models and physics simulation which was the main randomizing tool. Obviously, this approach suffers from the main disadvantage of current cinema production pipelines: high cost and high labor input. [Hodan et al, 2019] used only 6 scenes with 30 different objects. This was fundamentally different from previous approaches. Other disadvantages of the Hodan's approach include the use of non-freely available tools Maya and Arnold (which limits the adoption of this work), and slow rendering reported by authors – 15 to 720 seconds per image (depending on quality) on 16-core Xeon CPUs with 112 GB of RAM. Reasonably fast dataset generation is therefore possible only if significant computational resources are available. It is important to note that authors reported that accurate modeling of the scene context was more significant (+16% for CNN precision) in comparison to accurate light transport simulation (+6% for CNN precision).

Other works [Shah et al, 2017] show that modern game engines could also be used for AI training. The choice between a game engine or a cinema production rendering system should be done primarily basing on how easy to model target real-world situation.

2.4 Content Creation Pipeline

Unlike other works mentioned earlier a specialized content creation pipeline is proposed in [Denninger et al 2019]. And, as it was stated by the authors precisely, the design of open-source and universal pipeline was their goal. So, it is very close to our work. Sampler modules provide randomization capabilities which are the most interesting part of the pipeline. Sampler modules can generate positions for object placement (cameras, lights, 3d models) with various distributions and constraints like a proximity check. So, for example, object positions can be generated on the spherical surface but the objects will not be too close (for example, cameras will not look straight at the wall) and/or will not collide with each other. Sampler modules are also able to select objects basing on user-defined conditions and manipulate their properties (for example, enable physics simulation for 3d models). The MaterialManipulator and MaterialRandomizer modules were implemented to produce variation in appearance.

The main drawback of this work is the fact that until now it was not yet applied to any specific learning task unlike many previously mentioned papers. So, while it looks very good on a paper and in examples provided by authors, its performance in real-life applications for CNN training is not known yet. As mentioned before the authors intended their work to be a universal pipeline which can be adapted and used by CV researchers. Therefore, real evaluation of their work can be made only when its applications will be published. We believe that the [Denninger et al 2019] approach is right in general. However, having experience of similar pipeline creation and its application to various AI training tasks, we would discuss several modifications that need to be done in order to apply the Denninger approach in practice.

3. SUGGESTED APPROACH

The first difference between our work and existing approaches is reproducibility of scene generation results which allows generation of the same *desired features* of a scene for the same input setup. In fact, this turns dataset generation into a sampling problem. Having an input vector (x_0, x_1, ... x_n) of random numbers from 0 to 1 we assign to each random variable some specific meaning during randomization script development. For example, if we would like to render cars inside HDR environment, like [Movshovitz et al, 2016; Alhaija et al, 2018] did for 3D model pose/camera parameters estimation, we could:

1. Assign (x_0, x_1) pair for 3D model (car) rotation (additionally we need setting of allowable angle intervals, for example from 0 to 70 degrees for vertical angle and from 0 to 360 for horizontal).
2. Assign x_2 for car body color selection from palette (to restrict desired colors).
3. Assign x_3 for environment select.
4. Assign x_4 for environment rotation around vertical (Y) axis.
5. Assign x_5 for car 3D model selection.

We call this process *a scene sampling*. Thus, sampling of 6D vector (x_0 ... x_5) we obtain images for input samples which gives us important properties and thus powerful capabilities for further experiments:

- Applying quasi-random sequences (we used the Sobol sequence) we kill two birds with one stone: (1) Starting of the Sobol sequence from the beginning for each 3D model (i.e. generate x_0 ... x_5 with quasi random approach, but select 3D models one by one instead of sampling x_6) allows us to generate same camera positions for all 3D models which is important for training of pose estimation algorithms. (2) The Sobol sequence gives good uniform distribution in 5D-6D space. So, the generated samples would be also evenly distributed among all desired parameters: car colors, camera rotation and lighting conditions (which are set from environment map).
- Applying of non-uniform distribution for x_5, allows us to sample more cars of desired types and applying of tabulated distribution for x_2 we can use more cars of specified (for example, black and grey) colors.
- Setting of different values and distributions for training and validation datasets we can easily check hypothesis of our interest. For example, we can generate training dataset with camera rotation of only 25, 50 and 70 degrees but then check if this is enough for rotations 10, 30 and 60 degrees in our test dataset.
- When we move from the current frame to the next one, we would like to localize the scene changes. In such a case the rendering system does not have to perform expensive operations of loading content from disk to GPU memory often. And so, we efficiently apply caching technique. In our experiments we can automatically obtain desirable caching for rendering system by clustering the multidimensional input points. For example, we can group all input samples on (x_3, x_5) pair. In such a way we consequently render scenes with the same 3D model and the same environment map.

We would like to make a special note on the last point. One may suppose that this optimization could be omitted or achieved in other ways. We consider the following reasons support our position in practice:

- When a researcher writes randomization script (presumably a CV engineer) he most likely does not know details about the rendering system. So effective cache usage should be applied automatically without polluting the randomizer script logic with such optimization issues.
- Some specific procedural approaches could be done directly on GPU (that we actually did for procedural textures). But it is almost impossible to avoid costly interaction with disk or CPU simulation tools (for example, vector displacement, physics based animation or simulation) because for realistic simulation/modeling often we have to rely on a variety of existing CPU based products that could work for minutes or even hours (although giving realistic results).
- This optimization is critical for systems based on the real-time rendering algorithms. They directly feed their result to the neural network on GPU. Even in our case (we use the "offline" GPU path

tracing renderer) we gain acceleration from 1.5 to 3 times for considered case because the input HDR images have high resolution 8Kx4K (this is normal size for most of existing HDR environment assets). And it is simply not possible to load such texture from disk fast enough.

3.1 Suggested Solution in Details

We selected the 3ds Max and the Hydra Renderer [Frolov et al, 2018] due to full-fledged content creation pipeline, advanced GPU rendering and well-specified XML scene representation which is suitable to work with during randomization. The open source Natron software was used as post-processing and compositing tool. Post-processing is needed to produce an additional data (for example, 2d bounding boxes) or to combine the rendered images with photos in case of augmentation (compositing operations and screen-space effects).

3.1.1 Material Setup

Our material editor exploits two observations. Firstly, if we have two materials of the same nature (for example, wood) they actually cannot be interchanged in any arbitrary case. Let's consider a wooden pencil and a wooden floor for example. Both of these objects are constructed from wood but they have different microstructure of the wood and (most important!) they have different scale of texture matrices for applying of texture coordinates. Therefore, applying the same material for floor and pencil would not just look strange but is completely wrong. In the best case we will be able to see small copies of, for example, parquet boards on the pencil when the camera approaches to it. But most likely we will get just some undefined color (especially from far viewpoint). Second observation is the fact that there are many materials that can be applied for certain types of objects only. For example, the TV screen or computer monitor image may appear on an advertising poster and vice versa, but it cannot appear on a cup or a fork. So, there are a lot of objects in the interior scene where it cannot appear and we know such a relationship.

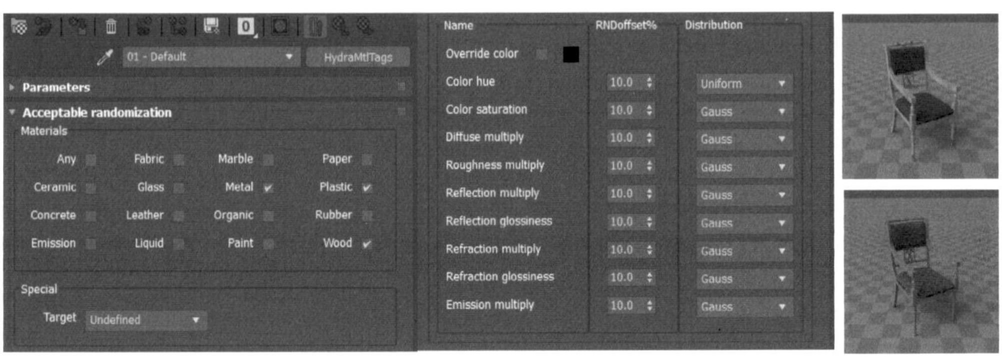

Figure 2. Material randomizer GUI. The "Acceptable randomization" tab is responsible for setting up universal (or tagged) materials. The "Special" tab is responsible for special (or targeted) materials. The middle part of GUI is responsible for distributions for separate material parameters. The right part is preview of object with assigned material

The artist's work was separated in two phases: creation of the material database and filling the database of objects. During *the first phase* artist creates *final materials* and indicates its *tags or target*. A single material is allowed to have several types. It can be combined with other materials or used as a part of some complex material model. This is why *we prefer the term material tag over material type*. And finally, the desired distribution parameters are set separately for each *final material* (see the right part of our GUI on *Figure 2*). The distribution is tested on some simple object (for example, sphere) during the first phase.

During the *second phase* artist takes 3D objects (floor, doors, walls, furniture or any other) and assigns *dummy materials* to them indicating material tags or targets.

3.1.2 Procedural Textures Setup

As we mentioned before, we heavily use procedural textures in our approach. The main goal of procedural textures usage is to provide variety of additional details to the rendered 3d models to produce more realistic images. The rendered objects usually have crisp and clear "idealistic" look. Usually real-life objects do not preserve the pristine condition for long. Various scratches, dirt and dust are almost always present on them. So, we implemented several procedural textures, simulating effects such as dirt, rust, scratches etc. (*Figure 3*) to improve the realistic look of our generated objects. It is important to note that in some cases the procedural approach is the only possible way. It is so when the input 3D models have not texture coordinates and usage of world-position 3D procedural textures is the only available option.

Figure 3. Examples of applying procedural textures in our pipeline during domain randomization

3.1.3 Interior Sampling

Our content creation pipeline for interiors was assembled from different implementations and is semi-automatic. We broke up "interior sampling" into three different subtasks: layout generation, furniture placement and object placement. For layout generation we have implemented a method based on combination of "dense packing" [Koenig and Knecht, 2014] and "inside-out" [Martin, 2006] methods. For furniture layout we have selected an artist-controlled approach which was implemented via the 3ds Max Scripting. Although existing advanced methods of furniture placement can be applied [Qi et al, 2016; Wang et al, 2018], but for us it was important to use a controlled method which in the same time fits in our sampling concept. Therefore, we first traverse the edges of the office perimeter and place furniture according to 1D pattern. Then an artist draws several binary 2D pattern images to arrange furniture inside the room. We assign four input random numbers to frequency and pattern number for 1D and 2D patterns. During sampling we randomly selected pattern and frequency.

Finally, we also used template-based method for object placement on tables and desktops. Performing some experiments with physics simulation in the beginning of our projects (analogously to [Hodaň et al, 2018]) we found that in practice it is difficult to achieve adequate and reproducible result with it: objects were piled in a heap, fell under a table or were in impossible configurations (like a book on the keyboard or a mouse on the monitor and etc.). We settled on approach when an artist prepares several templates with configured bounding boxes and rotation angles for each type of object on the table or on the floor surface: monitor, system unit, keyboard and etc. Now the objects can appear only within the allowed 2D bounding boxes on the floor or table planes. If a collision is happened, we apply "tabula rasa" method: clearing everything and regenerating it again until there are no collisions [Krauth, 2015]. The resulting generated content can be seen n rendered images on Figure 4 and Figure 1 (right).

Figure 4. Examples of our "interior sampling" approach

4. VALIDATION

We have validated our pipeline for road signs detection and segmentation and cars detection problems. For interiors, though, our validation is not yet ready. For cars we used KITTI-15 dataset [Geiger et al, 2013] for experimental evaluation. It consists of training and test parts. Each contains 200 frames. Since there is no labelling for the test set, we manually labelled bounding boxes for it. We used 50 different 3D models of cars, procedural texture for dirt and rust modeling, and random HDR environments for lighting. Car positions were sampled along the piecewise-linear trajectories that were drawn by artists in 3D (fig. 5, left) for all 200 images. Road plane was reconstructed based on the fact that all images were obtained with single camera parameters. We augmented each image of training set 20 times with 2-5 added random cars in each frame (example on fig. 5, right). As a result, we had 4000 frames in augmented training set. We also made experiments with random horizontal flips (probability of flipping is 0.5) of input images in order to estimate the benefits of our approach over simple methods of increasing training data size. We trained Faster-RCNN [Ren et al, 2015] with ResNet-50 FPN backbone on three training sets: (real images, real + flips, augmented).

We used mAP metric (average areas under curve for different IoU thresholds) for detector quality evaluation. Resulting mAPs are shown in table 1. Precision-recall curves for different IoU thresholds are shown on Figure 6. We clearly can see that our approach with augmentation of frames with rendered cars improves quality of detector.

Figure 5. Examples of augmented KITTI-15. Left column: images with marked trajectories for placing cars, right column: frames augmented with rendered cars

Table 1. mAP metric values for our experiments with cars

Dataset	Example
Real images	38.67 %
Real + flipped	40.30 %
Augmented (ours)	**43.26 %**

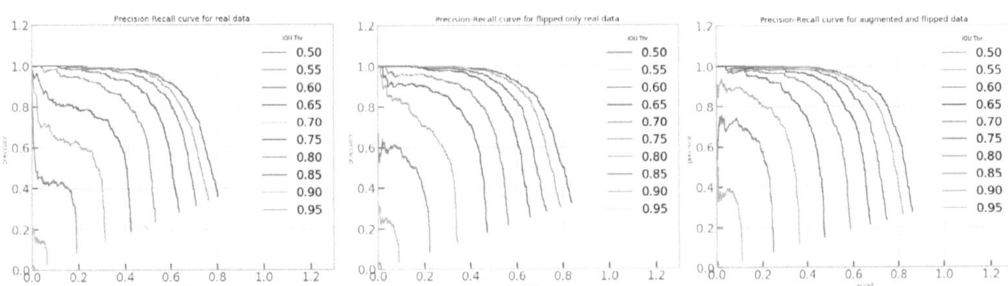

Figure 6. Real (left), real + flipped (middle) and augmented (ours, right) precision-recall curves

5. CONCLUSION

In this work we proposed the content creation pipeline for improving AI training by rendering synthetic datasets and augmenting them to real images. Unlike previous works, where the generator for single problem or the general-purpose pipeline but out of application (like [Denninger et al, 2019]) was proposed, we tested our pipeline in several scenarios, and therefore we can generalize results. Our solution is highly controllable and allows generating datasets with desired distribution of features in a reproduceable manner. This is achieved by the fact, that an artist, while tuning the distributions parameters and creating content, is guided by the requirements of CV researcher, on the one hand, and by the formalized scene sampling process, on the other hand. We always get the same rendered scene sampling the same point of input parameters in multidimensional space. In practice, this turned out to be one of the critical features for further use in neural network training. Because CNN is actually approximate multidimensional distribution, the generator/render should also "sample the scene from distribution" and the content creation pipeline should provide ability for tuning desired distribution, not just generate some random data.

REFERENCES

Alhaija, H. A., Mustikovela, S. K., Mescheder, L., Geiger, A., and Rother, C. 2018. Augmented Reality Meets Computer Vision: Efficient Data Generation for Urban Driving Scenes. *International Journal of Computer Vision,* vol. 126, No. 9, pp. 961–972.

Debevec, P., Image-Based Lighting: Tutorial *SIGGRAPH*, 2002, pp. 26–34.

Denninger, M., Sundermeyer, M., Winkelbauer, D., Zidan, Y., Olefir, D., Elbadrawy, M., Lodhi, A. and Katam, H. 2019. BlenderProc. arXiv preprint *arXiv:1911.01911.*

Frolov, V., Sanzharov, V., Trofimov, M., Pavlov, D. and Galaktionov, V. 2018 Hydra Renderer. Open source GPU based rendering system. https://github.com/Ray-Tracing-Systems/HydraAPI

Garon, M., Sunkavalli, K., Hadap, S., Carr, N., and Lalonde, J. F. 2019. Fast Spatially-Varying Indoor Lighting Estimation, *Proceedings of the IEEE Conference on Computer Vision and Pattern Recognition* pp. 6908-6917

Geiger, A., Lenz, P., Stiller, C. and Urtasun, R., 2013. Vision meets robotics: The kitti dataset. *The International Journal of Robotics Research,* Vol. 32, No. 11, pp.1231-1237.

Hodaň, T., Vineet, V., Gal, R., Shalev, E., Hanzelka, J., Connell, T., Urbina, P., Sinha, S.N. and Guenter, B. 2019. Photorealistic image synthesis for object instance detection. arXiv preprint *arXiv:1902.03334*

Hodan, T., Michel, F., Brachmann, E., Kehl, W., GlentBuch, A., Kraft, D., Drost, B., Vidal, J., Ihrke, S., Zabulis, X. and Sahin, C. 2018. BOP: Benchmark for 6D object pose estimation. *ECCV,* pp. 19-34

Kirsanov, P., Gaskarov, A., Konokhov, F., Sofiiuk, K., Vorontsova, A., Slinko, I., Zhukov, D., Bykov, S., Barinova, O. and Konushin, A. 2019. DISCOMAN: Dataset of Indoor Scenes for Odometry, Mapping And Navigation. arXiv preprint *arXiv:1909.12146.*

Koenig, R., Knecht, K. 2014. Comparing two evolutionary algorithm-based methods for layout generation: Dense packing versus subdivision. *AI EDAM.* Vol 28, No. 3, pp. 285-299

Krauth, Werner. 2015. Advanced Monte Carlo algorithms course lecture. pp 11-12. http://www.lps.ens.fr/~krauth/images/5/50/BadHonnef_2.pdf

Li, Z., and Snavely, N. 2018. Cgintrinsics: Better intrinsic image decomposition through physically-based rendering. *Proceedings of the European Conference on Computer Vision (ECCV)*, pp. 371–387.

Martin, J. 2006. Procedural house generation: A method for dynamically generating floor plans. *Proceedings of the Symposium on Interactive 3D Graphics and Games*, pp. 1-2.

McCormac, J., Handa, A., Leutenegger, S., and Davison, A. J. 2017. SceneNet RGB-D: Can 5M Synthetic Images Beat Generic ImageNet Pre-training on Indoor Segmentation. *Proceedings of the IEEE International Conference on Computer Vision,* pp. 2678-2687.

Movshovitz-Attias, Y., Kanade, T., and Sheikh, Y. 2016. How useful is photo-realistic rendering for visual learning. *European Conference on Computer Vision.*, pp. 202–217.

Qi, S., Zhu, Y., Huang, S., Jiang, C., and Zhu, S. C. 2016. Human-centric Indoor Scene Synthesis Using Stochastic Grammar. arXiv preprint *arXiv:1808.08473v1.*

Ren, S., He, K., Girshick, R., and Sun, J. Faster R-CNN: Towards Real-Time Object Detection with Region Proposal Networks. *Advances in neural information processing systems.* pp. 91-99

Risi, S., and Togelius, J. 2019 Increasing Generality in Machine Learning through Procedural Content Generation. arXiv preprint *arXiv:1911.13071*.

Sanzharov, V. and Frolov, V. 2019 Level of Detail for Precomputed Procedural Textures *Programming and Computer Software,* 2019, V. 45, No. 4, pp. 187-195

Shah, S., Dey, D., Lovett, C., and Kapoor, A. 2017. AirSim: High-Fidelity Visual and Physical Simulation for Autonomous Vehicles. arXiv preprint *arXiv:1705.05065*.

Song, S., Yu, F., Zeng, A., Chang, A.X., Savva, M. and Funkhouser, T. 2016. Semantic Scene Completion from a Single Depth Image. arXiv preprint, *arXiv:1611.08974*.

Song, Shuran and Funkhouser, Thomas. 2019. Neural Illumination: Lighting Prediction for Indoor Environments, *IEEE Conference on Computer Vision and Pattern Recognition*, pp. 6911-6919

Sorokin, M., Zhdanov, D., Zhdanov, A., Potemin, I., and Bogdanov N. 2020 Restoration of Lighting Parameters in Mixed Reality Systems Using Convolutional Neural Network Technology Based on RGBD Images. *Programming and Computer Software*, 2020, Vol. 46, No. 3, pp. 203-212

Spick, R.J., Cowling, P. and Walker, J.A. 2019. Procedural Generation using Spatial GANs for Region-Specific Learning of Elevation Data. *2019 IEEE Conference on Games (CoG)*, pp. 1-8.

Straub, J., Whelan, T., Ma, L., Chen, Y., Wijmans, E., Green, S., Engel, J.J., Mur-Artal, R., Ren, C., Verma, S. and Clarkson, A. 2019. The replica dataset: A digital replica of indoor spaces, arXiv preprint *arXiv:1906.05797*

Tremblay, J., Prakash, A., Acuna, D., Brophy, M., Jampani, V., Anil, C., To, T., Cameracci, E., Boochoon, S. and Birchfield, S. 2018. Training deep networks with synthetic data: Bridging the reality gap by domain randomization. arXiv preprint *arXiv:1804.06516*, 2018. 2

Tsirikoglou, A., Kronander, J., Wrenninge, M. and Unger, J. 2017. Procedural Modeling and Physically Based Rendering for Synthetic Data Generation in Automotive Applications. arXiv preprint *arXiv:1710.06270*

Valiev I., Voloboy A., Galaktionov V., Improved model of IBL sunlight simulation, *Proceedings of the 24-th int. Spring Conference on Computer Graphics (SCCG)*, 2008, pp.37-42. DOI:10.1145/1921264.1921274

Voloboi A.G., Galaktionov V.A., Kopylov E.A., Shapiro L.Z., Simulation of natural daylight illumination determined by a high dynamic range image, *Programming and Computer Software*, Vol. 32, No. 5, 2006, pp. 284-297. DOI:10.1134/S0361768806050057

Wang, K., Savva, M., Chang, A.X. and Ritchie, D. 2018. Deep convolutional priors for indoor scene synthesis. *ACM Transactions on Graphics (TOG)*. Vol. 37, No. 4, pp. 1-14.

Zhang, Y., Song, S., Yumer, E., Savva, M., Lee, J.Y., Jin, H. and Funkhouser, T. 2017. Physically-based rendering for indoor scene understanding using convolutional neural networks. *Proceedings of the IEEE Conference on Computer Vision and Pattern Recognition*, pp. 5287–5295.

LEARNING-BASED SEGMENTATION OF OPTIC DISC IN RETINAL IMAGES USING CLUSTERING TREES AND LOCAL MODE FILTERING

Michael Osadebey, Marius Pedersen and Dag Waaler
Norwegian University of Science and Technology, Norway

ABSTRACT

Delineation of the optic disc boundary in retinal images is the first step towards the computation of cup-to-disc ratio, an important indicator of ophthalmic pathologies such as glaucoma. This paper proposes the combination of learning-based clustering trees with local mode filtering for the segmentation of the optic disc region in retinal images. The algorithm identifies candidate optic disc region by extracting and pooling low-level features at different clustering resolutions from the filtered region-of-interest in two color channels. Thereafter, we use learned geometric properties such as area, eccentricity and solidity to extract high-level features for the identification of connected components, which most likely belong to the optic disc region. The final stage pools and fully connects these connected components into a single segmented region. Performance evaluation on three publicly available datasets from IDRID, DRISHTI-GS and MESSIDOR demonstrate promising results that are comparable to state-of-the-art algorithms.

KEYWORDS

Glaucoma, Retinal Images, Optic Disc, Clustering Trees, Local Mode Filtering

1. INTRODUCTION

The cup-to-disc ratio, defined as the diameter of the optic cup divided by the diameter of the optic disc, is one of several metrics used by ophthalmologists to assess the progression of glaucoma disease. The first step in the computation of cup-to-disc ratio is delineation of the boundaries covered by the optic disc and optic cup. Manual delineation in large-scale retina screening is time consuming, cumbersome and prone to fatigue-induced errors. Assessments from different experts can be subjective with high intra-reader and inter-reader variability. Therefore, automated methods are preferred because it is efficient and reproducible.

Prior work on optic disc segmentation combine several techniques, however, they can be broadly classified as template-based, deformable models and machine learning. Template-based methods exploit the generally accepted oval-shaped structure of the optic disc as well as its color and appearance. Aquino et al. (2010) identifies a region-of-interest where the optic disc region is located within the image. Next is the extraction of the optic disc boundary from the red and green channels by means of morphological operation and edge detection. The optic disc boundaries from both channels are then approximated using the circular Hough transform. Roychowdhury et al. (2015) combine thresholding and morphological reconstruction of the red color channel with region-based features and a Gaussian mixture model classifier to identify candidate optic disc region. The candidate optic disc region having the best-fit ellipse is regarded as the segmented optic disc.

Approaches based on deformable models generally adopt a template-matching technique to localize the optic disc region, followed by the use of a deformable model for segmentation of the optic disc boundaries. Lowell et al. (Lowell et al., 2004) localizes the disc region using a template in the form of a Laplacian of Gaussian filter. Segmentation of the optic disc is based on a global elliptical model and a local deformable model. Dey et al. (2019) localize the optic disc region before the application of an affine transformation-based snake model in a gradient vector field. The gradient descent technique was used to determine the initial parameters of the affine transformation. The snake evolves to enclose the desired boundary by calculating the partial derivatives and updating the affine transformation parameters.

In the past decade, there has been growing interest in applying machine learning to the segmentation of optic disc. Lim et al. (2015) proposed the fine-net convolutional neural network architecture, a variant of full-resolution residual networks (Pohlen et al., 2017) designed for semantic segmentation. The method begins with a preprocessing stage to remove blood vessels and localize a square region around the optic disc. Thereafter, following classification by a convolutional neural network, pixel-level probability maps of the optic disc, optic cup and background are generated. The predicted optic disc and cup boundaries are obtained after postprocessing the pixel-level probability maps.

This paper proposes a new approach to segment optic disc in retinal images. Three key contributions are:
Contribution 1: The application of clustering tree that overcomes the limitations of k-means clustering for segmentation of optic disc. Clustering tree is clustering at multiple clustering resolutions (Zappia et al., 2018).
Contribution 2: We exploit the noise reducing capability of the mode filter to reduce the effect of occlusion by blood vessels within the optic disc region.
Contribution 3: Feature extraction and pooling from two color channels to optimize segmentation.

2. MATERIALS AND METHODS

This study utilize three publicly available retinal fundus images from the Indian Diabetic Retinopathy Image Dataset (IDRID) (Porval et al., 2018, https://idrid.grand-challenge.org/}, the DRISHTI-GS dataset (Sivaswamy et al., 2014, https://cvit.iiit.ac.in/projects/mip/drishti-gs/mip-dataset2/enter.php), and the MESSIDOR consortium (Klein et al, 2016, http://www.adcis.net/en/third-party/messidor/.). The IDRiD database was part of 'Diabetic Retinopathy: Segmentation and Grading Challenge' workshop at IEEE International Symposium on Biomedical Imaging (ISBI-2018). It consists of two separate sets of images. The first set has 516 images (413 training and 103 testing) with manually marked OD center and fovea location. The second set that has 81 images (54 training and 27 testing) having manually marked optic disc ground truth for both the training and testing images and dimension 4288 × 2848 pixels. In this study, we utilized the second set. The DRISHTI-GS dataset consists of 50 images with resolution 2896 × 1944 and was downloaded from GitHub website (https://github.com/seva100/optic-nerve-cnn). The MESSIDOR database consists of 1200 retinal fundus images having three different resolutions of 1140 × 960, 2240 × 1488 and 2304 × 1536. The manually segmented optic disc rim for the MESSIDOR dataset is available at (Huelva, 2012, http://www.uhu.es/retinopathy).

2.1 Methodology

The four phases in our methodology are data preparation, learning, preprocessing and algorithm design.

2.1.1 Data Preparation

All datasets were manually divided into two categories; oculus sinister (left eye) and oculus dexter (right eye). They were further divided into learning and testing data. The learning data consist of 113 oculi sinister and 113 oculi dexter. The distribution of the learning data are 16, 10 and 200 images from IDRID, DRISHTI-GS and MESSIDOR, respectively. Corresponding distribution of the testing data are 65, 40 and 1000. The ground truth of oculus sinister and oculus dexter were separately summed. The major axis length of the summed image was computed and used to build separate region-of-interest template for each category. Since images from the three publicly available databases had different resolutions, we standardize these images by cropping the region-of-interest, without loss of image resolution, to a dimension of 850 x 850.

2.1.2 Learning

In this phase, we extract and analyze features from learning data to determine the algorithm operating parameters. Five region properties of the ground truth for each learning data was computed. They are area, eccentricity, solidity, major axis length and minor axis length. Using the k-means clustering algorithm (Lloyd et al., 1982}, we partition the red and green channels of each image into k=(1,2,...,8) predefined number of clusters. For each clustered image, clusters within the optic disc region were extracted and their region properties were computed. Region properties from the ground truth and the clustered images were analyzed using histogram to determine the algorithm operating parameters displayed in Table 1.

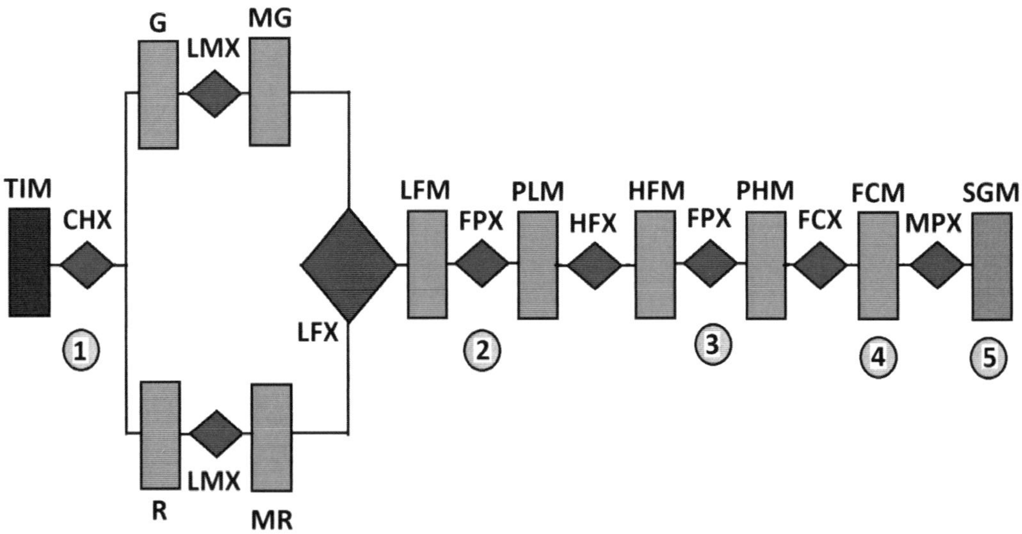

Figure 1. Flow chart of the five successive steps to implement the proposed method

Table 1. Algorithm operating parameters (in pixels) as determined from the learning phase of our methodology

Operating Parameters	**Area**	**Eccentricity**	**Solidity**	**Minor Axis Length**	**Major Axis Length**
Minimum Value	10000	0	0.3	60	60
Maximum Value	60000	0.7	1.0	300	300

For each learning data, pixel intensity levels of the red and green channels were resealed to lie between 0 and 255. Thereafter, each image was partitioned into distinct blocks of size 45 x 45. The maximum variance computed from the blocks for each image were analyzed using histogram. The minimum and maximum values of the variance are the parameters we use to scale the size of the mode filter from 7 x 7 to 45 x 45. The red and green channels typically have low and high variance, respectively.

2.1.3 Preprocessing

Our recent work (Osadebey et al., 2019) was adapted for the evaluation of contrast quality attribute in retinal images. A contrast quality score of 0.45 was fixed as the acceptable limit of quality score. Images with quality scores below the acceptable limits were enhanced by correction for illumination, using the method proposed in (Marrugo et al., 2015} to improve their quality.

2.1.4 Algorithm Design

The flow chart in Figure 1 describes the five successive steps through which the proposed method segments a typical color fundus image shown in Figure 2a to extract optic disc region shown in Figure 2f.

Step 1: Local Mode Filtering

From the image (TIM) shown in Figure 2a, we extract (CHX) the red (R) and green (G) color channels shown in Figure 2b-c, respectively. A duplicate copy of each image was partitioned into distinct blocks of size 45 x 45. Based on the maximum variance recorded from the blocks, the original red and green channel images were convolved with mode filter that varies from 7 x 7 and 45 x 45. The mode filter (LMX) was implemented using a sliding neighborhood operation. Local mode filter, like the median filter, is a nonlinear filter which reduces noise and potentially reduce occlusion by blood vessels. Figure 2d-e show the red and green color channels after filtering with a mode filter.

Step 2: Low Level Feature Extraction

The filtered red and green color channels undergo 8 successive k-means clustering operations. Figure 3b-g show low-level feature images (LFM) generated from 6 successive clustering operations, that is, k=(3,4,5,6,7,8) predefined number of clusters. In Figure 3b-g, it is evident that some pixels change clusters as the clustering resolution increases. Of a particular note is the red-colored cluster which gradually shrink in size until it stabilizes at the optic disc region. The mean pixel intensity of clusters in each feature image are sorted in ascending order. We carry out feature pooling operation (PLM) by thresholding the clustered image. The threshold is set at pixel label with maximum intensity level (in red color). This gives the pooled low-level feature image (PLM) (not displayed). The pooled features from all the clustered image is a binary image with dimension 850 x 850 x κ where κ is the clustering resolution.

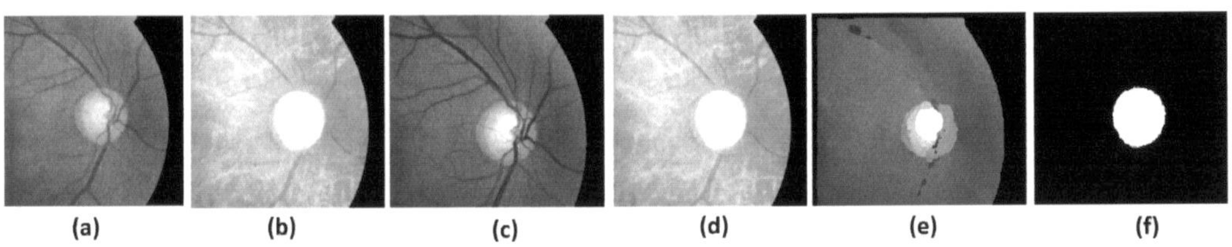

Figure 2. (a) Original color fundus image (b) Red color channel (c) Green color channel (d) Red colored channel in (b) filtered by a 7 x 7 mode filter (e) Green colored channel in (c) filtered by a 45 x 45 mode filter (f) Segmented optic disc region

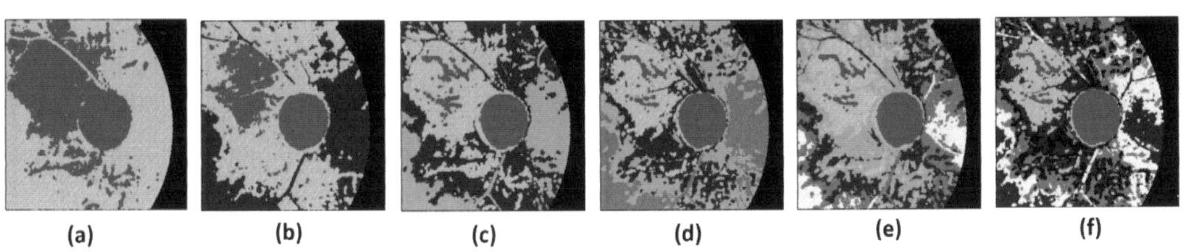

Figure 3. (a) The low-level feature images generated using k-means-based clustering tree at predefined number of clusters (a) k=3, (b) k=4, (c) k=5, (d) k=6, (e) k=7 and (f) k=8. The red-colored cluster, which describes possible optic disc location, gradually shrink in size with increasing predefined number of clusters until it stabilizes at the optic disc region

Step 3: High Level Feature Extraction

Region properties values derived during the learning phase are the thresholds we use for filtering the pooled low-level features (PLM) to extract (HFX) high-level feature image (HFM) (not displayed) that most likely contain the optic disc region. Feature pooling operation (FPX) is executed on the high-level feature image (HFM) by summing along the third dimension, resulting in a non-binary image which we refer to as pooled high level feature image (PHM) (not displayed) of dimension 850 x 850.

Step 4: Fully Connected Layer

The pooled high-level feature image from the red and green channels are fully-connected (FCX) by pixel-wise summation. Thereafter, we set a global threshold at zero-pixel intensity to obtain a binary image which we term as fully connected layer image (FCM) (not displayed).

Step 5: Segmented Object

In this final step, we eliminate false positives such as bright lesions that may have been segmented alongside the optic disc. Eccentricity region property of the fully connected layer image (FCM) is computed to extract connected component with maximum eccentricity. Thereafter, a hole filling operation (MPX) is executed to produce the segmented optic disc (SGM) shown in Figure 2f.

3. RESULTS

Table 2. Performance evaluation results recorded by proposed method and results published for four state-of-the-art algorithms on IDRID dataset. (-) indicates result not available

Metric	Dey et al. (2019)	Porval al. (2018)	Chalakkal et al. (2018)	Baid et al. (2019)	Proposed
Jaccard	0.90	0.71	0.86	-	0.91
Dice	0.94	0.80	-	0.88	0.95

Table 3. Performance evaluation results recorded by proposed method and results published for four state-of-the-art algorithms on DRISHTI-GS dataset. (-) indicates result not available

Metric	Zilly et al. (2015)	Kumar et al. (2015)	Mohan et al. (2018)	Joshi et al. (2011)	Dey et al. (2019)	Proposed
Jaccard	0.90	0.83	0.93	-	-	0.92
Dice	0.95	0.91	0.96	0.96	0.96	0.96

Table 4. Performance evaluation results recorded by proposed method and results published for eight state-of-the-art algorithms on MESSIDOR dataset

Algorithm	Morales et al. (2017)	Sigut et al. (2017)	Aquino et al. (2010)	Dey et al. (2019)	Zilly et al. (2017)	Cheng et al. (2013)	Kumar et al. (2015)	Mohan et al. (2018)	Proposed
Dice Score	0.90	0.95	0.92	0.91	0.95	0.93	0.85	0.96	0.92

Dice similarity score and Jaccard index were adopted as the performance evaluation metrics. Histogram distribution of Dice score recorded by the proposed method on IDRID, DRISHTI-GS and MESIDOR datasets are displayed in Figure 4a-c, respectively. Table 2-4 display the performance metrics recorded from the proposed method and prior contributions on IDRID, DRISHTI-GS and MESSIDOR datasets, respectively. The proposed method recorded mean Dice scores of 0.95, 0.96 and 0.92 on IDRID, DRISHTI-GS and MESSIDOR datasets, respectively. It recorded Dice score greater than 0.8 on 100 percent of the IDRID and DRISHTI-GS datasets with mean standard deviation Dice score of 0.02 and 0.06, respectively. Corresponding performance on the MESSIDOR dataset is 90 percent and mean standard deviation Dice score of 0.09. The proposed method failed to segment less than 1 percent of test data from MESSIDOR dataset (see Figure 4c). The proposed method is unique in comparison to current methods because it enhances the performance of k-means clustering technique by means of the clustering tree. Also, it exploits the noise reduction capability of the mode filter to reduce occlusions by blood vessels within the optic disc region. Furthermore, segmentation accuracy is optimized by feature extraction and pooling from the two color channels. Based on the formulation and performance of our proposed method as well as the performance evaluation results that was published from prior contributions, it is reasonable to state that the proposed method is comparable to current state-of-the-art algorithms.

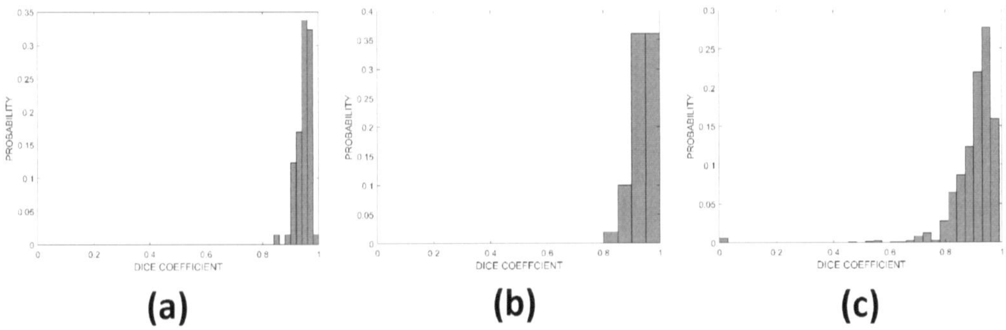

Figure 4. Histogram distribution of Dice scores recorded by the proposed method on (a) IDRID, (b) DRISHTI-GS and (c) MESSIDOR datasets

4. CONCLUSION

In this paper, we propose a new optic disc segmentation method that applies the k-means algorithm to generate a clustering tree. The clustering tree does not require the user to specify predefined number of clusters, thus it overcomes the major limitations of the k-means algorithm in automatic segmentation. The clustering tree generates low-level feature image from each color channel. The features were extracted and pooled from two color channels to optimize segmentation. The proposed method also exploits the noise reduction capability of the mode filter to suppress occlusions by blood vessels. Performance evaluation on three publicly available datasets shows that the proposed method is comparable to some state-of-the -art algorithms.

ACKNOWLEDGEMENT

This work is supported by the European Research Consortium on Informatics and Mathematics (ERCIM).

REFERENCES

Aquino, A., Gegúndez-Arias, M. E., & Marín, D. (2010). Detecting the optic disc boundary in digital fundus images using morphological, edge detection, and feature extraction techniques. *IEEE transactions on medical imaging*, *29*(11), 1860-1869.

Baid, U., Baheti, B., Dutande, P., & Talbar, S. (2019, October). Detection of Pathological Myopia and Optic Disc Segmentation with Deep Convolutional Neural Networks. In *TENCON 2019-2019 IEEE Region 10 Conference (TENCON)* (pp. 1345-1350). IEEE.

Chalakkal, R. J., Abdulla, W. H., & Thulaseedharan, S. S. (2018). Automatic detection and segmentation of optic disc and fovea in retinal images. *IET Image Processing*, *12*(11), 2100-2110.

Cheng, J., Liu, J., Xu, Y., Yin, F., Wong, D. W. K., Tan, N. M., ... & Wong, T. Y. (2013). Superpixel classification based optic disc and optic cup segmentation for glaucoma screening. *IEEE transactions on medical imaging*, *32*(6), 1019-1032.

Dey, S., Tahiliani, K., Kumar, J. H., Pediredla, A. K., & Seelamantula, C. S. (2019, May). Automatic Segmentation of Optic Disc Using Affine Snakes in Gradient Vector Field. In *ICASSP 2019-2019 IEEE International Conference on Acoustics, Speech and Signal Processing (ICASSP)* (pp. 1204-1208). IEEE.

Huelva, U. (2012). Expert system for early automated detection of OD by analysis of digital retinal images (http://www.uhu.es/retinopathy).

Joshi, G. D., Sivaswamy, J., & Krishnadas, S. R. (2011). Optic disk and cup segmentation from monocular color retinal images for glaucoma assessment. *IEEE transactions on medical imaging*, *30*(6), 1192-1205.

Klein, J. C., Menard, M., Cazuguel, G., Fernandez-Maloigne, C., Shaefer, G., Gain, P., ... & Charton, B. (2016). Methods to evaluate segmentation and indexing techniques in the field of retinal ophthalmology (MESSIDOR). *Ecole des Mines de Paris*.

Kumar, JR Harish, Aditya Kumar Pediredla, and Chandra Sekhar Seelamantula. "Active discs for automated optic disc segmentation." In *2015 IEEE global conference on signal and information processing (GlobalSIP)*, pp. 225-229. IEEE, 2015.

Lim, G., Cheng, Y., Hsu, W., & Lee, M. L. (2015, November). Integrated optic disc and cup segmentation with deep learning. In *2015 IEEE 27th International Conference on Tools with Artificial Intelligence (ICTAI)* (pp. 162-169). IEEE.

Lloyd, S. (1982). Least squares quantization in PCM. *IEEE transactions on information theory*, *28*(2), 129-137.

Lowell, J., Hunter, A., Steel, D., Basu, A., Ryder, R., Fletcher, E., & Kennedy, L. (2004). Optic nerve head segmentation. *IEEE Transactions on medical Imaging*, *23*(2), 256-264.

Marrugo, A. G., Vargas, R., Chirino, M., & Millán, M. S. (2015, December). On the illumination compensation of retinal images by means of the bidimensional empirical mode decomposition. In *11th International Symposium on Medical Information Processing and Analysis* (Vol. 9681, p. 96810D). International Society for Optics and Photonics.

Mohan, D., Kumar, J. H., & Seelamantula, C. S. (2018, October). High-performance optic disc segmentation using convolutional neural networks. In *2018 25th IEEE International Conference on Image Processing (ICIP)* (pp. 4038-4042). IEEE.

Morales, S., Naranjo, V., Angulo, J., & Alcañiz, M. (2013). Automatic detection of optic disc based on PCA and mathematical morphology. *IEEE transactions on medical imaging*, *32*(4), 786-796.

Osadebey, M., Pedersen, M., Arnold, D., & Wendel-Mitoraj, K. (2019). Local Indicators of Spatial Autocorrelation (LISA): Application to Blind Noise-Based Perceptual Quality Metric Index for Magnetic Resonance Images. *Journal of Imaging*, *5*(1), 20.

Pohlen, T., Hermans, A., Mathias, M., & Leibe, B. (2017). Full-resolution residual networks for semantic segmentation in street scenes. In *Proceedings of the IEEE Conference on Computer Vision and Pattern Recognition* (pp. 4151-4160).

Porwal, P., Pachade, S., Kadethankar, A., Joshi, A., Patwardhan, V., Kamble, R., ... & Meriaudeau, F. (2018, August). Automatic segmentation of optic disc by gradient minimization based approach. In *2018 International Conference on Intelligent and Advanced System (ICIAS)* (pp. 1-5). IEEE.

Porwal, P., Pachade, S., Kamble, R., Kokare, M., Deshmukh, G., Sahasrabuddhe, V., & Meriaudeau, F. (2018). Indian diabetic retinopathy image dataset (IDRiD): a database for diabetic retinopathy screening research. *Data*, *3*(3), 25.

Roychowdhury, S., Koozekanani, D. D., Kuchinka, S. N., & Parhi, K. K. (2015). Optic disc boundary and vessel origin segmentation of fundus images. *IEEE journal of biomedical and health informatics*, *20*(6), 1562-1574.

Sigut, J., Nunez, O., Fumero, F., Gonzalez, M., & Arnay, R. (2017). Contrast based circular approximation for accurate and robust optic disc segmentation in retinal images. *PeerJ*, *5*, e3763.

Sivaswamy, J., Krishnadas, S. R., Joshi, G. D., Jain, M., & Tabish, A. U. S. (2014, April). Drishti-gs: Retinal image dataset for optic nerve head (onh) segmentation. In *2014 IEEE 11th international symposium on biomedical imaging (ISBI)* (pp. 53-56). IEEE.

Zappia, L., & Oshlack, A. (2018). Clustering trees: a visualization for evaluating clusterings at multiple resolutions. *GigaScience*, *7*(7), giy083.

Zilly, J., Buhmann, J. M., & Mahapatra, D. (2017). Glaucoma detection using entropy sampling and ensemble learning for automatic optic cup and disc segmentation. *Computerized Medical Imaging and Graphics*, *55*, 28-41.

Zilly, J. G., Buhmann, J. M., & Mahapatra, D. (2015, October). Boosting convolutional filters with entropy sampling for optic cup and disc image segmentation from fundus images. In *International workshop on machine learning in medical imaging* (pp. 136-143). Springer, Cham.

REMOTE SENSING CLASSIFICATION USING MULTI-SENSOR SUPER-RESOLUTION ALGORITHM

Alexander Belov and Anna Denisova
Samara National Research University
34, Moskovskoye shosse, Samara, 443086, Russia

ABSTRACT

Super-resolution image fusion aims to produce an image with finer spectral and spatial details than the input images. However, the super-resolution fusion is mainly applied to enhance a visual representation of the images and its potential benefits to the final thematic classification is an open question. In this paper, we present an experimental investigation of the remote sensing image classification performance in the case of the multi-sensor super-resolution image fusion. The research aims to compare classification performance obtained for the fused image and the low resolution input ones using different standard-of-the-art classifiers and feature extraction methods. Input data are supposed to be multispectral data obtained in visible and near infrared spectral ranges by the different remote sensing systems. To perform a multi-sensor super-resolution image fusion, we used a gradient-descent optimization approach with a B-TV regularization successfully adapted for remote sensing images with different spatial and spectral sampling characteristics by the authors of the paper. As for features, we applied brightness in spectral channels, attribute profiles and local feature attribute profiles. The classification was performed using support vector machines and random forest classifiers that have been proved to be very effective for remote sensing data classification. The experimental research included the multi-sensor input data simulation for four remote sensing systems, the super-resolution image fusion of all simulated images and the thematic classification of the fused image and the images obtained as an average input for each of the simulated imaging systems. The spatial resolution of the fused image was in 2, 3, 4 and 5 times better than the spatial resolution of the modeled input images. The average bandwidth of the fused image was 29 nm whereas for the input low resolution images it was in the range from 37 to 83 nm. Experimental results have shown that random forest classification is better to use with fusion, whereas support vector machines demonstrated better results without fusion. The feature extraction test showed that extended attribute profiles enhance the random forest classification accuracy of the fused image. Thus, the classification results have shown that super-resolution image fusion leads to the classification accuracy increase in the case of random forest classifier and there is no need to apply fusion in the case of support vector machines.

KEYWORDS

Image Classification, Data Fusion, Super-Resolution, SVM, RF

1. INTRODUCTION

Remote sensing data fusion aims to enhance image quality in terms of spectral, temporal or spatial resolution. Among all super-resolution fusion algorithms, the most prominent algorithms seem to be spectral-spatial super-resolution algorithms which enhance both spectral and spatial resolution of the images simultaneously. Despite the evident visual enhancement of the images caused by spectral-spatial super-resolution algorithms, the potential effect on the image classification remains an open question. Therefore, our study aims to assess classification quality after spectral-spatial super-resolution.

In our study, we applied our own spectral-spatial super-resolution algorithm. The algorithm provides super-resolution image fusion in multi-frame case when input low resolution images (LR images) are supposed to be captured by different remote sensing systems with the different spectral and spatial sampling parameters (Belov and Denisova, 2018). The algorithm finds the estimate of the high resolution image (HR image) using the predefined spatial and spectral sampling parameters. We estimated the classification quality of the fused image using two well-known classifiers: Support Vector Machines with Radial Basis Functions (SVM-RBF) and Random Forest (RF). As shown in papers (Tuia et al.,2014; Belgiu and Drăguţ, 2016; Li et al.,2016; Khatami et al., 2016; García et al., 2019; Liao et al., 2015), these classifiers are the most frequently used for remote sensing data especially in the case of small training sets. As for features, we regarded brightness in spectral channels and two additional comprehensive feature extraction methods: Extended Attribute Profiles (EAP) and Local Feature Attribute Profiles (LFAP). The latter two feature extraction methods were effectively applied in remote sensing data analysis in papers (Pham et al., 2017; Pham, Aptoula and Lefèvre, 2018; Pham et al., 2018; Hong et al., 2020).

The goal of our experimental research was to answer the question whether the super-resolution image fusion is able to enhance image classification. We made our experimental research using simulated remote sensing data of four different remote sensing systems. The data for all of the four systems were used in the fusion process with the predefined parameters of the output spectral and spatial resolution. As a result, we assessed the classification quality in two cases for the fused image and for average input images of each system.

The rest of the paper is organized in the following way. Section 2 provides a description of our super-resolution image fusion algorithm. Section 3 describes the data simulation process. Section 4 contains a fusion parameters description and classification description. Section 5 concerns the experimental results.

2. SPECTRAL-SPATIAL SUPER-RESOLUTION IMAGE FUSION ALGORITHM

The described fusion algorithm was proposed in (Belov and Denisova, 2018) and it develops the ideas of the spatial super-resolution of the color images introduced by Fausiu et al. in (Farsiu et al., 2004, Farsiu et al. 2003). In contrast to the algorithms proposed in (Farsiu et al., 2004, Farsiu et al. 2003), our algorithm provides spectral resolution enhancement as well as the spatial one. In this paper, the spectral resolution is defined by the number of spectral channels and their average bandwidth.

The algorithm exploits the following observation model to describe the relation between input LR images and the reference HR image:

$$Y_{k\xi l} = D_k F_{k\xi} H_k \left(\sum_{\lambda=1}^{L} w_{kl}(\lambda) X_\lambda \right) + V_{k\xi l}, \tag{1}$$

$$k = 1,...,K,\ l = 1,...,L_k,\ \xi = 1,...,\xi_k,$$

where X_λ is the λ-th spectral channel of the reference HR image, $Y_{k\xi l}$ is the l-th spectral channel of the ξ-th LR image obtained by the k-th imaging system, $w_{k\xi}(\lambda)$ are the coefficients of the spectral transformation from L-channel reference spectral representation into L_k-th observed spectral representation of the k-th imaging system. Operator H_k defines an optical blur for the k-th system. Operator $F_{k\xi}$ is a frame geometry and frame motion transformation caused by the georeferencing errors. $F_{k\xi}$ is defined relatively to the reference frame position corresponding to the HR image X_λ. The operator D_k is the uniform sampling with averaging over the square are $T_k \times T_k$ where T_k is a ground sampling distance (GSD). The operators H_k, $F_{k\xi}$ and D_k are supposed to be linear and finite. $V_{k\xi l}$ is the Gaussian white noise in the l-th spectral channel of the image $Y_{k\xi}$. It is assumed that the GSD of the reference HR image is less than the GSDs of the input LR images $T < T_k, k = 1,...,K$, and the reference number of spectral channels is larger than the maximum channel number of the input LR images $L \geq \max\limits_{k=1,...,K}(L_k)$.

The fusion algorithm provides a gradient descent optimization of the following task:

$$\hat{X} = \arg\min_X \left\{ \sum_{k=1}^{K} \sum_{l=1}^{L_k} \left\| \frac{1}{\xi_k} \sum_{\xi=1}^{\xi_k} F_{k\xi}^{-1} I_k \sum_{\lambda=1}^{L} w_{kl}(\lambda) D_k H_k F_{k\xi} X_\lambda - Z_{kl} \right\|_1 + \beta \sum_{i=-p}^{p} \sum_{j=-p}^{p} \alpha^{|i|+|j|} \left\| X_L - S_1^i S_2^j X_L \right\|_1 \right\}, \tag{2}$$

$$Z_{kl} = \frac{1}{\xi_k} \sum_{\xi=1}^{\xi k} F_{k\xi}^{-1} I_k \left(Y_{k\xi l} \right), k = 1,...,K, l = 1,...,L_k, \tag{3}$$

where Z_{kl} is the l-th spectral channel of the average image Z_k for the k-th imaging system, I_k is the interpolation operator with the sampling step T/T_k, $F_{k\xi}^{-1}$ is the inverse operator of the frame geometry and frame motion transformation of the ξ-th observed image for the k-th imaging system. Both operators I_k and $F_{k\xi}^{-1}$ are assumed to be linear. Parameters p,α,β determine the weights of the B-TV regularization term.

The optimization task (2) is solved using the gradient descent method and results in the estimate $\hat{X}$ of the reference image with the sampling parameters T, L.

3. DATA SIMULATION

Experimental research was conducted using simulated data of four different imaging systems. We used 10 fragments of hyperspectral images as source data for simulation. All image fragments were derived from the images of the Hyperspectral scenes dataset (Graña et al., 2020) which have ground truth information. The source hyperspectral image fragments are described in Table 1.

Table 1. Hyperspectral image fragments used for simulation

Name	Size	Number of classes	Spectral range, nm
Botswana-1	240×240	6	447,17-1057,68
Botswana-2	240×240	5	447,17-1057,68
Pavia-1	420×420	8	430-808,75
Pavia-2	420×420	6	430-808,75
Pavia-3	420×420	5	430-808,75
PaviaU-1	240×240	6	430-812,5
PaviaU-2	240×240	8	430-812,5
PaviaU-3	240×240	8	430-812,5
Salinas-1	180×180	8	365,93-1262,96
Salinas-2	180×180	8	365,93-1262,96

The hyperspectral image fragments were used for the reference multispectral HR image simulation X and for the observed LR image $Y_{k\xi}, k = 1,...,4, \xi = 1,...,\xi_k$ simulation according to the observation model (1).

Spectral channels of the simulated images were determined using Gaussian spectral response function (SRF) $W_l(u)$ with the full width at half maximum (FWHM) and central wavelength u_l^0 parameters:

$$W_l(u) = \delta_l^{-1}(2\pi)^{-1/2}\exp\left\{-0.5\left(u-u_l^0\right)^2/\delta_l^2\right\}, \tag{4}$$

where $FWHM = 2\sqrt{2\ln(2)}\delta_l$ and l is the number of spectral channel.

Without loss of generality, we assumed that the GSD of the HR image is the same as the GSD of the hyperspectral image fragment and it is equal to $T = 1$. The number of spectral channels of the reference HR image was L=15 for all images except Pavia and PaviaU images for which it was L=11. The parameters of the spectral channels of the reference HR image are shown in Table 2.

Table 2. Parameters of the reference image spectral channels

№	1	2	3	4	5	6	7	8	9	10	11	*12*	*13*	*14*	*15*
u_l	463	492	521	550	580	609	638	665	694	724	753	*782*	*812*	*841*	*870*
FWHM	29	29	29	29	29	29	29	29	29	29	29	*29*	*30*	*30*	*30*

The GSDs T_k of four imaging systems were 2, 3, 4 and 5 correspondingly. The spectral channel configuration for the LR images was selected as spectral channels of four different real remote sensing systems: Geoton (Resurs-P), Spot-7, Kanopus-B and Sentinel-2A. Table 3 shows the parameters of the spectral channels for simulated imaging systems.

Table 3. Parameters of spectral channels for simulated imaging systems

№	k=1		k=2		k=3		k=4	
	u_0	FWHM	u_0	FWHM	u_0	FWHM	u_0	FWHM
1	485	70	490	70	490	30	490	65
2	560	80	560	60	555	45	560	35
3	645	70	660	70	660	30	665	30
4	685	30	*825*	*130*	*795*	*45*	705	15
5	715	30	–	–	–	–	740	15
6	750	100	–	–	–	–	783	20
7	–	–	–	–	–	–	*842*	*115*
8	–	–	–	–	–	–	*865*	*20*

Since the hyperspectral image fragments for images Pavia and PaviaU had smaller spectral range, the simulation for these images was made without spectral channels typed with an italic font in tables 2 and 3.

The reference HR image was generated as a result of spectral sampling of the hyperspectral image fragment.

LR images were generated according to the model (1). The coefficients of the spectral transformation for k-th imaging system were determined according to Gaussian SRFs (4) in the following way:

$$w_{kl}(\lambda) = \int_{\zeta_1(\lambda)}^{\zeta_2(\lambda)} W_{kl}(u)du \Bigg/ \int_{-\infty}^{+\infty} W_{kl}(u)du, \qquad (5)$$

where λ is the number of reference spectral channel, l is the number of channel for the k-th system, $\zeta_1(\lambda) = u_{kl}^0 - FWHM$, $\zeta_2(\lambda) = u_{kl}^0 + FWHM$.

The frame geometry and frame motion operator $F_{k\xi}$ was determined as a transient shift on $\chi_{\xi 1}$ and $\chi_{\xi 2}$ pixels in the horizontal and vertical directions:

$$X_{k\xi}^F(n_1,n_2,l) = F_{k\xi}\left(X_k^W(n_1,n_2,l)\right) = X_k^W(n_1+\chi_{\xi 1}, n_2+\chi_{\xi 2}, l). \qquad (6)$$

Operator H_k was defined as:

$$X_{k\xi}^H(n_1,n_2,l) = H_k\left(X_{k\xi}^F(n_1,n_2,l)\right) = \sum_{\tau_1=-\Delta k}^{\Delta k} \sum_{\tau_2=-\Delta k}^{\Delta k} h(\tau_1,\tau_2) X_{k\xi}^F(n_1-\tau_1, n_2-\tau_2, l), \qquad (7)$$

where $h(\tau_1,\tau_2) = A\exp\left(-0.5\sigma_k^{-2}\left(\tau_1^2+\tau_2^2\right)\right)$ is an impulse response of the Gaussian blur with radius σ_k.

The spatial sampling D_k was defined as two sequential operators of averaging D_1 and decimation D_2:

$$X_{k\xi}^{D1}(n_1,n_2,l) = D_{k1}\left(X_{k\xi}^H(n_1,n_2,l)\right) = \frac{1}{T_k^2} \sum_{\tau_1=-\lceil Tk/2 \rceil}^{\lceil Tk/2 \rceil} \sum_{\tau_2=-\lceil Tk/2 \rceil}^{\lceil Tk/2 \rceil} X_{k\xi}^H(n_1-\tau_1, n_2-\tau_2, l),$$

$$X_{k\xi}^{D2}(m_1,m_2,l) = D_{k2}\left(X_{k\xi}^{D1}(n_1,n_2,l)\right) = X_{k\xi}^{D1}(n_1,n_2,l)\Big|_{\substack{n_1=m_1T_k \\ n_2=m_2T_k}}. \qquad (8)$$

Table 4 contains parameters of spatial distortions for each of the simulated imaging systems.

Table 4. Spatial distortions parameters for the simulated imaging systems

Parameter	*k=1*	*k=2*	*k=3*	*k=4*
$\chi_{\xi 1}, \chi_{\xi 3}$	[-2,2]	[-3,3]	[-4,4]	[-5,5]
σ_k	5	7	9	11
T_k	2	3	4	5

The examples of the reference multispectral HR images are shown in Figure 1.

a) b) c) d)

Figure 1. The examples of the reference multispectral HR images: a) Botswana-1, b) Pavia-1, c) PaviaU-1, d) Salinas-1

4. FUSION AND CLASSIFICATION PARAMETERS

The fusion was carried out using the algorithm (Belov and Denisova, 2018) with the following regularization parameters: $\alpha_k = 0.1$, $p = 2$ and $\beta = 0.5$. The number of gradient descent method iterations was equal to 280. The step of the gradient descent process was 20.

We used the images of four systems for fusion. The number of the observed images for each imaging system was determined according to the rule of the optimal multi-frame image super-resolution (Farsiu et al., 2003) and it was equal to 4, 9, 16, 25 for the system 1, system 2, system 3 and system 4 correspondingly, the examples of fusion result and average input images for each system are shown in Figure 2.

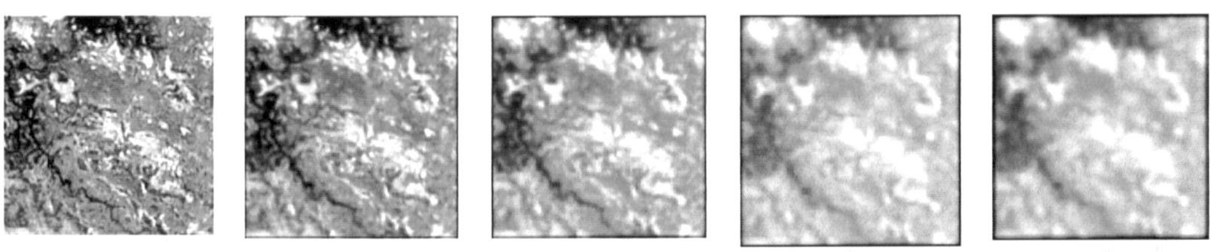

a) b) c) d) e)

Figure 2. The examples of: a) fusion result, b) average image for system 1, c) average image for system 2, d) average image for system 3, e) average image for system 4

To make the fused image and average images for each system comparable, we made the following kind of preprocessing. The input LR images for each of the K systems were transformed into average images Z_k using formula (3). For this purpose, we applied nearest neighbor interpolation and inverse frame motion operator with zero padding. Due to the zero padding, the images Z_k contained the lower values of pixels along the borders. Therefore, to make fused and average images comparable we reduced the size of all images in such a way that there were no incorrect border pixels in average images for each of the imaging systems.

The reference classification masks were divided into training and control sets with the ratio 7:3. The maximum number of pixels per class was equal to 15. The examples of the reference classification masks are shown in Figure 3.

Classification and feature extraction were performed using Matlab packages developed in studies (Marpu et al., 2013; Li et al., 2015). The SVM and RF algorithms were used with default parameters.

Classification accuracy was measured using the probability of true classification P that is defined as the ratio of correctly classified pixels to the total number of pixels in the test set. Further, we use average P value for 5 runs of the classification.

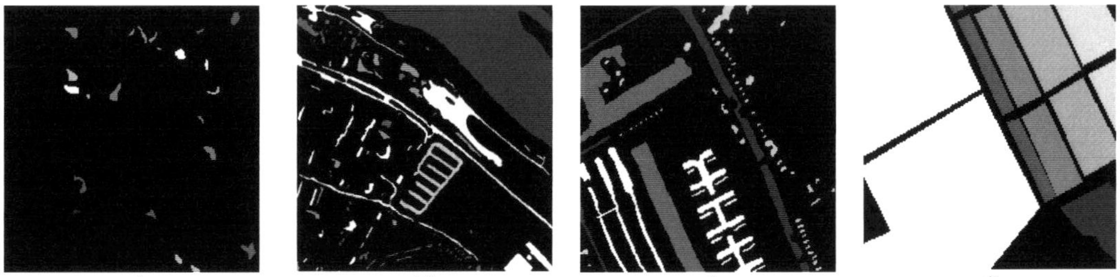

a) b) c) d)

Figure 3. Examples of the reference classification masks for images: a) Botswana-1, b) Pavia-1, c) PaviaU-1, d) Salinas-1. Black color is used for data without class label

5. EXPERIMENTAL RESULTS

5.1 Estimation of Fusion Influence on Classification Quality

To estimate how the fusion affects classification quality, we classified the fused image and average interpolated input LR images Z_k for each imaging system. The classification results for SVM and RF algorithms are shown in tables 5 and 6 correspondingly.

The data in table 5 show that for the SVM algorithm, the classification accuracy of the fused image was slightly worse than the classification accuracy of the average images for each system. The fusion results were classified with the average accuracy of 76.16, whereas for the system 1 and system 2, the classification accuracy was equal to 78 and 76.56 correspondingly. Thus, the smoother representation obtained after interpolation and averaging is better for SVM than a more detailed representation of the fused image.

Table 6 demonstrates that for the RF classification, the average classification accuracy of the fused image is higher than the accuracy of the images for each imaging system in 90% of the cases. Since system 1 had the smallest difference in spatial resolution with the fusion results, the results of system 1 image classification are the closest to the fused image classification results. Nevertheless, the classification accuracy of the fusion result was 4% higher than the classification accuracy of the system 1 image. Thus, the super-resolution fusion enhances the performance of the RF classifier.

Table 5. Accuracy of SVM classification

Image	**Fusion result**	**system 1**	**system 2**	**system 3**	**system 4**	**Reference image**
Botswana-1	89.84	**89.87**	77.11	78.98	79.33	87.18
Botswana-2	75.51	73.25	**82.75**	75.71	73.22	87.68
Pavia-1	71.74	76.43	**76.93**	69.84	60.90	82.44
Pavia-2	63.44	70.08	**76.62**	70.05	65.68	77.30
Pavia-3	77.44	85.19	**85.33**	77.93	53.10	78.54
PaviaU-1	79.71	78.83	**81.58**	75.48	63.54	74.88
PaviaU-2	63.61	66.67	57.02	**67.58**	62.82	69.00
PaviaU-3	**70.25**	66.55	59.24	65.16	65.79	70.59
Salinas-1	80.16	**83.26**	75.16	81.34	78.56	83.14
Salinas-2	89.92	89.84	**93.83**	92.83	91.75	90.90
Total average	**76.16**	**78.00**	**76.56**	**75.49**	**69.47**	**80.17**

Table 6. Accuracy of RF classification

Image	Fusion result	system 1	system 2	system 3	system 4	Reference image
Botswana-1	**85.85**	79.08	71.46	74.40	68.45	83.97
Botswana-2	**86.43**	81.64	86.44	82.74	86.17	81.82
Pavia-1	**81.35**	79.02	77.95	80.76	78.85	79.47
Pavia-2	**82.27**	74.72	79.53	77.16	74.35	84.17
Pavia-3	**86.37**	83.35	78.63	81.63	75.13	85.08
PaviaU-1	81.84	**85.01**	78.91	79.39	74.87	90.42
PaviaU-2	**64.25**	61.95	48.46	56.17	53.24	64.09
PaviaU-3	**72.80**	68.94	54.04	60.87	59.02	70.72
Salinas-1	**83.41**	81.58	80.13	77.24	77.92	85.17
Salinas-2	**88.41**	87.63	83.54	85.48	85.09	88.89
Total average	**81.30**	**78.29**	**73.91**	**75.58**	**73.31**	**81.38**

Overall, the results of the fusion with RF classification were better than the ones for SVM classifier. The average classification accuracy of the fused image with RF classifier was 81.3 in comparison with the best average classification accuracy of the SVM method equal to 78.

5.2 The Influence of Feature Extraction Methods on the Fused Image Classification

The experimental research of the feature extraction methods was performed only for RF classification of the fused image. The following feature extraction methods were considered:

1) Brightness in spectral channels,
2) Extended Attribute Profiles (EAP) (Pham et al., 2018),
3) Local Feature Attribute profiles (LFAP) (Pham et al., 2017).

EAP is constructed using different attribute filters applied to each spectral channel of the image. Attribute filters are the generalization of morphological filters with the appropriate criterion function of the connected components of the image. The threshold values of the criterion define a set of attribute filters. For example, the area attribute filter with the predefined threshold removes all connected components of the image having the area smaller than the threshold.

LFAP is formed from EAP by means of additional local filtration of EAP features. According to paper (Pham et al., 2017), both methods are very effective for hyperspectral remote sensing images. In (Pham et al., 2017) it was also considered the case of dimension reduction methods because hyperspectral images have hundreds of spectral channels. In our case, the fusion result is a multispectral image and there is no need for dimension reduction. We calculated EAP and LFAP for spectral brightness values of the fused image. We used EAP features proposed in (Pham et al., 2017) for the classification of Pavia University image (Graña et al., 2020). The EAP feature description is given in Table 7.

Table 7. The parameters of the EAP

Attribute	Threshold
Square	100, 500, 1000, 5000
Standard deviation	20, 30, 40, 50
Moment of inertia	0.2, 0.3, 0.4, 0.5
Diagonal	10, 25, 50, 100

As for LFAP features, we computed them from the EAP using local average and local range filers with the window size equal to 7×7.

The RF classification results using different feature extraction methods are shown in Table 8.

Table 8. RF classification accuracy using different feature extraction methods

Image	EAP	brightness	LFAP
Botswana-1	82.04	**83.55**	78.07
Botswana-2	**95.11**	86.49	85.48
Pavia-1	**84.11**	80.33	80.21
Pavia-2	**90.03**	84.31	77.24
Pavia-3	**96.46**	77.23	81.43
PaviaU-1	**91.51**	86.63	80.94
PaviaU-2	**68.50**	63.11	60.53
PaviaU-3	**79.88**	68.01	74.76
Salinas-1	**92.84**	83.23	82.25
Salinas-2	**94.41**	90.94	88.26
Total average	**87.49**	**80.38**	**78.92**

The best choice for the RF algorithm is EAP features. The classification accuracy of the fused image using EAP is from 70 to 95 % and it is higher on 9% than in the case without EAP. LFAP does not increase classification accuracy in comparison to the brightness features.

Thus, it can be concluded that RF classification of the fused image is more effective if the EAP features are used.

The examples of the RF classification with fusion and without fusion are shown in figures 4-7 correspondingly.

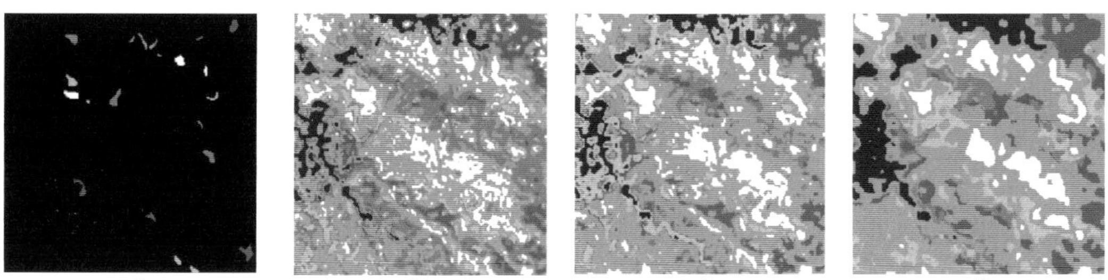

a) b) c) d)

Figure 4. Reference classification mask (a) and examples of the RF classification results for Botswana-1: b) fused image classification, c) system 1 classification, d) system 3 classification

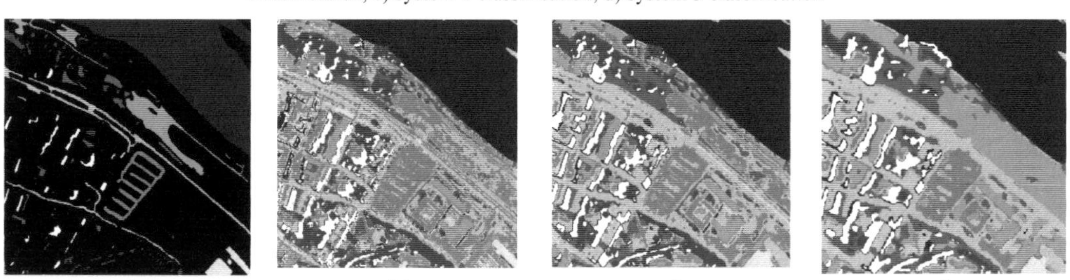

a) b) c) d)

Figure 5. Reference classification mask (a) and examples of the RF classification results for Pavia-1: b) fused image classification, c) system 1 classification, d) system 3 classification

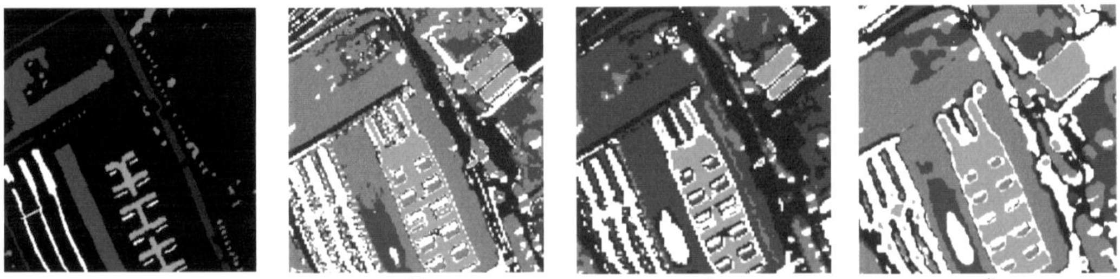

a) b) c) d)

Figure 6. Reference classification mask (a) and examples of the RF classification results for PaviaU-1: b) fused image classification, c) system 1 classification, d) system 3 classification

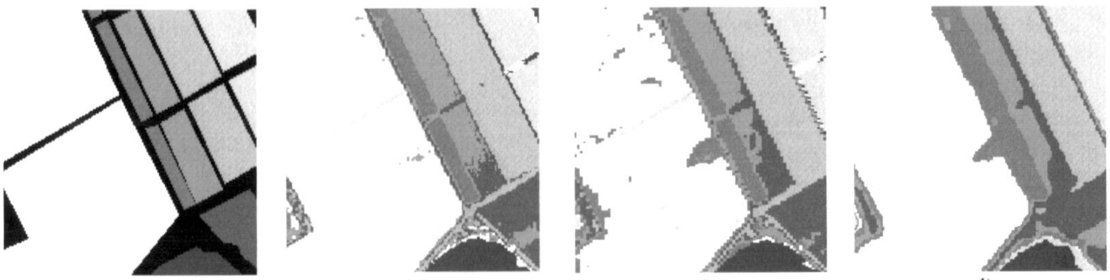

a) b) c) d)

Figure 7. Reference classification mask (a) and examples of the RF classification results for Salinas-1: b) fused image classification, c) system 1 classification, d) system 3 classification

Thus, super-resolution image fusion enhances the results of RF classification whereas SVM classification is better to use without fusion. The reason for this is that SVM performs better on the smother images whereas RF needs extra spatial and spectral details for better performance.

6. CONCLUSION

The paper concerns the question of the spectral-spatial super-resolution image fusion influence on the classification of remote sensing images. The experiments were conducted for simulated remote sensing images of four imaging systems with GSDs in 2, 3, 4 and 5 times larger than the GSD of the fused image. The fused image included 11 or 15 spectral channels with the average bandwidth of 29 nm according to the spectral ranges of the input images. Spectral channels of the simulated low resolution images included from 3 to 8 spectral channels with average bandwidth from 37 nm to 83 nm. Our experimental research showed that SVM classification is better to apply without fusion because the SVM performance for the smooth interpolated images is better than for the fusion result which has more detailed image representation. In contrast to SVM, RF classification of the fused image produces in 90% of the cases better results than without fusion. For example, for the image with spatial resolution two times worse than the spatial resolution of the fused image, the classification accuracy of the fused image was 4% higher. The classification results obtained for RF classifier with fusion are better than the classification results for SVM without fusion. In particularly, the average classification accuracy for the fusion with RF classification was 81.3 whereas the best classification accuracy of SVM without fusion was 78. The experiment with different feature extraction methods showed that extended attribute profiles are preferable for RF classification with fusion. The accuracy of the fused image classification with RF algorithm and EAP were on 9% higher than in the case of brightness features.

Thus, the best classification is obtained for the RF classifier with fusion whereas there is no need to apply fusion with SVM algorithm.

ACKNOWLEDGEMENT

The research was supported by RFBR project №18-07-00748.

REFERENCES

Belgiu, M. and Drăguţ, L., 2016. "Random forest in remote sensing: A review of applications and future directions" ISPRS Journal of Photogrammetry and Remote Sensing, vol. 114, pp. 24-31.

Belov, A.M. and Denisova, A.Y., 2018. "Spectral and spatial super-resolution method for Earth remote sensing image fusion" Computer Optics, vol. 42, pp. 855-863.

Farsiu, S., Robinson, M.D., Elad, M. and Milanfar, P., 2003. "Fast and robust super-resolution" Proceedings of the 2003 International Conference on Image Processing, vol. 3, pp. 291-294.

Farsiu, S., Robinson, M.D., Elad, M. and Milanfar, P., 2004. "Fast and robust multiframe super resolution" IEEE Transactions on Image Processing, vol. 13, pp. 1327-1344.

García, M.A., Moutahir, H., Casady, G.M., Bautista, S. and Rodríguez, F., 2019. "Using Hidden Markov Models for Land Surface Phenology: An Evaluation Across a Range of Land Cover Types in Southeast Spain" Remote Sensing, vol.11, No.5.

Graña, M., Veganzons, M.A. and Ayerdi, B. 2020. "Hyperspectral Remote Sensing Scenes", available at http://www.ehu.eus/ccwintco/index.php?title=Hyperspectral_Remote_Sensing_Scenes

Hong, D., Wu, X., Ghamisi, P., Chanussot, J., Yokoya, N. and Zhu, X.X., 2020. "Invariant attribute profiles: A spatial-frequency joint feature extractor for hyperspectral image classification" IEEE Transactions on Geoscience and Remote Sensing, pp. 1-18.

Khatami, R., Mountrakis, G. and Stehman, S.V., 2016. "A meta-analysis of remote sensing research on supervised pixel-based land-cover image classification processes: General guidelines for practitioners and future research" Remote Sensing of Environment, vol.177, pp. 89-100.

Li, J., Huang, X., Gamba, P., Bioucas-Dias, J.M., Zhang, L., Benediktsson, J.A. and Plaza, A. 2015. "Multiple Feature Learning for Hyperspectral Image Classification" IEEE Transactions on Geoscience and Remote Sensing, vol. 53, pp. 1592-1606.

Li, M., Ma, L., Blaschke, T., Cheng, L. and Tiede, D., 2016. "A systematic comparison of different object-based classification techniques using high spatial resolution imagery in agricultural environments" International Journal of Applied Earth Observation and Geoinformation, vol. 49, pp. 87-98.

Liao, W., Dalla Mura, M., Chanussot, J. and Pižurica, A., 2015. "Fusion of spectral and spatial information for classification of hyperspectral remote-sensed imagery by local graph" IEEE Journal of Selected Topics in Applied Earth Observations and Remote Sensing, vol. 9, pp. 583-594.

Marpu, P.R., Pedergnana, M., Dalla Mura, M., Benediktsson, J.A. and Bruzzone, L., 2013. "Automatic Generation of Standard Deviation Attribute Profiles for Spectral-Spatial Classification of Remote Sensing Data" Geoscience and Remote Sensing Letters, vol. 10, pp. 293-297.

Pham, M.T., Aptoula, E., and Lefèvre, S., 2018. "Classification of remote sensing images using attribute profiles and feature profiles from different trees: a comparative study" IGARSS 2018-2018 IEEE International Geoscience and Remote Sensing Symposium, pp. 4511-4514.

Pham, M.T., Lefèvre, S., and Aptoula, E., 2017. "Local feature-based attribute profiles for optical remote sensing image classification" IEEE Transactions on Geoscience and Remote Sensing, vol. 56, pp. 1199-1212.

Pham, M.T., Lefèvre, S., Aptoula, E. and Bruzzone, L., 2018. "Recent developments from attribute profiles for remote sensing image classification" arXiv preprint arXiv:1803.10036 2018.

Tuia, D., Volpi, M., Dalla Mura, M., Rakotomamonjy, A. and Flamary, R., 2014. "Automatic feature learning for spatio-spectral image classification with sparse SVM" IEEE Transactions on Geoscience and Remote Sensing, vol. 52, pp. 6062-6074.

IMPROVING DEEP MATRIX FACTORIZATION WITH NORMALIZED CROSS ENTROPY LOSS FUNCTION FOR GRAPH-BASED MOOC RECOMMENDATION

Thanh Le, Vinh Vo, Khai Nguyen and Bac Le
Department of Computer Science, Faculty of Information Technology, University of Science, Ho Chi Minh City, Vietnam
Vietnam National University, Ho Chi Minh City, Vietnam

ABSTRACT

Nowadays, with the fast growth of the Internet, the useful role of learning online is getting increasingly popular. MOOC platforms such as Coursera, Edx, Udemy, etc. are attracting many students from all over the world, with thousands of courses constantly continually being opened and updated. This raises the question of how to suggest courses that learners are interested in. To tackle this problem, we apply the Deep matrix Factorization model to the course suggestion along with the improved loss function. The experiment shows that our course recommendation system achieves better NDCG for top K courses than other methods. And the loss function has improved in NDCG measurement compared to the original DMF model.

KEYWORDS

MOOCs, Recommendation, Deep Matrix Factorization, Graph

1. INTRODUCTION

The recommendation system has gone through three decades of development across many fields, and today the most successful models are using deep learning because of having higher accuracy. In the Fourth Industrial Revolution, online learning became an indispensable need for students who yearn for knowledge, so MOOC platforms such as Coursera[1], Edx[2], Khan Academy[3], etc. contain thousands of courses and millions of students. The rapid increase in the number of courses on MOOCs poses a problem of how to choose the right course for learners themselves.

According to our survey, the current research on the recommendation system for MOOCs as well as its quality is not sufficiently high due to the complexity of assessing user knowledge and the continuity in the process. A good recommendation system enables learners to study more effectively. In 2016, (Jdidou & Khaldi, 2016) and in 2018, (Jdidou & Khaldi, 2018) showed that the course recommendation system would optimize students' profitability. (Yanhui et al., 2015) mentioned that 87.3% of the respondents were satisfied with the effectiveness of a course recommendation system. Furthermore, course recommendation systems have been developed to increase the completion rates of students (Labarthe et al., 2016).

Data from MOOCs is often the course name, content, as well as student information, etc. One person can study many different courses. From there, we can simulate in the form of knowledge graphs in which users, courses, etc. will be the vertices of the graph and the edge will be a relationship such as learning, voting, etc. This graph will get bigger and more complex as more courses are created and the number of learners grows. Recommending a suitable course for a specific user will be complicated both in time and accuracy. Because data can be represented in the form of knowledge graphs, we surveyed approaches in knowledge graph mining and combined them with collaborative filtering methods in the recommendation system.

Deep learning has exploded in recent years and has been applied in many fields (Salakhutdinov et al., 2007). In 2007, (Salakhutdinov et al., 2007) proposed a Restricted Boltzmann Machine model called RBM-CF, which

[1] https://www.coursera.org/
[2] https://www.edx.org/
[3] https://www.khanacademy.org/

was the first deep learning model used in the recommender system to bring higher results than the classical method, This model has a simple structure with only one hidden layer. (Elkahky et al., 2015) developed the MV-DNN model by combining multiple Deep Structured Semantic Model (DSSM) models to take advantage of common information across regions. (Kim et al., 2016) integrated convolution matrix factorization into probability matrix factorization (PMF) in the contextual analysis of the learners. (Tan et al., 2016) improved the RNN network by enhancing data to directly predict item embedding. (Y. Wu et al., 2016) suggested a Collaborative Denoising Autoencoder (CDAE) model that was improved from the Denoising AutoEncoder (DAE) model to solve the problem of the recommendation system, and CDAE also integrates human information to achieve greater accuracy.

Later, (Xue et al., 2017) proposed the Deep Matrix Factorization (DMF) method by combining matrix factorization and DMF model, while improving the loss function to achieve better effectiveness. (Wang et al., 2015) presented a new model called Collaborative Deep Learning (CDL) using a hierarchical Bayesian model and Stacked Denoising Autoencoders (SDAE) to solve the sparsity problem of data. (Li et al., 2017) use an autoencoder network to handle implicit and explicit information based on matrix factorization, and at the same time combining supervised learning and unsupervised learning to enhance model efficiency. In 2020, (Pan et al., 2020) upgraded the CDAE model by combining three small CDAE models to a new model called CoDAE (Correlation Denoising Autoencoder), this model was experimented and gave better results than the CDAE model in 2016.

Deep learning also is employed for MOOCs recommender systems, many works applied deep learning methods. (Raghuveer et al., 2014) introduced a reinforcement learning model to generate the learning context and analyze the learner's information. (Mi & Faltings, 2016) offered context trees applied to the online sequential recommendation. (Yang et al., 2014) use matrix factorization and context information forum apply on Forum thread. (Kardan et al., 2017) adopted social network analysis and association rule mining for MOOC forums. (Pardos et al., 2019) operated Recurrent Neural Networks to handle learner's time on each page for predicted courses. (Jing & Tang, 2017) construct a content-awareness framework using users' access information to represent students' interest and behavior features. (Zhang et al., 2017) used a deep belief network for the first time in MOOC recommendation. Then, (Zhang et al., 2019) improved a higher accurate recommendation model using learner's information and content features of the course by using learner-course feature vectors as inputs. While effectively, these methods need data that has a lot of information about courses, user's backgrounds like hobbies, actions, history, private information. This information is difficult to collect and handle. Additionally, these models have very high computation with a lot of calculation time.

Among the related works, we have found that DMF is suitable for the MOOC recommendation system because of its effectiveness. Therefore, in the next section, we present the basic theoretical principles of these methods, and improvements to increase the accuracy of the system.

The remainder of this paper is structured as follows. Part 2 presents the theoretical principle DMF model and our improvements. In Part 3, we conduct experiments and results on the travel-well dataset. Part 4 is the conclusion and our future works.

2. DEEP MATRIX FACTORIZATION

In the recommender system, data includes users and courses will be stored in a matrix. To use this matrix for later problems, we take methods in graph embeddings such as random walk approaches, deep approaches, factorization approaches, etc. Among them, the deep approaches are being applied more popularly. Therefore, we employ the matrix factorization using deep learning because of its effectiveness in our problem.

2.1 Deep Structured Semantic Model

Deep Structured Semantic Model (DSSM) is proposed by (Huang et al., 2013) for web search. Initially, DSSM maps query and documents into lower semantic space with a multi-layer non-linear projection. Then, for ranking webpage, cosine similarity is used.

Specifically, DSSM receives high dimensional vectors (converted from text features) as inputs. It transfers inputs to two multi-layer perceptrons. Then, map them into semantic vectors in a shared semantic space.

Suppose the input is vector **x**, the output is vector **y**, $\mathbf{l_i}$ is the ith hidden layer, $\mathbf{W_i}$ is the ith weight matrix, $\mathbf{b_i}$ is the ith biased. From interaction matrix **Y**, each user $\mathbf{u_i}$ is a vector of $\mathbf{Y_{i*}}$ meaning i^{th} user rates for all items. Each item $\mathbf{v_j}$ is a vector $\mathbf{Y_{*j}}$ meaning j^{th} item rated by all users. Multi-layer perceptrons (MLPs) use (1).

$$l_1 = W_1 x$$
$$l_i = f(W_{i-1} l_{i-1} + b_i), i = 2, \ldots N-1 \quad (1)$$
$$y = f(W_N l_{N-1} + b_N)$$

The similarity between the semantics of query and documents uses cosine similarity in (2).

$$R(Q,D) = cosine(p_i, q_j) = \frac{p_i^T . q_j}{\|p_i\| . \|q_j\|} \quad (2)$$

2.2 Deep Matrix Factorization Model

Deep Matrix Factorization (DMF) is a technique that combines the Matrix Factorization technique (MF) and DSSM. It receives explicit rating and zero implicit feedback and predicts courses based on the correlation of courses. The DMF model takes an interaction matrix. Similar to DSSM, this matrix split into two multi-layer perceptrons (MLPs in (1)). As the result, the output of these MLPs is latent representations. Finally, for calculating the correlation between two latent representations, we calculate cosine similarity. Fig. 1 illustrates DMF architecture.

Given a set include M users: $\mathbf{U=\{u_1,u_2,\ldots,u_M\}}$, and a set include N items: $\mathbf{I=\{i_1,i_2,\ldots,i_N\}}$. $\mathbf{R \in R^{MxN}}$ is the rating matrix with $\mathbf{R_{ij}}$ is rating of user **i** for item **j**, **unk** is unknown rating. Equation (3) present the user-item interaction matrix.

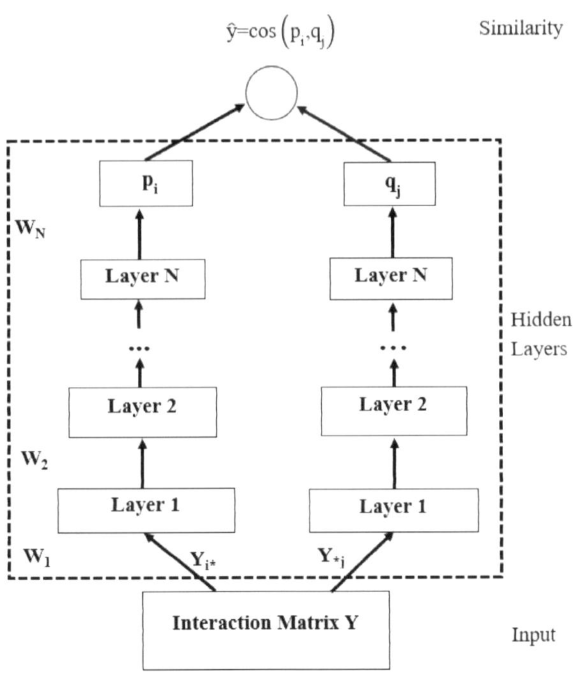

Figure 1. DMF architecture

$$Y_{ij}=\begin{cases} 0, \text{if } R_{ij}=\text{unk} \\ R_{ij}, \text{ otherwise} \end{cases} \quad (3)$$

where **u** is user, **v** is item; **i**, **j** is the index of **u**, **v**. **Y** is user-item interaction matrix, $\mathbf{Y}^+$is observed interactions, $\mathbf{Y}^-$ is zero elements in **Y**, $\mathbf{Y}^-_{\mathbf{sampled}}$ is a set of negative instances from Y (in part or in whole). $\mathbf{Y}^-\cup\mathbf{Y}_{\mathbf{sampled}}$ is a set of training interactions. Row **i** of matrix **Y** is $\mathbf{Y}_{\mathbf{i*}}$, column **j** of the matrix is $\mathbf{Y}_{\mathbf{*j}}$.

We use ReLU activation function in (4).

$$f(x) = \max(0,x) \quad (4)$$

This model has two MLPs, one for users and one for items, and outputs are mapped into low dimensional vectors in latent space in (5).

$$p_i = f_{\theta_N^U}\left(\ldots f_{\theta_3^U}\left(W_{U2} f_{\theta_2^U}(Y_{i*}W_{U1})\right)\ldots\right)$$
$$q_j = f_{\theta_N^I}\left(\ldots f_{\theta_3^I}\left(W_{V2} f_{\theta_2^I}(Y_{*j}^T W_{V1})\right)\ldots\right) \quad (5)$$

At that time, we calculate the cosine similarity of two latent representations p_i and q_j with (2).

In the next part, we will present an improved loss function which increases the accuracy of the model.

2.3 Loss Function

The general objective function in (6).

$$L=\sum_{u\in Y^+\cup Y^-} l(y,\hat{y})+\lambda\Omega(\theta) \quad (6)$$

where, $\Omega(\theta)$ is a regularizer and l(.) is a loss function.

The loss function is an important part of the objective function. The better loss function is, the better the objective function is. Hence, we optimize the objective function by improving the loss function.

Basically, binary cross-entropy is a popular loss function. There are many papers using binary cross-entropy in their works (J. Wu et al., 2009) (Equation (7)).

$$L_{BCE} = -\sum_{(i,j)\in Y^+\cup Y^-} Y_{ij}\log\widehat{Y_{ij}}+\left(1-Y_{ij}\right)\log\left(1-\widehat{Y_{ij}}\right) \quad (7)$$

Equation (7) works effectively with implicit feedback because it considers implicit feedback classification as binary classification. Since both zero implicit feedback and explicit rating are used, we deploy a new loss function by combining binary cross-entropy in (7) with max rating. The $\frac{Y_{ij}}{\max(\text{Rating})}$ is in range [0,1], so it is called Normalized cross-entropy loss (NCE) (Xue et al., 2017) (Equation (8)).

$$L_{NCE} = -\sum_{(i,j)\in Y^+\cup Y^-} \left(\frac{Y_{ij}}{\max(\text{Rating})}\log\widehat{Y_{ij}} + \left(1-\frac{Y_{ij}}{\max(\text{Rating})}\right)\log\left(1-\widehat{Y_{ij}}\right)\right) \quad (8)$$

In our data, we use max(Rating)=5 because 5 is the max rating.

This model uses direct input as an interaction matrix and is very useful in representing the final low dimensional. Normalized cross-entropy can make the predicted score of $\mathbf{Y}_{\mathbf{ij}}$ be negative so that we use (9) to solve this problem.

$$\widehat{Y_{ij}^O}=\max\left(\mu,\hat{Y}_{ij}\right) \quad (9)$$

where $\mu=10^{-6}$.

We represent the DMF with NCE loss function in Algorithm 1.

Algorithm 1: NCE_DMF (Iter, neg-ratio, R)
Inputs:
Iter # The number of iterations
neg-ratio #negative ratio
R # Interaction matrix
Outputs:
W_{Ui}(i=1...N-1)# weight matrix for user
W_{Vi}(i=1...N-1)# weight matrix for item

1. **Initialize:**
   a. Initialize randomly W_U and W_V
   b. Y := Use (3)
   c. Y^+:= All non-zero interactions in *Y*;
   d. Y^- :=All zero interactions in *Y*;
   e. $Y^-_{sampled}$:= sample neg _ ratio* $||Y^+||$ (interactions from Y^-)
   f. T:=$Y^+ \cup Y^-_{sampled}$
2. **Loop it** from 1 to *Iter*:
   Loop each interaction of user **i** and item **j** in T:
   p_i,q_j := Use (5)
   $\hat{Y}^O_{ij}$:= Use (2) and (9)
   L := Use (8).
   End for
   End for

3. EXPERIMENTS AND RESULTS

3.1 Dataset

The Travel-well dataset **Error! Reference source not found.**(Verbert et al., 2011) was collected from the learning resource exchange portal includes 20 content providers from Europe and elsewhere. It contains information about the ratings and tagging behaviors of 98 learners in over six months. Travel-well dataset is used for our experiment because some other datasets are not suitable for our model or not public. In our experiment, we only use rating information of this dataset.

Table 1. Travel-well dataset

#learners (#users)	#courses (#items)	#ratings	density
75	1608	2156	0.0178

3.2 Parameter Settings

We run at following requirements but not limited to: python = 3.7.6, with some libraries Tensorflow-gpu=1.5.0, numpy = 2.1.0.

Parameter settings: learning rates=0.0001, max epoch=50, batch size=256, early stopping = 5, K=1, 5, 10, 20, 30, 50. We choose the best hyper-parameter for the model by trying various parameter settings and then select ones that has the best accuracy. We applied k-fold cross validation for better validation with k = 10.

3.3 Metrics

To evaluate performance, we adopted the *leave-one-out* evaluation. Two metrics, *Normalized Discounted Cumulative Gain* (*NDCG*) in (He et al., 2015; Järvelin & Kekäläinen, 2002), are used to evaluate the ranking performance.

3.4 Results

To validate the effectiveness of our model, we have selected three following models to compare. They are good approaches in recommendation system based on explicit rating.

- **SVD** (Singular value decomposition) (Toroslu, 2010): This approach uses singular value decomposition to reduce the number of features of a dataset by reducing the space dimension from N-dimension to K-dimension (where K<<N). It applies a matrix structure where each row represents a user, and each column represents an item, and the elements of this matrix are the ratings that are given to items by users.
- **AutoRec** (Sedhain et al., 2015): AutoRec uses the autoencoder paradigm to design an item-based (user-based) by reconstructing the partially observed vectors.
- **DMF** (Xue et al., 2017): This model combines matrix factorization and deep structured semantic models.

Table 2 presents the detailed results on the NDCG@K metric with K = [1, 5, 10, 20, 30, 50] as in the original DMF, AutoRec, SVD and NCE_DMF models. The NCE-DMF shows better performance compare to SVD, AutoRec, and DMF models respectively. It is surprising with the NDCG@K of AutoRec model (<1% for all different K).

Table 2. NDCG@K with K = [1, 5, 10, 20, 30, 50] of the DMF, AutoRec, SVD, and NCE-DMF

K	DMF	AutoRec	SVD	NCE_DMF
1	0.3467	0.0019	0.4927	**0.5936**
5	0.3945	0.0039	0.4875	**0.7412**
10	0.4701	0.0040	0.4833	**0.7780**
20	0.5000	0.0043	0.4800	**0.7698**
30	0.5493	0.0059	0.4789	**0.7770**
50	0.5762	0.0070	0.4770	**0.6826**

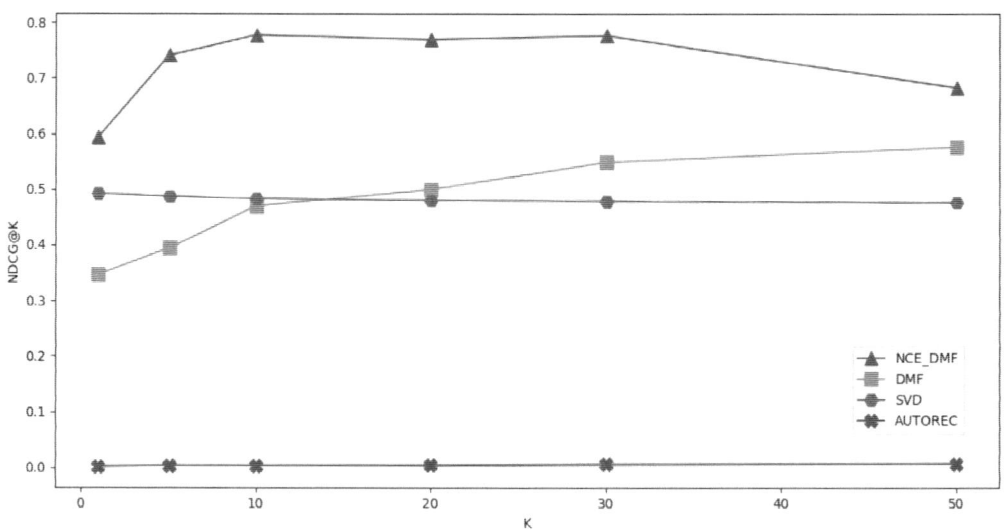

Figure 2. Comparison with NDCG@K on the Travel-well dataset

Figure 2 illustrates the NDCG@K metrics of the NCE_DMF, AutoRec, SVD and DMF models. In this chart, the AutoRec and DMF increase NDCG when K get bigger. However, the NDCG of SVD decreases when K increases. For NCE_DMF model, NDCG increases when $K \leq 30$, but decreases when K=50. The cause may come from the uneven distribution of data. Overall, the NCE_DMF model has higher NDCG ranking results than other related methods in the MOOC recommender system. This shows that we can apply NCE_DMF to improve the quality of the MOOC recommendation system.

4. CONCLUSION

In this paper, we improved the DMF model with a new loss function and applied it to the MOOC recommendation system. The experiment shows that the proposed approach is better than the other models on NDCG@K measurement. Specifically, our algorithm improved an average 25.09% compared to the DMF model, and 24.04% compared to SVD method. In the future, we will continue to improve DMF with some other loss functions. Moreover, this model can be expanded from zero of implicit feedback to implicit feedback containing user feedback.

ACKNOWLEDGEMENT

This research is funded by University of Science, VNU-HCM, under grant number CNTT 2020-05.

REFERENCES

Elkahky, A. M., Song, Y., & He, X. (2015). A multi-view deep learning approach for cross domain user modeling in recommendation systems. *Proceedings of the 24th International Conference on World Wide Web*, 278–288.

He, X., Chen, T., Kan, M.-Y., & Chen, X. (2015). Trirank: Review-aware explainable recommendation by modeling aspects. *Proceedings of the 24th ACM International on Conference on Information and Knowledge Management*, 1661–1670.

Huang, P.-S., He, X., Gao, J., Deng, L., Acero, A., & Heck, L. (2013). Learning deep structured semantic models for web search using clickthrough data. *Proceedings of the 22nd ACM International Conference on Information & Knowledge Management*, 2333–2338.

Järvelin, K., & Kekäläinen, J. (2002). Cumulated gain-based evaluation of IR techniques. *ACM Transactions on Information Systems (TOIS)*, *20*(4), 422–446.

Jdidou, Y., & Khaldi, M. (2016). Increasing the Profitability of Students in MOOCs using Recommendation Systems. *International Journal of Knowledge Society Research (IJKSR)*, *7*(4), 75–85.

Jdidou, Y., & Khaldi, M. (2018). Using Recommendation Systems in MOOC: An Innovation in Education That Increases the Profitability of Students. In *Enhancing Knowledge Discovery and Innovation in the Digital Era* (pp. 176–190). IGI Global.

Jing, X., & Tang, J. (2017). Guess you like: course recommendation in MOOCs. *Proceedings of the International Conference on Web Intelligence*, 783–789.

Kardan, A., Narimani, A., & Ataiefard, F. (2017). A hybrid approach for thread recommendation in MOOC forums. *International Journal of Social, Behavioral, Educational, Economic, Business and Industrial Engineering*, *11*(10), 2195–2201.

Kim, D., Park, C., Oh, J., Lee, S., & Yu, H. (2016). Convolutional matrix factorization for document context-aware recommendation. *Proceedings of the 10th ACM Conference on Recommender Systems*, 233–240.

Labarthe, H., Bachelet, R., Bouchet, F., & Yacef, K. (2016). Increasing MOOC completion rates through social interactions: a recommendation system. *Research Track*, 471.

Li, Q., Zheng, X., & Wu, X. (2017). Collaborative autoencoder for recommender systems. *ArXiv E-Prints*.

Mi, F., & Faltings, B. (2016). Adaptive Sequential Recommendation Using Context Trees. *IJCAI*, 4018–4019.

Pan, Y., He, F., & Yu, H. (2020). A correlative denoising autoencoder to model social influence for top-N recommender system. *Frontiers of Computer Science*, *14*(3), 143301.

Pardos, Z. A., Fan, Z., & Jiang, W. (2019). Connectionist recommendation in the wild: on the utility and scrutability of neural networks for personalized course guidance. *User Modeling and User-Adapted Interaction*, *29*(2), 487–525.

Raghuveer, V. R., Tripathy, B. K., Singh, T., & Khanna, S. (2014). Reinforcement learning approach towards effective content recommendation in MOOC environments. *2014 IEEE International Conference on MOOC, Innovation and Technology in Education (MITE)*, 285–289.

Salakhutdinov, R., Mnih, A., & Hinton, G. (2007). Restricted Boltzmann machines for collaborative filtering. *Proceedings of the 24th International Conference on Machine Learning*, 791–798.

Sedhain, S., Menon, A. K., Sanner, S., & Xie, L. (2015). Autorec: Autoencoders meet collaborative filtering. *Proceedings of the 24th International Conference on World Wide Web*, 111–112.

Tan, Y. K., Xu, X., & Liu, Y. (2016). Improved recurrent neural networks for session-based recommendations. *Proceedings of the 1st Workshop on Deep Learning for Recommender Systems*, 17–22.

Toroslu, Ġ. H. (2010). A singular value decomposition approach for recommendation systems. *The Graduate School of Natural and Applied Sciences of Middle East Technical University, Ph. D. Dissertation*.

Verbert, K., Drachsler, H., Manouselis, N., Wolpers, M., Vuorikari, R., & Duval, E. (2011). Dataset-driven research for improving recommender systems for learning. *Proceedings of the 1st International Conference on Learning Analytics and Knowledge*, 44–53.

Wang, H., Wang, N., & Yeung, D.-Y. (2015). Collaborative deep learning for recommender systems. *Proceedings of the 21th ACM SIGKDD International Conference on Knowledge Discovery and Data Mining*, 1235–1244.

Wu, J., Wang, Z., & Vojcic, B. R. (2009). Partial iterative decoding for binary turbo codes via cross-entropy based bit selection. *IEEE Transactions on Communications*, *57*(11), 3298–3306.

Wu, Y., DuBois, C., Zheng, A. X., & Ester, M. (2016). Collaborative denoising auto-encoders for top-n recommender systems. *Proceedings of the Ninth ACM International Conference on Web Search and Data Mining*, 153–162.

Xue, H.-J., Dai, X., Zhang, J., Huang, S., & Chen, J. (2017). Deep Matrix Factorization Models for Recommender Systems. *IJCAI*, *17*, 3203–3209.

Yang, D., Piergallini, M., Howley, I., & Rose, C. (2014). Forum thread recommendation for massive open online courses. *Educational Data Mining 2014*.

Yanhui, D., Dequan, W., Yongxin, Z., & Lin, L. (2015). A group recommender system for online course study. *2015 7th International Conference on Information Technology in Medicine and Education (ITME)*, 318–320.

Zhang, H., Huang, T., Lv, Z., Liu, S., & Yang, H. (2019). MOOCRC: A highly accurate resource recommendation model for use in MOOC environments. *Mobile Networks and Applications*, *24*(1), 34–46.

Zhang, H., Yang, H., Huang, T., & Zhan, G. (2017). DBNCF: Personalized courses recommendation system based on DBN in MOOC environment. *2017 International Symposium on Educational Technology (ISET)*, 106–108.

APPLICATION OF SLIDING WINDOWS TO SPELLING ERROR DETECTION IN MEDICAL DIAGNOSIS

Sutat Gammanee[1] and Sunantha Sodsee[2]
[1]*Doctoral student*
[2]*Assistant Professor*
King Mongkut's University of Technology North Bangkok, Faculty of Information Technology and Digital Innovation, King Mongkut's University of Technology North Bangkok, Bangkok, Thailand

ABSTRACT

Presently, problematic issues relative to health and public health in Thailand are underlined by an insufficient number of medical personnel. However, self-diagnosis, herein, is another option to help the mentioned limitation by identifying and monitoring unusual health conditions by oneself. To gain the diagnosis, history of medical data based on symptoms and disease of patients are needed significantly. In fact, especially in Thailand, medical data is recorded, not only presented by, such as: numeric data, images, but also describing by words or phrases. Then, the errors of medical data collection may be occurred by incorrect data or spelling errors of describing.

To enhance the performance of self-diagnosis, in this paper, the medical data in describing by medical words is focused. The detection of spelling errors and measuring similar words are coped with the proposed sliding window based methods, which are 1) sliding window based two-word inspection by once sliding method 2) sliding window based two-word inspection by initial word fixing method, and 3) sliding window based window size adjusting method.

For evaluating the proposed work, the example medical data (without patient information) is gained from the public hospital in Thailand. The results presented that the sliding window based two-word inspection by initial word fixing method presented the great accuracy of spelling errors detection about 80% in general words and 60 % of similar words measurement in medical terms.

KEYWORDS

Self-Diagnosis, Spelling Errors Detection, Sliding Windows

1. INTRODUCTION

Problematic issues in public health have currently become a major consideration, and a number of studies have been conducted in attempts to solve the problems. One of the underlined causes is an insufficient number of medical professionals—the ratio of medical personnel population was reported at 1:412 (Sawaengdee, 2017). Accordingly, a policy had been launched by government in order to promote self-care practices and reduce medical visits (Phalasuek, Thanomchayathawatch, & Songloed, 2018) by regularly doing exercises and performing self-diagnosis.

Self-diagnosis is the process of identifying and monitoring unusual health conditions by oneself for further medical treatments or basic self-care to prevent risk conditions and maintain the best curing conditions before the health problems become incurable. Currently, people are suffering from hard-working routines, and physical examination is often regarded as a very time-consuming task. As a result, a large number of patients decided to have medical visits when their health problems become incurable illness. Therefore, self-diagnosis could assist in reducing health problems, medical visits, and government budget in health promotion.

According to (Gammanee & Sodsee, 2018), raw data obtained by medical diagnosis had been categorized and gained two groups of patients—patients with normal conditions and patients with risk conditions. After categorization, the data of patients with risk conditions were analysed using the process of self-diagnosis performed by medical personnel.

The problem in this research is to diagnose the disease, based on the analysis of the medical diagnosis, Generally, medical diagnosis is recorded in forms of messages describing symptoms using medical terms which are uneasy for recording and spelling. Thus, spelling errors may occur during the recording process that may lead to false diagnosis e.g., 'Dysentery is the symptom of intestinal inflammation.', 'Hyperglycemia is the condition with too much glucose is blood circulation.', and 'Abdominal Discomfort is the symptom of pain that occurs between the chest and pelvic regions.' As seen from the above examples, a number of medical terms are similar in terms of spelling and could replace other words containing similar meanings—only written forms and word categories are different e.g., 'Abdomen' and 'Abdominal', both words refer to the symptom of stomachache and flatulence; as analyzed by machine learning, the words were interpreted as different words. Whereas, experts confirm similarity and interchangeability of both words. As a result, the analysis could be incorrect and lead to failure in medical treatment. The researchers propose of the concept of how Sliding Windows came to the application to group the vocabulary before processing it with a machine as the concept frame in Figure 1.

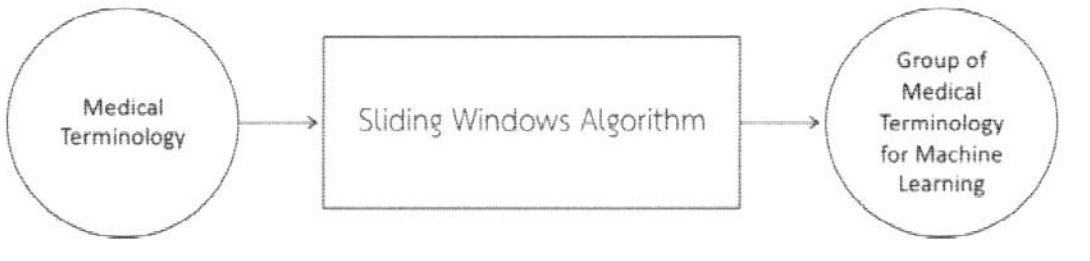

Figure 1. Appling Sliding Windows to Solve Research Problems

The concept of Sliding Windows is the process used in controlling accurate data-transmission with protocol between the sender and receiver by determining relative window sizes, sliding both sides at once, and detecting data until the process is complete. In this case, data detection of Sliding Windows is the pros that could handle with two similar meaning words. Sliding Windows was therefore adopted in this study to detect similarity of medical terms in order to categorize similar words into the same group. The researchers introduced the concept of sliding windows to the design to detect a similar word from a medical diagnosis to group the medical term that can be in the same group. In order to make the diagnosis more accurate. In addition, the benefits of this research can also learn similar words to solve problems with your doctor's information to correct them.

2. RELATED WORKS

2.1 Sliding Windows

Sliding Windows is the concept used in designing with arrays that is mostly selected for inspecting data-transmission between the sender and receiver by determining window sizes starting from the first point and continuing to slide to the right by point-by-point. The technique has been applied in various tasks. As seen in Figure 2:

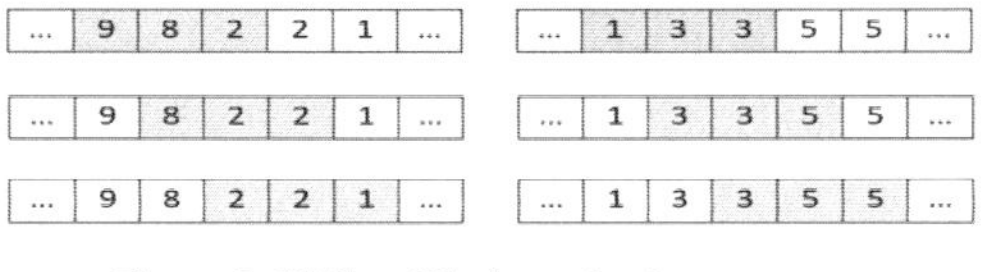

Figure 2. Sliding Windows for data accuracy

According to Figure 2, Sliding Windows is used as a protocol for inspecting data accuracy within the network (Moore & Papagiannaki, 2005), it is additionally adopted to identify a variable of arrays (Kohler, Gulati, Cao, Hart, & Ludascher, 2012).

2.1.1 Sliding Windows for Data Communication

Sliding Windows is used in data communication with multiple sets of data transmission to the receiver according to specified sizes for data inspection of both sides. The technique could assist in reducing memory storage use and maximizing data transmission speed. Besides, it is considered as a type of data transmission.

Some advantages of data transmission using Sliding Windows are multiple frames of data transmission and data inspect ability due to similar window sizes.

2.1.2 Sliding windows for Arrays

Sliding windows is used with arrays for accurate inspection of data steaming by determining suitable window sizes and sliding both sides at once. Besides, it could assist in arranging data and determining maximum values of arrays.

2.2 Commonly Misspelled Words in English

Commonly, misspelled words are seen in English writing. According to (Flor, 2012) (Mackay, 1969) (Healy, 1981), a number of misspelled words were retrieved and demonstrated as follows:

2.2.1 Correctly Spelled-Words Plus Additional Character

Words are correctly spelled, but an additional character (s) is inserted in. There are 3 patterns of the case—an additional character (s) at the final position e.g., computer – computers, an additional character (s) at the initial position e.g., computer – computer, and an additional character (s) at the middle position e.g., computer – computer.

Words are correctly spelled, but an additional character (s) is inserted in. There are 3 patterns of the case—an additional character (s) at the final position e.g., computer – computers, an additional character (s) at the initial position e.g., computer – computer, and an additional character (s) at the middle position e.g., computer – computer.

2.2.2 Partially Misspelled-Words

Words are incorrectly spelled by a wrong character (s). There are 2 patterns of the case—a wrong character (s) spelling, but containing the correct number of characters, e.g., computer – comtuter, and a wrong character (s) spelling and containing an incorrect number of characters e.g., computer –comtter.

2.2.3 Correctly Spelled-Words with Missing Characters

Words are correctly spelled with a missing character (s). There are 2 patterns of the case—missing a character (s) at the final position, e.g., computer – compute, and missing a character (s) at the initial position e.g., computer – omputer.

3. EVALUATING ALGORITHM EFFICIENCY

This study adopted Sliding Windows to detect of word similarity with an application of 3 Sliding Windows methods as follows:

3.1 Sliding Window Based Two-Word Inspection by Once Sliding Method

This method slides windows with 3 characters starting from left to right at once, then detects both windows for similarity of contained characters. As seen in Figure 3:

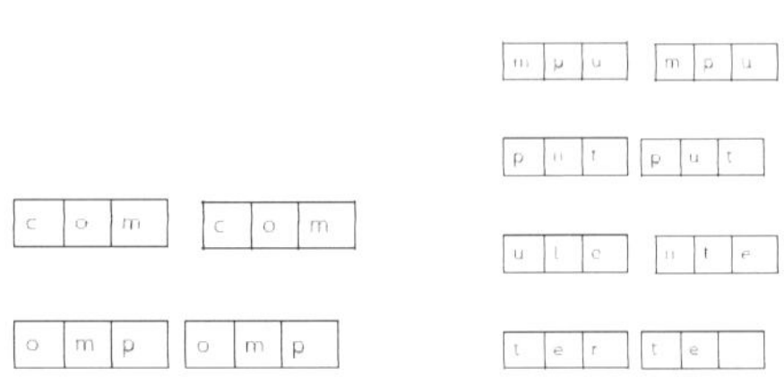

Figure 3. The working of Two-word Inspection by Sliding at Once method

An evaluation was conducted by counting points of inspection of both windows—correct point (similar spelling) as 1 and incorrect point (different spelling) as 0, then summarized all points, divided by a full point, and multiplied by 100 to determine percentage of correctness.

$$C_i(st1,st2) = \begin{cases} 1, & \text{When same all string} \\ 0, & \text{When not same all string} \end{cases} \qquad \text{Percentage} = \frac{\sum_{i=1}^{m} C_i(st1[i,i+1,i+2], st2[i,i+1,i+2])}{m} \times 100 \quad (1)$$

By Ci refers to function for checking same character
i refers to position of string
st1 refers to first string to compare
st2 refers to second string to compare
m refers to the number of string length

3.2 Sliding Window Based Two-Word Inspection by Initial Word Fixing

This method slides windows by remaining an initial word unmoved and moves the rest, then moves the initial word by point-by-point and the rest until all characters have been moved, then inspects for correctness. As seen in Figure 4: Inspection of 'comp' and 'comt'.

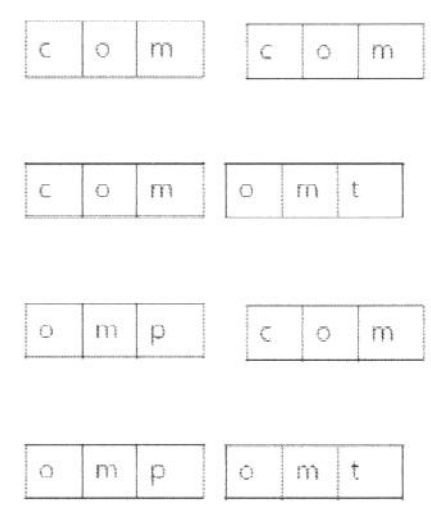

Figure 4. The working of Two-word Inspection by Fixing Initial Word method

$$\text{Percentage} = \frac{P}{(m-3) \times 3} \times 100$$

$$C_i(st1,st2) = \begin{cases} 1, & \text{When same all string} \\ 0, & \text{When not same all string} \end{cases} \qquad P = \sum_{i}^{m-3} C(st1[i,i+1,i+2], \sum_{j}^{m-3} st2(j,j+1,j+2)) \quad (2)$$

By Ci refers to function for checking same character
i refers to position of string
st1 refers to first string to compare
st2 refers to second string to compare
P refers to similarity score
m refers to the number of string length

3.3 Sliding Window Based Window Size Adjusting

An adjustment of window size was performed by increasing the window of characters from 1 to 2 until the window size contains the same size of word characters. Then, the first set of word is searched in comparison to the second word until the window size contains the same size of word characters. As seen in Figure 5.

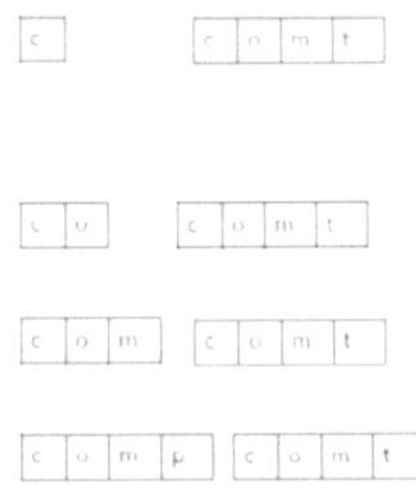

Figure 5. The working of Adjusting Window Sizes method

$$C_i(st1, st2) = \begin{cases} 1, & \text{When same all string} \\ 0, & \text{When not same all string} \end{cases} \qquad \text{Percentage} = \frac{\max \sum_i^m C\left(st1[i], \sum_j^m st2[j,\ldots,m]\right)}{m} \times 100 \quad (3)$$

By Ci refers to function for checking same character
i refers to position of string
st1 refers to first string to compare
st2 refers to second string to compare
m refers to the number of string length

Counting points was performed on each evaluation task and calculated in forms of percentage. The percentage was calculated using the number of characters divided by max number character, and multiplied by 100—the probability (P) was equivalent to the maximum value of percentage.

4. EXPERIMENT AND RESULTS

To evaluate the proposed sliding window based methods, the tests are divided in to two major parts, which are 1) spelling error detection in general words consisting of basic vocabulary and misspelled words retrieved from research (Fitzgerald, 1932), and 2) measuring similar word in medical terms.

4.1 Spelling Error Detection in General Words

4.1.1 Correctly Spelled-Words Plus Additional Character

In this subsection, the word "computer" is selected to test the proposed work by concerning major seven patterns of error (Flor, 2012). The results presented in Table 1 show that three proposed methods presented excellent detecting of spelling error on Pattern 1 and Pattern 6, which the accuracies are greater than 80%.

On the other hand, the method 1: sliding window based two-word inspection by once sliding method could not detect the error on Pattern 2 and Pattern 7 appropriately, which accuracies are 4.76% and 0%, respectively. Method 2: sliding window based two-word inspection by initial word fixing method showed accuracies of error detection that less than 80% only on Pattern 3 and Pattern 5. As well as, method 3: sliding window based window size adjusting method presented accuracies of error detection that less than 80% only on Pattern 3, Pattern 4 and Pattern 5.

Table 1. Accuracy of Spelling Error Detection in Basic Vocabulary

#Patterns	Patterns of Error	Method 1: Once Sliding	Method 2: Initial Word Fixing	Method 3: Window Size Adjusting
1	computers	95.23%	85.71%	88.88%
2	ccomputer	4.76%	85.71%	88.88%
3	commputer	33.33%	71.42%	66.67%
4	comtuter	83.33%	83.33%	50%
5	**comtter**	**40%**	**73.33%**	**37.5%**
6	compute	94.44%	94.44%	87.5%
7	omputer	0.00%	83.33%	87.5%
Average of Accuracy		50.16%	**82.47%**	72.42%

To conclude, the method 2 presented higher average accuracy of spelling error detection (82.47%) than others, especially on Pattern 5, that method 1 and method 3 achieved only 40% and 37.5%, respectively.

4.1.2 Correctly Spelled-Words Plus Additional Character

The misspelled words in this subsection are referred from (Fitzgerald, 1932). Herein, ten frequent misspelled words are selected to evaluate the proposed methods.

Table 2 shows that three proposed methods presented almost equally accuracy of error detection on Word 7, which are 72.22%, 72.22%, and 62.50%, respectively. Otherwise, the highest accuracies of words are performed by method 2.

Table 2. Accuracy of Spelling Error Detection in Misspelled Words

#Word	Misspelled Word	Method 1: Once Sliding	Method 2: Initial Word Fixing	Method 3: Window Size Adjusting
1	agressive	25%	91.67%	80%
2	**maintainance**	**40%**	**90%**	**41.67%**
3	personell	76.19%	90.47%	33.33%
4	facinating	11%	85.18%	72.72%
5	**restarant**	**50%**	**83.33%**	**40%**
6	experiance	87.50%	87.50%	30%
7	nieghbor	72.22%	72.22%	62.50%
8	**orignal**	**50%**	**77.78%**	**37.50%**
9	wellfare	40%	73.33%	62.50%
10	secratary	85.71%	85.71%	44.44%
Average of Accuracy		53.76%	**83.72%**	50.47

To conclude, the method 2 still presented higher average accuracy of spelling error detection (83.72%) than others, especially on Word 2, Word 5, and Word 8, that method 1 and method 3 achieved only 37.50% - 50%.

4.2 Measuring Similar Word in Medical Terms

The accuracy of similar word measurement in medical terms is focused in this section. Herein, the medical terms: the symptoms of abdomen are collected from the public hospital in Thailand. The spelling errors of symptoms are detected and measured as similar words.

To evaluate the performance for measuring similar words in the medical terms, the proposed sliding window based methods are tested on the regular ten symptoms of abdomen recommended by the medical professionals. The results are shown in Table 3.

Table 3. Accuracy of Similar Word Measurement in Medical Terms

#Word	Word	Similar Word	Method 1: Once Sliding	Method 2: Initial Word Fixing	Method 3: Window Size Adjusting	Replacement recommended by Experts
1	Abdomen	Abdominal	86.67%	86.67%	11.11%	✓
2	Antiemetics	Antinauseant	33.33%	59.25%	16.67%	✓
3	Backache	Back Pain	50%	72.22%	0%	✓
4	Cough, Chronic	Cough, Productive	50%	69.44%	5.88%	✓
5	Debility, General	Debilitating Disease	40%	57.78%	0%	✓
6	Sorensen	Sorethroat	50%	61.11%	0%	✓
7	Ankle Foot Pain	Ankle Pain	38.46%	69.33%	33.33%	✓
8	Arthritis	Arthralgia	57.14%	66.67%	0%	✓
9	Myocelialgia	Myalgia	10%	60%	41.67%	✓
10	Abdominal Discomfort	Abdominal Distention	66.67%	75.92%	5%	✓
Average of Accuracy			48.23%	**67.84%**	11.37%	

From Table 3, method 2: sliding window based two-word inspection by initial word fixing method showed the highest average accuracy of similar word measurement with 67.84%. To summaries, the method 2 performed excellent spelling error detection, and measuring the similarity among the medical terms. To compare with the experts' recommendation, the words can be replaced by the similar words when the measured values are greater than 50%.

5. CONCLUSION

This study presents a method for verifying the similarity of words using the innovative Sliding Windows concept that has been applied in 3 methods. 1. sliding window based two-word inspection by once sliding method 2. sliding window based two-word inspection by initial word fixing method and 3. sliding window based window size adjusting method. The evaluated is divided into 2 parts, 1) spelling error detection in general words consisting of basic vocabulary and misspelled words retrieved from research, and 2) measuring similar word in medical terms. All parts presented that when applied with subsection basic vocabulary, method 2 presented maximum efficiency and covered all pattern, while method 1 and method 3 could effective in some patterns.

When evaluated in subsection Misspelled Words , it was discovered that the method 2, which was effective from the first subsection, was still effective in evaluating this subsection as before, while method 1 and method 3 had reduced efficiency. And when evaluated in part 2 Measuring Similar Word in Medical Terms, it was discovered that all methods were reduced percentage, method 1 and method 3 decreased to less than 50%, while method 2 slightly decreased accuracy. The average is approximately 70%. All Examination presented that the performance of method 2 is the most effective, even through two forms of testing, and have the capability to group medical terminology.

REFERENCES

A. F. Healy., (1981). The effects of visual similarity on proofreading for misspellings. *Memory & Cognition*, Vol. 9, No. 5, pp. 453–460.

A. W. Moore and K. Papagiannaki., (2005). Toward the Accurate Identification of Network Applications. *Passive and Active Network Measurement*, Vol. 3431, pp 41-54.

D. G. Mackay., (1969). The repeated letter effect in the misspellings. *Perception & Psychophysics*, Vol. 5, No. 2, pp. 102–106.

Flor, M. (2012). Four types of context for automatic spelling correction. *Traitement Automatique des Langues (TAL)*. 53(3). pp 61-99.

Gammanee, S. and Sodsee, S., (2018). The application of clustering algorithms in screening patients. *The Fourteenth National Conference on Computing and Information Technology*. Chiang Mai, Thailand, pp. 462-467.

J. A. Fitzgerald., (1932). Words Misspelled most Frequently by Children of the Fourth, Fifth, and Sixth Grade Levels in Life outside the School. *The Journal of Educational Research*, Vol. 26, No. 3, pp. 213–218.

Köhler, Sven. et al, (2012). Sliding Window Calculations on Streaming Data using the Kepler Scientific Workflow System. *Procedia Computer Science*. Vol. 9, pp. 1639-1646

Phalasuek, R. et al, (2018). Participatory Action Research: Development of a Participatory Process. *The Southern College Network Journal of Nursing and Public Health*, Vol. 5, No. 1,pp 211-223.

Sawaengdee, K., (2017). Crisis of Nursing shortage in Health Service Facilities under Office of Permanent Secretary. *Journal of Health Science*, Vol. 26, No. 2, pp 456-468.

ON EFFICIENTLY CREATING TEMPORALLY BIASED SAMPLES OVER DATA STREAMS: BEYOND MEMORYLESS FUNCTIONS

George Lagogiannis[1] and Christos Makris[2]
[1]*Department of Agricultural Economics and Rural Development, Agricultural University of Athens, Iera Odos 75 11855 Athens, Greece*
[2]*Department of Computer Engineering and Informatics, University of Patras, 26504, Patras, Greece*

ABSTRACT

When creating a sample over a data stream, we sometimes need to give a priority to the recent past, over the distant one. This can be achieved if the probability of each stream element to exist in the sample decays as time passes, according to a bias-function. In order to obtain such a sample, one has to access some elements of the sample when a stream element arrives. For the exponential bias-function, according to which the probability of a sample-element to be deleted at each time-point, is the same for all sample elements, the number of needed accesses is O(1). For any other bias-function, one needs to access O(n) elements per incoming stream element, where n is the sample-size. In this paper we present an algorithm that achieves O(1) amortized accesses for any bias-function such that at each time-point, the probability of a sample-element to be deleted increases over time.

KEYWORDS

Temporally Biased Sample, Stream, Markov Chains

1. INTRODUCTION

Massive amounts of data are being produced each second in the Internet (call logs, clicks, sensor readings e.t.c.). For the theoretical study of the problems related to the exploitation of these data, we use the *data stream computational model*, according to which data arrive continuously through a possibly infinite stream. The huge volume of the incoming data and our limited primary memory dictate that we can afford to store a small part of the stream only, which we call *synopsis* or *sample* of the stream. This sample can be used for the training of machine learning models that will then be assigned with the task of processing the incoming stream elements, aiming to extract useful information (in applications related to security, marketing, data management e.t.c.). A survey on stream sampling methods can be found in (Haas 2016) and (Aggarwal 2007).

However, data tend to change over time and the efficiency of machine learning models depends greatly on their ability to accordingly adapt. Static machine learning models lack this ability, but this problem can be solved through a periodically retraining process that allows such models to be used in dynamic settings. This approach was proposed in (Hentschel et al 2018) in the setting of graph analysis algorithms and has recently been adopted in the MacroBase system (Bailis P. et al 2017). The only available data for this retraining process are the elements of the sample and for the retraining to be successful, the recent history of the stream must occupy a large enough portion of the sample.

Assuming that the main memory can store n stream elements, one could trivially include in the sample the n most recent stream elements. But then the more distant past of the stream is totally ignored, and this fact may be a little extreme. A more "mild" approach would be to create a *temporally biased* sample where the stream element that arrived at time r "survives" in the sample at time t (where $t \geq r$) with probability proportional to a *time-decay bias-function* $f(r,t)$ which is defined to be monotonically decreasing with t (for fixed r) and monotonically increasing with r (for fixed t). We say that such a sample is *consistent* with function $f(r, t)$.

In (Aggarwal 2006), an algorithm is introduced for creating a sample consistent with the exponential bias-function, $f(r, t) = e^{-\lambda(t-r)}$ where the parameter λ defines the bias rate and typically lies in the range [0, 1] with very small values. The interesting property of this algorithm is that only one sample element is accessed each time a new stream element arrives. This element is the one to be replaced in the sample by the incoming stream element. It follows that the number of elements in the sample remains the same at all times, it is thus a *reservoir sampling algorithm*. Clearly, the number of accessed sample elements per stream element is a major indicator of the efficiency of any sampling algorithm. In the following we name a sampling algorithm *time-efficient* if it achieves O(1) accessed sample elements per stream element.

The exponential function "treats" all the elements in a *memoryless* approach, meaning that the probability of each stream element to exist in the sample drops according to the same rate as time passes, no matter how old the element is in regard to the current time-point. More formally, a bias-function $f(r, t)$ is memoryless if the fragment $f(r, t) / f(r, t-1)$ (referred in the following of the paper as $g(r, t)$) is the same for all r, t ($t \geq r$). In (Aggarwal 2006) it was left open whether such a sample can be efficiently maintained for non memoryless functions, i.e. for functions $f(r, t)$ where $g(r, t)$ is not the same for all r, t ($t \geq r$).

Apparently, an algorithm that maintains such a sample for any given time-decay bias-function $f(r, t)$ is not difficult to be derived. According to Efraimidis (2010) there exist two such algorithms, i) an algorithm (referred as A-Chao) which had long ago been presented by Chao (1982) and ii) an algorithm (named A-ES) presented in (Efraimidis & Spirakis 2006). Indeed both algorithms can solve the problem, they dictate however that the weights of the elements in the sample must be recomputed at each time-point and this fact leads to a time complexity of O(n) per incoming stream element. The open problem stated by Aggarwal (2006), is whether or not an algorithm can be created such that given any non-memoryless bias-function $f(r, t)$, the algorithm creates a sample consistent with $f(r, t)$ without the need to access all the sample elements, each time a new stream element arrives. Ideally, such an algorithm should access only O(1) elements of the sample, achieving the time-complexity of the algorithm presented by Aggarwal (2006).

In this paper we provide an insight to this open problem, by focusing on the time-complexity and dropping the reservoir constraint. Said otherwise, the sample may grow or shrink and we are not interested in providing probabilistic guarantees on its size. We only care about the time-efficiency of the algorithm, matching the time-efficiency of (Aggarwal 2006) in an amortized sense, creating thus an *amortized efficient* algorithm for non-memoryless functions.

2. OUR RESULT

We divide all non-memoryless functions into 2 categories: i) the *harder to the older* category, contains all the functions for which $g(r, t)$ decreases as $t - r$ increases and ii) *the softer to the older* category, contains all the functions for which $g(r, t)$ increases as $t - r$ increases. Given the type of time bias we need (i.e. the need to give priority to the recent past instead of the distant one), it follows that the "harder to the older" category is our target.

Let M be the size of the available primary memory and $f(r, t)$ be a time-decay bias-function that belongs to the "harder to the older" category. We call $f(r, t)$ *M-implementable* if the average size of a sample consistent with $f(r, t)$ is at most equal to M. We present an amortized efficient algorithm that creates a sample consistent with any M-implementable time-decay bias-function $f(r, t)$ that belongs to the "harder to the older" category if:

- $0 \leq f(r, t) \leq 1$
- $f(t, t) = 1$
- $g(r, t) > 0.5$ for all r, t such that $t \geq r$

The first two constraints make sense, however the third may raise suspicion that the pool of available functions is significantly reduced. This is not the case because if $g(r, t) \leq 0.5$ for all the elements in the sample, then each stream element is expected to survive in the sample for at most two time-points on the average. It seems that such a function is too hard to be of practical interest. Nevertheless, a function where $g(r, t)$ becomes 0.5 or less for very old elements (i.e. for elements having inclusion probability close to 0) is certainly of practical use because the third constraint can easily be put aside without changing the time-complexity of our algorithm.

It must be made clear that our algorithm does not use a reservoir, meaning that the size of the sample is not kept unchanged during the execution of the algorithm. By "amortized efficient" we mean that the amortized number of sample elements accessed per stream element is O(1). Our algorithm requires a function that given r, t, returns $f(r, t)$. This is unavoidable since it works for any function following the above restrictions. In an amortized sense, it needs O(1) random numbers between 0 and 1 per incoming stream element. We adopt the framework given in (Aggarwal 2006) where time is defined by the arrival of the stream elements i.e. each time-point t defines the (one) stream element that arrived at time t. An alternative approach adopted in (Hentschel et al 2018) would be to use wall clock times, allowing empty time-points (i.e. time-points when no stream element arrives) and batch insertions (i.e. time-points when more than one stream elements arrive). However, the framework of (Aggarwal 2006) suffices for showing the efficiency of our algorithm. To the best of our knowledge this is the first time that a sampling algorithm able to "achieve" any function that matches the above restrictions is presented.

3. THE "TOOLS"

3.1 The Random Walk

Our algorithm is based on a random walk which we shall describe in this subsection. Let us assume that we have n sample elements u_1, u_2, … u_n, that have arrived (my means of a data stream) and been stored in a list according to their arrival time (i.e. each element has arrived after its neighbor on the left). The leftmost element u_0 of the list is artificial, and has not arrived through the stream.

Each sample-element (i.e. each node of the list) defines a slot which contains two states in the random walk. In particular, if u_i ($1 \leq i \leq n$) is an element of the sample, its slot contains the states u_i-go and u_i-select. A random walk performed by an entity which we call, *cursor* is defined on this list, as follows: The cursor starts from the leftmost slot and either moves to the slot on the right or jumps back to the leftmost slot. Each move (to the right) of the cursor between two consecutive slots, is called *hop*. The event $i \xrightarrow{t} i+1$ is the event that a hop from slot i to slot i+1 occurs at time t. The event $i \xrightarrow{t} j$ is a sequence of j - i consecutive hops from slot i to slot j that occur at time t.

When the cursor reaches a slot, we toss a fair coin in order to decide on the state of the slot that the cursor will visit. As a result, when the cursor visits a slot, each of the two states of the slot have equal probability of being visited by the cursor. The only slot where we do not toss a coin is the one corresponding to the artificial element because it contains only one state, which is a go-state.

The reason for the introduction of 2-state slots, is the need for inserting randomness into the task of choosing the element to be deleted. In particular, if each element accessed by the cursor is deleted (with probability 1), then the elements are deleted in a left to right order, and the sample always contains the n most recent elements of the stream. By setting an element candidate for deletion only if its select-state is accessed by the cursor, we introduce the necessary randomness for allowing the deletion of an element while older elements (than the one deleted) continue to exist in the sample.

The above described random walk on a list that contains 5 elements (plus the artificial one), is shown in Figure 1. In Figure 1, $p(i \xrightarrow{t} i+1)$ is equal to the sum of the probabilities corresponding to the two straight solid (red) arrows leaving any of the two states associated with slot i. For example, by assigning to each straight solid arrow in Figure 2 a probability of 0.45 there is a probability of 0.9 for moving to the next slot. Then, by assigning a probability of 0.1 to each solid curved arrow, it follows that there is a 0.1 probability of moving to the leftmost slot from any slot other than the rightmost one. The thick curved dashed arrows connecting the rightmost states to the leftmost slot, correspond to transition probabilities equal to 1.

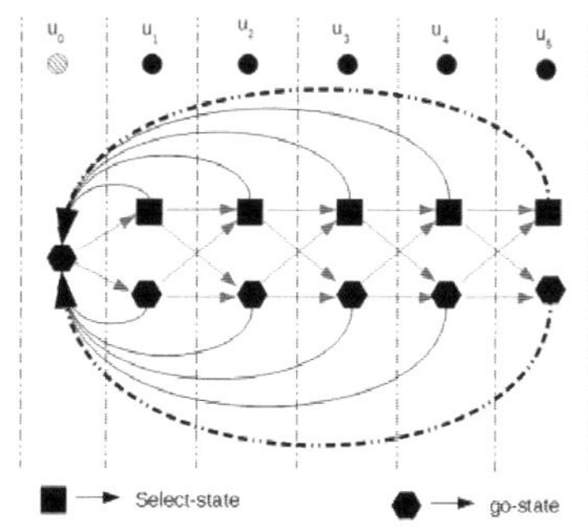

Figure 1. An example of the random walk upon which our algorithm is based

3.2 Basic Structures and Notation

Let S be a possibly infinite data stream and $f(r, t)$ be a "harder to the older" bias-function. Our algorithm will create a sample that is consistent with $f(r, t)$, i.e. the stream element that arrived at time r (denoted as $S(r)$) exists in the sample at time t ($t \geq r$) with probability $p(r, t) = f(r, t)$. Time is defined by the incoming stream elements, meaning that $S(r)$ arrives at time r.

The elements of the sample are stored in a list *sample-list*, where the most recent element becomes the rightmost element of the list therefore the sample-elements are sorted according to their arrival times. We assume that the leftmost element of the sample-list was inserted in the sample at time minus infinity i.e. it exists in the sample with probability 0 and cannot be deleted. This may seem to be a contradiction because no element of the sample exists in the sample with probability 0. Keep in mind however that this is an artificial element used for symmetry reasons and does not really exist in the sample. In the following, we name the elements of the sample-list using their distance from the leftmost (artificial) element. This way, we name the artificial element u_0, its right neighbor u_1 etc. Note that when element u_i is deleted from the sample, element u_{i+1} becomes u_i, u_{i+2} becomes u_{i+1} etc. Also note that the numbers do not play a role in the algorithm, and are only used for easing the description.

4. CREATING A TEMPORALLY BIASED SAMPLE

4.1 Description of the Algorithm

Each time a new stream element arrives, we increment time, we set the current time to be the arrival time of the element and we insert the new element in the rightmost position of the sample-list. Then we execute a *step* of the walk, and we define a step to be a "trip" of the cursor from the artificial element and back to it. This means that we increment time only when the cursor points to the artificial element and as a result, time remains frozen when the cursor walks the list rightwards. A sample element is deleted only if the cursor accesses its select-state, and when a slot (element) is accessed, each state of the slot has equal probability of being accessed. Let r_i, r_{i+1} be the arrival times of elements stored in slots i and j respectively. We set $p(i \xrightarrow{t} i+1)$ and $p(i \xrightarrow{t} 0)$ as follows:

- $p(i \xrightarrow{t} i+1) = \dfrac{1-g(r_{i+1},t)}{1-g(r_i,t)}$) if $i \neq 0$
- $p(i \xrightarrow{t} i+1) = 2-2*g(r_{i+1},t)$ if $i = 0$
- $p(i \xrightarrow{t} 0) = 1\text{-}p(i \xrightarrow{t} i+1)$

To create the random event $i \xrightarrow{t} i+1$ we first compute $p(i \xrightarrow{t} i+1)$, through a function that given *r*, *t* returns *f(r, t)*. Then we access a random number between 0 and 1, and the event occurs if this random number is at least equal to $p(i \xrightarrow{t} i+1)$.

Observe that when a new stream element arrives, the cursor always rests at the artificial element. The randomness introduced by the random walk involves the states accessed by the cursor during its traversal of the sample list, from the artificial element and back to it. A more formal description of the algorithm follows:

Algorithm for creating a temporally biased sample

$t \leftarrow t+1$
We insert the new stream element at the rightmost position of the sample-list (thus, when the first stream element arrives, it becomes the right neighbor of the artificial element).
delete_item $\leftarrow$ 0
$j \leftarrow 0$
Repeat
    $k \leftarrow j$
    We toss a biased coin with *p*(heads) = $p(j \xrightarrow{t} j+1)$
    if "heads" occur
        $j \leftarrow j+1$
        if delete_item = 1 then we delete element (slot) *k* **end if**
        We toss a fair coin.
        If "heads" occur then delete_item $\leftarrow$ 1 **else** delete_item $\leftarrow$ 0 **end if**
    else
        $j \leftarrow 0$
        if delete_item = 1 then we delete element (slot) *k* **end if**
    end if
Until $j = 0$

4.2 Analysis of the Algorithm

We must prove that our random walk is valid. Clearly, the sum of the probabilities of all the events occurring in any state are equal to 1 by definition (see Subsection 4.1). It remains to show that all transition probabilities are between 0 and 1.

Theorem 1: By setting the transition probabilities as shown in Subsection 4.1, all transition probabilities are between 0 and 1.

Proof: If $i = 0$, then $p(i \xrightarrow{t} i+1)$ is valid because:

$p(i \xrightarrow{t} i+1) < 1$ $ since $g(r_1,t) > 0.5$ and $p(i \xrightarrow{t} i+1) \geq 0$ since $g(r_{u_1},t) \leq 1$

If $i \neq 0$, then $p(i \xrightarrow{t} i+1) \geq 0$ because the enumerator and the denominator are both greater than 0. In advance, observe that $r_{i+1} > r_i$ because u_i is older than u_{i+1}. According to the definition of the "harder to the older" functions, it follows that $g(r_{i+1},t) > g(r_i,t)$. This means that $1-g(r_{i+1},t) < 1-g(r_i,t)$ and as a result, $p(i \xrightarrow{t} i+1) < 1$.

Theorem 2: The algorithm creates a sample consistent with the bias-function *f*(*r*, *t*).

Proof: Let us assume that element u_i, $(1 \leq i \leq n)$ arrived at time-point r_i. Then at each time-point *t* the cursor will reach the slot corresponding to element u_i with probability:

$$p(0 \xrightarrow{t} i) = p(0 \xrightarrow{t} 1) * p(1 \xrightarrow{t} 2) * \ldots * p(i-1 \xrightarrow{t} i) \Rightarrow$$

$$\Rightarrow p(0 \xrightarrow{t} i) = \left(2 - 2 * g(r_1,t)\right) * \frac{1-g(r_2,t)}{1-g(r_1,t)} * \ldots * \frac{1-g(r_i,t)}{1-g(r_{i-1},t)} \Rightarrow$$

$$\Rightarrow p(0 \xrightarrow{t} 1) = 2 - 2 * g(r_i, t)$$

According to our algorithm, if the cursor reaches slot i, the states of slot i have equal probabilities of being accessed. As a result, the probability that we reach state u_i-select during time-point t is:

$$p(u_i - select) = 1 - g(r_i, t)$$

Reaching the u_i-select state, means that we delete u_i, at time-point t. Therefore, the probability that u_i survives in the sample during time-point t is equal to $g(r_i, t)$. This way it follows that an element that arrived at time r continues to exist in the sample at time t with probability:

$$p(r,t) = g(r, r+1) * g(r, r+2) * \cdots * g(r,t) = f(r,t) \text{ since } f(r,r) = 1$$

The sample may shrink or grow but on the average its size is expected to be equal to $\lim_{t\to\infty} \sum_{i=1}^{t} f(i,t)$ since (according to Theorem 2) the sample is consistent with $f(r, t)$. In Section 2 we have assumed that $f(r, t)$ is M-implementable, therefore the average sample-size is a value at most equal to the size of the available primary memory.

The expected time-complexity per stream element at time t is proportional to the expected number of slots accessed by the cursor during time-point t. This number depends on the elements present in the sample at time t. More formally, given a time-point t and a set $H=\{u_1, u_2, \ldots, u_n\}$ that contains all the elements in the sample at time t so that u_i $(1 < i \leq n)$ has arrived after u_j $\forall$ $j < i$, let $EL_{H,t}$ be the expected number of slots accessed by the cursor at t. Then:

$$EL_{h,t} = 1 + p(0 \xrightarrow{t} 1) + p(0 \xrightarrow{t} 2) + \cdots + p(0 \xrightarrow{t} n) \Rightarrow$$

$$\Rightarrow EL_{H,t} = 1 + \sum_{i=1}^{n} \left(2 - 2 * g(r_i, t)\right)$$

Although the expected time complexity at time t depends on the existing sample at time t, we can derive an estimation of the expected time per stream element through an amortization approach over all the possible samples at time t. In particular, the algorithm will create a sample where the r-th element of the stream (i.e., $S(r)$) exists in the sample at time t with probability $f(r, t)$ and the cursor will reach $S(r)$ at time t with probability $2 - 2 * g(r,t)$. We define EL_t to be the expected number of slots accessed at time t, amortized over all possible samples having been created at time t. It follows that:

$$EL_t = \sum_{i=1}^{t} \left(2 - 2 * g(i,t)\right) * f(i,t)$$

and then the amortized expected time-complexity of our algorithm at time t is equal to $O(\lim_{t\to\infty} EL_t)$ The following theorem states that the amortized expected time-complexity of our algorithm is O(1).

Theorem 3: Let $f(r, t)$ be an M-implementable time-decay bias-function supported by our algorithm. Then, $\lim_{t\to\infty} EL_t = 2$

Proof: The proof is an immediate consequence of Theorem 2. According to Theorem 2, the algorithm creates a sample consistent with $f(r, t)$. By definition, the average size of this sample is at most M since $f(r, t)$ is M-implementable. Since the average sample-size is neither infinite nor 0 we conclude that in the long run, for each element that is inserted into the sample, an element is deleted from the sample (in any other case, the sample size would either grow to infinity or shrink to 0). Since at each time-point one element is inserted into the sample, we conclude that on the average one element is deleted per time-point. According to the algorithm, each accessed slot (element) is deleted with probability 0.5. As a result, the amortized number of elements accessed per time-point is 2.

5. EXPERIMENTS

For the experiments we define two different families of functions, i) increasing decay rate exponential-like bias-functions and ii) linear bias-functions.

A function $f(r, t)$ belongs to the increasing decay rate exponential-like family if:

$$g(r,t) = 1 - \frac{c*(t-r)}{2(t-r+1)}$$

We name constant c, ($c \leq 1$) *decay factor*. The smaller the value of c, the bigger the sample. Clearly, $g(r,t)$ drops as t - r increases (i.e. $f(r, t)$ belongs to the "harder to the older" category). If $t = r$, it follows that $g(r,t) = 1$ i.e. the cursor is not allowed to reach the rightmost element of the list which means that $p(t, t) = 1$. Furthermore: $\lim_{t-r\to\infty} g(r,t) = 1 - c/2$ i.e. $g(r,t) > 0.5$

Linear bias-functions are functions of the form $f(r, t) = 1-(t-r)*c$ where c (the decay factor) is less than 1. To our knowledge, such a function has never been used in the literature in the context of sampling over a data stream. It is obvious that $g(r, t)$ drops as t - r increases (i.e. $f(r, t)$ belongs to the "harder to the older" category). If $t = r$, it follows that $g(r, t) = 1$ and as a result, the cursor is not allowed to reach the rightmost element of the list (i.e. $p(t, t) = 1$). The problem is that if the arrival time r of an element is c-1 time-points away from the current time-point, it follows that $g(r, r+c-1) = 0.5$ which cannot be supported by our algorithm. However, in practice this is not a real problem, since if $g(r, t) = 0.5$, $f(r, t)$ is really small. In our experiments, we have chosen to set the forward probability equal to 1 for elements that arrived at least c-1 time-points away from the current time-point, forcing thus the cursor to visit each such element on every time-point. This means that each such element is expected to remain in the sample for two time-points. As a result, small inconsistencies may occur in regard to $f(r, t)$ in the area of inclusion probabilities that are very close to 0, but the portion of the sample that is inconsistent with $f(r, t)$ is negligible. The number of additional elements to be accessed per time-point is not affected asymptotically, because we introduce O(1) additional elements per time-point.

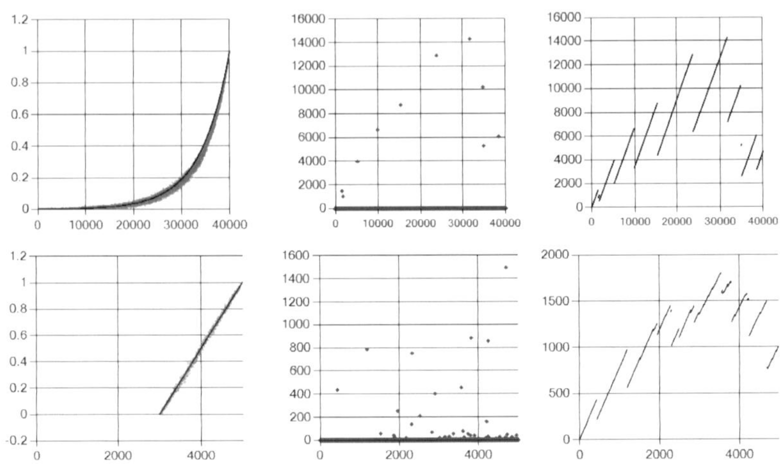

Figure 2. Experimental results

In Figure 2 we show the experimental results. In all of the graphs, the x-axis contains the time-points. The upper three graphs correspond to the increasing decay exponential-like bias-function produced by setting c=1/3000. The algorithm produces 500 samples, stops at 40000 time-points and $p(r, t)$ is experimentally computed (it is the number of samples containing $S(r)$ at time t, divided by the total number of samples). On the left graph, the black line corresponds to the theoretically calculated probability of each time-point to be represented in the sample at time t = 40000, according to the given bias-function. The gray (blue) zone around the black line consists of very dense points, where each point corresponds to the experimentally calculated probability of the corresponding time-point to be represented in the sample. Clearly, our algorithm works as proved. For each time-point we measure the time spent by the algorithm by measuring the sample elements accessed during that time-point. The graph in the middle shows the time spent per time-point. Observe that most of the measured time costs are very close to the 0 since only a few sample elements were accessed. The amortized expected time was found to be 1.84, i.e. less than 2 and there is a simple explanation for that: In the beginning, there exists a large number of time-points when no sample element is accessed because u_l is close to the current time-point and $p(0 \xrightarrow{t} 1)$ is very small. If the algorithm is allowed to be executed for more time-points, the measured time-complexity is found to approach 2. Finally, the graph on the right shows the sample size at each time-point. It appears to be composed by distinct straight lines that can be explained as follows: Most of the time-points, no element is accessed and when that happens, the sample grows by one element. When finally the event $0 \xrightarrow{t} 1$ occurs, it is very possible that the cursor performs a long walk over the sample-list, and each element accessed during this walk is deleted from the sample with probability 0.5. Then the sample size drops significantly.

The lower three graphs in Figure 2 correspond to the linear function produced by setting c=1/2000. The algorithm produces 500 samples and stops at 5000 time-points. Each graph visualizes the same information as the graph above it. The left graph clearly shows that the produced sample is consistent with the given bias-function. The middle graph shows the time-cost per time-point and the one on the right shows the sample size. Each graph looks like the graph on top of it, because the "behavior" of our algorithm is similar for both functions.

6. CONCLUSION

We showed that given a time-decay bias-function $f(r, t)$ that belongs to the "harder to the older" category, a sample consistent with $f(r, t)$ can be maintained by sparing O(1) amortized time per incoming stream element. This result has been made possible through the use of random walks and shows the superiority of this technique over existing ones in terms of time-complexity. Furthermore, we consider our algorithm to be simple and easy to implement.

REFERENCES

Aggarwal C., 2006. On Biased Reservoir Sampling in the Presence of Stream Evolution. *Proceedings of the 32nd International Conference on Very Large Data Bases (VLDB)*, Seoul, Korea, pp 607-618.

Aggarwal C. et al, 2007. A Survey of Synopsis Construction in Data Streams. In: *Aggarwal C.C. (eds) Data Streams. Advances in Database Systems*, vol 31, Springer, Boston, MA.

Bailis P. et al, 2017. MacroBase: Prioritizing Attention in Fast Data. *Proceedings the ACM International Conference on Management of Data*, Chicago, Illinois, USA , pp 541-556.

Chao, M. T., 1982. A general purpose unequal probability sampling plan. *Biometrika,* Vol. 69, No. 3 pp. 653-656.

Efraimidis P. S., Spirakis P. G., 2006. Weighted random sampling with a reservoir. *Information Processing Letters,* Vol. 97, No 5, pp 181-185.

Efraimidis P. S., 2010. Weighted random sampling over data streams. *arXiv preprint* arXiv:1012.0256.

Haas P. J., 2016. Data-Stream Sampling: Basic Techniques and Results. In *Data Stream Management – Processing High-Speed Data Streams*, Springer, 13-44.

Hentschel, B. et al, 2018. Temporally-Biased Sampling for Online Model Management. *Proceedings of EDBT/ICDT 2018 Joint Conference*, Vienna, Austria.

PERFORMANCE OF CORE METHODOLOGIES FOR CONSUMER PRICE PREDICTION SERVICES

Anne Falkenberg
Catholic University of Eichstaett-Ingolstadt, Auf der Schanz 49, 85049 Ingolstadt, Germany

ABSTRACT

The need to monitor prices gave rise to price comparison sites that have not yet adopted recommendation services to support customers in scheduling buying decisions. Using a large data set with 1.46 million daily minimum price observations for four product categories of electronic consumer goods, we outline reasons for the slow adoption of recommendation services, evaluate almost 1.1 billion price forecasts, and show that product prices are forecastable. We compare 16 different methods that can act as the core of price prediction services and give detailed insights on performance as well as advice on model selection for different product categories and advocate the transition towards prescriptive price analytics services.

KEYWORDS

Price Forecasting, Big Data, e-Commerce, Price Time Series, Predictive Analytics

1. INTRODUCTION

Consumers increasingly adopt online and mobile retail channels, which not only offer more convenient shopping experiences but also increase price transparency. Despite the universal availability of price information that allows comparing different offers, this also leads to a large amount of available prices especially for standardized products (Pan et al., 2002). Therefore, a key element of modern retail business models are pricing strategies that critically shape retailers' margins and profits (Bolton et al., 2006). Because price changes in traditional channels were rather rare, now that products are available online, pricing receives much more attention and price-setting behavior becomes more dynamic (Kannan et al., 2001; Kopalle et al., 2009; Levy et al., 2004). Price changes partially follow rational patterns and prices are adjusted based on demand and inventory considerations or as differentiation from other e-commerce platforms. Smaller or specialized retailers however often follow opportunistic patterns where the objectives are not transparent or price changing actions are not guided by algorithms. This uncertainty for the customer in combination with their high price sensitivity especially for homogeneous consumer goods gave rise to price aggregation platforms that act as a facilitator and allow customers to easily gain an overview of the retail landscape.

Apart from static or historical information, price comparison sites (PCS) like *idealo* or *shopbrain* recently started offering services to actively support customers in the buying process and enable them to use the provided information to optimize their purchase time decisions. The core of these services is usually a methodology to extrapolate prices based on historical information that allows condensing expectations about future price developments. However, compared to predictive or prescriptive analytics services found in the airfare industry, the approaches observable in the consumer goods retail market are quite elementary. While it seems surprising that there is such a difference between the airfare and consumer goods industries, this can be at least partially explained by characteristics of the underlying data generation process, the available data and, therefore, methodologies disposable to solve the underlying forecasting problem.

Given a product that a customer wants to purchase, s/he is usually not interested in the price from one specific seller. If a customer is not willing to choose from a range of quality-controlled sellers but sticks to one retailer, there will be no need for her/him to actually monitor the retail landscape via an aggregation platform. The entire business model of PCS, therefore, grounds on the users' flexibility about the place of purchase. The price of an individual retailer alone is no longer of primary interest to the customer. Instead, the minimum of all prices from the listed retailers constitutes the relevant reference price. The corresponding daily minimum prices are crucial to the customer and represent what PCS usually display in their historical pricing charts.

This process generates price time series with specific characteristics. Prices of consumer goods usually deteriorate over time, thus exhibit a time-dependent level. Price adjustments occur irregularly and with varying magnitude leading to calmer and more active price changing phases as well as to entirely constant segments. Time series of minimum prices exhibit similar characteristics than the ones from individual sellers but show more extreme values and shorter, more irregular segments with constant prices. When analyzing day-to-day price movements and thus the sequence of price changes, these constant segments lead to many observations that are zero, which is referred to as zero-inflation (Kömm and Küsters, 2015; Winkelmann, 2008). Many traditional forecasting techniques assume a strictly continuous distribution of the forecasted data (Hyndman and Athanasopoulos, 2018). This assumption is violated in the given case. However, methodological approaches that explicitly consider these shortcomings are rare, computational cumbersome and thus not scalable or directly applicable to forecast durable consumer goods prices (Buchwitz and Küsters, 2018; Kömm and Küsters, 2015; Rydberg and Shephard, 2003; Sucarrat and Grønneberg, 2016). The nature of the forecasting setting, as well as different challenges evolving from the concerning industry, customer environment and the time series characteristics, make forecasting minimum price time series for multiple product categories demanding. However, it is necessary if PCS want to enhance their service to help customers optimize their purchase time decisions.

In this paper, we aim to investigate the forecasting performance of available and scalable forecasting techniques for analytics services when applied to composed minimum price time series of consumer goods. In doing so, we evaluate and compare 16 methods for a forecast horizon of 8 weeks exemplary on 4 product groups: refrigerators, computer memory, graphic cards and smartphones. We focus on this short-term forecast horizon for two reasons: First, it is the most relevant for customers' buying decisions. Second, notification services like price alarms have an average waiting time up to two months for a 5% price reduction independent of the product category, showing that this time period is highly relevant for practical implementation (idealo, 2017). Our research is to the best of our knowledge the first contribution that benchmarks forecasting performance of core methodologies for prices of consumer durable goods for a broad range of product categories.

2. DATA SET

The analysis is based on a sample of daily minimum price observations from the German e-commerce market for 2,000 electronic consumer goods ranging from home appliances over computer hardware to smartphones, equally split into four categories. To make results comparable, we focus on the length of a typical life cycle for electronic consumer products and analyze the first two years of data resulting in 730 observations per item. In total, this yields a data set with 1.46 million daily observations. All items stem from well-known and established brands and each time series represents a specific entity with completely homogeneous properties and features, meaning different product configurations, sizes or colors constitute different time series.

Table 1. Descriptive statistics by product category

Category	Avg. Initial Price in €	Average Price in €	Average Daily Price Change in €	% of Constant Observations (zero-inflation)	N
Computer Memory	237.47	145.32	-0.17	38 %	500
Graphic Cards	279.86	235.14	-0.05	45 %	500
Refrigerators	829.04	709.79	-0.19	72 %	500
Smartphones	496.71	333.29	-0.29	64 %	500
All	460.77	355.89	-0.18	55 %	2,000

Table 1 provides the descriptive statistics for the nominal price level and the price changing frequency for the four product categories. The products with the highest average initial price are refrigerators with 829.04€ directly followed by smartphones with 496.71€. However, the single highest initial price with roughly 3,900€ comes from an AMD Graphic Card for Professional Workstations. Interestingly, the average daily price change is not directly linked to the price level so that computer memories reach an average daily price reduction of 0.17€, compared to graphic cards that only deteriorate with a rate of 0.05€ per day-to-day price movement.

The average daily price change of all products in the sample amounts to -0.18€. The most volatile products in terms of occurring price changes are memory modules, where only 38% of the observations do not change compared to the price from the previous day. Compared to this, refrigerator prices are more constant. With 72% zero-inflation in the data, the minimum price for a refrigerator changes on average about twice a week.

Figure 1 provides an aggregated overview of the utilized data. Each of the figures (1a-1d) shows the average relative price development over the first two years of the product life cycle for the respective category. Given a single time series $\{y_t\}_{t\in\mathbb{N}}$, each daily price y_t is divided by the initial price y_1 to obtain the relative price. The solid black line displays the relative price averaged over all products of the respective category. The shaded areas around the solid black line correspond to the 50%, 75% and 90% empirical confidence intervals of the relative prices. On average, all prices decrease over time but show different intensities of price deterioration. Besides, the longer the products are in the market, the wider the confidence intervals become. While this is nicely illustrated in figures 1c and 1d, for refrigerators the intervals stay almost constant independent of the products' time in the market. On average, the price level for the home appliance products (1a) drops rapidly but the steepness quickly decreases with the price level before stabilizing at around 85% of their starting price. While this is comparable to the price development of graphic cards shown in figure 1c, the average price level here starts to slightly increase at the end of the life cycle. Graphic cards show an identifiable global minimum approximately 1.5 years after their product launch, which cannot be observed in the other three categories.

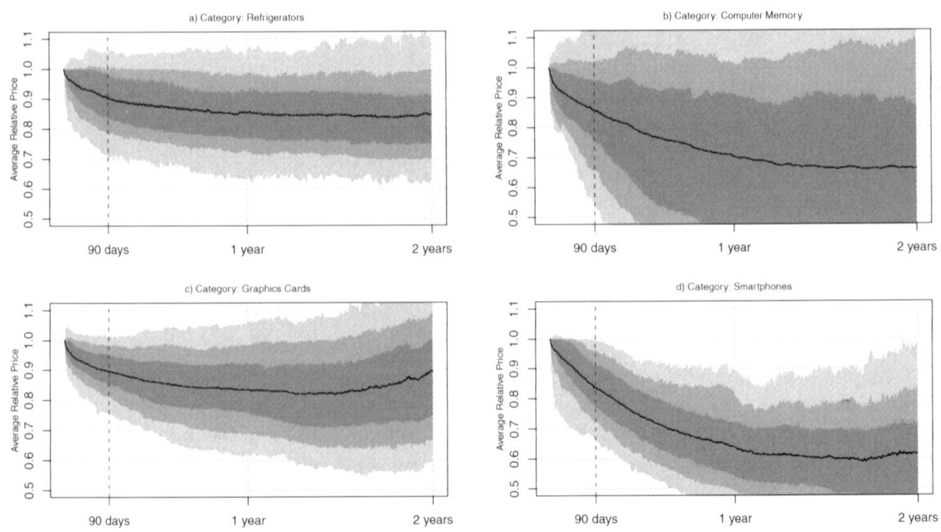

Figure 1. Relative price developments for each product category.

Both – computer memory modules and smartphones – show a comparably strong price deterioration. Even though their respective slope also decreases with the level, computer memory prices stabilize at around 65% of the starting price as shown in figure 1b. The settlement point for the smartphone product category is even lower with around 60%. However, while the general price dynamic of these two categories seem comparable, computer memories exhibit their own momentum. The intervals shown in figure 1b are almost three times wider than the ones shown in the remaining graphs despite representing the same quantiles. This indicates strong heterogeneity between individual items and may also be connected to the low zero-inflation within this category. Summing up the average price development, one can state that the overall shape is comparable for all average relative prices as each category shows deterioration, however, due to variations in slope and settlement levels, the average appearance varies.

3. METHODOLOGY

As shown by the descriptive statistics, forecasting approaches have to deal with a variety of paradigms that are present in the data. Besides the non-transparent data generation process, this includes time series with rapidly changing dynamics, potentially time-varying mean structures and local up- or downward movements that overlay the global price development. Due to this variety, it is unrealistic to expect a single method to deliver the best forecasts independent of these specific characteristics and independent of the forecast horizon. We, therefore, choose methodological corpora that possess different functionalities to deal with the features in the price data.

3.1 Forecasting Models

As several of the selected approaches belong to the same model families, represent simple or special cases of modified models or can be differentiated by pre- and post-processing options, the approaches can be grouped into the following seven classes. Due to the restricted length of this article, the technical details are not explained in-depth but cited accordingly. For each class, we focus on two to four configuration options, which leads to a selection of 16 methods that we elaborate on in the upcoming results section.

Global and Local Trend: Given the fact that the majority of electronic consumer product prices deteriorate over time, models that assume a global trend, present an intuitive benchmark for more complex approaches. We, therefore, include linear time series regression models (Makridakis et al., 1997) that are estimated using ordinary least squares as a benchmark. While the simplest form models a global linear trend (*Trend*), we also generate forecasts using an exponential trend (*Trend exp.*) and employ a configuration that contains a quadratic term (*Trend sq.*) to account for different shapes of price deterioration. As the data contains local dynamics, it may be plausible to restrict the amount of data used for the trend extrapolation to make the model more adaptive to local changes. For this reason, we generate forecasts based on a quarterly sliding window (*Trend 90*).

Mean Models formulate expectations for future price developments based on the arithmetic mean and, therefore, assume that deviations from the mean are based on random perturbations. Following the approach applied by *eBay* to signal price tendencies to their users, we include a global mean model (*Mean*) and the arithmetic mean based on the last 90 observations (*Mean 90*) in our comparison. Both trend and mean models together represent the forecasting approaches known to be currently in place and observable in practice and are, therefore, used mainly as a benchmark for more complex approaches.

Random Walk: Assuming the difference between two consecutive price observations is white noise, pure random walk models (*RW*) use the last available observation as the forecast for all future horizons. While mean and random walk models implement two divergent principles, the mean forecast converges towards a random walk prediction with increasing zero-inflation. Given that there are multiple constant segments in the price time series and that prices show strong price deterioration, we enhance the random walk with a drift term (*RW Drift*) (Hyndman and Athanasopoulos, 2018). This allows the model to incorporate a global tendency while eradicating some shortcomings of the presented trend approaches.

ARIMA: Autoregressive Integrated Moving Average models (ARIMA) depict the inherent dynamics in the price time series and therefore represent a more adaptive group of forecasting approaches. While such models are often described as short-term oriented, this is especially true for types that assume a stationary time series (Box et al., 1994). However, ARIMA models can also be applied to time series originating from an instationary data generation process and include coefficients to incorporate longer-term tendencies in the data. A fitted slope reflects the inherent direction of the price development after accounting for the partial autocorrelation (moving average) and autoregressive structure in the data. To estimate models, a concrete specification has to be determined, for which we revert to a procedure that automatically selects the model order that fits best to the price data (*AutoARIMA*) (Hyndman and Khandakar, 2008). This setting considers stationary as well as instationary model configurations and includes an appropriate number of autoregressive and moving average coefficients to capture the price dynamics. Additionally, we also employ forecasts that originated from models assuming instationary data generation processes, so that only the autoregressive and moving average orders are automatically selected (*AutoARIMA inst.*).

Exponential Smoothing: The inherent modeling idea of exponential smoothing models (EXS) is that forecasts are adjusted based on a local and time-varying level, trend and/or error estimates, while the speed of the adjustment is controlled via smoothing constants. Some model configurations allow for additive or multiplicative components in each case with or without damped trends (Holt, 2004) or combine these approaches with additive or multiplicative seasonality indices. An overview of the existing and considered configurations is given by Pegels (1969) and Gardner (2006, 1985). To estimate and forecast exponential smoothing models, we refer to their state-space representation that also enables automatic model selection

(*EXS*) (Hyndman et al., 2008). However, due to the good results in forecasting competitions (Makridakis and Hibon, 2000), we include some pure models in addition to the automated model selection approach – most importantly an exponential smoothing model with additive, damped trend (*EXS dHolt*). This allows us to derive conclusions based on the different components considered by the models.

Theta: The Theta method is a decomposition approach where the segmented components of a time series are called Theta-lines (Assimakopoulos and Nikolopoulos, 2000). Hyndman and Billah (2003) show that the generated forecasts are numerically equivalent to an exponential smoothing model combined with a drift term. This drift coefficient is equal to half of the slope coefficient when fitting a linear regression model to the data. For this reason, the Theta method is known to generate conservative predictions that show no extreme up- or downward tendencies. We employ an adapted version of the Theta method (*FourTheta*) (Nikolopoulos and Assimakopoulos, 2004) that is more tailored to the data in addition to the original version that we present in combination with a logarithmic transformation of the prices (*logTheta*) (Assimakopoulos and Nikolopoulos, 2000; Box and Cox, 1964).

Combination Methods have the potential to eradicate shortcomings from the individual methods through calculating the (weighted) average of the derived point forecasts (Clemen, 1989). Obviously, the resulting performance depends on the incorporated method. We consider static and equally weighted combinations for the automatic selection procedures of EXS and ARIMA models (*Combi EA*) as well as for a group of exponential smoothing models consisting of the simple exponential smoothing and exponential smoothing with and without damped trend (*Combi SHD*) that was also used in the M4 forecasting competition (M4 Competition, 2018).

3.2 Forecast Generation and Evaluation

To evaluate the forecasting accuracy of the presented methods, we use genuine out-of-sample forecasts. Each of the time series considered in the study contributes 730 observations to the sample. Because a sufficient amount of observations is needed to actually estimate an initial model, we reserve the first 90 time points as an introductory training set, while the remaining 640 observations are allocated to the initial test set. The forecast generation and evaluation scheme is illustrated in figure 2, where the black blocks represent observations that are incorporated in the model estimation, while grey and white circles in the boxes represent the generated forecasts. All forecasts that belong to the same forecast horizon are marked with the same color, e.g. the one-step-ahead forecasts shown in dark grey. In total, this cross-validation scheme yields 34,300 evaluable forecasts per method and time series pair. Given the 2,000 electronic consumer products and 16 considered model variants, we extract our findings from a basis of almost 1.1 billion evaluated predictions.

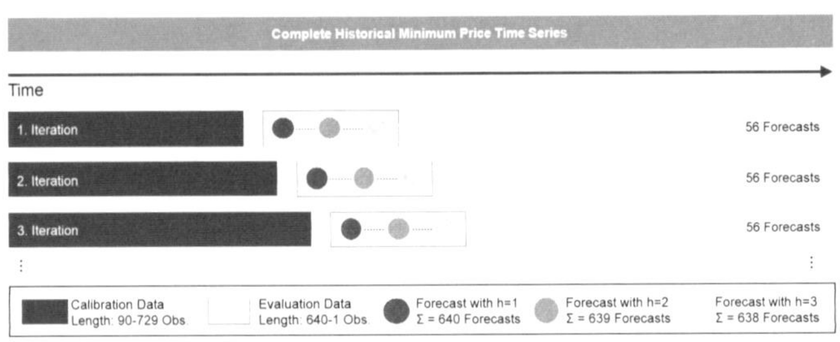

Figure 2. Rolling forecast evaluation scheme

Because we forecast prices, the generated predictions and their accuracy are related to the level of the respective time series. Thus, the need to make results comparable over all time points, forecast horizons, and products in the data set arises. For the evaluation, we, therefore, refer to the mean absolute percentage error (MAPE) per product as the main performance indicator. The MAPE for a specific forecast horizon h conditional on a specific product and method is given by

$$MAPE_h = \frac{1}{640 - h + 1} \sum_{k=1}^{640-h+1} \left| \frac{y_{90+h+k-1} - \hat{y}_{90+h+k-1}}{y_{90+h+k-1}} \right|$$

For each method, the evaluation measure is calculated over all forecasts that have been generated for one horizon (e.g. for $h = 1$ over the grey circles in figure 2). By being an aggregated measure, the MAPE allows gaining an understanding of the overall performance for the specific product and for different forecast horizons. We focus on presenting our findings for the traditional MAPE, which is not only more widely used but also allows comparability with other studies (Clements, 2005). However, results of other measures are consistent.

4. RESULTS

The following chapter presents overall performance as well as measures differentiated by product category for the different forecasting methods. As all performance differences between methods are highly significant due to the extremely large sample size, the following section does not present evidence and results from statistical tests for mean differences or predictive performance in general. In order to be able to visualize the results, the product-dependent evaluation measures have been condensed by averaging over all products in the sample or over the respective product category. The performance indicators for each method, therefore, represent 1.28 million in total respectively 320,000 forecasts per category for the first horizon.

Table 2 shows the resulting performance measure in percent for the 16 methods. When interpreting the MAPE, random walk, *AutoARIMA,* and *EXS* perform well, however, better performance is noted by *logTheta, FourTheta*, *EXS dHolt,* and *Combi SHD*. Interestingly, estimating the Theta method on a logarithmically transformed price series improves performance by 0.18% relative to the accuracy of the Theta model estimated on the nominal price values. The worst performances expectedly come from models that are not tied to the last observations of the series, so *Mean* as well as the linear trend, fail to deliver convincing results.

Table 2. Forecasting results in %

Method	*Trend*	*Trend sq.*	*Trend exp.*	*Trend 90*	*Mean*	*Mean 90*	*RW*	*RW Drift*	*Auto ARIMA*	*Auto ARIMA inst.*	*EXS*	*EXS dHolt*	*Four Theta*	*Log Theta*	*Combi EA*	*Combi SHD*
MAPE	13.23	11.61	9.8	7.14	20.77	8.35	5.01	6.31	6.06	5.98	5.21	4.99	4.98	4.93	5.37	4.99

Noteworthy insights are found when comparing models over time within their classes as shown in figure 3. As expected, the presented MAPE values increase with growing forecast horizons due to the rising uncertainty. This behavior is consistent throughout all methods. One should note that the value range of the axes between the first and second rows has been adapted to make results more legible. Figure 3 shows the forecast accuracy over a forecasting window from $h = 1$ to 56 for all methods. While the global mean is, without a doubt, the worst method to choose, Theta and Combination models complemented by the random walk produce suitable forecasts and show similar courses of their graphs over the forecast horizons. Additionally, *EXS dHolt* performs well throughout the shown 56 forecast horizons and exhibits a MAPE below 8% at $h = 56$ and by that delivers the third-best results after *logTheta* and *Combi SHD* and before *FourTheta* and *RW*. While the EXS and the ARIMA approaches deliver similar results for very short forecast horizons, ARIMA produces inferior results when horizons grow. This performance drift may explain why the combination of these two methodologies shows a deteriorated performance, while the combination of different EXS models (*Combi SHD*) delivers the second-best results at the end of the observation period.

Additionally, one should note that there are only a few crossing points between models and also between classes, meaning intersections, where it is favorable to switch from one method to another. In most cases, the performance order of the methods stays constant. An exception for that is the quadratic trend, which performs well for small forecast horizons, but its forecast error rises rapidly with increasing forecast horizons.

The results of trend models (3a) are very diverse compared to groups 3c and 3d. While the exponential and local (*Trend 90*) trend perform reasonably, the linear and quadratic trend appear to be not recommendable. Mean and random walk models (3b) also show very heterogeneous results with all random walk models outperforming the mean class. Within the random walk models, there is only a small difference between the *RW* and *RW Drift* in the short run. However, this quickly changes with increasing forecast horizons leading to highly deviating results – the random walk with drift being only the 10th-best model at $h = 56$, while the normal random walk shows suitable performance for the price data. ARIMA models (3c) perform reasonably on rather short horizons in general; however, as figure 3c shows both *EXS* models outperform the ARIMA class. The very good performance of the automatic exponential smoothing procedure can be easily overlooked when compared to configuration options within its model class. This is because the Holt exponential smoothing method with a damped trend delivers the second-best results in the analysis of the average performance and third best when looking at $h = 56$. As table 2 and figure 3d show, *FourTheta* is slightly inferior to the logarithmized configuration of the original Theta model. Finally, *Combi SHD* consistently outperforms the combination of the automatic selection procedures of EXS and ARIMA.

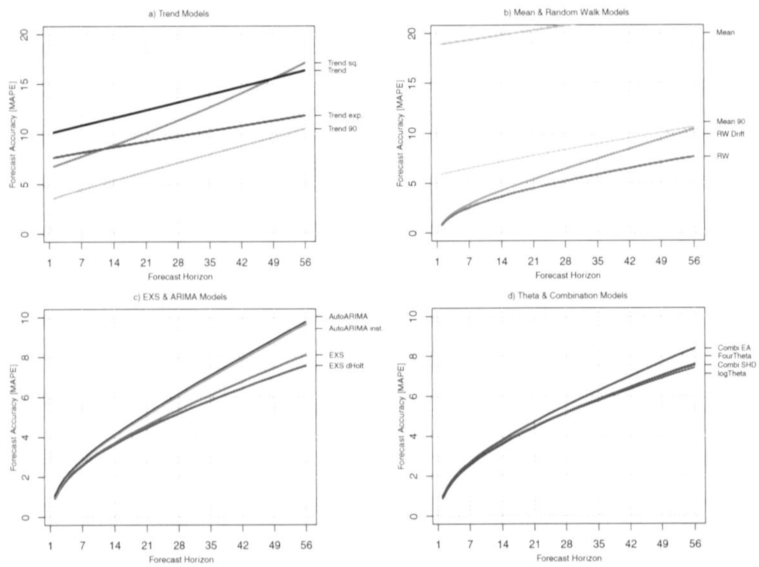

Figure 3. Result comparisons within model classes.

When discussing category-specific results, it is important to analyze which method delivers the best results for a given category. For refrigerators – from the 16 described methods – the *FourTheta* method delivers the best results directly followed by the random walk. Interestingly, the method including model adaptations with the lowest error is the single exponential smoothing model, which is the simplest form of exponential smoothing including only a weighted moving average and no components for trend or seasonality. For graphic cards, the pure *RW* model works best for all 56 horizons. However, the *RW* is narrowly outperformed by the *FourTheta* method for larger forecast horizons. The *Combi SHD* model delivers very good results for the smartphone product category. But pre- and postprocessing of the data in terms of applying the methods to logarithmic prices improves results significantly so that the *logTheta* method consistently outperforms all other methods independent of the forecast horizon. For the product category that is hardest to forecast – computer memory – *Combi SHD* works best overall. However, the Holt exponential smoothing model with a damped trend has very similar MAPEs resulting mainly from the good performance for larger forecast horizons.

All in all, it often seems to be advisable to transform the underlying data before generating predictions. Transformations like the exemplarily discussed logarithmic one, do not guarantee better performance but sometimes improve results and rarely lead to significantly worse outcomes.

5. CONCLUSION AND PRACTICAL IMPLICATIONS

In this paper, we presented an in-depth empirical analysis evaluating the forecasting performance of 16 methods for price prediction services based on a large sample of product price time series. We showed that univariate time series forecasting methods deliver suitable performance and that these methods are a viable option when planning and designing services, that support customers while buying consumer goods. By explicitly focusing on consumer goods prices, we help facilitate the transition towards data-driven services and dynamic business models for price aggregation sites and enable them to support customers to make better, more informed, less costly buying decisions.

Due to the large sample size and the variability of products and forecast horizons, the performance of particular forecasting configurations can be derived easily from our analysis. We showed that even though methods like Theta models perform well in a lot of cases, a one-fits-all solution does not exist – neither for every product category nor for every forecast horizon. When designing a recommendation service this should be taken into account and adapted depending on the application context.

Generally, we find that simple methods are hard to outperform, which is an indication that more complex approaches could not fully leverage the specific data characteristics. Thus, it would be interesting to investigate which data features contribute to forecast accuracy.

REFERENCES

Assimakopoulos, V., Nikolopoulos, K., 2000. The theta model: A decomposition approach to forecasting. *Int. J. Forecast.* 16, 521-530.

Bolton, R.N., Shankar, V., Montoya, D.Y., 2006. Recent Trends and Emerging Practices in Retailer Pricing, in: Krafft, M., Mantrala, M.K. (Eds.), *Retailing in the 21st Century - Current and Future Trends.* Springer, Germany, pp. 255-269.

Box, G.E.P., Cox, D., 1964. An analysis of transformations. *J. R. Stat. Soc. - Ser. B.* 26, 211-252.

Box, G.E.P., Jenkins, G.M., Reinsel, G.C., 1994. *Time Series Analysis: Forecasting & Control.* Wiley, Hoboken, NJ.

Buchwitz, B., Küsters, U., 2018. Should I buy my new iPhone now? Predictive Event Forecasting for Zero-Inflated Consumer Goods Prices. *Proc. 39th Int. Conf. Inf. Syst.* 1-16.

Clemen, R.T., 1989. Combining forecasts: A review and annotated bibliography. *Int. J. Forecast.* 5, 559-583.

Clements, M.P., 2005. *Evaluating Econometric Forecasts of Economic and Financial Variables.* Palgrave Macmillan, NY.

Gardner, E.S., 2006. Exponential Smoothing: The State of the Art - Part II. *Int. J. Forecast.* 22, 637-666.

Gardner, E.S., 1985. Exponential Smoothing: The State of the Art. *J. Forecast.* 4, 1-28.

Holt, C.C., 2004. Forecasting seasonals and trends by exponentially weighted moving averages. *Int. J. Forecast.*

Hyndman, R.J., Athanasopoulos, G., 2018. *Forecasting: Principles and Practice*, 2nd ed. OTexts.

Hyndman, R.J., Billah, B., 2003. Unmasking the Theta method. *Int. J. Forecast.* 19, 287-290.

Hyndman, R.J., Khandakar, Y., 2008. Automatic time series forecasting: The forecast package for R. *J. Stat. Softw.* 27, 1-22.

Hyndman, R.J., Koehler, A.B., Ord, K., Snyder, R.D., 2008. *Forecasting with Exponential Smoothing - The State Space Approach.* Springer, Berlin, Germany.

idealo, 2017. *Bestseller und ihr Preisverfall - Wann klingelt der Preiswecker.* Url: https://www.idealo.de/magazin/2017/07/31/bestseller-und-ihr-preisverfall-wann-klingelt-der-preiswecker/.

Kannan, P.K., Kopalle, P.K., Åsbrink, S., 2001. Dynamic Pricing on the Internet: Importance and Implications for Consumer Behavior. *Int. J. Electron. Commer.* 5, 63-83.

Kömm, H., Küsters, U., 2015. Forecasting zero-inflated price changes with a Markov switching mixture model for autoregressive and heteroscedastic time series. *Int. J. Forecast.* 31, 598-608.

Kopalle, P., Biswas, D., Chintagunta, P.K., Fan, J., Pauwels, K., Ratchford, B.T., Sills, J.A., 2009. Retailer Pricing and Competitive Effects. *J. Retail.* 85, 56-70.

Levy, M., Grewal, D., Kopalle, P.K., Hess, J.D., 2004. Emerging trends in retail pricing practice: Implications for research. *J. Retail.* 80, XIII-XXI.

M4 Competition, 2018. *Competitor's Guide.* University of Nicosia, Url: https://www.m4.unic.ac.cy/wp-content/uploads/2018/03/M4-Competitors-Guide.pdf

Makridakis, S., Hibon, M., 2000. The M3-Competition: results, conclusions and implications. *Int. J. Forecast.* 16, 451-476.

Makridakis, S., Wheelwright, S.C., Hyndman, R.J., 2008. *Forecasting Methods and Applications*, 3rd ed. Wiley India, New Delhi.

Nikolopoulos, K., Assimakopoulos, V., 2004. Generalizing the Theta model for automatic forecasting. *Int. Symp. Forecast.* ISF 2004, Sydney, Australia.

Pan, X., Ratchford, B.T., Shankar, V., 2002. Why Aren't the Prices of the Same Item the Same at Me. Com and You.Com?: Drivers of Price Dispersion Among E-Tailers. *SSRN 328820.*

Pegels, C.C., 1969. Exponential Forecasting: Some New Variations. *Manage. Sci.* 15, 311-315.

Rydberg, T.H., Shephard, N., 2003. Dynamics of Trade-by-Trade Price Movements: Decomposition and Models. *J. Financ. Econom.* 1, 2-25.

Sucarrat, G., Grønneberg, S., 2016. Models of Financial Return with Time-Varying Zero Probability. *MPRA Work. Pap.* 1-25.

Winkelmann, R., 2008. *Econometric Analysis of Count Data*, 5th ed. Springer, Germany.

A DATA MINING APPROACH FOR CUSTOMER SEGMENTATION USING A SAF-T BASED BUSINESS INTELLIGENCE SYSTEM

Rosa Silveira, Bruno Oliveira, Mariana Carvalho and Telmo Matos
[1]*CIICESI, Escola Superior de Tecnologia e Gestão, Politécnico do Porto, Portugal*

ABSTRACT

In 2018, 70% of the Portuguese companies produced thousands of Portuguese Audit Tax documents (SAF-T (PT)) files for tax validation. These documents represent a standardized procedure for the Portuguese companies, providing the necessary data about billing, accounting, and taxation. These files contain valuable information that can represent an important tool for analytical procedures to support decision-making processes. Thus, a Business Intelligence System based on SAF-T (PT) was created to support companies' analytical needs. An important decision-making process involves customer evaluation. So, the proposed system will begin, in a preliminary phase, with RFM analysis, for customer segmentation using Clustering techniques and results were cross-validated using Decision Tree and Linear Discriminant Analysis. Additionally, a brief interpretation of marketing strategies was suggested and a comparison between Rapid Miner and SPSS was synthesized. The results show that it is possible to explore SAF-T (PT) files to extract knowledge different than tax purposes, namely, the determination of customer profiles. Accuracy is superior to 80% in both software and techniques.

KEYWORDS

Data Mining, SAF-T (PT), Data Warehousing, Customer Segmentation, ETL

1. INTRODUCTION

Since 2017, the Portuguese Tax Authority (PTA) requires all companies that have organized accounting (approx.70%) to monthly submit the Standard Audit File for Tax Purposes[2] (SAF-T (PT)) for validation. The SAF-T (PT) documents represent valuable data extracted from the companies' operational systems. Despite having these data, several companies do not have mechanisms to create deeper knowledge from the data they produce. Owning data alone is not enough anymore to get practical results. Data need to make sense and be properly framed and aligned with the organization goals to become useful information for managers, who daily make decisions that affect the organization and consequently the stakeholders. This is nowadays the basis for growing business activities. In this paper, we explore the use of billing SAF-T (PT) documents to create a Business Intelligence (BI) System to support decision-making requirements. These documents store monthly data about several organization entities such as customers, products, and sales. This data can be very useful to provide data insights about the organization's business. Thus, a Data Warehouse (DW) can be generated based on SAF-T (PT) data and used within exploratory techniques to extract important findings about the business domain. We explore the customer perspective for data analyses, revealing how SAF-T (PT) data can be used to provide customer segmentation.

For data exploration, the Recency, Frequency and Monetary analysis (Bult and Wansbeek 1995) is performed. This is a customer equity analysis that companies can perform to evaluate and improve their relationship to this important stakeholder. RFM analysis is based on the following measures: Recency (R), which represents the period since customer's last purchase; Frequency (F), is the number of orders in a certain period and, Monetary (M) which represents the amount that the customer spent in the same interval. To perform the RFM method, we resort to Data Mining (DM) (Han, Kamber, and Pei 2012), more specifically, a clustering

[1] {8180717, bmo, mrc, tsm}@estg.ipp.pt
[2] https://www.oecd.org/tax/administration/45167181.pdf

technique, for grouping the customers based on its RFM values. DM allows us to extract knowledge of large datasets, which means, discover hidden and unknown patterns (or useful information) from large databases.

The rest of this paper is organized as follows: the second section is dedicated to a brief literature review; section 3 presents the case study and the validation of the results obtained from the different methods and tools and finally, in section 4 conclusions are addressed and future work suggested.

2. RELATED WORK

DM is widely used in decision support, forecasting, description and prediction in many application fields, like, banking, fraud detection, customer relationship management, and several other fields (Han, Kamber, and Pei 2012; Deshpande and Thakare 2010).

A review on DM techniques are presented in the work of Chen *et al.* (F. Chen et al. 2015) and Deshpande and Thakare (Deshpande and Thakare 2010). Both authors classify DM by the method used and their applications, in a specific domain. In both documents, clustering and classification analysis appear frequently. Clustering analysis is an unsupervised method widely used in the literature with several algorithms and techniques (Berkhin 2006). K-means is a widely used clustering technique that intends to group individuals according to its characteristics and use that information to support decision-making processes (Aviad and Roy 2011). In the order hand, classification is a supervised method that aims to create models used for predicting class labels within unknown records. DT and LDA are supervised methods used for classification or clustering validation.

As we are dealing with SAF-T (PT) data, where the document is oriented towards sales facts, we can perform several analyzes regarding the Customer Relationship Management (CRM) as discussed in (Tsiptsis and Chorianopoulos 2010). Introduced by (Bult and Wansbeek 1995), RFM is implemented to quantify customer equity and to focus on relationship management efforts. Later several approaches were carried out, for instance, weighted RFM in which weights are assigned to each variable according to business characteristics (Zaheri et al. 2012) and augmented RFM, where other variables are added, such as relationship duration, churn probability (Chan, Cheng, and Hsien 2011) or Count item (Khajvand et al. 2011). On the other hand, Chen et al. (Y. L. Chen et al. 2009) were the first to apply the RFM criterion in sequential patterns and, finally, Chan (Chan, Cheng, and Hsien 2011) combined RFM and prices optimization for on-line customers to personalize promotions and allow clients to bargain the conceded prices.

In several studies, thresholds are being specified by domain experts as shown in (Marcus 1998), (Khajvand et al. 2011) or in (Sohrabi and Khanlari 2007). In these papers, authors grouped individuals based on particular limits for each variable and then calculate the correspondent customer life value (CLV), as an index of importance for the company.

In this study, we do not intend to order or rank customers, but to distinguish and value each group of this special stakeholder. In the present study, clustering methods are used for "natural" customer segmentation instead of forcing customers into groups using specified thresholds. The objective is to identify customer characteristics that allow differentiating the company's response with appropriate marketing strategies. We consider that the analysis of natural clusters can help decision-makers identifying pattern clearly and associate market segments easily without partitioning customers *a priori* and, consequently, develop more effective strategies, for instance, targeted marketing (Marcus 1998).

3. RFM ANALYSIS

Even with limited organizational data (only billing and accounting business processes are covered), the SAF-T (PT) documents can represent the foundations to provide analytical procedures to support decision-making processes. This kind of standard data representation can be used to create a Data Warehousing System (DWS) as BI integral component, or, at least, a skeleton that can be used to ground the application of advanced DM techniques and the application of typical analytical procedures to support decision-making (considering perspectives presented in the billing SAF-T (PT) documents such as customer, products or suppliers).

However, even considering a standard data representation for SAF-T (PT), several problems can occur on data instances used to create each document. While structural constraints can be easily validated (using the correspondent XML Schema), the integrity of these data can be difficult to guarantee due to data entry errors or data changes framed on a specific time window. Additionally, history maintenance cannot be guaranteed using only SAF-T (PT) files because of each file stores self-contained data about customers, products, tax values, and invoices for a specific period. When analytical procedures are applied, data lineage and evolution are compromised because we have a small picture of the organization at a specific point in time. With a DW system, data that change over time can be captured, providing properly framed data states that can allow for deep data analysis.

We idealized a simple DW that captures sales events using a fact table and a set of dimension tables proving context and different perspectives for sales data analysis. The *Sales* fact table represents a sale line event with several measures. The amount is one of them, representing the Sale line *amount* obtained by the formula: *Quantity* * *UnitPrice*. Additionally, the DW schema comprises six dimensions: The temporal data dimension (*Calendar*); the *Customer* dimension, represented by the identification of the customer, type and an address hierarchy: *City* -> *Region* -> *Country* -> ALL; the *Invoice* dimension in which each fact belongs; the *Product* dimension; Tax dimension providing context about each sale; and the Company dimension holding the sales data. This is just an example of a possible configuration. Additional business processes could be included in the DW configuration. For example, the "movement of goods" related data could be a good candidate to extend the DW applicability.

In this study, we use this DW and propose a methodology (Figure 1) to perform the customer segmentation analysis and the validation of the outcome. First, it starts with the RFM analysis. A clustering algorithm is applied to the dataset in order to identify clusters according to the customers' characteristics (RFM variables). The first stage of the clustering algorithm implies to pre-process the available data. The second stage of the methodology consists of performing the clustering analysis (modelling phase), and it is previously required to determine the number of k clusters. After the modelling phase, the validation of the outcome of the clustering algorithm is performed, since the created clusters must be validated using supervised learning methods (Marôco, (2018)). So, DT and LDA are both used to validate the clustering outcome.

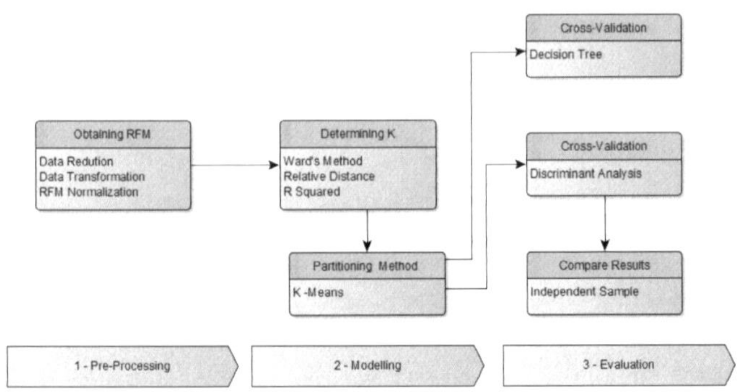

Figure 1. RFM analysis approach

To illustrate the proposed methodology, we randomly choose a company from the dataset. The following 5 attributes (from the original 84) were selected: SKCompany, CustomerID, SKInvoice; InvoiceDate and Amount. In the data pre-processing phase, the data is prepared and transformed into the application of the algorithm. The SKCompany attribute represents a particular company; the CustomerID is used to aggregate invoices with the right customer; using InvoiceDate we generate the new variable Recency by calculating the difference between the date of the last purchase with the actual one; the Frequency is a new attribute derived by the count of SKInvoices and finally to obtain Monetary the average purchase amount for one year was used. Total Monetary and Frequency trends to be correlated, hence the total amount spent in the same period was replaced by the average as proposed by (Marcus 1998). For illustrative purposes, we only perform the RFM analysis on the SKCompany number 8501 with 620 product lines, 124 invoices and 49 customers over one year. As shown in Table 1, in average, the period since a customer last purchase is 9.2 months, the number of purchases made within a year is approximately 13 and a customer usually spends about 4885 euros per year.

Table 1. Descriptive Statistics (SPSS)

Descriptive Statistics					
	N	Minimum	Maximum	Mean	Std. Deviation
Monetary	49	2920,20	7518,00	4885,3594	938,79433
Recency	49	4,99	16,46	9,2063	3,18958
Frequency	49	5	30	12,65	7,507
Valid N (listwise)	49				

3.1 Determining the Best k

Neither Rapidminer[3] nor SPSS[4] provides satisfactory indexes to assess the best number of clusters to be chosen to perform the k-means algorithm. Therefore, both distance between clusters and R^2 criteria will be used to decide the final number of clusters. R^2 represents the proportion of the total variability that is retained by the factor for all p-variables and k solutions and can be processed by applying three one-way ANOVA and comparing the sum of squares within groups with the sum of squares total. For both criteria, the square Euclidean distance (Johnson, Wichern, and others 2002) and the Ward's Method (Anderberg 1973) were used in SPSS, once Rapidminer does not have similar output. On the other hand, from the SPSS outputs, namely from the "Agglomeration Schedule", it is possible to select the last agglomerations and describe relative distances between clusters as shown in Figure 2.

As the number of clusters increases, R^2 increases since it accumulates more variability. On the contrary, as the groups aggregate, the relative distance between them decreases, until the final condition in which all objects are in the same final cluster, where the distance is zero.

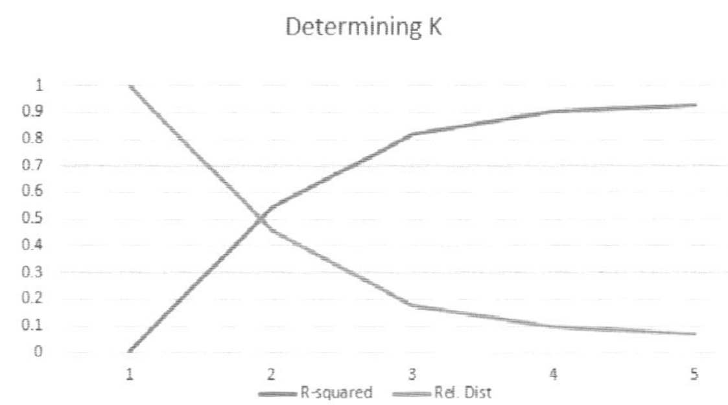

Figure 2. Relative distance and R squared

From the relative distance criteria, the best k is identified by the most pronounced "elbow" that is formed on the downward curve. This criterion is subjective, but in this case, it is visually clear that $k = 3$.

The R^2 criterion is more objective once we can determine that the best solution for k is the smallest number of clusters that retains a significant percentage of the total variability, let us say $R^2 = 80\%$. Then, the number of clusters satisfying those conditions is $k = 3$.

Once we have determined the number of clusters, the classification of each subject in the retained clusters may be refined with the non-hierarchical k-means procedure as follows.

[3] https://rapidminer.com/
[4] https://www.ibm.com/analytics/spss-statistics-software

3.2 K-means Application

While hierarchical algorithms gradually (dis)assemble objects into clusters, partitioning methods calculate distances based on the pre-defined 3 clusters. The output that is generated by each tool is the point in the center of each cluster – the centroids. Then, by centroids coordinates knowledge can be interpreted.

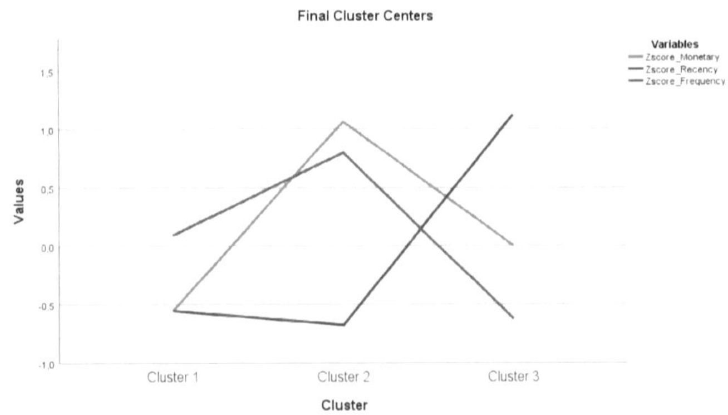

Figure 3. K-means centroids coordinates from customers (SPSS)

We can extract and interpret knowledge from the coordinates of the centroids shown in Figure 3. There are two centroids with the opposite behaviors, 2 and 3. While the type of customers represented in cluster 2 can be considered as a "heavy spender" (with high monetary values), its last purchase was very recent (low recency values) and frequently make purchases (high-frequency values), the type of customers represented in cluster 3 may be interpreted as a "minor spender" (with low monetary values), an infrequent customer (low-frequency values), and does not do purchases for a long time (high recency values). Finally, the type of customer represented in cluster 1 is a "light spender" (with low monetary values, in average), visits frequently the company (high-frequency values) and placed orders recently (low recency values).

The centroids analysis yields insights into marketing strategies and allows to address specific products, campaigns and optimize marketing costs. For instance, the customer in cluster 2 could be classified as an "easy customer", the one in cluster 3 "aversion to shopping" and finally customer in cluster 1 "adhering to promotions".

3.3 Validation of the K-means Outcome

According to (Marôco, 2018), the clusters formed by this heuristic method must be, *à posteriori*, validated using supervised learning methods. Both Rapidminer and SPSS produce a confusion matrix, which can be analyzed and interpreted and to consequently validate the k-means model performance. In both cases, the leave-one-out cross-validation is performed. This is a process in which one observation is left out of the sample then the model is redefined by the other cases and, finally, each case is reclassified by the new model including the one that was kept out.

3.3.1 Validation with Decision Tree

A DT algorithm generates a tree structure, where each internal node denotes a test on an attribute, each branch corresponds to an outcome of the test and each leaf holds a class label (Han, Kamber, and Pei 2012).

After performing the DT algorithm in our dataset, a tree structure is created. This structure allows to deduce the variable that best separates the groups is Recency, which defines high or low recency customers. Then, another decision is applied in the Frequency variable. These two variables are the main responsible for the partition of the groups by this method. Overall, both values are quite high: SPSS presents the higher accuracy value with 87,8%, while Rapidminer presents 85,7%, as shown in table below (Table 2).

Table 2. Validation using DT (Rapidminer and SPSS)

Validation by DT - Rapidminer

	true cluster_1	true cluster_2	true cluster_0	class precision
pred. cluster_1	12	0	0	100.0%
pred. cluster_2	3	26	3	81.3%
pred. cluster_0	0	1	4	80.0%
class recall	80.0%	96.3%	57.1%	85.7%

Validation by DT - SPSS

	true cluster_1	true cluster_2	true cluster_0	class precision
pred. cluster_1	20	2	1	87.0%
pred. cluster_2	1	9	2	75.0%
pred. cluster_0	0	0	14	100.0%
class recall	95.2%	81.8%	82.4%	87.8%

3.3.2 Validation with Linear Discriminant Analysis

The LDA can be performed by various methods. It is a very robust technique against the violation of assumptions although all assumptions were tested and confirmed. Wilks' lambda statistic measures the discriminant power of a variable; however, it is only valid if the variables are independent and if the samples come from a normal multivariate population whose variability is homogeneous in each group.

From the stepwise method, all the variables proved to be significantly important for differentiating groups (p-value<0.001). Recency was the first to enter with the minor value compared with the other variables in step 1 ($\Lambda_R = 0.312$). In step2, considering the remain variance, Monetary was chosen against Frequency ($\Lambda_M = 0.189$) and lastly Frequency joined the set in step 3 ($\Lambda_F = 0.150$). However, we are still unable to identify which clusters are distinguished from each variable. Therefore, two of Fisher´s Discriminant Functions (FDF) were extracted based on the canonical correlation between discriminant functions and groups. Table 3 presents the standardized coefficients of each RFM variable in the discriminating functions 1 and 2, the percentage of explained variances based on the eigenvalues and finally the statistics and the corresponding p-value. Note that each function is highly significant in discriminating groups ($\text{p} - \text{value} < 0.001$) however, the power of the first is vastly superior than the second once the percentage of variance retained is 76% against 24%, respectively.

Table 3. Discriminant Functions coefficients and statistics (adapted from SPSS output)

Standardized Coefficients in Discriminant Function							
Function	Recency	Frequency	Monetary	Eigenvalue	% of Variance	Wilk's Lambda	p-value
1	0.899	-0.437	-0.235	2,633	75.886	0.150	<0.001
2	0.312	0.427	0.957	0,837	24.114	0.554	<0.001

The structural coefficients were also considered but, since the correlation between variables and functions are weak, we obtained similar values, so we kept the standardized coefficients. Additionally, the first function is essentially defined by the variable Recency (0,899) and the second by Monetary (0,957). Thus, Figure 4 illustrates the positioning of each customer on the territorial map obtained by the scores of the FDF whose most significant variable is associated.

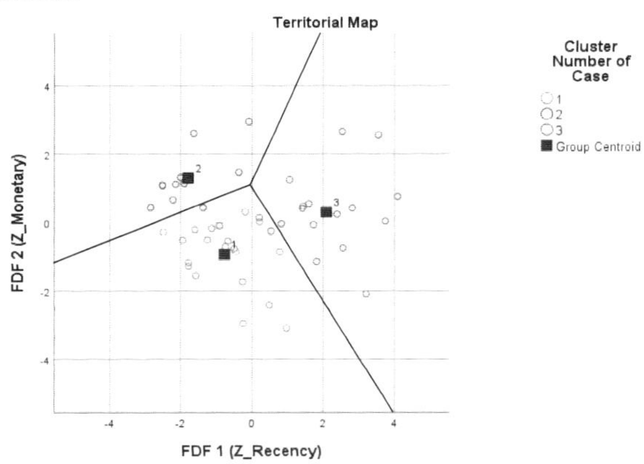

Figure 4. Territorial Map (adapted from SPSS output)

The black lines are the borders and were added manually since the SPSS territorial map is very rudimentary. Note that one instance classified in cluster 2 (in red) by K-means was classified by LDA in the first group and two individuals from cluster 3 fell into the predicted group 1. Using the interpretation of the clusters of Figure 4, the outcome of both tools of the application of the LDA algorithm and the composition of the final clusters represented in Table 4, we can conclude that the accuracy values are better but very similar to the ones in the DT validation approach. All values are quite high, over 83%. SPSS presents a higher accuracy value with 91,8%, while Rapidminer presents 85,7% accuracy value.

Table 4. Validation using LDA (Rapidminer and SPSS)

Validation by LDA - Rapidminer

	true cluster_1	true cluster_2	true cluster_0	class precision
pred. cluster_1	12	0	0	100.0%
pred. cluster_2	3	27	4	79.4%
pred. cluster_0	0	0	3	100.0%
class recall	80.0%	100.0%	42.9%	85.7%

Validation by LDA - SPSS

	true cluster_1	true cluster_2	true cluster_0	class precision
pred. cluster_1	20	1	2	87.0%
pred. cluster_2	1	10	0	90.9%
pred. cluster_0	0	0	15	100.0%
class recall	95.2%	90.9%	88.2%	91.8%

3.3.3 Independent Sample

Additionally, we applied the same methodology process in another randomly chosen company. Company 8585 contains information about 47 clients, 168 invoices from Jan 1, 2019 to Dec 31, 2019. The results were even better, compared with 8501's results (Table 5).

Table 5. Comparison of Accuracy from different techniques and tool

Company 8501, Accuracy

	D. T.	L. D. A.
RM	85.7	85.7
SPSS	87.8	91.8

Company 8585, Accuracy

	D. T.	L. D. A.
RM	87.2	95.7
SPSS	83	95.7

In both cases, in DT and LDA, accuracy values are also high (above 83%). These numbers lead us to look with optimism for a future validation with real data where, generally, the number of invoices is higher as also the number of customers. If these conditions are satisfied, according to the Central Limit Theorem, the approximation of distributions within groups to normal should be significant and the discriminating power of variables and functions should be higher what leads us to expected higher levels of accuracy for LDA.

4. CONCLUSIONS

In this work, we perform a customer segmentation analysis using the RFM criterion considering SAF-T (PT) data properly structured in a DW repository oriented to support selective strategies for sales. To perform the customer analysis, we apply a clustering technique and the consequent results were validated using supervised techniques, Decision Tree and Linear Discriminant Analysis.

The proposed methodology started with the pre-processing phase, which is essential to prepare the dataset to the application of the clustering technique. In the modelling phase, we applied the k-means algorithm to the dataset and afterwards, we used the leave-one-out cross-validation using two supervised methods. After the validation phase and interpreting the results, we obtained accuracy values greater than 83% in both tools and both algorithms. Concerning RFM analysis, a small number of clusters was determined, which facilitates interpretation. Understanding the characteristics of each group makes it possible to establish a relationship with customers to facilitate the direction of marketing strategies. Still, we would like to repeat this analysis with additional variables like geographic, demographic or customer preferences for future work.

From another perspective, data from real companies must be tested, for example, to test, if the position of a company in the distribution chain may affect the results, as well as the capacity for on-line business. The validations by DT and LDA from both tools obtained high levels of accuracy (above 83%). The best result was achieved by the LDA method in both programs, so this procedure should be considered for the classification and validation of clusters. It is intended to test the results with the application of Neural Network or other techniques for the validation of the clustering model. As for the dataset, it is expected that the application to other companies will produce also high levels of accuracy.

The RFM analysis has shown to be effective in the SAF-T (PT) dataset. It is suggested that the application of these techniques into real data could produce essential knowledge to decision-makers, helping them to drive their companies further into an increasingly competitive market. These findings are interesting since they prove the effectiveness of a self-service BI system that can be generated based on SAF-T (PT) data and possibly extended by companies' specific data. Thus, mainly the small companies can use it as a faster and cheaper way to initiate their BI system to support their tactical and strategic decisions. As future work, we intend to exploit this approach for BI implementation.

ACKNOWLEDGMENT

This work has been supported by national funds through FCT – Fundação para a Ciência e Tecnologia through project UIDB/04728/2020.

REFERENCES

Anderberg, M. R. 1973. *Cluster Analysis for Applications*. New York: Academic press.

Aviad, Barak, and Gelbard Roy. 2011. "Classification by Clustering Decision Tree-like Classifier Based on Adjusted Clusters." *Expert Systems with Applications* 38 (7): 8220–28.

Berkhin, P. 2006. "A Survey of Clustering Data Mining Techniques BT - Grouping Multidimensional Data." *Grouping Multidimensional Data*, no. c: 25–71.

Bult, J.R., and T.J. Wansbeek. 1995. "Optimal Selection for Direct Mail." *Marketing Science* 14(4): 378–95.

Chan, C. C.Henry, Chi Bin Cheng, and Wen Chen Hsien. 2011. "Pricing and Promotion Strategies of an Online Shop Based on Customer Segmentation and Multiple Objective Decision Making." *Expert Systems with Applications* 38 (12): 14585–91.

Chen, Feng, Pan Deng, Jiafu Wan, Daqiang Zhang, Athanasios V. Vasilakos, and Xiaohui Rong. 2015. "Data Mining for the Internet of Things: Literature Review and Challenges." *International Journal of Distributed Sensor Networks* 2015 (i).

Chen, Yen Liang, Mi Hao Kuo, Shin Yi Wu, and Kwei Tang. 2009. "Discovering Recency, Frequency, and Monetary (RFM) Sequential Patterns from Customers' Purchasing Data." *Electronic Commerce Research and Applications* 8 (5): 241–51. https://doi.org/10.1016/j.elerap.2009.03.002.

Deshpande, S.P, and V.M Thakare. 2010. "Data Mining System and Applications: A Review." *International Journal of Distributed and Parallel Systems* 1 (1): 32–44.

Han, Jiawei, Micheline Kamber, and Jian Pei. 2012. *Data Mining: Concepts and Techniques. Morgan Kaufmann Publishers*. Third Edit. Morgan Kaufmann Series.

Johnson, Richard Arnold, Dean W Wichern, and others. 2002. *Applied Multivariate Statistical Analysis*. Vol. 5. Prentice hall Upper Saddle River, NJ.

Khajvand, Mahboubeh, Kiyana Zolfaghar, Sarah Ashoori, and Somayeh Alizadeh. 2011. "Estimating Customer Lifetime Value Based on RFM Analysis of Customer Purchase Behavior: Case Study." *Procedia Computer Science* 3: 57–63.

Marcus, Claudio. 1998. "A Practical yet Meaningful Approach to Customer Segmentation." *Journal of Consumer Marketing* 15 (5): 494–504.

Marôco, João. 2018. *Análise Estatística Com Utilizaçao Do SPSS 25. Edições Sílabo, Lisboa*. 7th ed.

Sohrabi, Babak, and Amir Khanlari. 2007. "Customer Lifetime Value (CLV) Measurement Based on RFM Model." *Iranian Accounting & Auditing Review* 14 (47): 7–20.

Tsiptsis, Konstantinos, and Antonios Chorianopoulos. 2010. *Data Mining Techniques in CRM: Inside Customer Segmentation. Data Mining Techniques in CRM: Inside Customer Segmentation*. https://doi.org/10.1002/9780470685815.

Zaheri, Fayegh, Hiwa Farughi, Hersh Soltanpanah, Seiran Alaniazar, and Foruzan Naseri. 2012. "Using Multiple Criteria Decision Making Models for Ranking Customers of Bank Network Based on Loyalty Properties in Weighted RFM Model." *Management Science Letters* 2 (2): 697–704.

COMPARATIVE STUDY OF NOSQL DATABASES FOR BIG DATA STORAGE

Zirije Hasani[1], Blendina Destani[1], Samedin Krrabaj[1] and Jakup Fondaj[2]
[1]University "Ukshin Hoti" Prizren , Kosovo
[2]South East European University, Tetovo, Macedonia

ABSTRACT

Nowadays the amount of data that is required to be stored in databases relates to big data and that data is required to be stored in real time, but knowing that DBMSs cannot support such a thing, we use the NoSQL databases. NoSQL databases support dynamic scheme design, offering the potential for increased flexibility, scalability and adaptability over relational software. This makes them suitable for Web Applications, content management systems, and other uses that involve large amounts of non-uniform data that require more frequent updates and formats in different domains. There are already a large number of NoSQL databases, with a number of over 255. Their performance depends on various factors, so it is important to compare them based on the requirements of an application. So, during this research there will be made a comparison of some of the most popular NoSQL databases for big data storage.

KEYWORDS

Big Data, NoSQL Databases, Flexibility, Scalability, Web-Applications

1. INTRODUCTION

Today in the market are offered various database options which are available such as RDBMS, NoSQL, Big Data, Appliance Database, etc. Developers can be very confused with all these choices that are offered. They don't understand why they should consider a new database as an alternative when RDBMSs have been in use for more than 25 years. However, many large enterprises are already using alternative databases to save more money, and to complete projects faster. Structured data has been handled by traditional databases for many years. In traditional databases, data is stored in the form of strings and columns. Big data is the combination of structural, semi-structured and unstructured data. Many data are generated due to the interactions of social networks and mobile applications. Semi-structured and unstructured data cannot be stored in tabular form or by relational data (loginradious, 2020).

The number of internet users is increased globally. Smartphones and tablets have gained popularity, as the internet is accessible through these easy-to-handle devices. It is important to support a large number of competing users. At the same time, it is also important to dynamically support the rapid increase in the number of competing users. To support a large number of users in addition to the dynamic nature of application usage models, it is necessary for a technology database with an easier scalability. With relational technologies, it is difficult to have dynamic scalability while maintaining the performance of user requirements when using their applications.

The term NoSQL (Not Only SQL) was introduced by C.Strozzi in 1998 in which the SQL interface was not used. In 2009, NoSQL was re-introduced by Johan Oskarsson at the conference "open-source, distributed, non-relational databases". NoSQL databases will not replace relational databases but they will complement each other.

In this research we have study most popular NoSQL databases as Cloudant (Cloudant, 2019), MongoDB (MongoDB, 2020) and Neo4j (Neo4j, 2020). All these three databases are installed and tested and then is done comparative study between them based on different characteristics.

The rest of this paper has the following structure: in the second section is related work; in the third section is done classification of NoSQL databases, in the fourth section are the experimental results based on comparative study; and the last section contains conclusions and further work.

2. RELATED WORKS

As we mentioned in the introduction the term NoSQL (Not Only SQL) was introduced by C.Strozzi in 1998 in which the SQL interface was not used. Now there are many researches in this area and we are going to shown next some of them.

Adity Gupta,et.al., (Adity Gupta, 2017) the authors have conducted a research showing the differences between the different forms in which Nosql databases exist, as well as showing their importance compared to relational databases. Nosql databases they divided into four categories: key value stores, document store, graph databases, and column columns stores. These categories have been compared based on the features of their operation and their non-functioning. Non-functional features include performance, scalability, flexibility, structure and complexity, while functional features include de-normalization, connections, aggregation, keys. An example was taken for each of them and those databases were compared based on their data model, CAP theorem, as well as many other factors.

The author (Gupta, 2015) has made a comparison for storing Big Data in the Cloud by Nosql databases and relational databases. The large amount of data collected from different fields is a challenging aspect to analyze using the technologies available for their storage. In the modern world where data is presented in the form of documents, such as pdf, audio, video, all this in an unstructured form, so the tables and the definition of the scheme are no longer a concern that we have to deal with. Relative databases like MySql are no longer suitable for storing such a large amount of data. An alternative solution for them is to use developing databases, Nosql databases. So, during this study by this author a comparative analysis is given between some of the Nosql database platforms like MongoDB, HBase, Big Table with relational databases and specifies their limits when used for real life problems.

Next the authors (Hossain, 2013) is another study that talks about the new era of databases for storing big data, they do the classification, show the characteristics for them as well as comparing them. It also aims to help users, especially organizations, gain knowledge of the pros and cons that these databases offer to support applications that contain a large amount of data.

Pradeep Soni (Yadav, 2015) in his work he talks about one of the ways of storing big data based on the architecture of Nosql databases, which has to do with storing data in the form of "Document databases". In this paper he takes two types of databases that are mostly used for unstructured data MongoDB and Cassandra by making comparisons between them and reaching a conclusion as to which of them has better traced in terms of what he has tested.

The author (Harrison, 2015) in his book published in December 2015, made a division of databases throughout their development, dividing them into three stages: the first stage deals with the achievement of electronic computers, the second with the achievement of databases relational, and the third with non-relational databases. As for the third generation of databases which was born as a necessity, as modern applications are requiring constant availability and storage of large data, which relational databases cannot support. So, he has discussed these three stages and the advancement of technology that has brought the new generation of databases.

Based on this research we can see that there is not a comparative study for three NoSQL databases we chose to study Cloudant (Cloudant, 2019), MongoDB (MongoDB, 2020) and Neo4j (Neo4j, 2020).

3. CLASIFICATION OF NOSQL DATABASES

(Leavitt, 2010) classifies NoSQL databases into three types: key value stores (Memcached, Coherence, Redis), document-oriented databases (MongoDB, CouchDB, Cloudant), and NoSQL flat databases or column stores (BigTable, HBase, Accumulo). However, in this paper he classify NoSQL databases into four categories: Key-value stores; Document databases; Wide Column stores and Graph databases.

Document databases refer to databases that store their data in the form of documents. Each document has a special "ID" key, which is also unique within a collection of documents and for this reason identifies a document clearly. Compared to the key value storage method, the values are not permeable to the system and may also be required. Documents within an object-oriented database are somewhat similar to records in relational databases, but they are much more flexible as they are less common (V, 2014). The documents are in format such as XML, PDF, JSON etc. In relational databases, a row within the same database will have the same data field and unused fields remain empty, but in the case of storing the document, each document may have the same data and not the same. The documents in the database are addressed using a unique key that represents this document. Preservation of new documents during the execution time, which contain any kind of attributes, is very easy as well as the addition of new attributes to existing documents. Some of the most popular types of document storage are CouchDB, Mongo DB, Ravendb. CouchDB and RavenDB which store their data in JSON. Document-oriented databases should be used for applications where the data should not be stored in a table with fields of the same size, but instead of the data being stored as a document with special features, document storage should be avoided if the database will have a lot of connections and normalization (Hossain, 2013).

Graph stores are used to store information about network data, such as social links. Therefore, multi-link database applications are more suitable for graphical databases, as costly actions such as recursive links can be replaced by efficient traversals. Ne04j and GraphDB are based on direct graphics and very relational features. The length of keys and values can be defined within the scheme, from which the more complex presentation of constraints can be very easily described. Twitter maintains a lot of connections between people in order to provide service for their tweets. Cases of use for graphical databases are location-based services, displaying knowledge and finding ways to navigate problems displayed on systems, recommendation systems, and all use cases involving complex, complex connections. Graphical databases are best suited for larger connections over multiple nodes, while RDF is used for certain details in graphics. FlockDB is suitable for handling simple l-hop-neighbor connections with high scalability requirements (Hossain, 2013).

Key-values stores are the simplest NoSQL database. Each item in the database is stored as an attribute name (or 'key'), along with its value. The key value database model stores data in a completely free scheme. The procedure is similar to maps or dictionaries where the data is addressed by unique keys and since values are continuous strings of bits, which are completely impenetrable in the system, keys are the only way to recover stored data (Hossain, 2013). The data consists of two parts, a string which represents the key and the current data which is referred to as a value by creating the key-value pair. This way of storing is similar to hash tables where keys were used as indexes, making it faster than RDDBMS. Modern key value storage takes into account more scalability than inconsistency. High competition, fast search and massive storage options are saved by key-value. Examples of key value databases include Redis, Memcached, Berkeley DB, Amazon Dynamo DB. The Amazon Dynamo DB model offers a fast, secure, and cost-effective NOSQL database designed for the scalability of web applications. It offers scalability with low and predictable delays (Hossain, 2013).

Wide Column stores are optimized for query over large data (datasets) and store data columns in one place (together), instead of rows (Esha Awasthi, 2018). All storage is inspired by Google's Bigtable which is a distributed storage system for managing structured data, designed to scale a large amount of data. Saving columns in NoSQL are actually row / column hybrid storage, unlike relational database columns. Although it disseminates the concept of column-by-column database storage with columns and their expansion of row-based databases, column storage does not store table data but stores data with an architecture. massively distributed. In column storage, each key is connected to one or more attributes (columns). Column store storage stores its data in such a way that it can be collected quickly with less I / O activity. Provides high scalability in data storage. The data stored in the database is based on the colony family type ranking. Examples of family storage in columns include databases such as: Hbase, Hypertable, Cassandra. (Hossain, 2013)

Table 1. Comparison of classified NoSQL databases (Hossain, 2013)

Type	Performance	Scalability	Flexibility	Complexity	Examples
Key-value store	Hight	Hight	Hight	None	Product purchase invoice (Amazon)
Column store	Hight	Hight	Medium	Low	Saving user details (Facebook)
Document store	Hight	Variable	Hight	Low	Companies
Graph database	Variable	Variable	Hight	Hight	Movies

4. COMPARATIVE STUDY OF NOSQL DATABASES FOR BIG DATA STORAGE

To compare the NoSQL databases, we have installed all of best selected as Cloudant (Cloudant, 2019), MongoDB (MongoDB, 2020) and Neo4j (Neo4j, 2020). Based on the experiments we have developed the comparative table bellow where the comparison is based on different parameters like the programing language they support, operating system, the method of distributing data, if they have implemented MapReduce logic, if they support foreign key method, the replication method, the transaction concepts, etc.

Table 2. Comparative study of NoSQL databases

	Cloudant	MongoDB	Neo4j
Description	Database as a service provided by Apache CouchDB	One of the most popular databases based on documents which is also provided as a cloud service and as a self-management infrastructure.	Database offered as open-source
The model of database	Document store databases	Document store databases	Graph stores
The implemented language	Erlang	C++	Java, Scala
Operating system	hosted	Linux, OS X, Solaris, Windows	Linux, OS X, Solaris, Windows
The programing languages	C#, Java, JavaScript, PHP, Objective-C, Ruby	C#, C++, Clojure, Dart, Erlang, GO, Java, JavaScript, MatLab, PHP, Python, Ruby, Scala, Prolog, Lisp, Lua, PowerShell, Groovy	.Net, Clojure, Elixir, Go, Haskell, JavaScript, Java, Perl, PHP, Ruby, Python, Scala
Distributing method	Sharding	Sharding	None
The replication method	Replication master-master and master-slave	Replication with master-slave	Random Clustering by Raft Protocol
MapReduce	Yes	Yes	No
Foreign key	No	No	Yes
The transaction concept	No	Multi-document transactions ACID	ACID
Sustainability	Yes	Yes	Yes
Competition	Yes	Yes	Yes
Triger	Yes	Yes	Yes

Cloudant (Cloudant, 2019) database is a cloud-based database for storing data as JSON-style documents. Target has web and mobile app developers, for quick and easy data storage and access only through the Cloud system. They cannot be installed, so they are only accessible through the Cloud system. Therefore, if we refer to scalability, availability, security become more attractive to users. The popularity of these systems if we look at it based on the overall percentage (db-engines.com, 2020) of all DBMs has increased from 0.1% as it was in 2013 to 1.6% in 2017, so far in December 2019 it has gone to 3.7% the popularity of this type of database, which is being seen to continue to have a steady rise.

On the other hand, we have the MongoDB (MongoDB, 2020) database, which is a modern leader platform designed to share the power of software and data for developers and the applications they build. Starting from the world's most sophisticated organizations to large companies, government agencies use MongoDB to create applications that previously were no longer possible with a portion of the cost of legacy data. MongoDB was created to meet the requirements of modern applications which enables us: the best way to work with data, through the document storage model, design of distributed systems, thus enabling the intelligent placement of data wherever you want, a unified experience that gives you the opportunity to get anywhere (run), allowing you to try your future work (projects you will do in the future). MongoDB also offers the global MongoDB Atlas service fully managed in the public cloud. Atlas enables customers to take advantage of MongoDB's capabilities in AWS, Azure or GCP without having to decide, operate and scale the software or infrastructure itself. The MongoDB Atlas is available with the pay-as-you-go model and is billed based on the hours used.

MongoDB (MongoDB, 2020) contains the most valuable features of relational databases: ACID transactions, strong consistency, expressive questionnaire language, secondary indexes. As a result, developers can build applications with high and fast functionality.

Some data extracted regarding the use of the MongoDB database:

- million downloads (downloads) - (increasing more than 30 thousand downloads per day)
- 15,000+ customers in more than 100 countries around the world
- Appointed as a leader in "Forrester Wave ™: Database-As-A-Service Q2 2019"
- 1M + university enrollment in MongoDB courses
- More than 1,000 technology and service partners
- Ranked in the highest positions of non-relational databases in DB Engines positions.

As for the Neo4j (Neo4j, 2020) database, it is considered the most popular graphical database in the world, with more than 15+ million downloads (downloads), about 200K active cases and somewhere around 300+ clients of enterprises. Neo4j is a graphical database platform that is built to store, extract data through questionnaires, analyze and manage a large amount of data more efficiently than other databases. The Neo4j database has a high degree of scalability which is scaled vertically and horizontally, without introducing integrated data or consistency issues (logical connection) using the "Causal Clustering" architecture, which now supports "multi-clustering". Customers have placed graphs with 10 million nodes and links. Neo4j is following the path of the paradigm by focusing on data links rather than the way relational databases and these NoSQL focus, on data collection. Graphics use cases are being used everywhere, and all of this is being covered by the Neo4j database.

So, as we saw above based on some statistics, the knowledge we gave about the three types of Nosql databases we saw that the MongoDB database is the most used database, which based on its architecture, the benefits it offers, users prefer more about the projects they create. In the following, we will present the graph for the growth of these databases over the years, from 2013 to March 2020.

In the following figure are shown statistics[1] for the use of three databases from 2013 to 2020. All calculations made below by DB-Engines are taken by calculating some of the parameters of all DBMSs, parameters such as the number of searches made for their websites (example taken from Google), general interest in system, frequency for technical discussions about the system, number of jobs offered where they mentioned the system, number of profiles of professionals they mentioned on their professional networks (like LinkedIn), mention on social networks (Twitter) (DB-Engines, 2020).

[1] Taken from www.DB-Engines.com, accessed on:20.02.2020

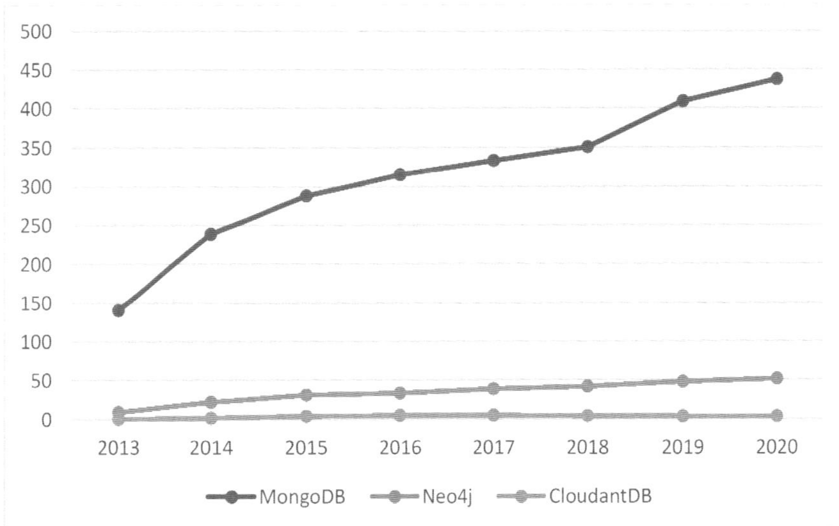

Figure 1. The use of MongoDB, Neo4j and Cloudant

5. CONCLUSION AND FUTURE WORKS

Today, with the global growth of internet use, there has been a significant increase in the number of users and the time they spend online. It is therefore important to support a large number of competing users. At the same time, it is also important to dynamically support the rapid increase in the number of users and the need to maintain the performance of user requirements when using their applications.

In this way, there is a need to use databases that support this data, data that we otherwise known as Big Data, which are generated in large quantities, change quickly and come in different forms as structured, unstructured, and semi-structured, and that is difficult to manage using old traditional databases or technologies, such as relational databases.

To manage this data already used databases known as NoSQL databases, or otherwise Non-SQL. So, these databases provide horizontal scalability, better control over the availability of data and many other benefits that offer and that have made it easier for users to manage their data. We currently have a large number of NoSQL database types.

During this study, the NoSQL database was divided into four types as key-value, based on documents, graphically and as a Column database, and for each of them an example of NoSQL platforms was taken and discussed by getting to know more about doing the same at the same time and making comparisons between them, a study that can help their users a lot if they decide to work on their projects have knowledge of them and can decide which of them can suits them and is best for projects they want to work on in their future.

Finally, a practical demonstration was made where three types of databases were selected such as MongoDB, CloudantDB and Neo4j, these were tested and compared based on the characteristics they possess. During the testing and based on the reports that have been made regarding them, we concluded that the MongoDB database is one of the most used.

REFERENCES

Adity Gupta, S. T. (2017). NoSQL databases: Critical analysis and comparison. *2017 International Conference on Computing and Communication Technologies for Smart Nation (IC3TSN)* (pp. 293-299). IEEE.

Cloudant, I. (2019, 03 02). *https://www.ibm.com.* Retrieved from ibm.com: https://www.ibm.com/cloud/cloudant

DB-Engines. (2020, 02 15). *Method of calculating the scores of the DB-Engines Ranking.* Retrieved from DB-Engines: https://db-engines.com/en/ranking_definition

db-engines.com. (2020, 02 11). *DB-Engines Ranking.* Retrieved from db-engines.com: https://db-engines.com/en/ranking

Esha Awasthi, S. A. (2018). A Survey on Nosql and Newsql Data Stores For Big Data Management. *Global Journal of Engineering Science and Researches*, 269-277.

Gupta, S. (2015). Comparative Analysis of Nosql Specimen with Relational Data Store for Big Data in Cloud. *International Journal of Distributed and Cloud Computing*, 10-21.

Harrison, G. (2015). *Next Generation Databases, NoSQLand Big Data.* Apress.

Hossain, A. B. (2013). NoSQL Database: New Era of Databases for Big data Analytics - Classification, Characteristics and Comparison. . *International Journal of Database Theory and Application*, 1-14.

Leavitt, N. (2010). Will NoSQL Databases Live Up to Their Promise? *Computer*, 12-14.

loginradious. (2020, 04 20). *Relational Database Management System (RDBMS) vs noSQL.* Retrieved from loginradius.com: https://www.loginradius.com/engineering/relational-database-management-system-rdbms-vs-nosql/

MongoDB. (2020, 02 05). *https://www.mongodb.com.* Retrieved from mongodb.com: https://www.mongodb.com

Neo4j. (2020, 02 10). *https://neo4j.com.* Retrieved from neo4j.com: https://neo4j.com/

V, M. (2014). Comparative Study of Nosql Document, Column Store Databases and Evaluation of Cassandra. *International Journal of Database Management Systems (IJDMS)*, 11-26.

Yadav, P. S. (2015). Quantitative analysis of Document Stored Databases. *International Journal of Computer Applications (IJCA)*, 1-37.

FEATURE FUSION BASED ON AUDITORY AND SPEECH SYSTEMS FOR AN IMPROVED VOICE BIOMETRICS SYSTEM USING ARTIFICIAL NEURAL NETWORK

Youssouf Ismail Cherifi and Abdelhakim Dahimene
IGEE, Universite de M'Hamed Bougara, Boulevard de l'independance, 35000 Boumerdes, Algeria

ABSTRACT

In today's world, identifying a speaker has become an essential task. Especially for systems that rely on voice commands or speech in general to operate. These systems use speaker-specific features to identify the individual, features such as Mel Frequency Cepstral Coefficients, Linear Predictive Coding, or Perceptual Linear Predictive. Although these features provide different representations of speech, they can all be considered as either auditory system based (type 1) or speech system based (type 2).

In this work, a method for improving existing voice biometrics system is presented. A method fusing a type 1 feature with a type 2 feature is implemented using artificial neural network and evaluated on in-campus recorded data set. The obtained results demonstrate the potential of our approach in improving voice biometrics system, regardless of the underlying task being speaker identification or verification.

KEYWORDS

Speech Processing, Neural Network, Pattern Recognition, Speaker Recognition, Feature Extraction

1. INTRODUCTION

It is a well-known fact that speech itself contains several levels of information conveyed to the auditor. Mainly, speech is used to communicate a message to the auditor, a message that is carried in words. However, speech also contains information about the speaker himself, this is due to the way it is produced. This information could be for instance the speaker's gender, emotions, age, origin and obviously identity. Recognizing a person's identity by analyzing a portion of his speech is known as Speaker Recognition (Reynolds, 2002).

Depending on the number of identities involved, speaker recognition can be one of two tasks: speaker verification or speaker identification. In speaker verification, the objective is to verify that the speaker is the exact person he claims to be. On the other hand, speaker identification goal is to assert the identity of a speaker among a closed set of known speakers. In addition to the number of speakers involved, speaker recognition tasks can be either text-dependent or text-independent based on the user level of control and cooperation.

The development of speaker recognition methods and techniques has been an active field of research for well over five decades and continues to be. These methods have extended from using spectrogram comparisons to basic template matching, to dynamic time-warping algorithms, to more advance statistical pattern recognition algorithms such as Artificial Neural Networks (ANNs) and Hidden Markov Models (HMMs). In fact, most of the research that has been done in order to improve the accuracy of speaker recognition tasks focuses on the development of high-performance pattern recognition algorithms or the adjustment of existing algorithms. An example of this would be the use of Gaussian Mixture Model (GMM) (Chakroum et al, 2016) or Artificial Neural Network (ANN) (Srinivas et al, 2014) to obtain a better recognition rate.

Continuous research and effort are ongoing, involving the combination of two modelling techniques (Al-Shayea & Al-Ani, 2016. Chakroborty & Saha, 2009. Singh et al, 2016. Awais et al, 2014) or the implementation of specific hardware (Gaafar et al, 2014).

Having a better recognition rate does not depend only on the modelling techniques, as shown in previous work (Paliwal et al. in 2010), where a better is obtained by adjusting the width of the window at which the feature was extracted. Similar conclusions were deducted (Gulzar et al. 2014; Dave, 2013), but instead of adjusting the frame width, the effect of changing the set of features entirely was studied. In some other work (Eringis and Tamulevicius, 2014) it was shown that by adjusting the frame width and increment for different features, an improvement of 4.15% (from 88.75% to 92.9%) can be achieved.

Based on the aforementioned work, an improved speaker recognition scheme is suggested in this paper. This scheme has a high accuracy that makes it well suited for applications in various fields such as security and crime investigations.

2. MATERIALS AND METHODS.

2.1 Proposed Approach

The adopted approach for improving the recognition rate is to fuse two different types of features. The fused features are a combination of auditory system-based feature (type 1) with a speech system-based feature (type 2). To ensure that both features are kept isolated and not grouped under the same vector space, Artificial Neural Networks (ANN) algorithm is used to model the voice print. Using ANN, each set of features is connected to a dedicated input layer and are only fused/merged at the hidden layer (Figure 1).

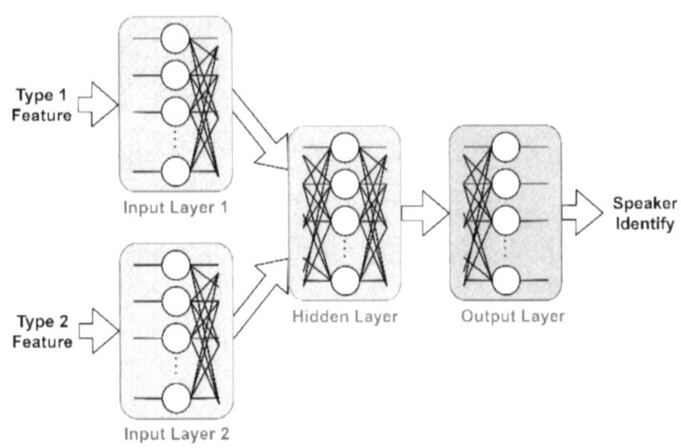

Figure 1. The proposed system for feature fusion. Type 1 feature is auditory system-based feature and type 2 is speech system-based feature

The structure shown above was implemented using MATLAB 2017a Deep Learning Toolbox (Figure 2). Each of the input layer as well as the hidden layer contained 44 perceptrons, to account for all possible phonemes in the English language. While the output layer contained a number of perceptrons equivalent to the number of speakers.

To reduce the influence of extreme values or outliers in the dataset without having to remove them, a SoftMax function was used as the activation function for the output layer. For input layers and hidden layers perceptrons, the tangential sigmoid activation function was used. This function has a steeper derivative which make it a good candidate for extracting intermediary features (Meena et al, 2011).

To train the structures shown above, the conjugate gradient backpropagation algorithm is used to reduce the Sum of Square Errors (SSE) between the outputs of the network and a vector of desired targets. This algorithm has a better accuracy when compared with other algorithms as shown in Table 1.

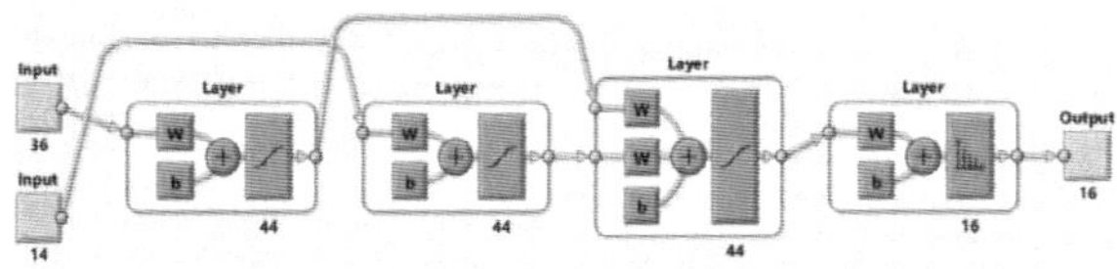

Figure 2. Feature fusion ANN structure

Table 1. Performance of different training functions in MATLAB's NN toolbox (Vacic, 2015)

Function name	training		validation		testing		time	
	mean	stdev	mean	stdev	mean	stdev	mean	stdev
trainb	0.6456	0.7246	0.6302	0.6946	0.6386	0.7081	2.511	3.3835
trainbfg	0.0096	0.0032	0.0199	0.0084	**0.0209**	0.0046	7.3219	4.5702
trainbr	7.6088	3.5328	18.9761	10.219	149.8294	32.2893	18.5063	8.927
traincgb	0.0102	0.0026	0.0193	0.0069	**0.0203**	0.0059	4.3389	1.886
traincgf	0.0112	0.0033	0.0199	0.0091	**0.0202**	0.0051	4.9752	2.4127
traincgp	0.0114	0.003	0.0213	0.0093	**0.0216**	0.0045	4.0544	1.9337
traingd	0.0265	0.0055	0.0332	0.0099	0.0323	0.0029	13.003	4.4432
traingdm	0.5528	0.34	0.5556	0.3221	0.5592	0.3499	1.2875	0.3697
traingda	0.0244	0.0063	0.0293	0.0084	0.0310	0.0037	5.2	2.222
traingdx	0.0394	0.0312	0.0448	0.0317	0.0445	0.0274	5.4219	3.526
trainlm	0.0065	0.0027	0.0199	0.0066	**0.0231**	0.0037	8.5762	3.494
trainoss	0.013	0.0038	0.0204	0.0081	**0.0205**	0.0035	5.1703	2.8221
trainrp	0.0137	0.0045	0.0207	0.0059	0.0229	0.0035	7.4954	3.8277
trainscg	0.0114	0.0035	0.0213	0.0109	**0.0218**	0.0073	4.3171	1.7394

Overall, 3 set of features were extracted to test the effectiveness of the suggested approach. The extraction was also done in MATLAB using the Auditory Toolbox (Malcom Slaney) and VOICEBOX (Mike Brooks).

2.1.1 Mel Frequency Cepstral Coefficient

The MFCC are among the most dominant and common features in the field of Natural Language Processing. They represent the short-term power spectrum of a given audio clip but what set them apart from the cepstrum is the fact that use a Mel-scaled filter banks. These filter banks are equally spaced, and they approximate the human auditory system more than the linearly spaced bands used in the cepstrum. This makes MFCC the best candidate as a type 1 feature.

To extract MFCC from an audio signal, the signal is processed as shown in Figure 3. At the end of this pipeline 13 coefficients were extracted. The 0th coefficient is discarded since it does not contain any significant information. The delta and delta-delta were added to the remaining 12 coefficients to ensure that the model is getting sufficient information about the fluctuation of the signal.

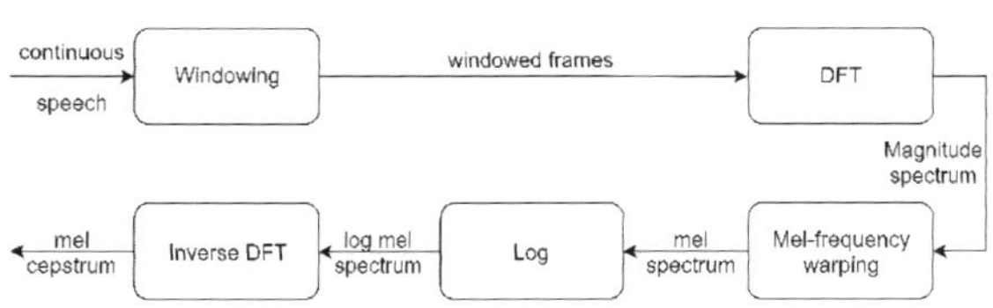

Figure 3. MFCC derivation

$$\Delta_k = f_k - f_{k-1} \tag{1}$$
$$\Delta\Delta_k = \Delta_k - \Delta_{k-1} \tag{2}$$

2.1.2 Linear Predictive Coding

LPC is a good candidate for speech analysis due to the nature of the speech generation process. The entire process can be represented by a digital filter as modelled in Fig 4 which makes LPC one of the most powerful type 2 features for speech analysis (Buza et al, 2006).

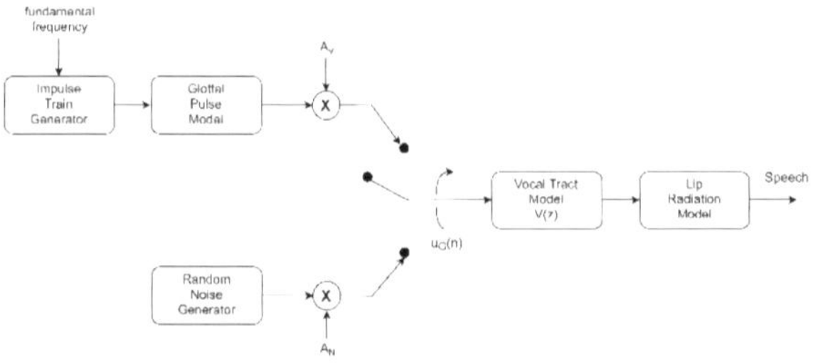

Figure 4. Speech Production Model. A_v is the voiced sound gain, A_n is the unvoiced sound gain and $u_G(n)$ is voiced/unvoiced switching function

To extract LPC from an audio signal, the signal is first framed using short time Hamming windows. For each frame 14 formants or coefficients are extracted. This ensures that all possible speech segments (voiced and unvoiced) are covered and for both genders as well. Formants are extracted by computing coefficients that link the current speech sample with the previous samples with the same window. This can be expressed by the following equation:

$$s(n) = \sum_{k=1}^{p} \alpha_k s(n-k) \tag{3}$$

Where s is the speech signal, n is the sample point, α is the formant and p is the number of the required formants (14 in our case).

2.1.3 Perceptual Linear Prediction

Similarly to LPC, PLP models the human speech based on how speech is produced. PLP differs from LPC on the fact that it discards irrelevant information of the speech and thus approximating the human speech system in a way that improves the recognition rate.

2.2 Data Collection

To carry out this work, sixteen participants were recruited from the Institute of Electrical and Electronic Engineering (IGEE) to record a corpus of 51 to 54 English sentences each. All participants were PhD students with ages ranging from 24 to 27 (8 females, 8 males; mean age: 25.37 ± 0.88). They were all non-native English speakers from Algeria, with a relatively high level of proficiency in English (mean TOEFL score: 89.75 ± 6.75 with a mean of 26.06 ± 2.93 in the speaking section).

All recordings were carried out in the same room located within the institute, (6.0m(L) x 3.5m (W) x 4m(H) as shown in Figure 5). Participants were sitting on a chair, facing a wall at a distance of 0.75m with a monitor in front of them displaying the sentence to be read. The recording device (Honeywell CN51 Personal Digital Assistant (PDA)) was placed between the monitor and the participant.

The recorded sentences differ from one student to the other to ensure that the task remains text-independent and the collaboration of the speaker to a minimum.

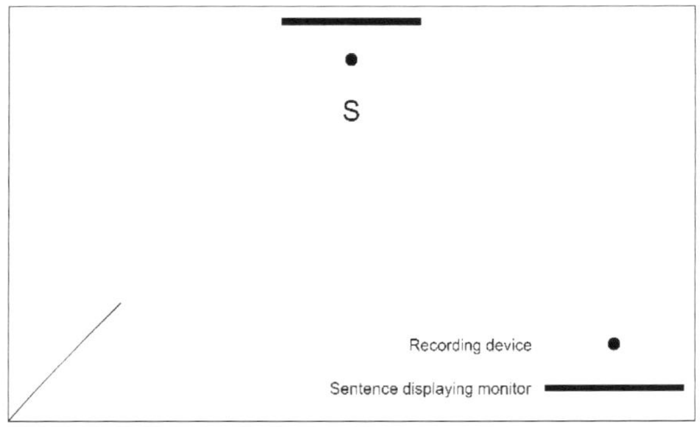

Figure 5. Recording room layout. S is the speaker/participant

To demonstrate that the approach is effective for a wider range of scenario, the LibriSpeech ASR corpus (Vassil et al, 2015) was implied. The corpus however was only used to confirm the recognition accuracy and was not used for all procedures due to hardware limitations.

2.3 Procedures

To assess the performance of the feature fusion approach, a specific pipeline was put in place.

2.3.1 Tuning the Parameters for Feature Extraction

The first step for improving the recognition rate is to adjust the frame width and increment during feature extraction. This improvement has already been shown (Paliwal et al, 2010. Eringis & Tamulevicius, 2014) given that these parameters determine whether the modeling algorithms are getting a sufficient level of information from the speech segment as input.

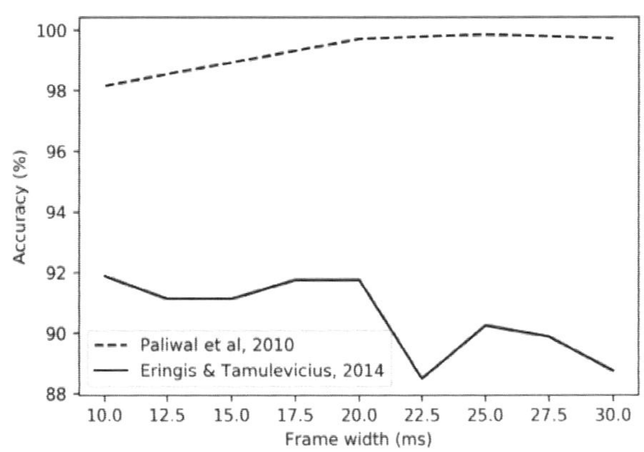

Figure 6. The effect of adjusting the frame width during MFCC extraction on the overall accuracy, blue for the work done by Paliwal et al, 2010 and orange for the work done by Eringis and Tamulevicius, 2014

There is some discrepancy in the literature regarding the frame width values which optimize accuracy (see Figure 6). To confirm which frame width to choose, the structure shown in Figure 7 is trained with MFCC features extracted using different frame widths. Thirty random segments for each speaker in the data set are used for training while the remaining 21 segments are used for testing. This training was carried out in a cross-validation setup to avoid any overfitting due to the complex nature of chosen model. Once the overall accuracy was obtained, the frame width was increased by 5 ms. This procedure was repeated until a frame width of 30.0 ms was reached.

The second parameters to consider for tuning the feature extraction was the frame increment. For this, 3 values were considered: Overlapping (50%), Slightly-Overlapping (75%) and Non-Overlapping (100%). For each of these values the same network shown in Fig 7 was trained with 30 cross-validated speech segments.

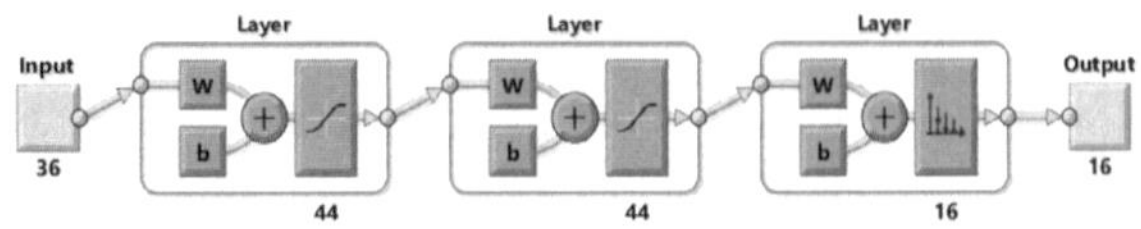

Figure 7. The single feature ANN structure

2.3.2 Fusing, Training and Testing

To study the effect of fusing features on the overall recognition rate, the structure shown in Figure 2 is trained using two features extracted at the optimal frame width and increment. For each speaker, 30 random segments are used for training while the remaining 21 segments are used for testing. The selected segments were cross-validated and the resulting performance was compared to that of training the structure shown in Figure 7 using a single feature extracted at the same optimal parameters.

The same procedure was repeated for the LibriSpeech corpus. To ensure that the approach works on a larger dataset (921) and on native English speakers. Although the corpus contains more than 51 segments for each speaker, only 51 segments were used between training and testing similarly to the recorded corpus.

3. RESULTS & DISCUSSION

When adjusting for the frame width during feature extraction, the best recognition rate was obtained for a frame width of 10 ms, which coincides with the results obtained by Eringis and Tamulavicius, 2014. These results are depicted in Figure 8. This pattern of improvement was found across all three features that were extracted.

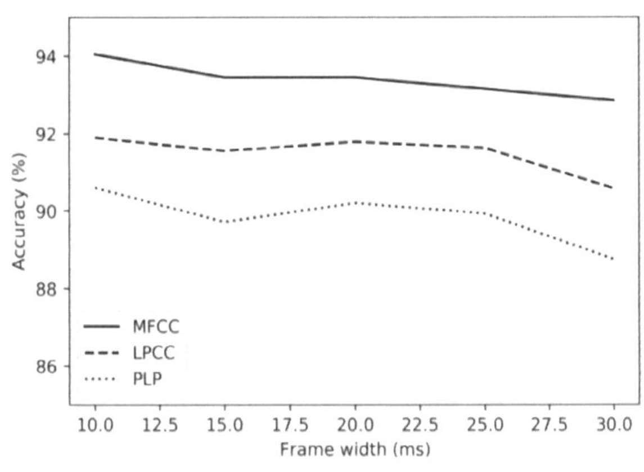

Figure 8. The results of frame width tuning tasks

Examining the 3 different frame increments for the optimal frame width of 10 ms, we found that a frame increment of 75% provided the highest recognition rate on average compared to the 50% and 100% increments (see Fig 9). This implies that by only adjusting the extraction parameters, 3 additional speech segments were correctly identified.

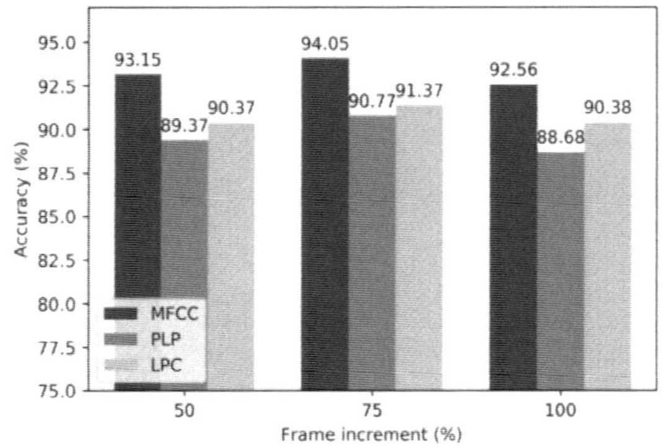

Figure 9. The results of frame increment tuning task

The fusion of type 1 and type 2 features improved the accuracy of the recognition tasks. As seen in Figure 10, any combination of type 1 and type 2 feature would result in a better recognition rate than using just a single feature. The best result was obtained when combining MFCC and LPC (99.4% accuracy), this is due to the fact that these two sets of features are uncorrelated.

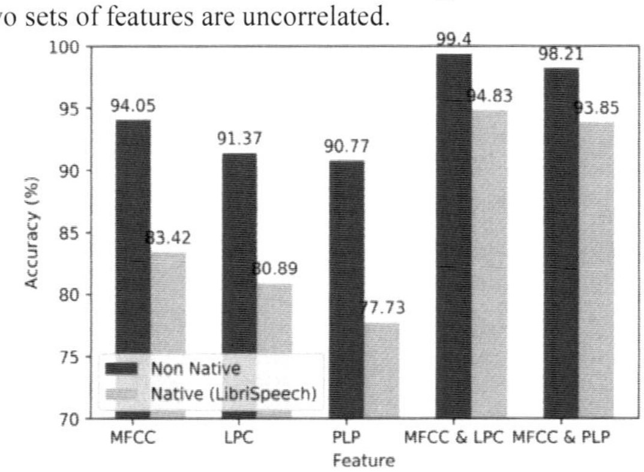

Figure 10. Feature fusion effect on the overall accuracy for speaker recognition. MFCC: Mel-frequency cepstral coefficients; LPC: Linear predictive coding; PLP: Perceptual linear predictive

Figure 10 also demonstrates that the approach works well for native speakers and for a larger set of speakers. In fact, the improvement obtained when testing for the larger corpus was higher. This was due to the fact that this approach created higher dimensionality allowing for a better discrimination. Of course, the approach resulted in a slight increase in the training time. Fig 11 shows the required training time for each of the trials described in section 2.5. These results were obtained using the 4710MG i7 CPU with a RAM of 8GB.

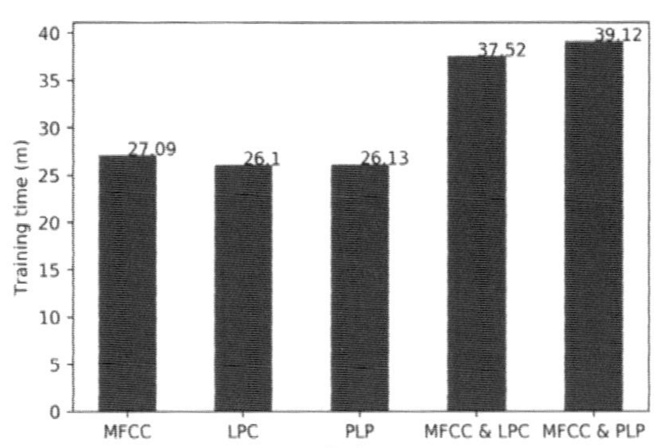

Figure 11. Feature fusion effect on the required training time for speaker recognition. MFCC: Mel-frequency cepstral coefficients; LPC: Linear predictive coding; PLP: Perceptual linear predictive

The difference in training time between the best performing single feature structure and the best performing fused features structure is 10 minutes and 25 seconds. This means an increase of 38.50% in training time for an improvement of 5.35% in speaker-recognition accuracy if we consider only the effect of feature fusion without the parameter tuning and 6.55% when considering the parameters tuning. This is in fact very significant if we consider and application such as criminal investigation where 6.55% means that 22 cases or suspects are correctly being recognized using, for example, a phone call.

In addition, the training time can be significantly reduced, if a better hardware is used such as a more performing GPU or/and by reducing the duration of the recordings that are used for training the model as feature fusing allows to recognize the speaker much earlier as shown in Figure 12 and Table 2.

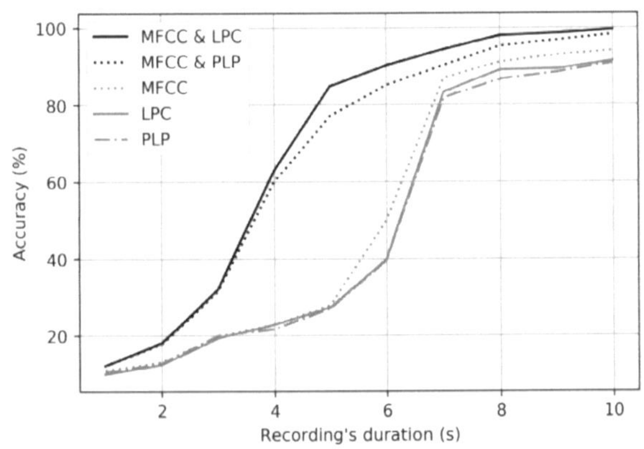

Figure 12. Speaker recognition accuracy over time. MFCC: Mel-frequency cepstral coefficients; LPC: Linear predictive coding; PLP: Perceptual linear predictive

Table 2. Speaker recognition accuracy over time. MFCC: Mel-frequency cepstral coefficients; LPC: Linear predictive coding; PLP: Perceptual linear predictive

Input	**Time (s)**									
	1	**2**	**3**	**4**	**5**	**6**	**7**	**8**	**9**	**10**
MFCC	11.01	13.09	19.94	22.91	27.97	50	86.9	91.07	92.85	94.05
LPC	10	12.5	19.34	22.91	27.38	39.88	83.33	88.89	89.28	91.37
PLP	10.5	12.79	19.94	21.72	27.08	39.58	81.84	86.60	88.39	90.77
MFCC & LPC	12.20	18.15	32.14	63.09	84.82	**90.17**	**94.34**	97.91	98.57	99.4
MFCC & PLP	12.20	17.85	31.54	60.11	77.08	85.11	90.17	95.23	96.72	98.21

By using 6 seconds of recording the model was able to reach 90.17% when fusing MFCC with LPC. What is even more important about these results is the fact that the fusion approach was able to outperform the single feature approach by utilizing 7 seconds out of the provided 10 seconds of recording, this reduced training time in the fusion approach from 37 minutes and 32 seconds to 24 min and 41 seconds. This time is less than the time required to train the model for any of the features independently. These results are significant when taking into consideration the applications of speaker recognition. For fields such as security, this means less data storage, and for crime investigation this means the ability to identify a suspect even if the provided audio is short.

4. CONCLUSION

The speech signal does not only convey a message, it conveys information about the speaker themselves, their gender, origins, health and age. The aim of this work was to improve the task of recognizing a person based on speech segments.

The approach we used proved to be very effective in improving the speaker recognition rate. This improvement was achieved with the use of two sets of features instead of just one. These two feature sets are completely uncorrelated and each one represents different characteristics of the speech signal. The drawback of such approach is the long training time (over 39 minutes for 480 speech segments). Nevertheless, this can be mitigated by using an approach such as deep features, where the trained model input and hidden layers are kept. The output layer however could be replaced by a less time demanding classification or clustering technique such as Support Vector Machines (SVM) or Gaussian Mixture Models (GMM).

The demonstrated approach improved the recognition rate by 6.55%, which means it recognized 22 more segments out of the 336 speech segments used for testing. This was achieved at the cost of a 10 minutes and 26 seconds increment in the training time and no change in the testing time.

REFERENCES

Al-Shayea Q.K., and Al-Ani M.S., 2016. Speaker Identification: A Novel Fusion Samples Approach. *In International Journal of Computer Science and Information Security*, Vol. 14, No. 7, pp 423-427.

Awais M., Mansour A., and Ghulam M., 2014. Automatic Speaker Recognition Using Multi-Directional Local Features (MDLF). *In Arabian Journal for Science and Engineering*, Vol. 39, No. 5, pp 3379-3811.

Buza O., Toderan G., Nica A., and Caruntu A., 2006. Voice Signal Processing for Speech Synthesis, *In International Conference on Automation, Quality and Testing, Robotics*. Cluj-Napora, Romania, pp. 360-364.

Chakroborty S. and Saha G., 2009. Improved Text-Independent Speaker Identification using Fused MFCC & IMFCC Feature Sets based on Gaussian Filter. *In International Journal of Electrical, Computer, Energetic, Electronic and Communication Engineering,* Vol. 3, No. 11, pp 1974-1982.

Chakroum R., Zouari L.B., Frikha M., and Ben Hamida A., 2016. Improving Text-independent Speaker Recognition with GMM. *In International Conference on Advanced Technologies for Signal and Image Processing,* Monastir, Tunisia, pp. 693-696.

Dave N., 2013. Feature Extraction Methods LPC, PLP and MFCC in Speech Recognition. *In International Journal for Advance Research in Engineering and Technology,* Vol. 1, No. 6 , pp 1-5.

Eringis D., and Tamulevicius G., 2014. Improving Speech Recognition Rate through Analysis Parameters. *In Electrical Control and Communication Engineering,* Vol. 5, pp 61-66.

Gaafar T.S., Abo Baker H.M., and Abdalla M.I., 2014. An improved method for speech/speaker recognition. *In International Conference on Informatics, Electronics & Vision*, Dhaka, Bangladesh, pp. 1-5.

Gulzar T., Singh A., and Sharma S., 2014. Comparative Analysis of LPCC, MFCC and BFCC for the Recognition of Hindi Words using Artificial Neural Networks. *In International Journal of Computer Applications,* Vol. 101, No. 12, pp 22-27.

Meena K., Subramaniam K., and Gomathy M., 2011. Gender Classification in Speech recognition using Fuzzy Logic and Neural Network. *In The International Arab Journal of Information Technology,* Vol. 10, No. 5, pp 477-485.

Paliwal K.K., Lyons J.G., and Wojcicke K.K., 2011. Preference for 20-40 ms window duration in speech analysis. *In International Conference on Signal Processing and Communication Systems,* Gold Coast, Australia, pp. 1-4.

Reynolds D.A., 2002. An Overview of Automatic Speaker Recognition Technology. *In International Conference on Acoustics, Speech, and Signal Processing,* Orlando, Florida, USA, pp. 4072-4075.

Singh S., Assaf M.H., Das S.R., Biswas S.N., Petriu E.M., and Groza V., 2016. Short Duration Voice Data Speaker Recognition System Using Novel Fuzzy Vector Quantization Algorithm. *In International Instrumentation and Measurement Technology Conference Proceedings,* Taipei, Taiwan, pp. 1-6.

Srinivas V., Santhi C.R. and Madhu T., 2014. Neural Network based Classification for Speaker Identification. *In International Journal of Signal Processing, Image Processing and Pattern Recognition,* Vol. 7, No. 1, pp 109-120.

Vacic V., 2015. Summary of the training functions in Matlab's NN toolbox. *In MSc, University of California,* Riverside, California, USA.

Vassil P., Guoguo C., Daniel P., and Sanjeev Khudanpur., 2015. LibriSpeech: an ASR corpus based on public domain audio books. *In International Conference on Acoustics, Speech, and Signal Processing,* South Brisbane, Queensland, Australia, pp. 5206-5210.

PARALLEL SOLVERS COMPARISON FOR AN INVERSE PROBLEM IN FRACTIONAL CALCULUS

Pasquale De Luca[1], Ardelio Galletti[2] and Livia Marcellino[2]
[1]*Department of Computer Science, University of Salerno, Fisciano, Italy*
[2]*Department of Science and Technology, University of Naples Parthenope, Napoli, Italy*

ABSTRACT

High-Performance Computing (HPC) is a fundamental tool for improving the performance of many algorithms in terms of time, especially for large-scale problems. In the last years, various HPC architectures have been developed to quickly process data in many research areas and at the same time the HPC tools has become very important. In addition, the development of scientific libraries for parallel computing plays a key role in achieving better performance. In particular, thanks to the computational power of Graphic Processing Units, the most popular and inexpensive accelerators, the parallel computing field has become almost a standard process for data management. Hence, the porting of many standard numerical libraries on these architectures produced excellent results. In this work, we deal with a two-dimensional time fractional diffusion problem. More in detail, we analyze the performance of some parallel codes, specifically designed to solve it, implemented in different architectures. Moreover, a further GPU version is proposed and compared with the above implementations.

KEYWORDS

Parallel Algorithms, Multicore, GPU Computing, CUDA, Fractional Calculus

1. INTRODUCTION

The data size to be processed has been growing exponentially in the last years in the digital era. Therefore, the computational time and memory requirements, which characterize large problems, have been increased. The parallel computing approach represents the main source of speed improvement. In fact, there are many application fields, such as Mathematical Modeling, Computational Fluid Dynamics, Numerical Analysis etc., which benefit from the use of parallelization techniques. So, an accurate performance analysis certainly plays a key role. Clearly, the performance of a parallel algorithm depends on both the algorithms and the architectures used. Moreover, each architecture has a specific role for each problem and this is the major cause and the greatest motivation of the hardware evolution. For many decades the development of HPC technologies has focused on the need to work with machines with more processing units, in order to obtain the best performance. Today, thanks to modern multicore and Graphic Processing Units (GPUs) architectures, many problems can be investigated and the analysis of related performance, in terms of accuracy and efficiency, is possible as well as mandatory. Moreover, the rapid increase in the performance of graphics hardware and software has made GPUs, and related parallel numerical libraries, strong candidates for performing many computing intensive tasks.

This paper aims to provide a comparison analysis of some parallel codes, in terms of performance. These codes have been developed to solve a numerical problem in fractional calculus. Briefly, the theory of fractional calculus has become more and more central in several application fields, both in engineering and science. Indeed, inherent features of several chemistry, mechanics, and physics processes are potently described by means of mathematical fractional models (Mohebbi et al. 2013, Piret et al. 2013, Aslefallah et al. 2015). Here, we are focused on a two-dimensional inverse Caputo time fractional diffusion equation. The numerical procedure, we consider, is based on the discretization of the Caputo fractional derivative and on the use of a meshless localized collocation method exploiting the radial basis functions (RBFs) properties. In fact, nowadays the use of RBFs in fractional calculus is a well established procedure (Fasshauer 2007, Cuomo et al. 2017). This is mainly because they do not require the mesh construction, which is a well known too expensive task. The numerical scheme we deal with has been previously parallelized both in multicore and GPU architectures (De Luca et al. 2020, De Luca et al. 2020). Those implementations have been proven to be very efficient, but no comparison to find the best performance, in terms of execution time, has been discussed. Hence, here the objective is first of all to provide a clear comparison between the two versions. Then, we will exploit the potentiality of the GPU algorithm, for investigating the use of other library solvers to tackle the main computational kernel which consists in the numerical solution of a large and sparse linear system of equations. More precisely, starting by the previous GPU-parallel version of our software in (De Luca et al. 2020, De Luca et al. 2020) based on ad hoc parallel CUDA-kernels and efficient usage of parallel numerical libraries available on CUDA (Compute Unified Device Architecture) environment, we propose a further solver and measure the effects in terms of execution times and accuracy. Tests show that the new version can overcome in accuracy the other ones.

The rest of the paper is organized as follows: in section 2 the numerical problem and the related sequential algorithm are recalled; section 3 deals with the description of the main details of both parallel implementations, multicore and GPUs, of the algorithm. The use of different solvers is also a contribution in this section; in section 4 we provide tests and experiments to analyze and compare our codes in terms of performance and reliability; finally, in section 5 conclusions close the paper.

2. FRACTIONAL MODEL AND ALGORITHM

The starting model is the two-dimensional inverse time fractional diffusion equation [6, 7, 8], defined as follows:

$$ {}_0^c\boldsymbol{D}_t^{\alpha}\boldsymbol{v}(\boldsymbol{x},\boldsymbol{t}) = \boldsymbol{\kappa}\boldsymbol{\Delta}\boldsymbol{v}(\boldsymbol{x},\boldsymbol{t}) + \boldsymbol{f}(\boldsymbol{x},\boldsymbol{t}), \qquad (1) $$

where: $\boldsymbol{x} = (x,y) \in \boldsymbol{\Omega} \subseteq \boldsymbol{R}^2$ and $t \in]0,T]$. Here, the expression: ${}_0^c\boldsymbol{D}_t^{\alpha} = \frac{\partial^{\alpha}}{\partial t^{\alpha}}$ denotes the Caputo fractional derivative (Cuomo et al. 2016, Podlubny 1999). The order α is in $]0,1]$. The model also includes following initial and Dirichlet boundary conditions:

$$ \begin{aligned} \boldsymbol{v}(\boldsymbol{x},\boldsymbol{0}) &= \boldsymbol{\varphi}(\boldsymbol{x}), \boldsymbol{x} \in \boldsymbol{\Omega}, \\ \boldsymbol{v}(\boldsymbol{x},\boldsymbol{t}) &= \boldsymbol{\psi}_1(\boldsymbol{x},\boldsymbol{t}), \boldsymbol{x} \in \boldsymbol{\Gamma}_1, \boldsymbol{t} \in]\boldsymbol{0},\boldsymbol{T}], \\ \boldsymbol{v}(\boldsymbol{x},\boldsymbol{t}) &= \boldsymbol{\psi}_2(\boldsymbol{x})\boldsymbol{\rho}(\boldsymbol{t}), \boldsymbol{x} \in \boldsymbol{\Gamma}_2, \boldsymbol{t} \in]\boldsymbol{0},\boldsymbol{T}], \end{aligned} \qquad (2) $$

and the solutions sought $v(\boldsymbol{x},t)$ and $\rho(t)$ are unknown functions that verify the additional non-local boundary condition:

$$ \iint_{\Omega} \boldsymbol{v}\,(\boldsymbol{x},\boldsymbol{t})\boldsymbol{dx} = \boldsymbol{h}(\boldsymbol{t}), \boldsymbol{t} \in]\boldsymbol{0},\boldsymbol{T}] \qquad (3) $$

2.1 Numerical Model

Following the time discretization described in (De Luca et al. 2020), let: $\tau > 0$ be a time step and set: $t^n = n\tau$ for $n = 0, \dots, T/\tau$

By putting $t = t^{n+1}$ in (1), we get:

$$ {}_0^c\boldsymbol{D}_t^{\alpha}\boldsymbol{v}(\boldsymbol{x},\boldsymbol{t}^{n+1}) = \boldsymbol{\kappa}\boldsymbol{\Delta}\boldsymbol{v}(\boldsymbol{x},\boldsymbol{t}^{n+1}) + \boldsymbol{f}(\boldsymbol{x},\boldsymbol{t}^{n+1}), \qquad (4) $$

where: $(\boldsymbol{x}, t^{n+1}) \in \Omega \times (0,T]$.

Then, by using the second-order time discretization (Tian et al. 2015, Kibas et al. 2006), we obtain:

$$ [{}_0^c\boldsymbol{D}_t^{\alpha}\boldsymbol{v}(\boldsymbol{x},\boldsymbol{t})]_{t=t^{n+1}} = \sum_{j=0}^{n+1} \frac{\omega^{\alpha}(j)}{\tau^{\alpha}} \boldsymbol{v}(\boldsymbol{x},\boldsymbol{t}^{n+1-j}) - \frac{t^{-\alpha}}{\Gamma(1-\alpha)}\boldsymbol{v}(\boldsymbol{x},\boldsymbol{0}) + \boldsymbol{O}(\boldsymbol{\tau}^2) \qquad (5) $$

where the parameters are:

$$\boldsymbol{\omega}^{\alpha}(j) = \begin{cases} \frac{\alpha+2}{2}\boldsymbol{p}_0^{\alpha}, & j = 0, \\ \frac{\alpha+2}{2}\boldsymbol{p}_j^{\alpha} - \frac{\alpha}{2}\boldsymbol{p}_{j-1}^{\alpha}, & j > 0, \end{cases} \qquad p_j^{\alpha} = \begin{cases} 1, & j = 0, \\ \left(1 - \frac{\alpha+1}{j}\right) p_{j-1}^{\alpha}, & j \geq 1. \end{cases}$$

Finally, combining equations (4) and (5), we have following discrete time model:

$$\frac{\omega^{\alpha}(0)}{\tau^{\alpha}}\boldsymbol{v}^{n+1} - \boldsymbol{\kappa\Delta v}^{n+1} = -\sum_{j=1}^{n}\frac{\omega^{\alpha}(j)}{\tau^{\alpha}}\boldsymbol{v}^{n+1-j} + \frac{t^{-\alpha}}{\Gamma(1-\alpha)}\boldsymbol{v}^{0} + \boldsymbol{f}^{n+1} \qquad \textbf{(6)}$$

where for $j = 0, \dots, n+1$ we set $\boldsymbol{f}^{n+1} = \boldsymbol{f}(\boldsymbol{x}, \boldsymbol{t}^{n+1})$ and $\boldsymbol{v}^{n+1-j} = \boldsymbol{v}(\boldsymbol{x}, \boldsymbol{t}^{n+1-j})$.

Now, to get a discretized solution we use a meshless localized collocation method. More in detail, we partition the global domain Ω into local sub-domains Ω_i $(i = 1, \dots, N)$, related to every point, that cover Ω. So, we define radial point interpolation shape functions, ϕ_i for all Ω_i, each of which corresponds to a unique local field point $\boldsymbol{x}_i$. The chosen RBFs are the generalized multiquadric radial basis function (GMQ-RBF): $\boldsymbol{\phi}(\boldsymbol{r}) = (\boldsymbol{r}^2 + \boldsymbol{c}^2)^{\boldsymbol{q}}$

where c is the shape parameter and $q = 2.5$ is fixed. Assuming that v can be approximated by:

$$\boldsymbol{v}(\boldsymbol{x}) = \sum_{i=1}^{N}\boldsymbol{\phi}_i(\boldsymbol{x})\boldsymbol{v}_i \qquad (7)$$

where the norm $\boldsymbol{\phi}_i(\boldsymbol{x}) = \boldsymbol{\phi}(\| \boldsymbol{x} - \boldsymbol{x}_i \|_2)$ denotes the classical Euclidean distance. Finally, by using expansion (7) in (2), (3) and (6), the equations of the discrete model are obtained:

$$\sum_{i=1}^{N}\left[\frac{\boldsymbol{\omega}^{\alpha}(\boldsymbol{0})}{\boldsymbol{\tau}^{\alpha}}\boldsymbol{\phi}_i(\boldsymbol{x}_j) - \boldsymbol{\kappa}\left[\frac{\partial^2\boldsymbol{\phi}_i}{\partial \boldsymbol{x}^2} + \frac{\partial^2\boldsymbol{\phi}_i}{\partial \boldsymbol{y}^2}\right](\boldsymbol{x}_j)\right]\boldsymbol{v}_i^{n+1} =$$

$$-\sum_{j=1}^{n}\frac{\omega^{\alpha}(j)}{\tau^{\alpha}}\sum_{i=1}^{N}\phi_i(\boldsymbol{x}_j)v_i^{n+1-j} + \frac{t^{-\alpha}}{\Gamma(1-\alpha)}\sum_{i=1}^{N}\phi_i(\boldsymbol{x}_j)v^0 + f^{n+1}, (j = 1, \dots, N_\Omega) \qquad (8)$$

$$\sum_{i=1}^{N}\phi_i(\boldsymbol{x}_j)v_i^{n+1} = \psi_1^{n+1}(\boldsymbol{x}_j), (j = N_\Omega + 1, \dots, N_\Omega + N_{\Gamma_1}) \qquad (9)$$

$$\sum_{i=1}^{N}\phi_i(\boldsymbol{x}_j)v_i^{n+1} = \psi_2^{n+1}(\boldsymbol{x}_j)\rho^{n+1}, (j = N_\Omega + N_{\Gamma_1} + 1, \dots, N_\Omega + N_{\Gamma_1} + N_{\Gamma_2}) \qquad (10)$$

$$\sum_{i=1}^{N}\left(\int_\Omega \phi_i(\boldsymbol{x})d\Omega\right)v_i^{n+1} = h^{n+1}. \qquad (11)$$

We notice that equations (8) concern the N_Ω interior points in Ω, while the N_{Γ_1} equations (9) and the N_{Γ_2} equations (10) are related to the initial and boundary conditions, respectively. Lastly, equation (11) arises from integral in (3), which is discretized with a Gauss-Legendre bidimensional quadrature rule of order 15.

2.2 Algorithm

The above described approach identifies a $(N+1) \times (N+1)$ linear system where the size problem depends on both boundary and interior points, that is: $\boldsymbol{N} = \boldsymbol{N}_\Omega + \boldsymbol{N}_{\Gamma_1} + \boldsymbol{N}_{\Gamma_2}$.

In this scenario, the discrete solution entries: $\boldsymbol{v}^{(n+1)} = (\boldsymbol{v}_1^{n+1}, \dots, \boldsymbol{v}_N^{n+1}, \boldsymbol{\rho}^{n+1})$ are determined by solving the linear system:

$$\mathcal{A}\boldsymbol{v}^{(n+1)} = \mathcal{B}^{(n+1)}, \qquad \textbf{(12)}$$

where $\mathcal{A}$ *is a* $(N+1) \times (N+1)$ *sparse coefficient matrix;* $\mathcal{B}^{(n+1)}$ *is a* $(N+1)$ *column vector.*

We emphasize that $\mathcal{B}^{(n+1)}$, unlike $\mathcal{A}$, has to be upgraded along time steps. The sparsity of $\mathcal{A}$ arises from the local approach, that is only nearby points of each field point $\boldsymbol{x}_i$ are considered. Since number of neighbors can change, the $\mathcal{A}$ structure cannot be shown here explicitly. The discrete model is summarized in Algorithm 1.

Input: $\kappa, \alpha, T, \tau, \varphi, \Psi_1, \Psi_2, h.$

1: generate $\{\mathbf{x}_i\}_{i=1}^{N_\Omega}$, % interior points

2: generate $\{\mathbf{x}_{i+N_\Omega}\}_{i=1}^{N_{\Gamma_1}}$ % Γ_1 boundary points

3: generate $\{\mathbf{x}_{i+N_\Omega+N_{\Gamma_1}}\}_{i=1}^{N_{\Gamma_2}}$ % Γ_2 boundary points

4: build $\mathbf{A}$ % *by following (8,9,10,11)*

5: evaluation of $\nu(\mathbf{A})$ % condition number of $\mathbf{A}$

6: for $n = 0, 1, \ldots, T/\tau - 1$ % *loop on time slices*

7: build $\mathbf{B}^{(\mathbf{n+1})}$ % *by following (8,9,10,11)*

8: compute $\mathbf{v}^{(n+1)}$: % *solution of* $\mathcal{A}\mathbf{v}^{(n+1)} = \mathcal{B}^{(n+1)}$ *in (12)*

9: endfor

Output: $\left\{\{v_i^{T/\tau}\}_{i=1}^{N}\right\}$, $\{\rho^{T/\tau}\}$ $\nu(\mathbf{A})$.

Algorithm 1. Pseudo-code

3. PARALLEL CODES

The algorithm proposed in previous section can reach a good accuracy (De Luca et al. 2020), but executing the software on a latest-generation CPU, we observe a very large execution time. This is essentially due to the fact that, when we deal with a huge practical problem, with a large domain, the computational complexity increases considerably. Starting from these considerations we have implemented two different parallel versions of Algorithm 1: in the first one we developed a parallel algorithm specifically designed for multicore architectures and based on the Pthreads library[1], while in the second one, we implemented a GPU software based on ad hoc parallel CUDA-kernels and the efficient usage of numerical libraries available for GPUs[2]. Here, we want to compare these two implementations and to propose a variant of the second version, which allows us to investigate the possibility of using a different solver for the main computational task.

3.1 Multicore Parallel Code Details

A first attempt of parallelization strategy, presented in (De Luca et al. 2020) focused on employment of multicore processors, which are widely used across many application domains. The parallel approach is based on a functional decomposition combined with a classical domain decomposition. More specifically, a pool of threads works exploiting an asynchronous parallelism by solving different tasks of the overall work in a parallel way. In particular, lines 1–4 perform the domain decomposition strategy; while a combination of domain decomposition and functional decomposition approach is used to perform in parallel lines 5–9. This combination is made as follows: the condition number of the sparse matrix is computed by a single thread, and concurrently, other threads build the right-hand side vectors (using a classical domain decomposition) and solve the sparse linear system, for each time step. Sparse linear systems are solved by using a specific routine of the CSPARSE library[3]. Note that, well-suited semaphores[4] help the execution for critical regions, protecting the routines which are not *thread-safe*. This ensures a correct data consistency.

[1] https://computing.llnl.gov/tutorials/pthreads/

[2] https://docs.nvidia.com/cuda/cuda-c-programming-guide/index.html

[3] http://faculty.cse.tamu.edu/davis/suitesparse.html

[4] https://pubs.opengroup.org/onlinepubs/7908799/xsh/semaphore.h.html

3.2 GPU-Parallel Code Details: LU Version

In (De Luca et al. 2020) another parallel approach, based on GPUs, is presented. Thanks to this last generation parallel machines, we achieve a satisfying execution of our code by using the powerful characteristics of CUDA environment, which allow us to overcome the limited memory problem, allocating the memory dynamically. In this way we reduced the transfer of host-device data. Moreover, also for this version, we combine the domain decomposition with a functional decomposition more sophisticated with respect to the multicore implementation. Therefore, following the domain decomposition-based parallelization strategy, each thread is linked at a single input point in order to perform the operations required to build the final sparse matrix (lines 1–4). Instead, to solve the main linear system, and evaluate $\nu(\boldsymbol{A})$ (lines 5–9), a functional decomposition strategy is implemented. This phase makes use of a synchronization by the __syncthreads() routines, in order to avoid any memory contention. In particular, the *loop for* , related to time discretization, runs in parallel on T/τ threads, to build the system and to copy of the sparse matrix in the local memory using the *compressed sparse row* format CSR [5] . Finally, the main sparse linear system is solved from the host by cusolverSpDcsrlsvlu() routine of the cuSOLVER library[6].

3.3 Another GPU Implementation: QR Version

The results obtained in the two previous parallel versions seemed to us satisfactory, especially from a performance point of view, but also as regards the accuracy of the results. However, the sparse linear system preserves the ill conditioning problem. Therefore, in order to investigate about an accuracy improvement, here, we analyze the results which can be obtained by modifying the solver choice. More precisely, in line 8 we use the *cusolverSpDcsrlsvqr*() routine, instead of the *cusolverSpDcsrlsvlu*() previously used in the LU version. The *cusolverSpDcsrlsvqr*() routine implements the sparse QR factorization. Also for this routine it is necessary to store the coefficient matrix in CSR format and the functional decomposition strategy has slightly modified to ensure data consistency and to manage efficient storage of the new data structures used. This highlights the potential of our software which is written in modular blocks that can be easily adapted to new solvers.

4. PERFORMANCE COMPARISON

In this section we present a behavior analysis of the three parallel versions of Algorithm 1, described in section 3. The experimental tests are carried out in order to compare the different approaches for solving the inverse time fractional problem (1). Although several parallel software are available to solve many fractional problems, currently, to our knowledge, no one exists to this specific aim. In order to investigate about possible gain of performance or accuracy, several executions with different input size parameters, are presented. The three parallel codes run on a computer machine with the following technical specifications: two CPU Intel Xeon with 6 cores, E5-2609v3, 1.9 Ghz, 32GB of RAM 4 channels 51Gb/s memory bandwidth; two NVIDIA GeForce GTX TITAN X, 3072 CUDA cores, 1 Ghz Core clock for core, 12 GB DDR5, 336 GBs as bandwidth.

All experiments in this section are referred to the same case study (see De Luca et al. 2020). More in detail, we set:

- a uniform two-dimensional grid in $\Omega = [0,1]^2$, with: $N = \left(1 + \frac{1}{h}\right)^2$, h stepsize along x, y directions;
- boundaries: $\Gamma_2 = \{(x,y) \mid x = 1,\ 0 < y < 1\}$ and $\Gamma_1 = \partial\Omega \backslash \Gamma_2$;
- the source function: $f(\boldsymbol{x},t) = 2\left(\frac{t^{2-\alpha}}{\Gamma(3-\alpha)} - t^2\right) exp(x+y)$,
- initial and Dirichlet conditions: $\varphi(\boldsymbol{x}) = 0,\ \ \psi_1(\boldsymbol{x},t) = t^2 exp(x+y),\ \ \psi_2(\boldsymbol{x}) = exp(x+y)$.

[5] https://docs.nvidia.com/cuda/cusparse/index.html#csr-format
[6] https://docs.nvidia.com/cuda/cusolver/index.html

The true solutions are given by: $v(\boldsymbol{x}, t) = t^2 exp(x + y)$ and $\rho(t) = t^2$.

Execution times shown are taken as averages of 10 simulations.

Test 1 – The following test deals with the performance of the different implementations of Algorithm 1. In particular, Table 1 highlights the best performance among the three proposed approaches by varying the input sizes N, and for $\tau = 1/100$. Here, we report the execution times, obtained for the best configuration, both for multicore and GPU implementations, that is: the threads number for multicore version is set to 12 (one per core); the Block × threads for GPU versions is set to 1×512. These optimal configurations emerged from the analysis carried out in (De Luca et al. 2020) and (De Luca et al. 2020).

Table 1. Execution times (s) comparison: serial, multicore, GPU-LU and GPU-QR

		Parallel Time		
N	Serial Time	MULTICORE	GPU-LU	GPU-QR
3.6×10^3	1.6×10^3	1.99	1.40	2.38
8.1×10^3	1.2×10^4	7.98	1.86	2.84
1.0×10^4	3.19×10^4	11.01	3.60	5.47
1.69×10^4	1.66×10^5	29.01	5.20	7.53
1.98×10^4	2.46×10^5	38.80	8.12	11.48
2.25×10^4	3.9×10^5	68.01	8.12	11.95

An very appreciable improving of performance, with respect to serial execution times, has already obtained by the multicore version. Better results, in terms of execution times, are provided by the GPU versions. Such an acceleration level mainly depends on the higher optimization of the parallel versions compared to the sequential one. Finally, we observe that the GPU-LU version returns the best gain of efficiency, regardless of the size problem. We highlight that the execution times in Table 1 refer to the whole computational process, including all phases described in Algorithm 1. Conversely, next experiment concerns the performance analysis, for the GPU codes, of just a portion of the process, that is the sparse linear system task.

Test 2 – Here, a specific comparison between GPU versions is presented. Since, the two versions mainly differ from each other for the routine used for solving the main task, i.e. the sparse linear system, we just limit out attention to their behaviour. We recall that GPU-LU version uses the routine cusolverSpDcsrlsvlu, which is based on the sparse LU factorization, while the GPU-QR version employs the routine *cusolverSpDcsrlsvqr*, based on the sparse QR factorization. The experiments, shown in Table 2, include several values of $\boldsymbol{N}$ and $\boldsymbol{\tau}$ and exploit the best configuration Block \times thread = $\mathbf{1 \times 512}$.

Table 2. GPU solvers execution times (in milliseconds) *cusolverSpDcsrlsvlu*(LU) vs *cusolverSpDcsrlsvqr*(QR)

N	*solver*	$\tau = \frac{1}{10}$	$\tau = \frac{1}{20}$	$\tau = \frac{1}{40}$	$\tau = \frac{1}{80}$	$\tau = \frac{1}{160}$
20^2	LU	71.12	100.81	137.37	212.88	387.68
	QR	93.23	153.24	221.93	322.09	540.15
40^2	LU	83.12	180.82	180.82	271.96	488.67
	QR	94.58	133.07	229.39	368.60	592.78
60^2	LU	108.47	156.92	230.32	329.03	460.15
	QR	153.23	247.86	364.96	506.71	703.76
80^2	LU	132.88	198.70	279.86	412.81	586.94
	QR	195.73	294.35	392.18	576.19	848.12
100^2	LU	150.31	268.95	379.55	489.77	823.36
	QR	263.15	342.99	518.57	742.91	1096.57

Experimental results emphasize that the QR solver requires more time with respect to LU solver, also when a small input size is given. In detail, LU routine is about 1.5 times faster than the QR routine. Moreover, looking at execution times in Table 2, separately for LU and QR versions, values monotonically increase both with the size problem $\boldsymbol{N}$ and the number of time steps $\boldsymbol{T/\tau}$, in agree with the expected computational cost. Despite the different execution times both versions offer similar behaviour regard the provided accuracy.

Test 3 – Here, we are interested in measuring the effect of using the two GPU versions, in terms of accuracy. The accuracy is computed as the error, due to the numerical approximation introduced by using both time discretization and the local collocation approach, that is the error defined as the RMSE between $\boldsymbol{v}$ and its computed value $\tilde{\boldsymbol{v}}$. Table 3 highlights the accuracy provided for N=10^4 and by varying the time step τ between from 1/10 to 1/160.

Table 3. Accuracy for several executions by using different decomposition approaches, varying time stepping

version	$\tau = \frac{1}{10}$	$\tau = \frac{1}{20}$	$\tau = \frac{1}{40}$	$\tau = \frac{1}{80}$	$\tau = \frac{1}{160}$
GPU-LU	**5.50e-05**	**3.54e-05**	2.95e-05	**2.75e-05**	2.64e-05
GPU-QR	3.63e-04	9.94e-05	**2.80e-05**	2.85e-05	**2.17e-05**

The results in Table 3 show that both versions can offer the same level of accuracy, regardless the time step value. Moreover, the best results (in bold) are alternatively provided from the two codes. So, we can conclude that both implementations, despite the execution times required, can be used for an accurate computation. We point out that previous conclusions do not change as the number of centers $\boldsymbol{N}$ varies.

5. CONCLUSION

In this paper, we analyzed the performance of three parallel codes, specifically designed for solving a two-dimensional time fractional diffusion problem. We started from two previously implemented versions of the parallel algorithm: one on multicore architecture and the other in a GPU environment. Then, we also provided a new GPU version, based on QR factorization, and compared all parallel algorithms in terms of performance and accuracy. Tests showed that the proposed new version can offer better accuracy results.

ACKNOWLEDGEMENT

This paper has been supported by project *Algoritmi innovativi per interpolazione, approssimazione e quadratura* (AIIAQ) and project *Algoritmi numerici e software per il trattamento di dati su larga scala in ambienti HPC* (LSDAHPC)

REFERENCES

Abbasbandy, et al. Comparison of meshless local weak and strong forms based on particular solutions for a non-classical 2-D diffusion model, Engineering Analysis with Boundary Elements, 39 (2014) 121-128.

Aslefallah, Mohammad et al. "Nonlinear fractional integro-differential reaction-diffusion equation via eadial basis functions." The European Physical Journal Plus 130.3 (2015): 47.

Cuomo, et al. "A GPU-Parallel Algorithm for ECG Signal Denoising Based on the NLM Method," 2016 30th International Conference on Advanced Information Networking and Applications Workshops (WAINA), Crans-Montana, 2016, pp. 35-39.

Cuomo, S., et al. Reconstruction of implicit curves and surfaces via RBF interpolation (2017) Applied Numerical Mathematics, 116, pp. 157-171. DOI: 10.1016/j.apnum.2016.10.016

D'Amore, L. et al. (2011, September). A Parallel Three-dimensional Variational Data Assimilation Scheme. In AIP Conference Proceedings (Vol. 1389, No. 1, pp. 1829-1831). American Institute of Physics.

De Luca P., et al. (2020) Performance Analysis of a Multicore Implementation for Solving a Two-Dimensional Inverse Anomalous Diffusion Problem. In: Sergeyev Y., Kvasov D. (eds) Numerical Computations: Theory and Algorithms. NUMTA 2019. Lecture Notes in Computer Science, vol 11973. Springer, Cham

De Luca, P., et al. (2020) A gpu-cuda framework for solving a two-dimensional inverse anomalous diffusion problem. In: Foster, I., Joubert, G.R., Kuˇcera, L., Nagel, W.E., Peters, F. (eds) Parallel Computing: Technology Trends, Advances in Parallel Computing. Vol 36. pp 311 - 320. IOS Press, 2020.

Fasshauer, Gregory E. Meshfree approximation methods with MATLAB. Vol. 6. World Scientific, 2007.

Kilbas, et al. Theory and Application of Fractional Differential Equations, North Holland Mathematics Studies, 204 (2006).

Mohebbi, Akbar, et al. "The use of a meshless technique based on collocation and radial basis functions for solving the time fractional nonlinear Schrodinger equation arising in quantum mechanics." Engineering Analysis with Boundary Elements 37.2 (2013): 475-485.

Piret, CeCile et al.. "A radial basis functions method for fractional diffusion equations." Journal of Computational Physics 238 (2013): 71-81.

Podlubny, Fractional Differential Equation, Academic Press, 1999.

Q. Liu, et al. An implicit RBF meshless approach for time fractional diffusion equations, Comput Mech, 48 (2011) 1-12.

Tian et al. A class of second order difference approximations for solving space fractional diffusion equations, Mathematics of Computation, 84 (2015) 1703-1727.

Yan, et al. The method of approximate particular solutions for the time-fractional diffusion equation with a non-local boundary condition, Computers and Mathematics with Applications, 70 (2015) 254-264.

USER BEHAVIOR MODEL DEVELOPMENT IN THE TILE LOGIC FOR AUTOMATING USABILITY EVALUATION

Vladimir V. Devyatkov and Evgeny A. Tipsin
Bauman Moscow State Technical University, Russia

ABSTRACT

The paper is devoted to the direction of automating usability evaluation. This paper presents the methodology of an intelligent agent user model formation; contains the model requirements to reliable modelling of a real user behavior on which the choice symbolic approach of an intelligent model development is based. The factors affecting user behavior are presented. The mathematical model of an intelligent agent is introduced. This model is based on the aspects formal description of an agent's activities, such as goal-directed, planning, and knowledge organization. The tile logic is used as a formal language. In conclusion, we present the future of use and development of the proposed approach.

KEYWORDS

Software Applications, Usability, Usability Testing, Intelligent Agents, Tile Logic, Human-Machine Interaction

1. INTRODUCTION

Widespread development of information technology has led to a large number of software applications development. They are installed on different platforms and designed for users without education in the information technology area. Such applications are, for example, online banks, city navigator, monitoring public transport and others. More and more, these applications have a complex structure and behavior. Therefore, unexperienced users have difficulties by interacting with them. In order to reduce difficulties, many companies provide human-oriented design of applications. There is a wide range of traditional means of usability evaluation. The most in-demand of them are: standards/guidelines review, heuristic valuation, cognitive walkthrough, pluralistic walkthrough, feature inspection, task analysis, focus groups, surveys, interviews, questionnaires and benchmarking, eye tracking, analysis of user's electroencephalogram (Alfimtsev et al., 2015) and others. Usability evaluation methods with invitation of real users are the most effective, because they provide quantitative and qualitative data (Sakulin et al., 2018). However, all these usability evaluations are rather labor-intensive. This is reflected in spending time for preparing for benchmarking, selection of respondents and further analysis of obtained results by experts of human-machine interaction. In some cases, availability of special equipment is necessary. In order to reduce complexity, unexperienced users' difficulties with interacting and amount of manual work, increase accessibility usability testing for a large number of developers, the direction of automated usability evaluation is relevant.

The previous paper (Devyatkov and Tipsin, 2019) contains an overview of automating usability evaluation approaches, including analysis of user logs properties, parametric analysis of page properties and model-oriented proof of properties existence. The solution was proposed to automate usability testing by modelling interaction of an application model and an user intelligent agent after analyzing the approaches and identifying the advantages and disadvantages of each. The conclusion on application usability is based on analysis of this interaction. The models architecture and interaction principles were presented in the paper. The tile logic (Bruni, 1998) was selected as a formal language for adequate models representation.

In real situations, user's behavior is determined by many external and internal factors, including psychological characteristics, user experience and much more (Alfimtsev et al., 2016). In other words, intelligent agent development is not a trivial task, because many aspects of user behavior must be considered.

This article presents the methodology of an intelligent agent formal development, which is based on aspects formal description of agent's activities, such as goal-directed, planning, and knowledge organization.

The tile logic is convenient for developing an agent user model, because it allows to form general behaviour by separate bidirectional tiles, each of them adequately represents elements of user behavior during interaction with applications. Tiles composition forms behavior of any complexity (Devyatkov, 2016).

Below are the basic user model requirements, the factors affecting user behavior; the explanation of approach choice to intelligent model development; the mathematical model of an intelligent agent with description of formal aspects, such as goal-directed, planning, and knowledge organization. In conclusion, we present the future of use and development of the proposed approach.

2. REQUIREMENTS TO INTELLIGENT USER MODEL

Users do not solve problems by random interaction with a product, but they form a sequence of actions to achieve a goal mentally, so-called problem solution plan. The question arose: how can a user form a problem solution plan for a previously unknown product? Each user knows how any product works and how to use it according to their mental model (Boicho and Kokinov, 2001). Users interact with new products based on previous experience expecting similar behavior for similar products. According to human-machine interaction expert Jacob Nielsen: «A mental model is based on belief, not facts: that is, it's a model of what users know (or think they know) about a system such as your website.» (Nielsen and Loranger, 2006). Thus, the developed intelligent model must have the ability to form problem solution plans for reliable modelling of user behavior.

User interaction with applications looks like moving from a one interface element to another. An user can attend to a one group of interface elements, and leave others immediately. This is related to fact, that the user evaluates each interface element as it is useful for solving a problem or for compliance with solution requirements. This assessment is based on the possessed knowledge or acquired in process of interacting with a product. Knowledge provides to make right decisions for quick achievement of a goal. Similar requirements apply to the intelligent user model.

Differences between a user's mental model and a real product or lack of knowledge for well-informed decisions are possible. Therefore, the intelligent model should include the simplest human behavior aspects, such as decision-making under conditions of uncertainty, imperfect knowledge.

Traditional methods of evaluation usability - questionnaires and interviews are used to understand user decisions and a user model for thinking. The intelligent user model should be able to explain its behavior for complete user replacement in a testing usability process.

3. APPROACH SELECTION TO INTELLIGENT USER MODEL DEVELOPMENT

There are two main approaches to development of artificial intelligent systems. One of them is based on modelling biological system of a brain - neural network artificial intelligence, and the other is based on human reasoning - symbolic artificial intelligence. The comparison of symbolic and neural network approaches was carried out according to the requirements formulated in the previous section in selection of approach to the intelligent agent development:

- Knowledge acquisition. Neural network methods require a large amount of data for training, therefore, they do not allow to effectively solve the problem of acquiring knowledge. The symbolic approach does not have such limitations, therefore, modelling dynamics of acquiring declarative knowledge is well modeled using symbolic methods;
- Planning. Traditionally, artificial neural networks are used for pattern recognition, classification, clustering, forecasting and control tasks. However, tasks of forming problem solution plans relate to problems called «NP-complete». The difficulties of a topology selection and neural network parameters selection prevents the solution of the planning problem based on neural networks. Therefore, planning is based on the formal logics, and the reasoning is carried out by logical inference in artificial intelligence symbolic models in most of the most popular and common approaches;
- Decision explanation. The neural network is actually a black box model. It is impossible to get any static data, understand the process of the result conclusion and decision-making process (Ivashkin et. all,

2018). Neural network models are too mathematically abstract and complex to view and understand. The symbolic approach is able to represent the reasoning stages unlike the neural network model;

- Decision-making under conditions of uncertainty and imperfect knowledge. Neural networks provides the correct result based on imperfect or previously unknown data that makes it possible to use to solve complex problems. However, a large amount of data is required for effective neural network training. In turn, symbolic artificial intelligence approach does not depend on training data amount and have a lof of formalisms. It provides to model any aspects of human thinking and decision-making under conditions of uncertainty and imperfect knowledge.

It was concluded that the symbolic artificial intelligence approach is the most appropriate for creating a user model.

4. USER BEHAVIORAL FACTORS

Consider the factors F, that affect user behavior during on interaction with a application, among which:

- $page$ description. Gestalt principles (Ellis, 1999) are applied in human-machine interaction design. The one core idea is that people tend to identify elements initially in general form. In other words, the human brain recognizes the whole faster than the component. Based on this idea and experiments, that confirm its truth, it is concluded that users identify a page initially in a general form. Despite the fact that users did not interact with each element of a product interface, they have a general representation of a page structure that affect user behavior during on interaction with an application.
- description structure $block$. According to two Gestalt principles - proximity (Emergence) and common region. The principle of proximity states that things that are close together appear to be more related than things that are spaced farther apart. The principle of common region states that when objects are located within same closed region, people perceive them as being grouped together. Let's introduce the concept of a structural block, it is related or grouped user interface elements (Sakulin et al., 2019). Each structural block has a specific purpose or function. Thus, based on these principles, it follows that users perceive a page in a general form, as a set of structural blocks, users interact with one specific structural block at one time.
- interaction $context$. Context is a system of factors that provide to explain actions and understand respondent's motivation during on interaction with an application. Each action takes on special content taking into consideration context.
- individual $feature$ of the user. Each user has individual characteristics that affect the behavior during on interaction with a product, for example, preferences, interests, expectations, behavior patterns and others.

5. FORMAL DESCRIPTION OF THE USER MODEL

In this article, the tile logic with aspects, such as goal-directed, planning, and knowledge organization, is proposed to be used by describe the user model. A nonempty finite set of base tiles $T = \{t_0, t_1, ..., t_m\}$, corresponding to user behavior should be created to use the tile logic. In other words, the logic is formed by set of base tiles T and several auxiliary tiles which can be composited. Tiles can be composited horizontally (denoted by symbol $*$), vertically (denoted by symbol $\cdot$), and in parallel (denoted by symbol $\otimes$) to define complex behavior of systems. A tile is a single user action, the coordinated composition of individual tiles represents the common user behavior. Let's introduce the tiles composition function $T \times K \rightarrow T$, mapping the current tile T and knowledge base K to the new tile T composition.

The basic tiles T describe single user actions in a specific situation, which can be described by the factors presented in the previous section, such as $page$ and structure $block$; interaction $context$; individual of the user. These factors are reflected in the tile interfaces: the tile initial input interface $?i_i$, the tile initial output interface $!o_i$, the tile final input interface $?i_o$, the tile initial output interface $!o_o$. Interfaces set restrictions on individual tiles composition. Horizontal and vertical composition is enough to simulate user behavior. Compositions are responsible for certain processes, which will be discussed below.

The agent interacts with the application by receiving – perception $?A$ and sending messages - reaction $!A$. Agent's perception - nonempty finite set $?A$ and an element of this set $?a \in ?A$ is a message from an application presenting a formal description of an user interface structural block. The agent needs to form correct reaction $!a \in !A$ to received message, where $!A = \{click, double\_click, input, track\}$ nonempty finite set, where $click$ - single click, $double\_click$ - double click, $input$ - entering data, $track$ - the transition from one element to another (moving eyes). To that end, it is necessary to determine block description, that is block semantic meaning, which has an impact on making the right decision. The agent has a knowledge base K for such reasoning.

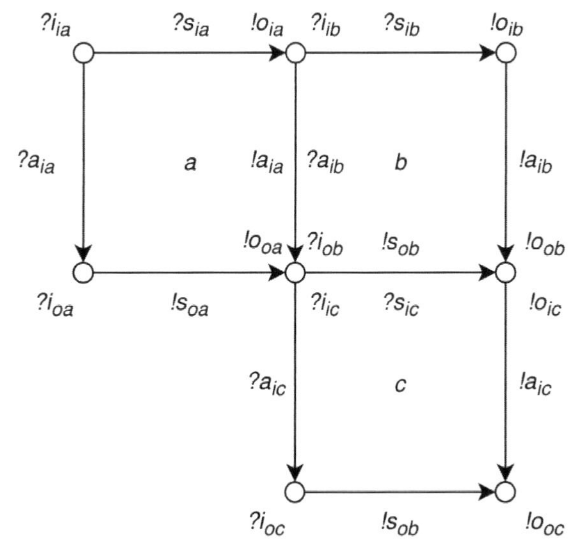

Figure 1. Horizontal and vertical tile composition

The agent's knowledge base K – a set of facts and rules that describe relationships between objects of domain area that help make decisions and agent actions plan. Facts describe objects presence in domain area, their properties, the relationship between them. Rules define relationships between classes, facts, and the rules themselves. In process of modeling, the knowledge base can be dynamically edited: add, delete and modify facts. Information can be obtained from the knowledge base on the basis of facts and rules by inference mechanism. Facts and rules are represented as predicate characters $predicate\_symbol(Term_1, Term_2, ..., Term_n)$ followed by ordered set of terms $Term_1, Term_2, ..., Term_n$, corresponding to objects.

The agent internal activities are presented as a horizontal composition, as shown in Figure 1. Horizontal composition is possible only if $!o_{ia} = ?i_{ib}$ and $!o_{oa} = ?i_{ob}$.

The vertical composition is performed after internal activities to perform an action $!a \in !A$, that is sending a message to the application, as shown in Figure 1. Vertical composition is possible only if $!i_{ob} = ?i_{ic}$ and $!o_{ob} = ?o_{ic}$.

A goal is a state or a set of states that agent's current behavior is directed towards. The goal is described by the criterion function $goal(T, K) \rightarrow \{completed, continue\}$, mapping the current tile T and knowledge base K to one of the values: $completed$ goal achieved; $continue$ agent in the process of achieving the goal (goal not achieved at calculation time). If the goal is achieved $goal(T, K) = completed$ agents interaction is terminated. There are many ways to describe function criteria, for example, a set of statements in temporal or dynamic logic and other.

Consider the general statement of the planning problem. If T is a set of tiles describing user behavior; the tile $t_0 \in T$ represents the initial state; G set of tiles of the target state, then problem solution plan is

$plan = \langle T, t_0, G \rangle$. Ordered set $T_{pln} = \langle t_0, t_1, ..., t_n \rangle$, where $t_i \in T$, called the problem solution plan if the tiles composition sequence $t_0, t_1, ..., t_n$ leads to the target state. An ordered set T_{pln} is called a plan. Plan realizes the goal, if the condition $goal(T, K) = continue$ for the current tile T and knowledge base K.

As previously stated, users can form a problem solution plan for a previously unknown product based on previous experience. A predicate is introduced to formalize knowledge $product(?a, !a, ?a')$ containing 3 terms: $?a$ - perception; $!a$ - reaction; $?a'$ - perception. If $product(?a, !a, ?a')$ is true, then to the reaction $!a$ with the perception $?a$ the future perception will $?a'$. This agent knowledge is similar to an application behavior description, in fact, that is an application model in terms of the agent. The agent's plan based on knowledge may differ from the actual plan results if the agent's knowledge does not match with reality. The plan is not static, it can be rebuilt when changing agent knowledge or changes in the external environment were not provided for by the original plan. Let's introduce plan revision function: $K \times plan \times T_{pln} \rightarrow plan'$, mapping knowledge base K, the current $plan$ and the current tile T_{pln} to the new $plan'$.

6. CONCLUSIONS

In this paper provides methodology of intelligent agent user model formation. The basic user model requirements and explanation of the approach choice to intelligent model development are reviewed. The factors affecting user behavior are presented. The mathematical model of an intelligent agent is introduced. It is based on aspects formal description of agent's activities, such as goal-directed, planning, and knowledge organization. The tile logic is used as a formal language. In the future research, it is planned to conduct an experiment using eye tracking technology to extract user behavior patterns. The basic set of tiles will be formed from behavior patterns. Special attention will be paid to three areas of agent model improvement: planning for achieving goals; experience accumulation and analysis; inclusion of unobserved variables which is human behavior characteristics used in psychology and sociology. The direction of automating usability evaluation has good prospects. Any development of modelling human behavior will be claimed in many domains of knowledge.

REFERENCES

Alfimtsev, A., Sakulin, S., & Levanov, A. (2016). Formalization of expert knowledge about the usability of web pages based on user criteria aggregation. International Journal of Software Innovation (IJSI), 4(3), 38-50.

Alfimtsev, A. N., Basarab, M. A., Devyatkov, V. V., & Levanov, A. A. (2015). A new methodology of usability testing on the base of the analysis of user's electroencephalogram. Journal of Computer Sciences and Applications, 3(5), 105-111.

Boicho, D. G. K. J. H., & Kokinov, N. (2001). The analogical mind: Perspectives from cognitive science. MIT press.

Bruni, R., Meseguer, J., & Montanari, U. (1998). Process and term tile logic.

Devyatkov V.V. Verification of Intelligent Interface Properties in the Tiles Logic. Vestn. Mosk. Gos. Tekh. Univ. im. N.E. Baumana, Priborostr. [Herald of the Bauman Moscow State Tech. Univ., Instrum. Eng.], 2016, no. 3, pp. 65–87.

Devyatkov, V. V., & Tipsin, E. A. (2019, July 16). Automating usability evaluation of visual user interfaces in the tile logic. International Conferences Interfaces and Human Computer Interaction 2019.

Ivashkin, Y. A., Blagoveschensky, I. G., & Nikitina, M. A. (2018). Neural network and agent technologies in the structural-parametric modeling of technological systems. In 2018 School-Seminar on Optimization Problems and their Applications, OPTA-SCL 2018 (pp. 169-180).

Nielsen, J., & Loranger, H. (2006). Prioritizing web usability. Pearson Education.

Sakulin, S., Alfimtsev, A., Solovyev, D., & Sokolov, D. (2018). Web page interface optimization based on nature-inspired algorithms. International Journal of Swarm Intelligence Research (IJSIR), 9(2), 28-46.

Sakulin, S., Alfimtsev, A., Tipsin, E., Devyatkov, V., & Sokolov, D. (2019). User Interface Distribution Method Based on Pi-Calculus. International Journal of Distributed Systems and Technologies (IJDST), 10(3), 1-20.

BIDIRECTIONAL RAY TRACING WITH CAUSTIC PHOTON AND INDIRECT IMPHOTON MAPS

Andrey Zhdanov[1], Dmitry Zhdanov[1] and Vladimir Galaktionov[2]
[1]*ITMO University, Russia*
[2]*Keldysh Institute of Applied Mathematics, Russia*

ABSTRACT

The current article presents methods aimed at the acceleration of realistic images synthesis by bidirectional ray tracing, which is based on the simultaneous use of photon maps for caustics illumination and imphoton (visibility) maps for indirect illumination. The usage of two separate maps allows to reduce the size of the maps and as result to increase the processing speed while keeping the image quality.

KEYWORDS

Rendering, Ray Tracing, Photon Maps, Imphoton Maps, Caustic Illumination

1. INTRODUCTION

The problem of physically correct light propagation modeling and luminance calculation arise while solving a wide range of applied problems, for example, synthesis of the photorealistic images, modeling, and design of the optical effects, virtual prototyping of complex optical systems, etc. The synthesis of realistic images is in high demand in various areas such as assessing the appearance and visual perception of various objects; architectural design, creating demo images for advertising or presentation purposes; synthesis of photorealistic images for the moves industry, animation, and computer games. Physically accurate modeling of the light propagation effects in optical systems is in high demand in various areas such as analysis of the human perception of various optical systems, for example, car dashboards; design of lighting systems and analysis of ergonomics and comfort of workplaces; analysis of the scattered light and glare effects in optical systems. Virtual prototyping of complex optical systems is in demand when analyzing the performance of optical systems in the real environment without creating real prototypes of these devices, such as an analysis of the visual perception of a mixed reality system.

The synthesis of realistic images is being researched by a wide group of authors. The synthesis of a physically correct realistic image is the solving of the rendering equation presented by Kajiya (1986) for each image point. This equation is an equation with infinite recursion and traditionally it is solved by the ray tracing methods, both forward and backward. At the moment, a large number of works were published devoted to the synthesis of photorealistic images by ray tracing using both central and graphic processors. The ray tracing methods are either deterministic or stochastic. Despite the apparent simplicity of deterministic calculation methods, they have some fundamental limitations related to the inability to use the complex optical properties of scene materials, the complexity of evaluating the accuracy of calculations, problems of integrating luminance, etc. So, to achieve the physical correctness of the synthesized image, it is required to use the stochastic ray tracing methods. These methods could be forward or backward ray tracing methods as it was shown in works of Veach (1988) or modifications of bidirectional ray tracing methods as it was presented in the work of Georgiev et al. (2011), methods based on the photon mapping presented by Jensen (1996) and later discussed by Hachisuka et al. (2011) and Keng et al. (2016), the Veach's et al. (1997) Metropolis light transport method and others. Kim (2019) described a method of separate caustics calculation. In the scope of the current research, authors have developed the method of bidirectional ray tracing that uses two separate maps to account caustic and indirect illumination separately within the single computation workflow.

2. RAY TRACING METHOD

As it was said before, one of the ways to solve the rendering equation is to use the method of stochastic bidirectional ray tracing with photon maps. In its simplest form the stochastic bidirectional ray tracing with photon maps algorithm is illustrated in the Figure 1 and consists of the repeating phases consisting of the three main steps:

1. Forward rays from light sources are generated and traced in the scene. The photon map is formed at the ray paths points with diffuse surface properties.
2. Backward paths are generated and traced in the scene. The direct luminance is accumulated from the path points with diffuse events by using the light sampling (sampling shadow ray for the point on the light source) and BDF sampling (sampling shadow ray direction based on the bidirectional scattering distribution function of the surface). The indirect and caustic illumination is accumulated from intersecting backward ray paths with the previously formed photon map.
3. Final image if formed and the accuracy is estimated. If the attained accuracy is not enough, then calculations continue from the first step.

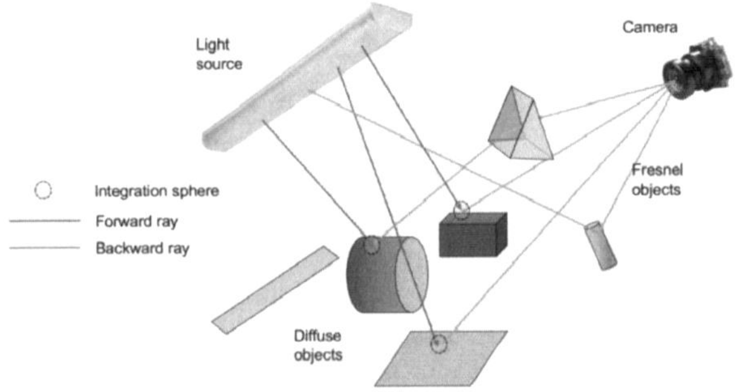

Figure 1. The bidirectional ray tracing with photon maps method

Opposite to the traditional method, authors have modified bidirectional ray tracing with photon maps algorithm to form the visibility maps instead of photon maps to account indirect illumination, as result backward paths are traced first and the intersection of forward rays with visibility maps is analyzed. These visibility maps are built for the most optimal points where the diffuse event occurs in the backward ray path, which are chosen basing on the point general illumination conditions (distance to the light sources, the shape of the surface BDF, etc.). As the first diffuse event might lead in the edge effects as, for example, the decreased luminance at the object edges, generally the second or the third diffuse event point is chosen. This modification allowed to decrease the size of the visibility map comparing to the initial photon map, however, it is applicable only in case if the scene lacks the caustic illumination. Also, opposite to the photon map, that stores points, the visibility map might store spheres, as the integration sphere radius depends on the distance from the camera while this information, in its turn, is known only at the backward ray tracing stage. However, when the traditional photon map is used, the integration sphere radius is known only at the backward ray tracing stage, so the photon map is intersected with the sphere which would require more processing time. As result, the intersection check with the visibility map is much faster compared to the photon map but might require more time to build an optimization structure.

To account the caustic illumination, authors propose to use the additional photon map, that is formed only for rays that might result in caustic illumination: the forward rays that encounter the diffuse event after one or more specular events. To form the caustic photon map an additional preliminary forward ray tracing step is added. At this stage rays are traced until the first diffuse event occurs, then the photon map is built for all points of the forward ray trace paths with diffuse surface properties. As result, the backward ray tracing step is used not only to form the visibility map but also to account the caustics illumination from the photon map. Opposite to the photons emitted from the light sources, we called the "objects" emitted from the camera the imphotons and the map that is formed – the imphoton map.

So, in the scope of the current research, the authors have developed an approach to bidirectional ray tracing that uses two separate maps that account the caustic and indirect illumination separately. Comparing to the traditional ray tracing with photon maps method which utilizes the same photon map to account both the caustic and indirect illumination, the proposed method uses two smaller size maps to account caustics and indirect illumination components separately. The workflow of the developed method is presented in Figure 2.

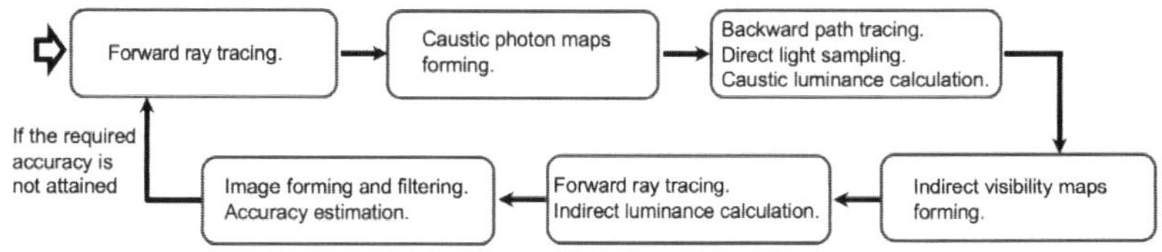

Figure 2. The workflow of the bidirectional ray tracing with caustic and photon maps method

The method workflow consists of repeating phases and each of them consists of the following steps to calculate the image components:

1. Forward rays are generated, and the forward ray tracing is performed. Rays are traced specularly until the first diffuse event. The final states of the traced rays are stored for photon map forming and further use in the next forward ray tracing stage.
2. The caustic illumination photon maps are formed for all points of the forward ray trace paths with diffuse surface properties that occur after at least one specular event in the ray path. The acceleration structure is built for the formed caustic photon map.
3. Backward paths are generated, and the backward path tracing is performed. Direct light and BDF samplings as described in the book by Pegoraro (2016) are performed during backward path tracing to account the direct illumination. By analyzing the hits with previously formed caustic photon maps the caustic illumination is accumulated in the image pixels.
4. The indirect illumination imphoton map is formed. This imphoton map stores spheres with centers in the points of the second or farther diffuse event of backward paths and radius that depends on the path length from the camera to the intersection point. The depth of the diffuse event to form the imphoton map is chosen basing on hit point illumination conditions (distance to the light source, the shape of the surface BDF, etc.). The acceleration structure is built for the imphoton map.
5. Rays that were stored when forming caustic photon maps are traced further through the scene. By analyzing the hits with previously formed indirect imphoton maps the indirect illumination is accumulated in the image pixels. In case if the number of the stored rays is not enough, then additional rays are generated and traced.
6. The image data accumulated at the current phase is formed and filtered. The data accumulated in image pixels at the current phase is added to the final synthesized image. Final image accuracy is estimated. If attained accuracy is not enough then calculation continues from the first step with the next phase.

As a result, when tracing backward rays, an intersection with photon maps is checked to account the caustic illumination, and when tracing forward rays, an intersection with imphoton maps is checked to account the indirect illumination. While the traditional ray tracing with photon maps method requires the creation of relatively big photon map which in its turn occupies a lot of memory and requires more time to build an acceleration structure, authors propose to use two smaller maps (one for caustics illumination and another one for indirect illumination) that reduce the memory usage and speed ups map processing and as result the image synthesis process. The ratio between the number of forward and backward rays traced can be varied basing on which component implies the bigger gain in the final image.

3. SIMULATION RESULTS

The simulation of the real head-up display (HUD) system was done using the presented method. The simulation goal was the analysis of the possibility to use the optical scheme shown in Figure 3 in the real environment so that the augmented image formed by the HUD is clearly seen while the bright spot caused by the rear projection effect is not noticeable.

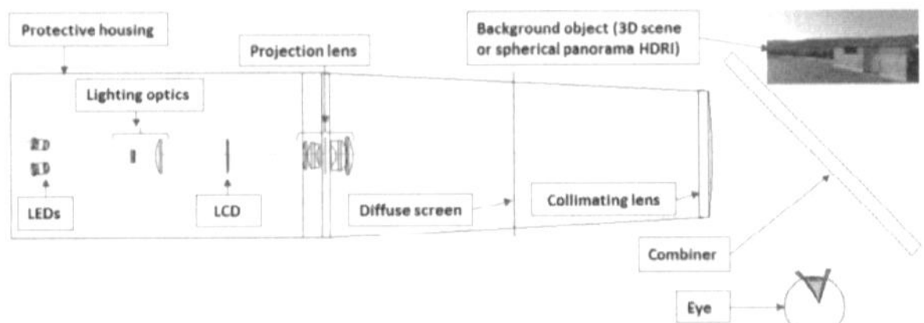

Figure 3. HUD system optical scheme

The augmented image is formed on the LCD screen and projected to the device user eye through projection optics and combiner. At the same time, the device user observes the real world environment through the same combiner. As the LCD screen is not absolutely contrast the rear projection effect arises and results in the bright spot being seen clearly by the device user. By varying the power of the LED light sources the rear projection effect might be lowered while keeping the augmented image visible. Figure 4 shows the simulation results of augmented information perception in different real-world conditions.

Figure 4. Simulation results. Top row from left to right: the rear projection effect shown with the real environment channel disabled; the daytime environment with high LED luminance (10000 cd/m^2). Center row: the nighttime environment with relatively high LED luminance (200 cd/m^2); the nighttime environment with medium LED luminance (30 cd/m^2); the nighttime environment with low LED luminance (6 cd/m^2). Bottom row from left to right: the cloudy daytime environment with high LED luminance (10000 cd/m^2); the cloudy daytime environment with medium LED luminance (1600 cd/m^2); the daytime environment with the direct Sun view and medium LED luminance (1600 cd/m^2)

The specific of the given optical system is that the augmented reality image is formed solely by the caustic illumination, while the real world environment might have any type of illumination, however mainly it is formed by indirect and direct illumination. In the previous work (2018) authors showed that this type of optical system can be simulated by combining the results obtained by stochastic forward and bidirectional ray tracings while using only one of these ray tracing is not effective. The proposed approach allowed to simulate the image formed by the HUD system more effectively comparing to bidirectional ray tracing with photon maps only. In case if the scene lacks either caustic or indirect illumination then the presented method gives no speedup but at the same time it does not slow down the calculations.

4. CONCLUSION

The method of bidirectional ray tracing using both photon and imphoton maps is developed. The usage of separate photon maps for caustic illumination and imphoton maps for indirect illumination allowed to decrease the total size of maps and as result to speedup both the construction of maps acceleration structure and the intersection of the ray with maps methods. Because caustics illumination is accounted by the separate photon map, the imphoton map is shifted farther from the first diffuse event and it resulted in more uniform imphoton distribution in the scene that finally would reduce the indirect illumination noise.

ACKNOWLEDGEMENT

This work was funded by the Russian Science Foundation (project No. 18-79-10190). The design and calculation of the optical scheme of the head-up display system were done by V. A. Galaktionov.

REFERENCES

Georgiev, I. et al, 2011. Bidirectional light transport with vertex merging. *Proceedings of SIGGRAPH Asia 2011*. New York, NY, USA, pp. 27:1-27:2.

Hachisuka, T. et al, 2012. State of the art in photon density estimation. *Proceedings of SIGGRAPH Asia 2013*, New York, NY, USA, Article No.20.

Jensen, H. W. 1996. Global illumination using photon maps. *In Proceedings of the eurographics workshop on Rendering techniques '96*, Springer-Verlag, London, UK, 21–30.

Kajiya, J.T., 1986. The rendering equation. *Proceedings of SIGGRAPH '86*. New York, NY, USA, vol. 20, pp. 143-150.

Kang, C. et al, 2016. A survey of photon mapping state-of-the-art research and future challenges. *In Frontiers Inf Technol Electronic* Vol 17, 185–199

Kim H., 2019. Caustics Using Screen-Space Photon Mapping. *In: Haines E., Akenine-Möller T. (eds) Ray Tracing Gems*, Apress, Berkeley, CA, USA.

Pegoraro, V., 2017. *Handbook of Digital Image Synthesis: Scientific Foundations of Rendering*, CRC Press, USA.

Veach, E. and Guibas, L.J., 1997. Metropolis light transport. *Proceedings of SIGGRAPH '97,* New York, NY, USA, pp. 65-76.

Veach, E., 1998. *Robust monte carlo methods for light transport simulation. Ph. D. thesis.* Stanford, CA, USA.

Zhdanov, D.D., Galaktionov, V.A., Voloboy, V.G., Zhdanov, A.D., Garbul, A.A., Potemin, I.S. and Sokolov, V.G, 2018. Photorealistic Rendering of Images Formed by Augmented Reality Optical Systems. *In Programming and Computer Software*, Pleiades Publishing, vol. 44, no. 4, pp.213-224.

AN OPEN-SOURCE, HARDWARE ACCELERATED INDUSTRY PROTOTYPE FOR MULTIDIMENSIONAL GLYPHS

Dylan Rees[1] and Robert S. Laramee[2]
[1]*Swansea University, Swansea, UK*
[2]*University of Nottingham, Nottingham, UK*

ABSTRACT

Data-glyphs are a common, useful metaphor for visualizing multidimensional data. However, to represent a larger number of glyphs requires an increasing amount of computational power to derive the data-dependent geometry of each glyph. We present a novel visualization implementation for computing and rendering customized data-glyphs for an industry application. Our software utilizes the parallel processing power of the Graphics Processing Unit (GPU) to enable interactive exploration of thousands of multidimensional data-glyphs. This is achieved by passing normalized data values to the OpenGL geometry shader to construct the geometry of each glyph reflecting the data values. The technique is applicable to a variety of glyph designs and supports fast selection between different designs. We demonstrate this technique to render more than 100,000 glyphs at interactive frame rates. To address the challenge of reproducing the technique, we provide a simplified open-source code example implementation that can be used by anyone, including our industry partner.

KEYWORDS

Glyphs, OpenGL, Rendering

1. INTRODUCTION

Glyphs provide a popular means for conveying multidimensional data; however, their shape and layout can be complex and therefore computationally intensive to calculate their geometry. This is especially true for glyphs where the geometry of the glyph is dependent on the data dimensions to be represented. With an increasing number of glyphs required for ever growing data-sets, this issue is amplified, requiring longer computational time to render a complete image. This becomes a challenge where glyphs are used for interactive exploration of data, with scenes requiring continuous update. Scenes that are slow to update can be frustrating for users, making adoption of a tool with such a feature difficult.

In this paper we provide technical details of our software implementation for rendering a large number of multi-dimensional glyphs such as seen in Figure 1 (left). This is done by leveraging the parallel processing capabilities of a Graphics Processing Unit (GPU).

The contributions of this paper are:

- A novel implementation for calculating and rendering large numbers of multidimensional data-glyphs
- A method to support easy and fast selection of glyph design
- The provision of a self-contained open-source code implementation to demonstrate the technique

2. RELATED WORK

A survey of data visualization books by Rees and Laramee (Rees & Laramee, 2019) highlight six OpenGL textbooks that introduce and detail the operation of OpenGL (Angle & Shreiner, 2011), (Wolff, 2011), (Movania, 2013), (Wright Jr, et al., 2015), (Kessenich, et al., 2016).

McNabb and Laramee (McNabb & Laramee, 2017) describe four surveys addressing glyph design (Ward, 2002), (Borgo, et al., 2013), (Fuchs, et al., 2017), (Ropinski, et al., 2011). The work of Ward presents a taxonomy of glyph placement strategies (Ward, 2002). Borgo et al. provide design guidelines for glyphs (Borgo, et al., 2013). The work of Fuchs et al. surveys glyph based user-studies (Fuchs, et al., 2017) and Ropinski et al. survey glyphs for medical visualization (Ropinski, et al., 2011). Consultation of these surveys fails to identify work that discusses rendering implementation techniques for glyphs.

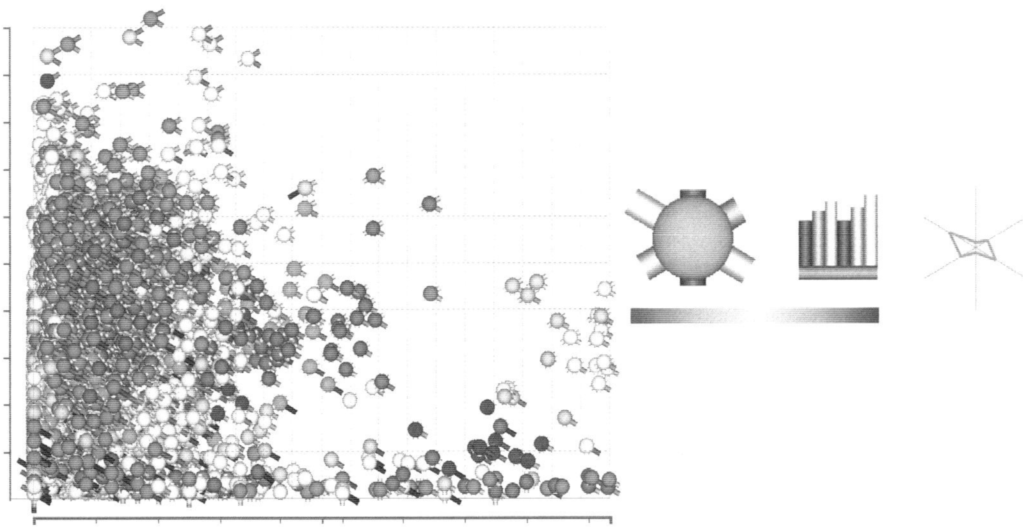

Figure 1. (Left) Over 6,500 glyphs drawn utilizing the technique presented in this paper. Each glyph features six continuous variables plus a categorical variable mapped to color. The x and y position of the glyph on the canvas are also mapped to variables. (Right) Three glyph designs, each of which feature six continuous variables represented by the size of the bars in the left two glyphs and by the radar on the right glyph. A categorical variable is also represented by color, indicated by the orange in these examples. Color is also used to redundantly map to the bar size on the right two glyphs, as indicated by the pictured colormap

The use of glyph optimization work is most prominent in scientific visualization, with glyphs often used to represent flow (Peng, et al., 2009), (Peng, et al., 2011) and for molecular visualization (Grottel, et al., 2014). Because of the large number of glyphs required to effectively visualize the flow or molecules, optimizations through the use of GPU rendering techniques are widely developed (Crawfis & Max, 1993), (Reina & Ertl, 2005), (Grottel, et al., 2009), (Peeters, et al., 2009), (Alharbi, et al., 2019).

Falck et al. compile and provide detailed explanations of GPU accelerated algorithms for rendering and processing scientific data (Falk, et al., 2016). As such, we recommend readers consult this work for a comprehensive overview of GPU accelerated glyph rendering.

Our work differs from others as we utilize GPU shaders for the construction of multi-dimensional data glyphs for information visualization rather than scientific visualization. In contrast to previous work, the technique we present leverages the geometry shader to construct each individual data-glyph geometry. We also provide a seldom-seen open-source implementation.

3. GLYPH RENDERING

In this section, we discuss step-by-step the process for replicating the technique that we present in this paper. The technique treats each glyph as a point primitive and passes the data variables from a vertex buffer through the vertex shader to the geometry shader. Once in the geometry shader, data values are used to determine the complex geometry of each glyph before being passed on in the pipeline to be rendered. This technique enables for complex glyphs to be rendered using a single draw call.

Before glyphs can be rendered, data must first be processed into a format that can be loaded into vertex buffers for rendering. The first step is to find the maximum and minimum value for each of the variables. Once this has been established, the next step is to normalize each of the variables to a range [0,1].

The data is then ready to be stored into vertex buffers to be transferred to the GPU memory. Before this, the number of variables each glyph is to represent must be established a priori. We demonstrate glyph designs in Figure 1 (right), inspired by the work of Rees et al. (Rees, et al., 2020), featuring six continuous variables plus a categorical value mapped to color. As well as the glyph variables, we also map the position of the glyphs to a two-dimension scatterplot enabling each glyph to represent an additional two variables. For the construction of these glyphs therefore requires nine data variables to be copied into vertex buffers and onto the GPU memory to be processed by the rendering pipeline.

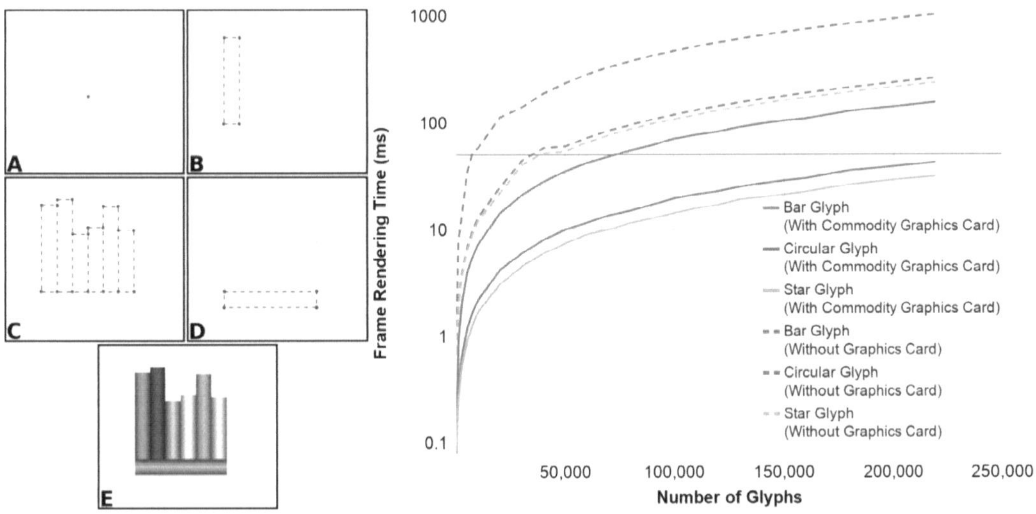

Figure 2. (Left) OpenGL shader glyph construction. A shows the single vertex position output from the vertex shader. B shows the output of a single bar from lines 42-57 of the geometry shader, while C shows the output of all bars in the encapsulating for loop, lines 28-58. The category indicator bar shown in D is output from lines 60-75 from the geometry shader. Finally, color is added in E by the fragment shader (see supplementary material). (Right) Rendering performance against the number of glyphs drawn for three different glyphs with and without a commodity graphics card

The vertex shader determines the positioning of the glyph, and simply passes the other data through to the geometry shader.

The geometry shader is used to determine the shape of the glyph according to the data variables passed from the vertex shader. The geometry shader for each of the glyphs in Figure 1 (right) can be found in the supplementary material or on the online repository (Anon, 2020).

The geometry shader takes in the point vertex position from the vertex shader and outputs a series of vertices in a triangle strip to build a bar chart glyph, this is demonstrated in Figure 2 (left). First the shader calculates the position in the screen-space, then iterates through each data variable to calculate the size of each corresponding bar, emitting five vertices for each bar to the fragment shader using the `EmitVertex()` function. Details being emitted are the positions for each new vertex, a color attribute to map the bar color to the data value, a 2D vector for shading effects, and an attribute to distinguish the data bars from the categorical identifying bar. Once the data bars have been emitted, vertices for an additional categorical identifying bar are emitted.

A variety of different geometry shaders, creating different styles of glyphs, can be used and easily switched by re-running the OpenGL program with the different shader, without the need to reload the data into the graphics memory buffers.

Once a vertex has been emitted by the geometry shader, it is processed by the fragment shader. The fragment shader adds shading effects and color to the vertices emitted from the geometry shader. A texture can also be added to the glyphs, therefore, if a glyph design incorporates an identifying symbol, this can be added as a texture at this stage of the process.

A self-contained, simplified open source implementation of the code is available in the supplementary material and on GitHub: https://github.com/glyph-renderer/glyph.

The open-source implementation developed for this article features three individual glyph designs, however additional user specified glyphs can be added with the addition of a new geometry shader.

4. DISCUSSION

A limitation exists in the amount of data that can be passed between shaders. This is dependent on the graphics hardware, for our consumer grade Nvidia GeForce GTX 1060 6 GB graphics card this is 1024 floating points of data. The number of glyphs that can be interactively draw utilizing this method is only limited by the hardware capabilities. However, with the games industry driving GPU development, this limitation becomes less relevant as new GPUs increase capabilities.

Drawing so many glyphs highlights an overplotting issue where the glyphs are drawn on top of one another become indistinguishable, as can be seen in Figure 1 (left). Because the technique introduced in this paper allows for interactive frame rates, a user can interactively zoom and explore the glyphs, partially alleviating this issue. Another solution to this is to cluster overlapping glyphs as previously presented by several works (Yang, et al., 2003), (Fuchs, et al., 2016), (Rees, et al., 2020).

To gauge the performance of the presented technique, the rendering time for each frame was measured for a varying number of glyphs. Results are shown in the supplementary material. Figure 2 (right) shows the performance of the open-source implementation presented in this paper. Performance is measured on two separate personal computers (PC). The first PC features an Intel i7-6700HQ processor, 8GB of RAM, and an NVIDIA GeForce GTX 1060 6 GB graphics card. The second PC features an Intel i5-6500 processor, 16GB of RAM, and has no dedicated graphics card, relying on integrated graphics (Intel HD Graphics 530). For compatibility, testing was performed using OpenGL version 4.5. Performance is measured for three glyph types, a bar chart glyph, a circular glyph, and a star chart glyph all depicted in Figure 1 (right).

Due to a limitation on array sizes, the maximum number of glyphs rendered is limited to 220,000. The PC including the graphics card achieved higher frame rates in comparison to the PC without for the same number of glyphs. Due to more calculations being required to compute the geometry, the circular glyph is slower than the bar chart glyph. In all scenarios, a frame rendering time of less than 17 ms was achieved for up to 2,500 glyphs (equivalent to 60 fps) and 50 ms (20 fps) for up to 7,500 glyphs. Over 50 ms the user will notice severe roughness. The PC without a graphics card takes 35 ms to render a frame with 5,000 circular glyphs, and 58 ms to render 10,000 circular glyphs but remains under the 17 ms threshold for 10,000 bar chart and star glyphs. The 50 ms frame rendering threshold is only crossed for 40,000 bar chart or star glyphs.

The PC with the graphics card remains under a 17 ms frame rendering time for over 20,000 glyphs, with over 70,000 circular glyphs rendered before the frame rendering time increases over the 50 ms threshold. For the bar chart glyphs, the PC with the graphics card remains under 17ms for 90,000 glyphs and under 40 ms for 200,000 glyphs. Over 120,000 star glyphs are rendered before the frame rendering time increases over 17ms and remains under 30ms for 200,000 star glyphs. With every glyph design tested, both with and without a graphics card, overplotting becomes a greater issue before frame rates drop below an interactive rate.

5. CONCLUSION

We describe a technique for generating and interactively rendering many unique multidimensional data glyphs based on instance variables. This technique utilizes GPU parallelization to calculate the individual geometries of each glyph instance. Source code for a simple version of the technique presented are provided to enable ease of recreation. In the future we aim to performing an exploratory analysis of the limits of the presented technique, gauging the maximum number of glyphs that can be rendered while still achieving interactive frame rates (5 fps). A solution for overplotting previously mentioned is another future work aim.

REFERENCES

Alharbi, N. et al., 2019. Hybrid Visualization of Protein-Lipid and Protein-Protein Interaction. *Proceedings of Eurographics Workshop on Visual Computing in Biology and Medicine (VCBM).* Brno, Czech Republic.

Angle, E. & Shreiner, D., 2011. *Interactive Computer Graphics: A Topdown Approach with Shader-Based OpenGL.* Addison-Wesley, Boston USA.

Anon, 2020. *glyphRenderer – GitHub* https://github.com/glyph-renderer/glyph Accessed Apr 27, 2020.

Borgo, R. et al., 2013. Glyph-based Visualization: Foundations, Design Guidelines, Techniques and Applications. *Proceedings of Eurographics 2013 - State of the Art Reports*. Girona, Spain, pp. 39–63.

Crawfis, R. A. & Max, N., 1993. Texture splats for 3D scalar and vector field visualization. *Proceedings of Visualization'93.* San Jose, USA, pp. 261–266.

Falk, M. et al., 2016. Interactive GPU-based Visualization of Large Dynamic Particle Data. *Synthesis Lectures on Visualization,* Vol 4, pp. 1–121.

Fuchs, J. et al., 2017. A systematic review of experimental studies on data glyphs. *IEEE Transactions on Visualization and Computer Graphics,* Vol 23, pp. 1863–1879.

Fuchs, J. et al., 2016. Leaf Glyphs: Story Telling and Data Analysis Using Environmental Data Glyph Metaphors. *Proceedings of Computer Vision, Imaging and Computer Graphics Theory and Applications.* Berlin, Germany, pp. 123–143.

Grottel, S. et al., 2014. MegaMol—a prototyping framework for particle-based visualization. *IEEE transactions on visualization and computer graphics,* Vol 21, p. 201–214.

Grottel, S. et al., 2009. Optimized data transfer for time-dependent, GPU-based glyphs. *Proceedings of 2009 IEEE Pacific Visualization Symposium.* Beijing, China, pp. 65–72.

Kessenich, J. et al., 2016. *OpenGL Programming Guide: The Official Guide to Learning OpenGL.* Addison-Wesley Professional, Boston, USA.

McNabb, L. & Laramee, R. S., 2017. Survey of Surveys (SoS) - Mapping The Landscape of Survey Papers in Information Visualization. *Computer Graphics Forum,* Vol 36, pp. 589-617.

Movania, M. M., 2013. *OpenGL Development Cookbook.* Packt Publishing Ltd., Birmingham, UK.

Peeters, T. H. J. M. et al., 2009. Fast and sleek glyph rendering for interactive HARDI data exploration. *Proceedings of IEEE Pacific Visualization Symposium.* Beijing, China, pp. 153–160.

Peng, Z. et al., 2011. Mesh-driven vector field clustering and visualization: An image-based approach. *IEEE Transactions on Visualization and Computer Graphics,* Vol 18, pp. 283–298.

Peng, Z. et al., 2009. Glyph and Streamline Placement Algorithms for CFD Simulation Data. *Proceedings of NAFEMS World Congress (NWC) Conference,* Crete, Italy, pp. 66.

Rees, D. & Laramee, R. S., 2019. Survey of Information Visualization Books. *Computer Graphics Forum,* Vol 38, pp. 610-646.

Rees, D. et al., 2020. AgentVis: Visual anaysis of agent behaviour with hierarchical glyphs. *IEEE Transactions on Visualization and Computer Graphics.*

Reina, G. & Ertl, T., 2005. Hardware-accelerated glyphs for mono-and dipoles in molecular dynamics visualization. *Proceedings of EUROVIS 2005: Eurographics / IEEE VGTC Symposium on Visualization,* Leeds, UK, pp. 177–182.

Ropinski, T. et al., 2011. Survey of glyph-based visualization techniques for spatial multivariate medical data. *Computers & Graphics,* Vol 35, pp. 392–401.

Ward, M. O., 2002. A taxonomy of glyph placement strategies for multidimensional data visualization. *Information Visualization,* Volume 1, pp. 194–210.

Wolff, D., 2011. *OpenGL 4.0 Shading Language Cookbook.* Packt Publishing Ltd., Birmingham, UK.

Wright Jr, R. S. et al., 2015. *OpenGL SuperBible: Comprehensive Tutorial and Reference.* Addison-Wesley Professional, Boston, USA.

Yang, J. et al., 2003. Interactive hierarchical displays: a general framework for visualization and exploration of large multivariate data sets. *Computers & Graphics,* Vol 27, pp. 265-283.

THE EFFECTIVE BIDIRECTIONAL RAY TRACING ON MULTIPROCESSOR WORKSTATIONS

Andrey Zhdanov[1], Dmitry Zhdanov[1], Vadim Sokolov[1] and Vladimir Galaktionov[2]
[1]*ITMO University, Russia*
[2]*Keldysh Institute of Applied Mathematics, Russia*

ABSTRACT

The computing power and complexity of computation architecture of modern computer systems used for image rendering is constantly rising, so effective parallelization of rendering methods is an urgent challenge. Modern workstations might have several CPUs with NUMA that makes traditional parallelization methods ineffective and requires research of the new approaches. In the scope of the current research, authors present a CPU parallelization algorithm for bidirectional ray tracing with photon maps that use three-level parallelization thread architecture and asynchronous calculations to achieve the high rendering scalability.

KEYWORDS

Photon Mapping, Rendering, Ray Tracing, Parallel Computing

1. INTRODUCTION

The problem of physically correct light propagation modeling and luminance calculation arise while solving a wide range of applied problems, including synthesis of the photorealistic images, optical effects modeling, virtual prototyping of the complex optical systems, and so on. With increasing computing power and complexity of the computation architecture of the modern computer systems, both the complexity of image synthesis tasks and the required calculation accuracy raise. The photon mapping method introduced by Jensen (1996) allows us to solve the rendering equation and account all types of illumination. Methods based on photon mapping are being developed by various groups of researchers. In their work, Kang et al. (2016) presented the current state of research in the area of the photon mapping methods. There are approaches aimed at using GPU, CPU, or both these types of calculators. Effective parallelization of photon mapping methods is an urgent challenge for the modern workstations which might have several CPUs with Non-Uniform Memory Access and dozens of cores, GPUs, and other types of calculators. Despite there are CPU and GPU manufacturers solutions aimed at the effective ray tracing as, for example, Intel Embree, presented by Wald et al. (2016), Nvidia RTX, examined by Frolov et al. (2019) or RadeonRays by AMD, the problem of the effective processing of the traced rays still exits. According to Amdahl's law (1967), the theoretical speedup of algorithm parallelization is limited and depends on a percent of work that cannot be parallelized. In the scope of the current research, authors have developed a CPU parallelization algorithm for bidirectional ray tracing with photon maps that pretend to minimize the non-parallelizable part of the calculation process by using three-level parallelization architecture and asynchronous calculations.

2. PARALLELIZATION METHOD

One of the methods to solve the rendering equation is to use the method of stochastic bidirectional ray tracing with photon maps. In the scope of the current research, we used the modified method of bidirectional ray tracing with photon mapping, where instead of photon map an imphoton (or visibility) map is formed. The general method algorithm consists of 3 main steps:

1. Backward paths from the camera are generated and traced in the scene. The direct light and BDF samplings are performed at path points with diffuse properties to account the direct luminance. The imphoton (visibility) map is formed at the points of paths with diffuse properties and an acceleration structure is built to speed up the further maps access.
2. Forward rays from light sources are generated and traced in the scene. By intersecting with previously formed imphoton maps, the indirect and caustic luminance is accumulated in the corresponding pixels of the intermediate image.
3. An intermediate image formed at the current phase is added to the final image and accuracy is estimated. If attained accuracy is not enough, then calculations continue from the first step.

The bidirectional ray tracing with imphoton maps is hardly parallelized and requires special techniques to use all computation resources of a modern workstation in the most effective way. The main problems arise when implementing this algorithm to be used on a modern workstation with several CPUs and a big number of computation cores. Traditionally, the rendering parallelization method is as following: the high-resolution image is split into blocks (mainly of 32x32 pixels size) and these blocks are rendered on CPU cores one by one in a single task scheduler queue. If the number of CPU cores is relatively high and is close to the number of computation blocks, then it is highly possible that some threads would finish their job earlier and would stay unoccupied until all threads finish their jobs as all blocks are already either finished or being rendered. Taking into account that most computer graphics scenes are not uniform, these blocks would require different time to be calculated which would also result in a significant difference in the computation load for different cores. When using single-level parallelization, it is not possible to proceed to the next step before the previous step is finished. For example, it is not possible to start imphoton map forming step before all backward rays are traced. Also, the single level parallelization would result in a huge size of the imphoton map that requires advanced parallelization algorithms for processing and optimization. So, the authors developed the three-level parallelization method that allows performing part of the operations asynchronously, as a result, reducing the synchronization time loss and speeding up the algorithm performance on multi-CPU workstations.

The first parallelization level utilizes several computation threads that perform rendering of the whole scene in parallel and renders only the part of the whole image. This part is defined by a random 32x32 pixel mask that is applied to the whole image. Each of the first level group thread uses the same shared memory, shared scene, shared maps, and runs synchronously through the whole rendering process steps. In general, it the simple single-level parallelization method for a random part of the whole synthesized image.

Each of the second-level group threads is the main thread of the first level group, each of them computing their own part of the image basing on the random mask assigned by the main thread. Once in several predefined number of phases, the whole intermediate image is formed, added to the final image, and masks are re-randomized. The randomization of masks leads to the more uniform task distribution between the level 1 thread groups. The level 2 thread groups run partly synchronously. These threads use the same shared memory, however, each of them uses their own maps and render their own part of the whole image at the same time having access to the other threads maps when they do exist to calculate the indirect and caustic luminance components. The group of first and second level threads is shown in Figure 1.

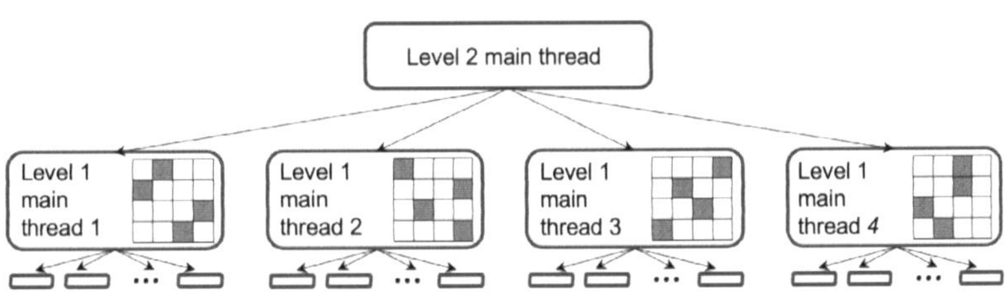

Figure 1. The first and second level thread groups

By using synchronous and asynchronous calculation at the same time authors have achieved almost full utilization of single CPU resources with shared memory. However modern workstations might have Non-Uniform Memory Access (NUMA) architecture. In NUMA architecture the CPU cores are split between several NUMA nodes and each of these NUMA nodes has its own local memory. At the same time, NUMA nodes have low-speed access to other NUMA nodes memories. In this case, the shared memory usage is no longer effective, so authors have introduced the third level of parallelization that is aimed at effective usage of the whole resources of a workstation that has several NUMA nodes. The third level uses groups of the second level threads and binds each of them to a specific NUMA node. These groups have no shared resources and do not communicate with each other directly in any way. Each of these groups works solely on their own NUMA node and utilizes only local memory. The main thread of the third level group is at the same time the main thread of the second level group. Once in several, relatively big number of phases, the main thread fetches the current state of the image from all other second level main threads, forms the total image, and updates the total accuracy. This is performed without interrupting the calculations of the second level groups and keeping the asynchronous nature of calculations. The group of the third level threads is shown in Figure 2.

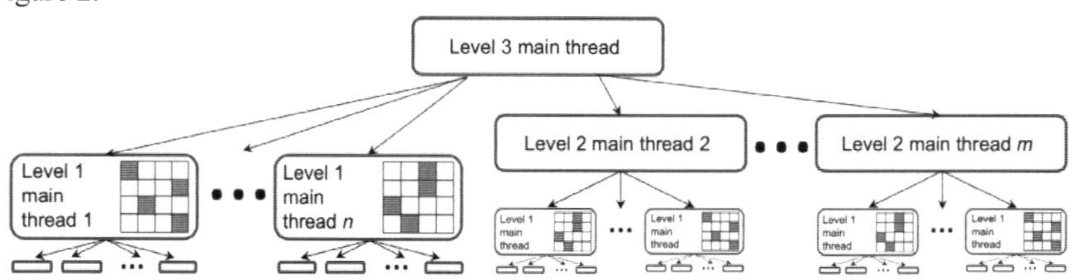

Figure 2. The three levels of threads

As this computation model is highly asynchronous it can utilize all the CPU resources in a quite effective way and have high scalability when changing the number of cores used for computation.

To sum up, the computation process parallelization levels are:

1st. Completely synchronous level. Threads compute the same image with the same random mask.

2nd. Partly synchronous level. Thread groups of the first level compute their own parts of the whole image with partly shared memory (scene and imphoton maps) and synchronize after several phases. At synchronization points masks are re-randomized.

3rd. Completely asynchronous level. Thread groups of the second level compute their own whole images and the main thread accumulates current computed images from these groups over several phases interval to form the final image without interrupting the computation process.

3. SIMULATION RESULTS

We have implemented the proposed parallelization method and tested it on the Cornell Box scene and the light guides placed in the Judge II viewing booth scene. The test equipment was a workstation with double AMD EPYC 7281 16 cores CPUs resulting in a total of 32 cores. All simulations were performed with the spectral color model. The speedup estimation was based on the number of rays traced and processed when rendering a scene with the 10 minutes time limit. Table 1 shows the bidirectional ray tracing with the imphoton maps speedup test for the Cornell box scene using the developed method. Table 2 shows the speedup test of a simple single-level parallelization method. Figure 3 shows the speedup graph based on the number of cores used and the final synthesized image when all 32 cores were used.

Table 1. The number of rays traced when varying the number of used cores. Three-level method. Cornell box scene

Number of cores	1 core	4 cores	8 cores	16 cores	24 cores	32 cores
Backward paths	35 936 168	71 797 941	138 834 968	263 419 810	403 687 733	514 062 277
Forward rays	27 682 024	155 974 036	300 251 153	564 103 834	867 447 398	110 1151 351
Speedup	1	3.58	6.90	13.01	19.98	25.39

Table 2. The number of rays traced when varying the number of cores used. Singe-level method. Cornell box scene

Number of cores	1 core	4 cores	8 cores	16 cores	24 cores	32 cores
Backward paths	36 495 918	80 342 047	112 646 486	98 916 448	70 904 587	61 734 479
Forward rays	28 104 980	173 091 798	339 242 857	392 582 996	409 392 886	455 235 368
Speedup	1	3.92	7.00	7.61	7.43	8.00

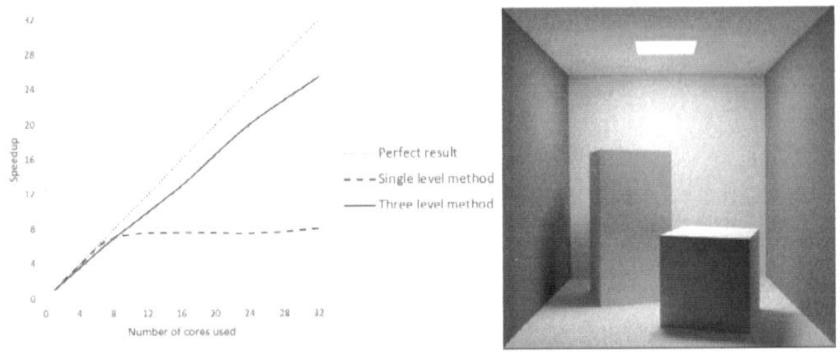

Figure 3. To the left: the speedup of the calculations depending on the number of used cores. To the right: synthesized image with 32 cores and three-level method. Cornell box scene

Tables 3 and 4 show the speed test for light guides in the Judge II viewing box scene. Figure 4 shows the speedup graph based on the number of cores used and the synthesized image when all 32 cores were used.

Table 3. The number of rays traced when varying the number of cores used. Three-level method. Light guides scene

Number of cores	1 core	4 cores	8 cores	16 cores	24 cores	32 cores
Backward paths	12 933 960	24 560 276	47 597 995	93 309 854	147 415 145	191 567 253
Forward rays	1 241 843	22 673 023	44 330 204	81 280 703	133 191 853	176 613 858
Speedup	1	3.33	6.48	12.31	19.79	25.97

Table 4. The number of rays traced when varying the number of cores used. Singe-level method. Light guides scene

Number of cores	1 core	4 cores	8 cores	16 cores	24 cores	32 cores
Backward paths	13 566 182	30 072 348	31 856 759	24 031 276	20 370 604	16 356 663
Forward rays	1 308 936	27 687 893	71 095 408	79 462 634	93 799 644	98 508 600
Speedup	1	3.88	6.96	7.57	7.68	7.72

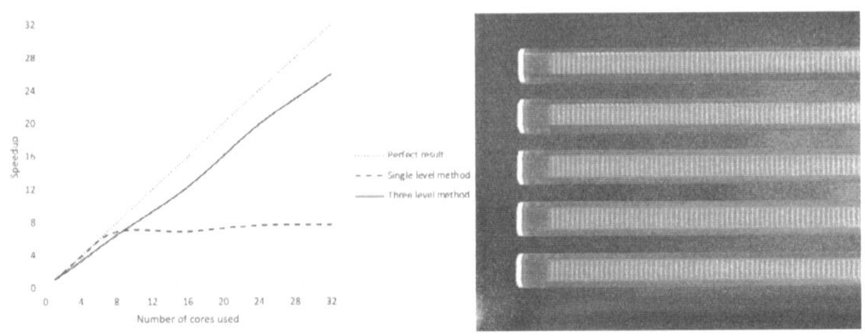

Figure 4. To the left: the speedup of the calculations depending on the number of used cores. To the right: synthesized image with 32 cores and three level method. Light guides scene

From the presented simulations results the advantages of the presented method can be seen clearly. The speedup of the proposed approach on test scenes is close to the linear one. The authors have also tested the proposed approach on workstations with up to 64 cores with similar results.

4. CONCLUSION

In the scope of the current research, the parallelization of the bidirectional ray tracing with imphoton maps was developed that allows keeping the calculation speedup at an almost linear rate when rising the number of used computation cores on modern multiprocessor workstations. In the following research, authors are going to extend this method to use modern heterogeneous workstations with both several CPUs and GPUs.

ACKNOWLEDGEMENT

This work was funded by the Russian Science Foundation (project No. 18-79-10190). The design and calculation of the light guides scene were done by V. G. Sokolov and V. A. Galaktionov.

REFERENCES

Amdahl, G.M., 1967. Validity of the single processor approach to achieving large scale computing capabilities. *In Proceedings of the April 18-20, 1967, spring joint computer conference (AFIPS '67 (Spring))*, New York, NY, USA, pp. 483–485.

Frolov, V.A., 2019. Examination of the Nvidia RTX. *In Proceedings of Computer Graphics and Vision 2019*, Bryansk, Russia, pp7-12.

Jensen, H. W., 1996. Global illumination using photon maps. *In Proceedings of the eurographics workshop on Rendering techniques '96*, Springer-Verlag, London, UK, 21–30.

Kang, C. et al, 2016. A survey of photon mapping state-of-the-art research and future challenges. *In Frontiers Inf Technol Electronic* Vol 17, 185–199

Wald, I., 2016. Embree ray tracing kernels: overview and new features. *In SIGGRAPH'16,* New York, NY, USA, Art. 52.

REAL-TIME RENDERING WITH HETEROGENEOUS GPUS

Xiao Lei and Vetria L. Byrd
Purdue University, Department of Computer Graphics Technology
401 North Grant Street, West Lafayette, IN 47907, United States

ABSTRACT

A large portion of recent personal computers are equipped with both integrated and discrete GPUs. However, most of the time these two GPUs are not utilized concurrently in the same application. This paper provides an exploration into utilizing integrated plus discrete GPUs to improve real-time rendering performance with Vulkan API. Specifically, our approach includes offloading asynchronous computation workload from the discrete GPU to the integrated GPU, and multi-threading and render graphs are adopted to saturate GPUs utilization. Through benchmarking, we validate that our approach can speed up the overall performance by up to 4% with the utilization of combinations like Intel UHD 630 plus NVIDIA RTX 2070. Our results reveal that with tools like Vulkan, such heterogeneous-GPU system is exploitable.

KEYWORDS

Heterogeneous-GPU, Vulkan API, Rendering Performance

1. INTRODUCTION

With previous API like OpenGL, an application running on a computer equipped with both integrated and discrete GPUs cannot make use of both GPUs without context switching. This makes either the integrated or discrete GPU remain idle while the other GPU is loaded. This scenario suggests that there could be potential benefits if all the available GPUs can be enabled.

The introduction of low-level command and resource control brought by Vulkan makes it possible to manage resource and task scheduling across vendor-independent graphics hardware in application-level. This explicit control inspired the idea of utilizing modern personal computers' heterogeneous GPUs (integrated plus discrete) feature to obtain performance improvement.

A similar approach for exploiting parallelism offered by integrated GPU (Peek, et al., 2014) has been applied to head-mounted displays, in which the integrated GPU is utilized to do image warping. A former multi-adapter experiment (Yeung, 2015) also claimed a noticeable framerate improvement with the discrete plus integrated GPUs combination. In recent GDC 2020, Intel presented their idea (Hux, 2020) of utilizing integrated GPU to speed up the n-Body particle rendering. Despite these advances, the literature shows there is very little overlap with implementing heterogeneous GPUs system with Vulkan and evaluating the outcome.

This paper aims to identify, design, and evaluate the methods that could allow the integrated GPU to assist real-time rendering through offloading workloads from the discrete GPU with Vulkan implementation. Towards achieving these aims, we implemented and benchmarked a real-time rendering program based on Vulkan and C++. The program resembles a pure graphics engine that supports 3D rendering with several shading techniques and could offload certain workloads from the discrete GPU to the integrated GPU.

2. METHODS

2.1 Offloading Workload from Discrete GPU

Through the physical device querying and logical feature wrapping interfaces provided by Vulkan, the integrated GPU (iGPU) and the discrete GPU (dGPU) can be encapsulated as two logical devices.

Since the resources created on different logical devices are not interchangeable, the heterogeneous GPUs renderer manages two sets of resources: one set used by the dGPU and the other set used by the iGPU. Data from one GPU is transferred to the other GPU through explicit buffer copying. This schema is illustrated in Figure 1. Under such schema, swapchain presentation is handled by the dGPU, and there is no read back from video memory to system memory as all data transfers are unidirectional.

In each frame, certain application data is copied into iGPU resources to perform asynchronous update, while the original values from the previous frame are used for output image rendering in the dGPU. The input data is read and written as an image in the iGPU.

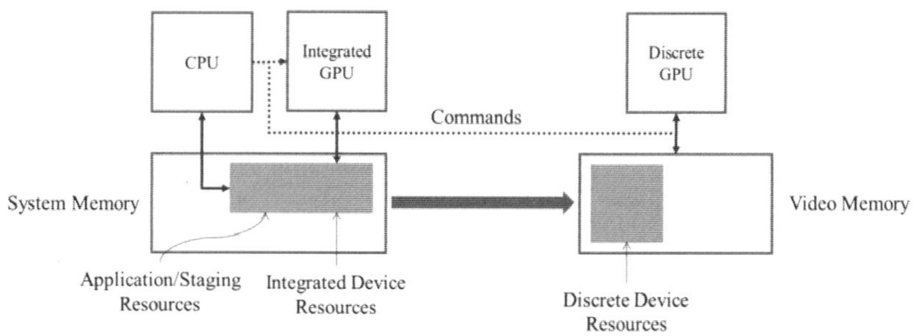

Figure 1. Integrated GPU works on asynchronous computation

2.2 Saturating the GPUs

One of the valuable features that Vulkan provides is improved compatibility with multi-threading. To better utilize this multi-threading capability, render graph (Persson, 2017) is adopted in our approach.

A render graph is an acyclic graph that describes the render pass behaviors and organizes their dependencies. The basic unit of a render graph is pass node. Each pass node consists of 5 components: node properties, render context, input resources, output resources, and render pass functions. The two GPUs (iGPU and dGPU) each own an exclusive render graph specifically for task description.

Multi-threading can be implemented on top of the render graph as illustrated in Figure 2. During one frame, each command-recording thread takes one pass node from the render graph by priority sequence and executes the pass functions. All the command recording threads hold individual command buffer pools for command buffer allocation.

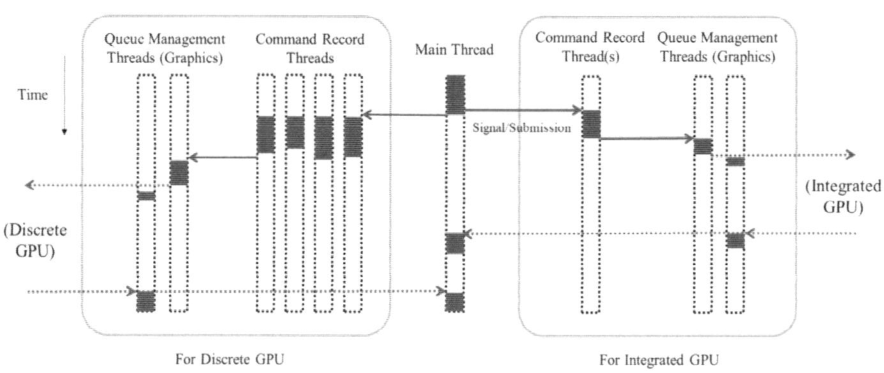

Figure 2. Multi-threading design for heterogeneous GPUs

When recording with multiple threads, the finished command buffers may arrive in any sequence. The renderer running on the main thread or cycle management thread is therefore responsible for checking and holding each arrived command buffer and ensuring they are submitted in the correct sequence.

The main thread is in synchronization with the dGPU since the dGPU directly controls when a frame is finally presented. Since in our settings the iGPU is expected to complete its job inside the same frame, the two GPUs work under the same task execution cycle in parallel. Timeline semaphore is used as the main synchronization primitive between CPU and GPU.

The complete process can be outlined as follows:

Begin ↓

Query physical devices and setup logical devices

Initialize ↓

Generate render graphs and allocate corresponding resources

Frame Loop ○

Copy asynchronous task data to iGPU's buffer

Generate and submit command buffers to iGPU and dGPU (parallel)

Copy results back from iGPU's buffer (parallel)

Recycle frame resources (parallel)

Present final image on dGPU

3. RESULTS AND DISCUSSION

A scene with 512 objects was used during the test, as shown in Figure 3. Each object is a textured amago fish mesh with 6.3K triangles. In each frame, the positions of all the objects are put into asynchronous update while the original values are used for rendering in the current frame. The position data is read and written as a 32×16 image in the iGPU. Two personal computers with different hardware combinations were used as testing devices. Their detailed specifications are given in Table 1.

Figure 3. Screenshot: the test scenario with 512 objects. Background strokes are part of the post-processing step and are not related to asynchronous computation

With default test workload, the average (discrete) GPU frame time on device A is 6.6ms and this value is 19ms on device B. The fraction taken up by the asynchronous computation step on device A and B are 0.8ms and 2.3ms, respectively. When applying Amdahl's law (Hill & Marty, 2008) in the theoretical estimation, the fraction of asynchronous computation can be treated as completely taken out from the sequential workflow. The speedup is also upper bounded by hardware capabilities as listed in individual GPU theoretical performance in Table 1. Thus, the final theoretical speedup upper bound would be 1.080 for device A (0.441/5.46 + 1.0) and 1.137 for device B (1.0 / (1.0 – (2.3/19.0) + 0.0)).

Table 1. Specifications of the testing devices

	Device A	Device B
CPU	Intel Core i7 9750H	Intel Core i5 7300HQ
Discrete GPU	NVIDIA GeForce RTX 2070 Max-Q	NVIDIA GeForce GTX 1050
Performance (discrete)	5.460 TFLOPS	1.911 TFLOPS
Integrated GPU	Intel UHD Graphics 630	Intel HD Graphics 630
Performance (integrated)	441.6 GFLOPS	384.0 GFLOPS
System Memory	DDR4 2666 16GB 64-bit × 2	DDR4 2133 8GB 64-bit
Vulkan Runtime	1.2.131.2	1.2.131.2

The simulated workload consists of a series of trigonometric and pseudo-random computations. The default test load contains 5000 computation loops, and the extra test case (4×load) increased this loop count to 20000. Note that the load increase is not necessarily proportional to the actual time to complete the asynchronous task.

The results measured on both devices are presented in Table 2. The major additional overhead comes from issuing commands for the iGPU, which would delay the command recording for the dGPU, as illustrated in Figure 5. In the meantime, as depicted in Figure 4, this overhead can get covered by the workload fraction taken out from the dGPU.

Table 2. Measured average frame time in milliseconds (lower is better)

	Device A	Device A (4×load)	Device B	Device B (4×load)
Discrete GPU	6.913ms	7.231ms	20.063ms	20.134ms
Heterogeneous GPUs	6.639ms	9.329ms	19.708ms	19.498ms

In three of the four test cases, a maximum of 4.1% frame time improvement is observed. Although in the second case there is a performance downgrade, it can be expected with the given test conditions. The default workload would take the iGPU on device A about 5ms to complete, which is within the time required by the dGPU to complete a full frame. But as the computational load increased, the iGPU became the bottleneck on device A, resulting in the performance decrease. In the meantime, the iGPU on device B only has slightly lower performance than the iGPU on device A, thus the time required by the iGPU on device B to complete the same computational task can be expected to be well within 19ms when the computational load increased.

Such observation suggests that when offloading asynchronous computation workload to the iGPU, the relative performance of the iGPU and application target frame rate should be carefully balanced.

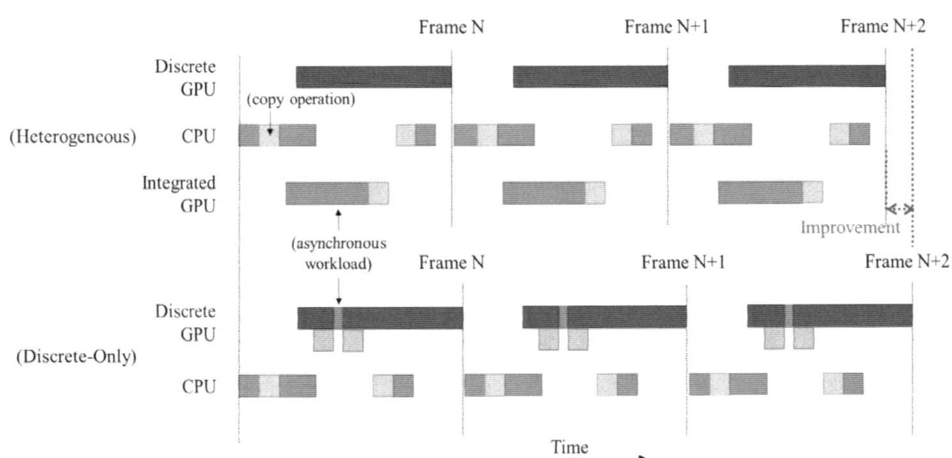

Figure 4. Source of frame time improvement. This is an illustration, not accurate time mapping

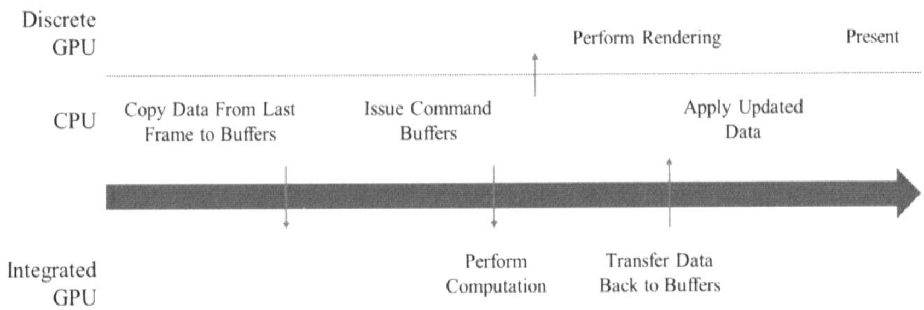

Figure 5. Timeline of a frame with heterogeneous GPUs

Aside from asynchronous computation workload, we have also experimented offloading post-processing workload that includes copying 3 full-screen images from dGPU to iGPU. However, due to the limit of PCI-e transfer bandwidth, the average data transfer overhead (5ms in total) exceeds the workload fraction that can be offloaded from the dGPU. The best outcome we observed is an average of 8.9% framerate downgrade comparing with single dGPU setup (39.572ms/frame vs. 36.324ms/frame) on device A.

4. CONCLUSION

This paper validates that offloading asynchronous computation workload from the dGPU to the iGPU, with Vulkan implementation, can provide up to 4% performance improvement. Tested combinations include Intel UHD 630 plus NVIDIA RTX 2070, and Intel HD 630 plus NVIDIA GTX 1050.

The necessary conditions include:

1. The data transfer overhead between the iGPU and the dGPU must be less than the workload fraction taken out from the dGPU.
2. The iGPU must be able to complete the offloaded task within the time required by the dGPU to complete a full frame unless the task is not frame-aligned.

This work contributes to the body of knowledge on real-time rendering with heterogeneous GPUs. The approach presented in this work is applicable in graphics applications with asynchronous procedures involved. Examples include character flock behavior update, particle physics simulation with low or fixed refresh rate, and resource pre-processing. Our approach can be further improved through analyzing the performance stability when other GPU-demanding program is present in the system and identifying the sweet spot in the size of data transferred for the offloaded workload.

REFERENCES

Hill, M. D., & Marty, M. R. (2008). Amdahl's Law in the Multicore Era. *Computer*, 41(7), 33-38.

Hux, A. (2020, March 17). *Multi-Adapter with Integrated and Discrete GPUs*. Retrieved from https://devmesh.intel.com/projects/multi-adapter-particles

Peek, E., Wünsche, B., & Lutteroth, C. (2014). Using Integrated GPUs to Perform Image Warping for HMDs. *Proceedings of the 29th International Conference on Image and Vision Computing New Zealand*, 172-177.

Persson, T. (2017, August 28). *High-Level Rendering Using Render Graphs*. Retrieved from Our Machinery: https://ourmachinery.com/post/high-level-rendering-using-render-graphs/

Yeung, A. (2015, April 30). *DirectX 12 Multiadapter: Lighting up dormant silicon and making it work for you*. Retrieved from DirectX Developer Blog: https://devblogs.microsoft.com/directx/directx-12-multiadapter-lighting-up-dormant-silicon-and-making-it-work-for-you/

IMAGE PROCESSING TECHNIQUES FOR FAST AND ACCURATE ESTIMATION OF POSE OF A DOUBLE PENDULUM

Muhammad Haris, Junaid Ahmed Memon and Muhammad Farhan
School of Science and Engineering, Habib University, Karachi, 75290 Sindh, Pakistan

ABSTRACT

Double pendulum exhibits a rich dynamic behavior and is often used to study nonlinear dynamics, instability, and chaos. In order to devise a method for its control, the angles and the angular velocities of its two arms need to be measured accurately with sufficiently fast sampling rate. Generally, encoders and other sensors are used which are costly, difficult to install for custom built pendulums, and require continuous calibration to measure the angles. Therefore, in this paper we present a comparison of four image processing based methods to estimate the angles of double pendulum. The first two methods are widely used involving variants of Canny edge detection in conjunction with Hough transform. The third method extracts the skeleton of the thresholded pendulum and then applies Hough transform on the skeleton to compute the angles. The fourth method, never before used for double pendulum, segments the pendulum arms and uses basic matrix operations to extract the angles. The results focus on the speed-accuracy-memory tradeoff for all the methods and manifest that the fourth method is satisfactorily accurate with minimum computational complexity and memory usage.

KEYWORDS

Double Pendulum, Pose Estimation, Canny Edge Detection, Hough Transform, Speed-Accuracy Tradeoff

1. INTRODUCTION

Accurate position control is a problem in robotic systems. In many applications, robot bodies are assumed to be rigid, however, it is not true for all cases. Therefore, the analysis and control of the physical model of a flexible robot and solving its tracking problem is a useful topic in robotics and has been considered in many literature (Artega, 2000), (Lee, 1998). Double pendulum is one such system, where two arms are linked with non-rigid joint. The study of double pendulum is important in the field of physics and especially in control engineering (Ataei, 2007) where the general interest lies in its control. In order to control the system it is necessary to track pendulum arms by knowing the angles of the double pendulum. There are a few ways to track pendulum arm e.g., with Inertial Measurement Unit using sensors (accelerometer and gyroscopes), using encoders and via image processing (Kiril, 2013). Error accumulation (Kiril, 2013) and noise, and requirement to modify setup are major problems when sensors are used whereas use of image processing algorithm enables a rather accurate tracking at a lower cost with ease in installation.

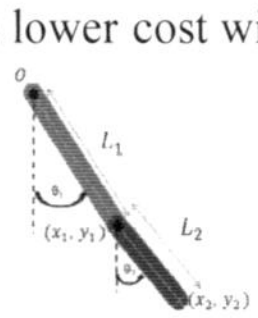

Figure 1. Diagram demonstrating the project

In order to control the pendulum, the angles the arms make with the vertical axis need to be fed into the mathematical model to produce appropriate output voltage for the motors. Our focus is to extract the pose of double pendulum i.e. θ_1 and θ_2 as shown in Figure 1. There can be a variety of algorithms to move forward with the angle estimation from a series of images of a pendulum. One method is by marking the joints physically (Kulp, 2007) where background color and light intensity plays an important role and extracting coordinates of joints. After discriminating the joints, the displacement, (x_i, y_i), from the reference origin can be calculated. This displacement can be converted to angles, θ_i using the following mathematical formula (Kulp, 2007).

$$\theta_i = atan2(y_i - y_{i-1}, x_i - x_{i-1}) \quad (1)$$

There can be a number of ways to segment out joints. For the ease of the process, markers be physically placed on joints so that bounding boxes can be obtained easily. Other approaches include detecting edges of the pendulum arms and segmenting it. There are quite a few approaches within this domain as well. For example, the authors in (Ali, 2015) proposed to use Hough transform on lines, corresponding to arms, extracted from the image to measure angles of the double pendulum by applying appropriate trigonometry, and their method reported maximum error of 0.4°. It is to go from the (x, y) space to the (ρ, ϕ) space in order to detect simple shapes like line, circle or ellipse. Figure 2 demonstrates the mapping.

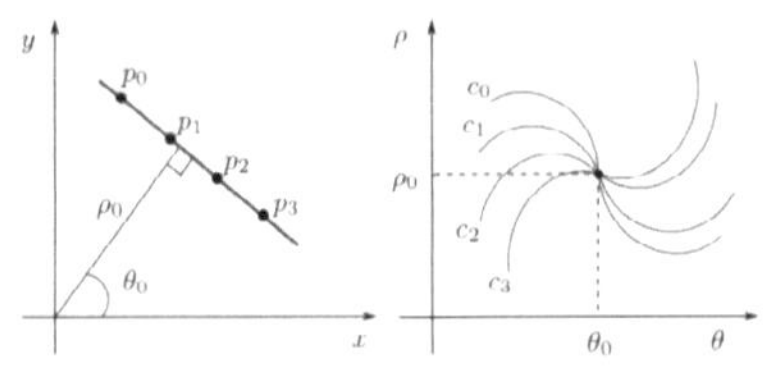

Figure 2. Change of space during Hough transform (Bergues, 2019)

We can see that where there are intersection in the (ρ, ϕ) space, they correspond to a line in the (x, y) space. The same paper proposes other ways which include detecting pointers or markers corresponding to end-points as well as defining points in space and using pattern recognition to find the angles. However, the paper concludes that use of Hough transform yields the most accurate angles.

Another paper (Kavithaa, 2013) used vision algorithm called Lukas Kanade's Optical Flow to track the blob. The histogram equalization based pre-processing is applied and thresholding is performed to detect the blob. They used a blob library in OpenCV to detect the blob. Repeated edge detection and Hough transform is applied on each image to get the track in another paper (Ngyuyen, 2009).

Another paper (Robinson, 2010), cited that it was very difficult to extract actual angular measurements from the radial and tangential accelerations provided by the accelerometer and that the resolution provided was insufficient to yield clear data, even after filtering. Therefore, they shifted to vision-based approach to track the double pendulum arms. They extracted 8-bit image frame of the captured video. The 8-bit image is then morphologically opened to remove noise in the binary image. Following opening, thinning is applied to the image to extract the "skeleton" of the image and the endpoints are found which are used to get the angles.

From literature, it was found that Canny edge detection followed by Hough transform is a reliable way to get angles, however these algorithms are slow. We present a comparison of four methods in terms of speed, accuracy and memory consumption so that one can choose a method based on the performance requirement.

2. METHODOLOGY

In this paper we compare four methods to estimate the pose of a double pendulum. The machine used to run the algorithms had a 64-bit 2.4 GHz processor with 4 GB RAM. The camera captures video at a resolution of 1080p at a frame rate of 30 fps. Before applying any of these methods, pre-processing is required to remove noise and sharp edges in the background occurring mainly due to uneven lighting. Blurring using average filter is applied on the image after it is converted to grayscale from RGB.

In order to evaluate performance we run each of the following algorithms on 300 frames. The metrics used to compare these methods include memory consumption, time taken to compute angles for each frame and RMS error in angles from the true values. These true values are obtained by segmenting out small markers from the pendulum. For the benchmark data we use images of pendulum with markers on it. Using basic thresholding, $T_1 > P(x,y) > T_2$, the markers placed on arms are segmented out. The markers are labelled and three points on pendulum are extracted out and the angles are computed using the formula given in equation (1).

2.1 Canny Edge Detection Followed by Hough Transform (Method 1)

This method uses Canny edge (Canny, 1986) detection to extract single pixel thick edges of the double pendulum. Hough transform (Richard, 1972) is then applied on these edges and the three peaks with the highest values, in the Hough space, are used which gives the angles of these lines. These three peaks correspond to the two lines for the upper arm and one for the lower arm. The first two peaks have the same angle. The two unique angles are chosen, directly from the Hough space. Figure 3 shows a frame being processed using the described method.

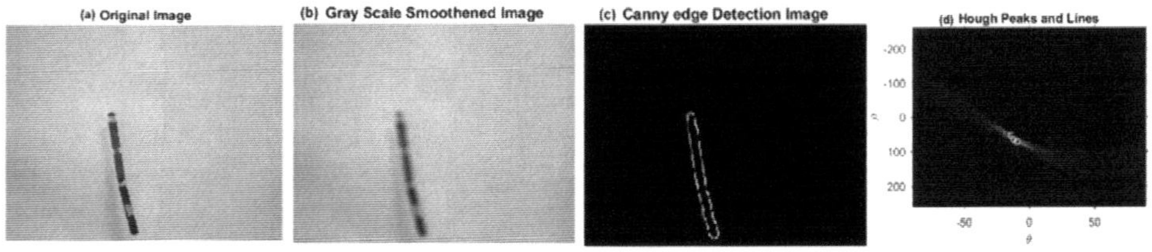

Figure 3. Processing via method 1. (a) Original Image. (b) Gray Scale Image. (c) Canny Edge Image. (d) Hough Peaks

2.2 Optimized Canny Edge Detection Followed by Hough Transform (Method 2)

Approximate Canny Edge (Miroslav, 2018) is builtin function in MATLAB and it makes the entire procedure nearly 2.7 times faster than the above method. The optimal function in Canny's detector is described by the sum of four exponential terms, but it can be approximated by the first derivative of a Gaussian. This method is exactly like method 2. *Approximate Canny Edge* is used to detect edges of the segmented pendulum. Once the edge is found, the method uses Hough transform for detecting angles as was in the previous case, by connecting lines in the edge image. This yields lines and their corresponding angles. The first and the third peaks' angles are selected since they are unique and correspond to the upper and lower arm respectively.

2.3 Hough Transform of Skeleton Image (Method 3)

This method computes the skeleton, by repeated application of morphological operations, namely erosion and dilation, on the pendulum image followed by applying Hough transform on it. In this method only the two highest valued peaks are utilized. The two peaks taken into consideration correspond to the upper and the lower arm respectively. Once again, the angles are extracted directly from the Hough space. Figure 4 (a), (b) shows a frame being processed using the described method. Hough transform detects two lines (pendulum arms) in the (ρ, ϕ) space, which directly yields the angle.

2.4 Constraints based Image thresholding (Method 4)

In this method we exploit the white background and threshold the image to separate foreground from the background. This method requires some information about the fixed joint of the pendulum, O, and the length of both the arms, L_1 and L_2. The algorithm searches for the closest high pixel in the vicinity of O, then looks for a high pixel at a distance L_1 from the first point. The last step is to detect a high pixel at a distance L_2 from the second point. Algorithm makes sure that the third point does not end up on the first arm rather it is chosen depending on the angle θ_1. Each search returns an array of pixels, and for whilst searching for the third point either the first index or the last index is chosen, depending on whether the first arm makes a negative or a positive angle with the vertical axis, respectively. The operations are simple which greatly increases its speed, unlike other methods where morphological and complex algorithms are being used. Figure 4 (b), (c) shows a frame being processed using the described method. However, this method places some constraints on the length of the pendulum, hence if the working distance is altered the length needs to be calibrated manually.

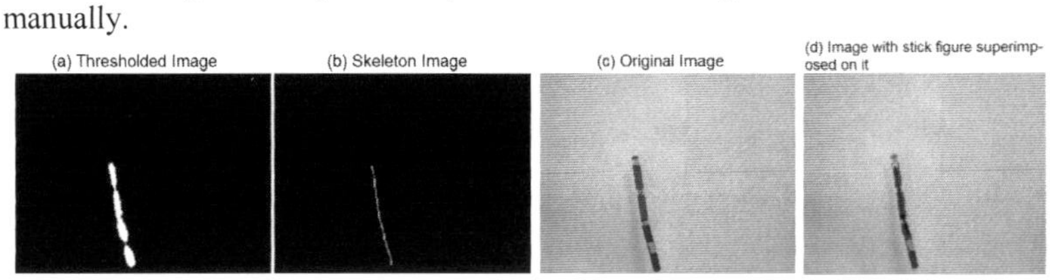

Figure 4. Frame being processed using method 3, 4. (a) Thresholded Image. (b) Skeleton Image (c) Original Image. (d) Image with stick figure superimposed on it

3. RESULTS AND DISCUSSION

Figures 5 and 6 compare the error in angles, $\theta_1$and θ_2, the computation time, and memory usage for the four methods with respect to changing image scale. The first 3 methods are satisfactorily fast, whereas the last method is the fastest. Method 3 improves the speed of computation by optimizing the edge detection procedure. The last method yields the least error for the first limb, however, for the second limb the last method yields the highest error. The error for second limb stays the same for the first three methods, so they are consistent. The memory consumption is the lowest for the last method, and nearly the same for the first three methods.

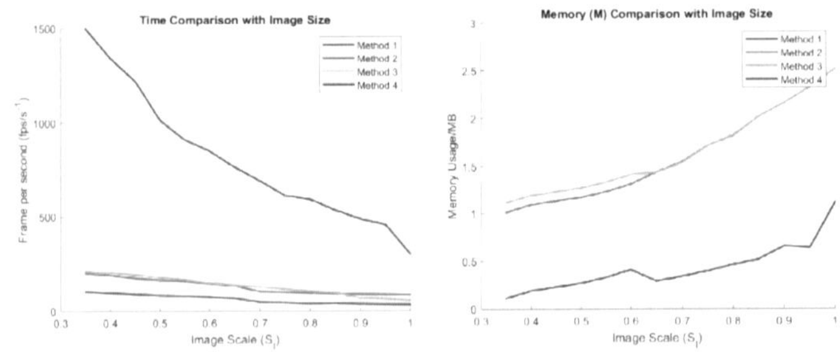

Figure 5. Speed and Memory for different methods. (a) Time Comparison for different Methods from reference data. Frames processed per second fps against Image Scale (left). (b) Memory Usage Comparison for different Methods from reference data (MBs used against Image Scale) (right)

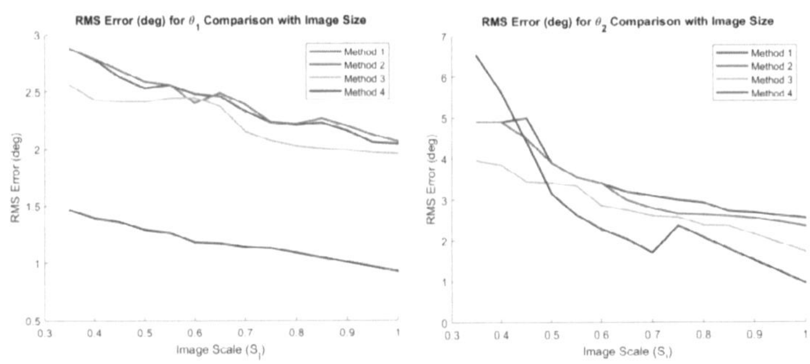

Figure 6. Accuracy Comparison for different methods from reference data. (a) RMS error (deg) for limb-1 against Image Scale) (left). (b) RMS error (deg) for limb-2 against Image Scale) (right)

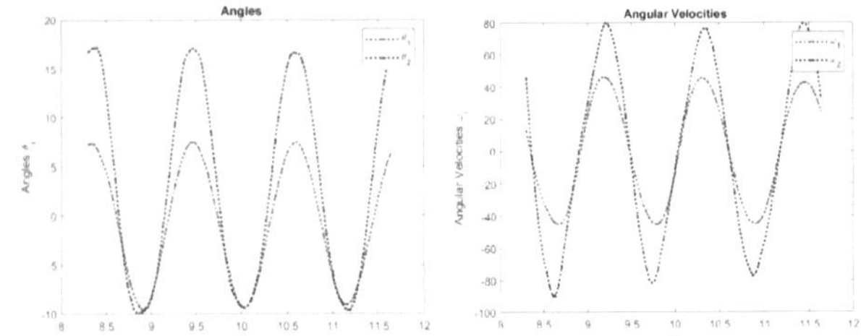

Figure 7. Results obtained (a) Angles obtained (Left), (b) Angular velocities (Right)

For the graph comparing time in Figure 5(a), the first three methods demonstrate a nearly constant behavior, however, a quadratic function best fits the data for the fourth method. The method used to derive the relation is obtained using least squares method. Here S_I is the image scale. For the graph comparing memory consumption, 5(b), a similar trend is seen; the first three methods fit a single quadratic function and the fourth method fits a separate linear function.

In the graphs comparing the RMS error in θ_1, in Figure 6(a), we can see that a single linear functions fits the first three methods and a separate linear function fits the data for the fourth method. In the graphs comparing RMS errors in θ_2, in Figure 6(b), we can see that all the curves can be approximated by a single quadratic function, with a reasonable degree of error.

The following table shows standard deviation in error in angles for different methods.

Table 1. Standard deviation in error in angles for different methods

-	Method 1	Method 2	Method 3	Method 4
θ_1	3.5361	3.3476	8.4567	0.4176
θ_2	2.9545	3.2314	6.9928	1.3136

The results also include angular trajectory and angular velocity of both pendulum arms and speed of computation. Figure 7 shows the angles obtained and the angular velocities. Since the readings are noisy so Savitzky Golay smoothing filter is applied. It smoothens the movement of the first arm. The algorithms miss out the movement of the second limb if the movement is really fast. This can be dealt with by increasing the camera resolution. Use of a better camera with a frame rate of nearly 72 fps (Ali, 2015) can improve the results significantly. If the lighting of the image acquisition platform is made better, the results can be further improved significantly.

4. CONCLUSION

In this paper we explored the efficacy of estimating the pose of a double pendulum using image processing thus reducing the cost of installing setups based on encoders, accelerometers and gyroscopes. Four methods were compared against a reference method using metrics such as accuracy, the speed of computation, and the memory usage. The results suggest that 4th method has the highest computation speed and the lowest error for the first limb. This method's (4th) error is highly dependent on the width of the pendulum. Since this method searches for a white pixel in a certain specified region, the smaller is the width of the pendulum, the smaller is the deviation from the truth. However for the second limb the Canny edge detection followed by Hough transform gives the lowest error (1st method). All the methods require a uniform background. The results highlight the speed-accuracy-memory tradeoff between the methods and could be used to identify the appropriate method for a given application based on the required performance metric.

REFERENCES

Ali D. and Teerapong D., 2015, Control of Double Inverted Pendulum First Approach, *Blekinge Institute of Technology*

Artega M. A. and Siciliano B., 2000, On Tracking Control of Flexible Robot Arms, *IEEE Transactions on Automatic Control*, vol. 45

Ataei M. et al, 2007, The control of a double-pendulum system, *International Conference on Control, Automation and Systems*

Bergues G. J., 2019, Straight Line Detection Through Sub-pixel Hough Transform, *Intelligent Computing*, vol. 998

Canny J., 1986, A Computational Approach to Edge Detection, *IEEE Transactions on Pattern Analysis and Machine Intelligence*, vol. PAMI-8

Gonzalez C., 1977, Digital Image Processing, *Upper Saddle River, NJ: Pearson/Prentice Hall*

Kavithaa R. et al, 2013, Simple Pendulum analysis – A Vision based approach, *Fourth International Conference on Computing, Communications and Networking Technologies*

Kiril A., Iva N., 2013, An algorithm for error reducing in IMU, *2013 IEEE INISTA*

Kulp C. W. et al, 2007, Tracking the Motion of a Double Pendulum Using Mathematica, *Journal of Planning Education and Research*, vol. 12

Lee J. D. and Wang B. L., 1998, Optimal control of a flexible robot arm, *Computers and Structures*, vol. 29

Miroslav H. and Peter K., 2018, About Edge Detection in Digital Images, *Radio Engineering*, vol. 27, no. 4

Nguyen T. T., 2009, Rectangular object tracking based on standard Hough transform, *IEEE International Conference on Robotics and Biomimetics*

Richard O. D. and Peter E. H., 1972, Use of the Hough Transformation To Detect Lines and Curves in Pictures, *Communications of ACM*, vol. 15, no. 1

Robinson J., 2010, Double Pendulum, *Georgia Institute of Technology*

COMPARATIVE EVALUATIONS OF CNN BASED NETWORKS FOR SKIN LESION CLASSIFICATION

Evgin Goceri and Ayse Akman Karakas
Akdeniz University, Engineering Faculty, Biomedical Engineering Department, Antalya, Turkey

ABSTRACT

The aim of this work is to classify Hemangioma, Rosacea and Acne Vulgaris diseases from digital colored photographs automatically. To determine the most appropriate deep neural network for this multi-class classification, network architectures have been examined. To perform a meaningful comparison of deep networks, they should be (i) implemented with the same parameters, (ii) applied with the same activation, loss and optimization functions, (iii) trained and tested with the same datasets, (iv) run on computers having the same hardware configurations. Therefore, in this work, five deep networks, which are applied widely in image classification, have been used to compare their performances by considering these factors. Those networks are VGG16, VGG19, GoogleNet, InceptionV3 and ResNet101. Comparative evaluations of the results obtained from these networks have been performed in terms of accuracy, precision and specificity. F1 score and Matthew's correlation coefficient values have also been computed. Experimental results indicated that ResNet101 architecture can classify images used in this study with higher accuracy (77.72%) than the others.

KEYWORDS

VGG, GoogleNet, ResNet, Inception, Skin Disease, Lesion Classification

1. INTRODUCTION

Traditional diagnosis of Hemangioma, Rosacea and Acne Vulgaris is mainly based on visual examinations of lesions by a dermatologist. Therefore, computer assisted diagnosis for these diseases with pattern recognition can be performed. By this way, the number of patients in dermatology can be reduced and subjective diagnosis problem can be eliminated.

Superiority of deep neural networks, particularly Convolutional Neural Networks (CNNs), in image classification (Lai, 2019; Korotcov et al., 2017; Lee et al. 2017) was the main motivation behind this study to use a deep network for this multi-class classification. However, there are several deep network architectures designed with different number of layers, different activation, loss and optimization functions, which have an important role in accuracy of a classifier.

To determine the most appropriate deep network, architectures should be examined and their performances should be compared. To perform a meaningful comparison, these networks should be (i) implemented with the same parameters, (ii) applied with the same activation, loss and optimization functions, (iii) trained and tested with the same datasets, (iv) run on computers having the same hardware configurations. Therefore, in this work, different CNN based deep networks have been implemented by considering the above factors and their image performances have been compared. These networks that are used widespread in image classification have been applied; VGG16, VGG19, GoogleNet, InceptionV3 and ResNet101.

Skin lesion images segmented from photographs have been used in this study. Figure 1 shows example photographs (Figure 1.a, b, c) and lesion images (Figure 1.d, e, f). Images have been obtained from several public databases (Web_1, 2020; Web_2, 2020; Web_3, 2020).

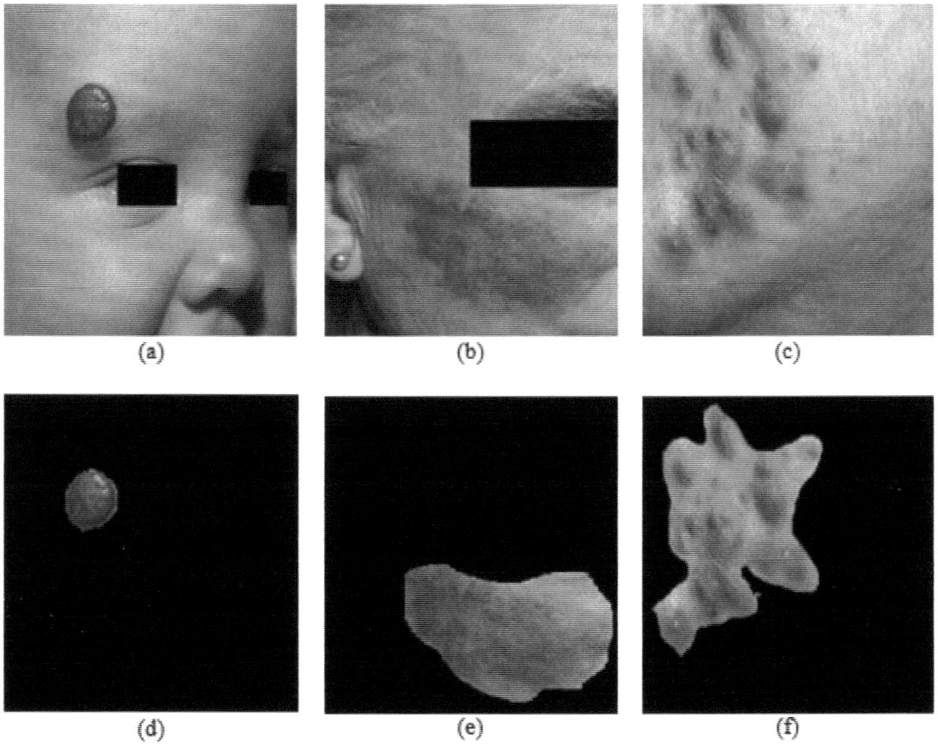

Figure 1. Hemangioma (a), Rosacea (b), Acne Vulgaris (c), Hemangioma lesion (d), Rosacea lesion (e), Acne Vulgaris lesion (f)

In this study, the image dataset has been constructed with equal number of images (101 images) from each disease class. The dataset has been divided into two groups as training and testing. The training (testing) group includes 60 (41) images from each class.

The chosen activation function in this study is ReLU (Rectified Linear Unit) and optimization function is Adaptive Moment Estimation (ADAM). To consider pixel-wise similarities, cross entropy has been used as a loss function. Initial learning ratio, epoch and iteration numbers are 0.0003, 6 and 108 respectively.

Implementations have been performed using Matlab (R2019b) on the same computer, which includes 16 GB RAM memory and Core i7-4930 K processor.

This paper has been structured as follows: Section 2 gives a short information about the network architectures applied in this work. Section 3 explains measurement metrics used to compare classification performances of those networks. Section 4 gives results, finally, Section 5 presents conclusions.

2. CNN BASED NETWORKS APPLIED IN THIS WORK

The deep neural network architectures applied widespread for image classification have been used in this work. Those networks are Visual Geometry Group (VGG) network, GoogleNet, InceptionV3 and ResNet101, which are pretrained on images from ImageNet (Web_4, 2020). In this section, these architectures are explained.

2.1 VGG16 and VGG19

VGG network was proposed by the Visual Geometry Group, Engineering Science Department at the University of Oxford (Simonyan et al., 2015). VGG16 is a 16-layer network. In this architecture, 224x224 colored images are passed through five blocks of convolution layers where each block is composed of increasing numbers of 3x3 filters. The stride is set to one. The blocks are separated using maximum pooling layers, which reduce volume size. A maximum pooling operation is applied over 22 windows with stride two. The five blocks of convolution layers are connected to three fully-connected layers. The top layer is called as soft-max layer to obtain class probabilities as outputs. Similar to VGG16 architecture, VGG19 network model has been used. The "16" and "19" stand for the number of weight layers in the network (Simonyan et al., 2015).

2.2 GoogleNet

GoogleNet architecture has 22 layers and uses Inception modules as the main structural contributions of the network. Therefore, GoogleNet is also known as InceptionV1. Inception module was developed by considering how an optimal local sparse structure in a CNN can be approximated using dense components (Szegedy et al., 2015). GoogleNet architecture uses 3 different filters, which are 1x1, 3x3 and 5x5 dimensional, for the inputs. The 1x1 convolution operation with 128 filters is applicable for dimension reduction. Also, to use less number of parameters, the fully-connected layers are replaced with the one including global-average-pooling after the last convolutional layer. Because the pooling operation calculates mean values of the channel values across the two-dimensional feature map (Szegedy et al., 2015).

2.3 InceptionV3

InceptionV3 is a further version of GoogleNet and was introduced in (Szegedy et al., 2016). Main differences between GoogleNet and InceptionV3 are presented in Table 1.

Table 1. Main differences between GoogleNet and InceptionV3 architectures

Network	Convolution Filters	Pooling Operation	Layers	Feature Map Downsizing	Inception Module	Auxiliary Classifier
GoogleNet	1x1filter, 3x3 filter and 5x5 filter is used	Average value is computed from feature maps and global average pooling is applied	22	Max. pooling	Convolutions using 1x1, 3x3 and 5x5 filters, and max pooling using 3x3 filter is performed together	2
InceptionV3	Two 3x3 filters are used instead of 5x5 filter	Pooling is performed with an appropriate grid size reduction. Convolution and pooling operations are applied to construct feature maps.	42	Grid size reduction	Convolutions are divided into smaller and asymmetric processes. So, a novel inception module is constructed	1

2.4 ResNet101

ResNet architecture was proposed to solve the degradation problem that occurs in deep networks. The problem affects accuracy of deep networks, which saturate during convergence and degrade rapidly (He et al., 2016). Like GoogleNet, a global average pooling is applied before the classification layer in

ResNet. Unlike sequential neural network architectures such as VGG, ResNet includes residual building blocks. Every block in the ResNet architecture accomplishes an identity mapping and produces element-wise addition of the features obtained from convolutional layers. A major novelty in this architecture is to apply a batch normalization step and skip connections to train deeper network structures. ResNet101 is deeper than previous networks.

3. RESULTS

Classification performance have been evaluated in terms of accuracy, precision, specificity, F1 score and also Matthew's Correlation Coefficient (MCC)) (Web_5, 2020). These parameters have been computed using the following formulas;

$$Accuracy = \frac{TP + TN}{TP + FP + TN + FN} \quad (1)$$

$$Precision = \frac{TP}{TP + FP} \quad (2)$$

$$Specificity = \frac{TN}{TN + FP} \quad (3)$$

$$\mathrm{F1}_{score} = 2\left(\frac{PPV * TPR}{PPV + TPR}\right) = \frac{2 * TP}{2 * TP + FP + FN} \quad (4)$$

$$MCC = \frac{TP\,x\,TN - FP\,x\,FN}{\sqrt{(TP + FP)(TP + FN)(TN + FP)(TN + FN)}} \quad (5)$$

where TN (True Negative), FN (False Negative), TP (True Positive) and FP (False Positive) terms for a disease, let's say Psoriasis, have the following meaning: TP: Psoriasis images are classified as Psoriasis; FP: non-Psoriasis images that are classified as Psoriasis; FN: Psoriasis images that are not classified as Psoriasis; TN: non-Psoriasis images that are not classified as Psoriasis.

F1 score, which is also known as Dice similarity measure, is computed by considering both precision and sensitivity. It is the harmonic mean of these two parameter values. In (5), the term PPV (Positive Predictive Value) is obtained by TP/(TP+FP) and the term TPR (True Positive Rate) is obtained by TP/P, which is TP/(TP+FN). To obtain F1 score, PPV and TPR values are taken into account equally. However, TN values are not used. Therefore, we also calculated MCC, which is another important metric used in machine learning to analyze quality of classifiers. Table 2 presents numerical values obtained by these six-evaluation metrics.

Table 2. Quantitative values obtained by five network architectures for multiclass lesion classification

Network	Accuracy (%)	Specificity (%)	Precision (%)	F1 score (%)	MCC (%)
VGG16	57.72	78.89	58.11	52.63	37.47
GoogleNet	66.17	90.16	67.41	65.18	58.37
VGG19	69.32	91.41	69.01	68.43	62.47
InceptionV3	72.86	93.02	71.53	71.30	65.00
ResNet101	77.72	94.76	79.81	77.82	72.61

In Figure 2, the lines with light-blue and black color show the training and testing accuracy values obtained by ResNet101, which classifies images with the highest accuracy. The line with dark-blue color shows the training accuracy values after normalization.

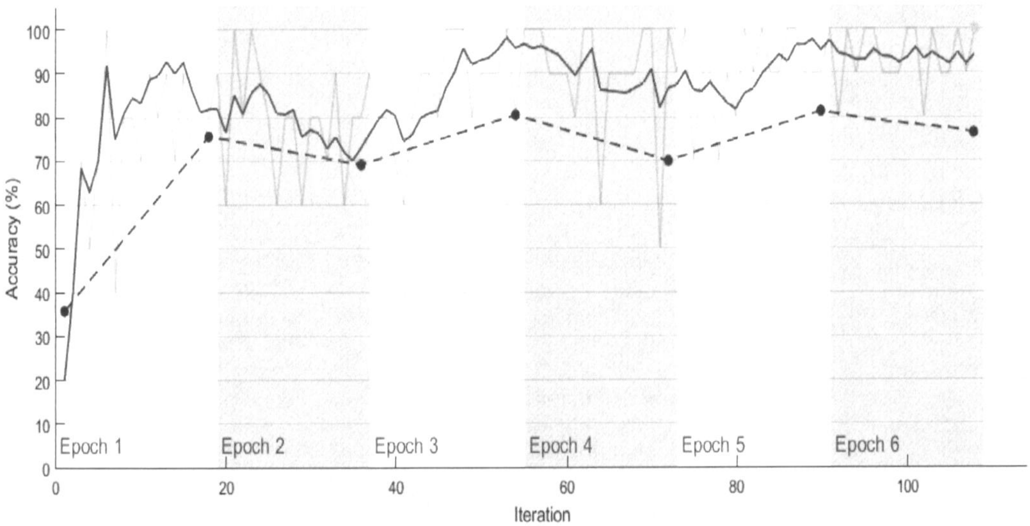

Figure 2. Accuracy values according to epoch obtained by ResNet101 network

In Figure 3, the lines with light-red and black color show the loss values obtained by ResNet101in the training and testing stages. The line with dark-red color shows normalized loss values obtained in the training stage.

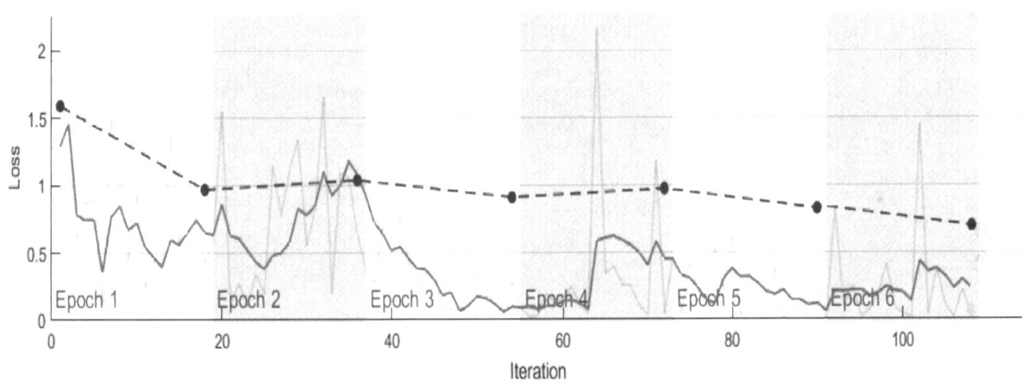

Figure 3. Loss values according to epoch obtained by ResNet101 network

4. CONCLUSION

In this study, classification performances of five deep network structures have been evaluated to classify three skin diseases. Comparative evaluations have been performed using accuracy, specificity, precision, F1 metric and MCC. Quantitative values indicated that ResNet101 can classify images with higher accuracy than the other networks.

ACKNOWLEDGEMENT

This work has been supported by The Scientific and Technological Research Council of Turkey (TUBITAK - 118E777).

REFERENCES

He, K., Zhang, X., Ren, S., Sun, J., 2016. Deep residual learning for image recognition. *In Proceedings of the IEEE Conference on Computer Vision and Pattern Recognition (CVPR)*, Las Vegas, USA, pp. 770–778.

Korotcov, A., Tkachenko, V., Russo, D.P., Ekins, S., 2017. Comparison of Deep Learning with Multiple Machine Learning Methods and Metrics Using Diverse Drug Discovery Data Sets. *Mol. Pharmaceutics*, Vol.14, No.12, pp.4462-4475

Lai, Y., 2019. A Comparison of Traditional Machine Learning and Deep Learning in Image Recognition. *Journal of Physics: Conference Series, 3rd International Conference on Electrical, Mechanical and Computer Engineering (ICEMCE2019)*, 9–11 August 2019, Guizhou, China, Vol. 1314, No.012148, pp.1-9

Lee, J.G., Jun, S., Cho, Y.W., Lee, H., Kim, G.B., Seo, J.B., Kim, N., 2017. Deep Learning in Medical Imaging: General Overview. *Korean Journal of Radiology*, Vol. 18, No. 4, pp.570-584.

Simonyan, K., Zisserman, A., 2015. Very Deep Convolutional Networks for Large Scale Image Recognition. *International Conference on Learning Representations*, San Diego, USA, pp.1-15

Szegedy, C., Liu, W., Jia, Y., Sermanet, P., Reed, S., Anguelov, D., Erhan, D., Vanhoucke, V., Rabinovich, A., 2015. Going Deeper with Convolutions. *In Proceedings of the IEEE Conference on Computer Vision and Pattern Recognition*, Boston, USA, pp. 1–9.

Szegedy, C., Vanhoucke, V., Ioffe, S., Shlens, J., 2016. Rethinking the Inception Architecture for Computer Vision, *IEEE Conference on Computer Vision and Pattern Recognition (CVPR)*, Las Vegas, USA, pp. 2818-2826.

Web_1, 2020. Dermatoweb, http://www.dermatoweb.net (Access date: April 24, 2020)

Web_2, 2020. DermNet New Zealand. http://www.dermnetnz.org (Access date: April 24, 2020)

Web_3, 2020. DermQuest Image Library. https://www.dermquest.com/image-library (Access date: April 24, 2020)

Web_4, 2020. ImageNet. http://www.image-net.org (Access date: April 20, 2020)

Web_5, 2020. Matthew's Correlation Coefficient. https://en.wikipedia.org/wiki/Matthews_correlation_coefficient (Access date: May 1, 2020)

EXPLORING CORRELATION USING CIRCLE WAVES

Dhruv Ishpuniani
Trinity College Dublin, The University of Dublin, Ireland

ABSTRACT

Correlation is widely used in data analytics applications to measure association between various variables. The common approaches to visualize multivariate correlation are clustered heatmaps and scatterplot matrices, however, they do not scale well when the number of variables is large. This paper presents a new animated, aesthetically pleasing alternative to the aforementioned approaches which also reduces the information overload experienced by the viewer. The proposed technique is applicable to scenarios where the analysis requires multiple target variables to be investigated and a high-level intuition about the correlation magnitude is enough.

KEYWORDS

Correlation, Exploratory Data Analysis, Multivariate Data, Circle Waves

1. INTRODUCTION

Correlation is a method to gauge the strength of association between two discrete or continuous, quantitative variables. Pearson's correlation coefficient is a widely used metric to measure correlation and it captures a magnitude of the linear relationship between features. Pearson's correlation has a wide variety of applications, from selecting features for machine learning models (Blum and Langley, 1997) to finding genes that are related to a specific disease network (Horvath and Dong, 2008). Visualizing correlation helps in exploratory data analysis by providing the investigator with a platform to test new hypotheses.

Idioms such as clustered heatmaps and scatterplot matrices are generally utilized to visualize correlation. Both these approaches are reasonably effective in visualizing correlations; however, they lose their effectiveness when the number of features increases. Additionally, they both suffer from screen space limitations.

The main contribution of this paper is to provide an alternative to heatmaps and scatterplots to visualize correlations in the case where a high-level intuition about the variables highly correlated with the target variable is enough and the number of variables is very large. Additionally, the technique is useful where the analysis requires investigating multiple such target variables. The animated, aesthetically pleasing, novel technique to visualize multivariate correlation presented in this paper, reduces the information overload experienced by the viewer and is able to convey the correlation information better.

2. BACKGROUND AND RELATED WORK

A Scatterplot is one of the most basic idioms used to visualize the correlation between two variables (Rensink and Baldridge, 2010). The two axes represent variables and each plotted point indicates the value observed for the two variables. The magnitude of correlation is measured by calculating the deviation from the straight line produced by the point cloud. Scatterplot matrices are used to compare more than two variables. A scatterplot matrix (figure 1(a)) contains scatterplots where each scatterplot has the target variable on one axis and a variable with which the correlation has to be visualized on the other axis. This approach provides a very rich visualization, but at the same time, it also requires a lot of screen-space. Additionally, scatterplot matrices do not scale well to explore more than a few dozen variables in a dataset (Friendly, 2002).

Another standard approach is to compute correlation coefficients between all variable pairs and visualizing the correlation coefficient matrix using clustered heatmaps (Wilkinson and Friendly, 2009) (figure 1(b)). Colour is used to encode the pairwise correlation information. Clustering helps with detecting patterns; however, the detection of patterns depends on the clustering technique used. Along with that, due to the relative nature of colour perception, it is challenging to accurately interpret the visualization (Wong, 2010).

The original idea for circle waves as a visual was proposed by Dave Whyte (Whyte, 2014). The idea of using circle waves to show correlation between various fields was inspired from the solar correlation map (Zapf and Kraushaar, 2017). This approach visualizes the Pearson's correlation coefficients using the model of a solar system, with the target variable being in place of the sun. The magnitude of correlation is encoded in the radius of orbit, higher the correlation, shorter the radius. The kind of correlation (positive or negative) is encoded by the colour of the label.

Research has suggested that viewers find it easier to interpret visualizations containing animated elements (Robertson et al., 2008). In addition, aesthetics play an important role in engaging the viewer with a particular visualization (Cawthon and Moere, 2007). The technique proposed in this paper builds upon the concepts of motion and aesthetics to effectively visualize correlation while combating the limitations of the previous approaches at the same time.

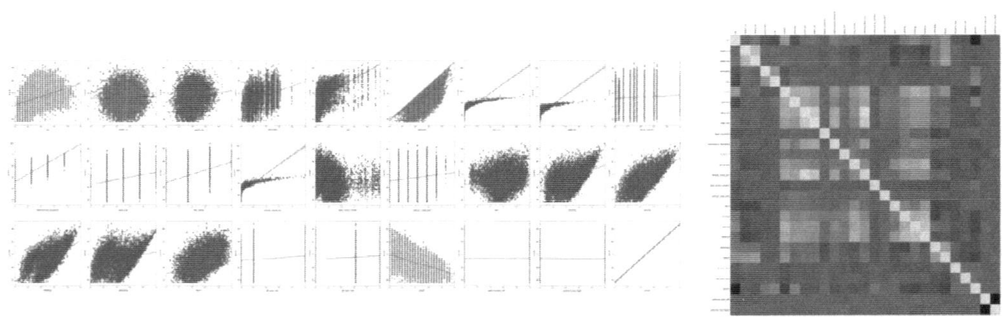

(a) (b)

Figure 1. (a) Scatterplot matrix having the target value "overall" rating of a player and (b) Pearson's correlation coefficient heatmap for the FIFA 20 complete player dataset

3. VISUALIZATION METHODOLOGY

3.1 Design

The circle wave was proposed by Dave White (Whyte, 2014) as a screen loading animation, programmed in processing. It was adapted to D3.js by Mike Bostock (Bostock, 2019) which was further extended to be used as a medium to visualize correlation in this paper. The original implementation by Bostock has three circle waves with constant amplitude. In this paper, the amplitude of each wave is computed dynamically on the basis of the degree of correlation. Each circle wave is a cosine signal revolving around a pivot, representing a variable. Multiple cosine signals are superimposed, each cosine signal having the same speed and some phase shift, depending on the number of variables to be correlated. The amplitude of each wave gives an idea about the Pearson's correlation coefficient between the variable it represents and the target variable. The amplitude is inversely proportional to the correlation coefficient. This means that higher the correlation of a field, the more its circle wave approximates an exact circle. Circle waves of different colours are used to represent different variables. The attributes having the highest correlation with the target attribute are also ranked in the legend of the visualization.

3.2 Exploring a Dataset

The proposed visualization technique is applied to explore the FIFA 20 complete player dataset (Leone, 2019). This dataset is primarily selected because it contains a comprehensive list of all currently active football players. Secondly, the dataset has a wide set of features which can be used for analysis and has almost negligible missing data. This dataset is present in a tabular form where the columns are various variables and a row represents a player. The dataset has 104 attributes for each of the 18278 players.

It was imperative that a few fields are filtered out from the dataset in order to narrow down the scope of the visualization. Majority of the fields were ratings for granular attributes like "sprint speed", "shot power" and "long pass". These fields were removed from the dataset since they had parent attributes with aggregated scores i.e. "pace", "shooting", "passing", "dribbling", "defending" and "physicality" present in the dataset. Using these parent attributes paints a better picture about the correlation between the players' intrinsic (pace, passing, skill level, etc.) and extrinsic (wage, market value, etc.) attributes. The visualization focuses only on the outfield players, leading to the omission of attributes related to goalkeeping like "diving" and "reflexes" from the dataset. A Pearson's correlation coefficient matrix is generated once the dataset has been cleaned up and all categorical data has been encoded.

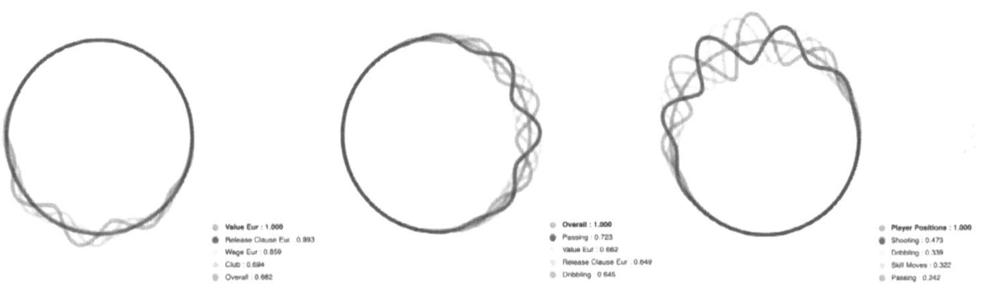

(a) (b) (c)

Figure 2. Using circle waves to show variables highly correlated with the target variables. The target variable is "Value Eur" in (a), "Overall" rating of a player in (b) and "Player Positions" in (c)

Figure 2 shows how circle waves can be utilized to view variables highly correlated with the target variable. Consider figure 2(a), the target value is "value eur", and the highest correlated variables are "release clause eur", "wage eur", "club" and "overall". This makes sense as a player's value, logically, should be highly correlated with their wages, the club they play for and their release clause. The variable "release clause eur" has the highest correlation coefficient, 0.993 and the circle wave associated with it is hardly differentiable from the circumference itself. In contrast, consider figure 2(c), the target variable is "player positions" and the highest correlated variable is "shooting" having a correlation coefficient of 0.473. The circle wave associated is far away from the circumference. The circle wave associated with the field "passing" is further away since it has a correlation coefficient of 0.242.

4. CONCLUSION

This paper introduces a novel visualization technique to examine multivariate correlation and demonstrates its application on the FIFA 20 complete player dataset. To the best of my knowledge, idioms used to visualize correlation have been limited to solar correlation maps, scatterplots, heatmaps and their variations. Using circle waves to visualize correlation tasks is the novel concept presented in this paper.

The viewer can intuitively understand the magnitude of correlation between different attributes since it utilizes their subconscious perception of visual harmony. Highly correlated attributes will have a neat and orderly visualization whereas attributes having low correlation will lead to a chaotic visualization. This visualization provides a clean depiction of the correlation task and does not overload the viewer with a profusion of information. However, the visualization is restricted to correlating a limited number of attributes for it to remain elegant. Additionally, despite being a novel concept, the visualization can solely be used for very specific tasks where the analysis requires multiple target variables to be investigated and a high-level intuition about the correlation magnitude is enough.

This paper lays the groundwork for applying circle waves to visualize correlation tasks. The future work includes testing the technique with different datasets and evaluating its efficacy with a user study. Furthermore, this visualization idiom can be extended to include multiple encoding channels. For example, wave specific features like the stroke width, speed, phase shift and radius of movement can also be utilized to encode information in the visualization. The visualization can be extended to the third dimension, thus achieving another level of information encoding. Extending this visualization to be projected in an augmented reality environment seems achievable as well. With the advancements in technology, applications of the proposed visualization technique's potential know no bounds.

REFERENCES

Blum, A.L. and Langley, P. (1997). Selection of relevant features and examples in machine learning. *Artificial Intelligence*, [online] 97(1–2), pp.245–271. Available at: https://www.science direct.com/science/article/pii/S0004370297000635.

Bostock, M. (2019). *Circle Wave*. [online] observablehq.com. Available at: https://observablehq.com/@mbostock/circle-wave.

Cawthon, N. and Moere, A.V. (2007). The Effect of Aesthetic on the Usability of Data Visualization. *2007 11th International Conference Information Visualization (IV '07)*.

Friendly, M. (2002). Corrgrams. *The American Statistician*, 56(4), pp.316–324.

Horvath, S. and Dong, J. (2008). Geometric Interpretation of Gene Coexpression Network Analysis. *PLoS Computational Biology*, 4(8), p.e1000117.

Leone, S. (2019). *FIFA 20 complete player dataset*. [online] kaggle.com. Available at: https://www.kaggle.com/stefanoleone992/fifa-20-complete-player-dataset#players_20.csv.

Rensink, R.A. and Baldridge, G. (2010). The Perception of Correlation in Scatterplots. *Computer Graphics Forum*, 29(3), pp.1203–1210.

Robertson, G., et al. (2008). Effectiveness of Animation in Trend Visualization. *IEEE Transactions on Visualization and Computer Graphics*, 14(6), pp.1325–1332.

Whyte, D. (2014). *Circle wave II*. [online] dribbble.com. Available at: https://dribbble.com/shots/1698964-Circle-wave-II.

Wilkinson, L. and Friendly, M. (2009). The History of the Cluster Heat Map. *The American Statistician*, 63(2), pp.179–184.

Wong, B. (2010). Color coding. *Nature Methods*, [online] 7(8), pp.573–573. Available at: https://www.nature.com/articles/nmeth0810-573.

Zapf, S. and Kraushaar, C. (2017). *A new visualization to beautifully explore correlations*. [online] O'Reilly Media. Available at: https://www.oreilly.com/content/a-new-visualization-to-beautifully-explore-correlations [Accessed 26 May 2020].

KNOWLEDGE DISCOVERY AND FRAMEWORK FOR PURCHASE BEHAVIOR ANALYSIS IN MOBILE GAMING APPLICATIONS

Martins Jansevskis and Kaspars Osis
Faculty of Engineering, Vidzeme University of Applied Sciences, Valmiera, Latvia

ABSTRACT

The gaming industry is a fast expanding industry with a large global market and is projected to hit $300 billion by 2025. The total number of players in 2019 was projected to hit 2.4 billion (Taylor, 2019). Knowledge discovery is achieved by collecting and analyzing data from within the gaming applications. The data collected is used to understand players, gain insights and to improve products for the gaming community based on feedback and user interaction. And as a result, obtained knowledge contributes to monetization in a way that is especially interesting in the e-sports and streaming space. Machine learning is one of the technologies that can assist in knowledge discovery as it provides potential to obtain insights into previously overlooked data. This paper provides insight in a work of how machine learning algorithms are applied to gain behavior understanding whithin mobile gaming applications in a way compliant with European General Data Protection Regulation (GDPR). The paper is a part of a larger research work and contributes to the domain of knowledge discovery within in-app purchase behavior data and serves as a step towards further research in this area.

KEYWORDS

Knowledge Discovery, Data Analysis, GDPR, Mobile Gaming Applications

1. INTRODUCTION

In mobile games usually exists an imbalance between players that spend money and those who do not. The vast majority of players are the ones that do not. One of the key challenges in mobile games is to convert players from non-spending to spending, and by doing so ensuring that the lifetime value (LTV) of players is higher than the User Acquisition Cost (UAC) (Sifa et al., 2015). To increase LTV and lower UAC, knowledge discovery by collecting and analyzing data from within the game in a manner that would be compliant with the European General Data Protection Regulation (GDPR) has to be implemented in a way that would satisfy players. The goal of the knowledge discovery process for this research is to determine if existing players or devices would ever become a paying customers and what behavioral incentives increase LTV.

In accordance to address the defined challenges, authors defined three main tasks – determine and define the potential data set that can be collected without violating GDPR, develop mobile packages to integrate into existing games, collect data to carry out analysis and apply machine learning (ML) algorithms. In the process authors were adopting methods that rely on publicly available ML algorithms, to keep results relevant for the gaming industry. The proposed framework is based on prior research in the field of knowledge discovery using machine learning (Jansevskis and Osis, 2018) and applies the previously introduced approach for potential business use. The results presented are the preparatory steps in providing a potential solution for determining if a player will contribute to a company's revenue streams.

2. DEVELOPMENT PROCESS

As initially defined, knowledge discovery in this research resolves around predicting if existing players will become paying customers. To carry out this research with long term goals authors have chosen to develop a framework that would accumulate data, provide mobile packages and integrate in existing mobile gaming applications as well as develop machine learning solutions to further carry out the learning process.

2.1 Dataset

The research included determining potential datasets that could be used for developing the ML algorithms. Authors based their assumptions on similar researches (Sifa et al., 2015) (Han and Windsor, 2013) (Pantano and Priporas, 2016) (Xudong et al., 2016) and potentially available data from within the game. Authors chose to collect data of player's behavior in the following categories: sessions, product views, and purchases. The session is being registered when a player launches the game with the included author's developed package. The product view is being registered when a player's mobile device requests product data from mobile packages. The purchase is registered when a player spends money on in-game merchandise and creates an order. To make this research repeatable in the long term, authors chose to connect mobile packages with an online store and provide different products for purchasing. The items added to the online store and on sale are t-shirts, socks, gift-cards and 3D figurines with custom made designs for a specific game. Table. 1 lists dataset authors were including in mobile packages.

Table 1. Defined metrics dataset for behavior analysis

Category	Type	Example
Device data	**Device**	iPhone10.6
	OS version	9,1
	Region	en_US
	Apple/Google Pay status	Active
Game data	**Category**	Puzzle
	Publisher	Blizzard
	Total number of players	1224
Design	**Date of install**	2020-02-20
	Date of update	2020-02-20
	Trigger	t-shirt
User	**Game time**	455
	Last session	2020-02-20
	Session time	707
	Start of session	2020-02-20
	End of session	20:20:06.56554+02
	Time until first product view	45
Encounters	**Dismissal clicks**	3
	Number of dismissals	45
	Dismissal ratio	1
Purchase behavior	**Spending amount**	6,52
	Number of purchases	1
	Currency	USD
Customer	**City**	Atlanta
	State	Georgia
	Country	US
	Product	t-shirt

The defined dataset for mobile packages had to be GDPR (General Data Protection Regulation (GDPR), 2020) compliant and must not include personal information. Since real purchases are being made and the order fulfillment process has to be carried out it is required to collect personal data. To accomplish GDPR compliance authors were using an online store from the Shopify platform (Shopify, 2020) and does not include data with the player's name, age, gender and detailed address in the dataset for analysis.

2.2 Proof of Concept Algorithm Development

The development process of potential purchase behavior algorithms included data pre-processing, outliers` removal, category variables encoding and variable normalization. The main task at this phase was removing features without enough data, removing features with constant values and removing features that can be only calculated after purchase has been made. Feature engineering was applied to derive new features from the historical data of player's interactions with a game. A skewed distribution towards non-paying behavior was expected as from data it was known that only a small amount of players are the paying customers (Sifa et al., 2015). To solve the problem of imbalanced datasets, it was possible for testing purposes to synthetically generate paying players following Synthetic Minority Over-sampling Technique-Nominal Continuous (SMOTE-NC) method (Chawla et al., 2002). The correlation analysis on the dataset was applied to evaluate which features were relevant to improve player engagement in the game (an increase of LTV). Feature selection techniques were used to limit the number of features by selecting only the important ones.

For evaluation the F-Score (F1-Measure) (DeepAI, 2020) the harmonic mean over the precision and recall values for predicting the paying players was used. Additionally, the geometric mean of the classification accuracy values for each of the classes (G-mean) (DeepAI, 2020) was also applied. For the baseline solution the following models have been chosen for training:

- decision trees with reduced error pruning;
- support vector machines with polynomial and radial basis function kernels;
- random forests by selecting the square root of number of possible features.

Of particular interest in the process was to determine the features that have a significant impact on predicting if player will be a paying customer.

Exists two main approaches of collaborative filtering which recommend products based on history and content-based, which is based on product descriptions and how they match with the player's profile. The advantage of the first solution is described in details with matching products to customers (Candellier et al., 2009), the main disadvantage is that the player has to have historical data.

Collaborative filtering does have a higher accuracy and is being developed based on deep learning methods (Chen, Lin, and Pan, 2017). This approach faces another challenge - the problem of scalability. New models on top of costly methods used in collaborative filtering introduced the time cost of using neural networks. The solution to this challenge with new methods of sampling was presented in research (Chen, Lin, and Pan, 2017). In the work of Weia et al. (2017) an approach of solving cold start (players without historical data) challenge has been proposed.

Based on research papers the baseline solution was developed on item-item collaborative filtering. In this phase product is a content triggered by a developed SDK. Purchasing products is a desired interaction with the given player.

2.3 Technology Framework

In process of planning and designing the framework for purchase behavior analysis authors carried out mobile gaming market analysis to determine potential technology stack that would cover the most common technologies used for mobile games (MarketWatch, 2020). Figure 1 shows the initial framework proposed by authors to implement player purchase behavior analysis. Proposed technology framework roots in the earlier research work done in the field of knowledge discovery and further elaborates previously proposed technological stack solutions framework (Jansevskis and Osis, 2018). The framework consists of five components that support data gathering and is designed around central data storage that is being accessed through application programming interface (API).

Data storage in the proposed framework provides functionality such as data continuity, integrity, and availability as those considerations have to be taken into account. The primary task of a cloud storage facility is to deliver data for connected mobile packages. As there are significant volumes of data produced by mobile games and player`s devices the main task was to choose solutions that can be easily extended and scaled.

Security considerations and role-based access controls (RBAC) had to be implemented between all of the components of the frameworks. To cover user privileges requirements authors propose to use OAuth 2.0 (Oauth.net, 2020) industry-standard protocols for every connected mobile software development kit (SDK) and limit access to read-only scopes for public API access. To cover data security considerations authors were using building security in the maturity model (BSIMM) (Bsimm.com, 2020).

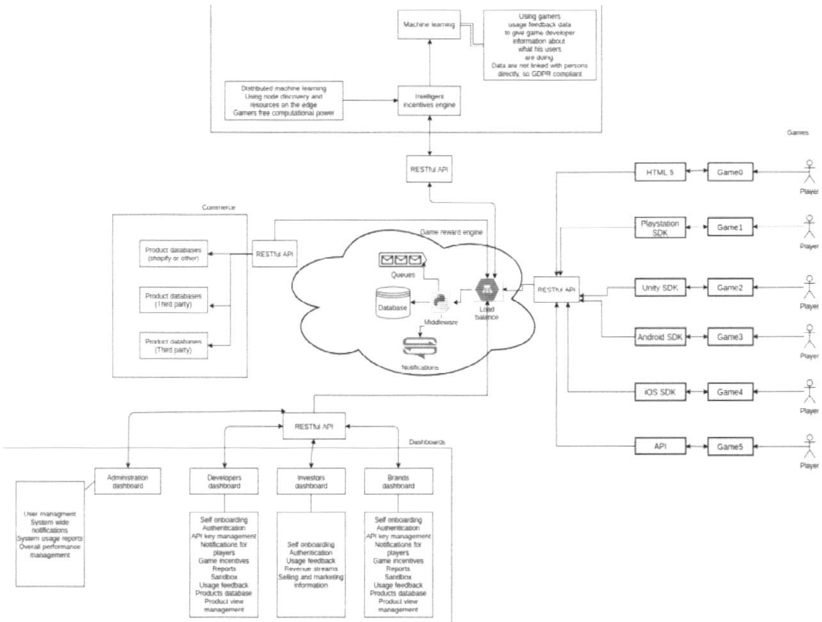

Figure 1. Proposed technology framework for purchase behavior analysis in mobile gaming applications

As data has to be collected from within the mobile gaming applications, SDKs for most common platforms have to be developed and connected to public API. In framework development process authors were including Android, iOS and Unity platforms. As in-app purchases data had to be collected authors were using Apple Pay (Apple, 2020), Google Pay (Pay.google.com, 2020) and Stripe (Stripe.com, 2020) integrations for mobile platforms.

2.4 Algorithm Results

To test the developed algorithm a dataset had to be prepared based on initially defined available metrics. The primary key in available data was device identifier that identifies a unique device. Based on device identifier information about purchases from stores was extracted and used as a target variable for learning task. In the preprocessing stage a subset of data was prepared using data from two-week time span and a dataset with more than 50 thousand records containing about 500 monetized devices. Learning models were tested using balancing. That was necessary because dataset contained a high imbalance as only approximately 1% of devices were monetized.

Two approaches of balancing were applied - SMOTE_NC and Random OverSampling. Following classification models were used: Dummy Classifier, AdaBoost Classifier, Logistic Regression and Random Forest Classifier. The AdaBoost Classifier model with Random OverSampling balancing method provided the most promising results with accuracy 0.854158. For this model 85.03% of true negatives and 0.39% of true positives were returned. This indicated that approximately 50% of monetized devices were correctly recognized, while just a small percentage of non-monetized were falsely recognized.

3. CONCLUSION

In this paper, a framework is being described that aims to gather in-game purchase data and described the ML algorithms development process to further analyze player's behavior to determine if one is going to become a paying customer. The described framework and its related mobile SDKs have been implemented in three existing games. The ML algorithms have been applied to collected data and further research has to be carried out to determine if applied techniques and chosen algorithms hold business value.

To advance the development of the research, it is necessary to apply framework to a larger set of mobile games and carry out further research on ML algorithms and player purchase behavior analysis. The most important and challenging task is the attempt to onboard mobile game developers and publishers to apply this framework.

REFERENCES

Apple. (2020). Apple Pay. [online] Available at: https://www.apple.com/apple-pay/ [Accessed 16 Feb. 2020].

Bsimm.com. (2020). Building Security In Maturity Model | BSIMM. [online] Available at: https://www.bsimm.com/ [Accessed 15 Feb. 2020].

Chawla, N., Bowyer, K., Hall, L. and Kegelmeyer, W. (2002). SMOTE: Synthetic Minority Over-sampling Technique. Journal of Artificial Intelligence Research, 16, pp.321-357.

Candiller, L., Jack, K., Fessant, F., i Meyer, F. (2009). State of the Art Recommender System. DOI: 10.4018/978-1-60566-306-7.ch001.

Chen, L., Lin, M. and Pan, Y. (2017). Find crucial factors of in-game purchase using neural networks. 2017 IEEE 8th International Conference on Awareness Science and Technology (iCAST), [online] pp.334-338. Available at: https://ieeexplore.ieee.org/document/8256473 [Accessed 20 Feb. 2020].

DeepAI. (2020). F-Score. [online] Available at: https://deepai.org/machine-learning-glossary-and-terms/f-score [Accessed 20 Feb. 2020].

General Data Protection Regulation (GDPR). (2020). General Data Protection Regulation (GDPR) – Official Legal Text. [online] Available at: https://gdpr-info.eu/ [Accessed 10 Jan. 2020].

Han, B. and Windsor, J. (2013). An investigation of the smartphone user's in-game purchase intention. International Journal of Mobile Communications, 11(6), p.617.

Jansevskis, M. and Osis, K., 2018. Machine Learning and on 5G Based Technologies Create New Opportunities to Gain Knowledge. 2018 2nd European Conference on Electrical Engineering and Computer Science (EECS).

MarketWatch. (2020). Mobile Gaming Market 2019 Global Industry Analysis, Emerging Technology, Sales Revenue, Competitive Landscape, Emerging Technologies, Gross Margin Regional Forecast To 2023. [online] Available at: https://www.marketwatch.com/press-release/mobile-gaming-market-2019-global-industry-analysis-emerging-technology-sales-revenue-competitive-landscape-emerging-technologies-gross-margin-regional-forecast-to-2023-2019-05-09 [Accessed 10 Feb. 2020].

Oauth.net. (2020). OAuth 2.0 — OAuth. [online] Available at: https://oauth.net/2/ [Accessed 5 Feb. 2020].

Pantano, E. and Priporas, C. (2016). The effect of mobile retailing on consumers' purchasing experiences: A dynamic perspective. Computers in Human Behavior, [online] 61, pp.548-555. Available at: https://www.sciencedirect.com/science/article/pii/S0747563216302448?via%3Dihub [Accessed 20 Feb. 2020].

Pay.google.com. (2020). Google Pay (UK) – Pay in apps, on the web, and in stores. [online] Available at: https://pay.google.com/about/ [Accessed 16 Feb. 2020].

Sifa, R., Hadiji, F., Runge, J., Drachen, A., Kersting, K., Bauckhage, K (2015). Predicting Purchase Decisions in Mobile Free-to-Play Games. Proceedings, The Eleventh AAAI Conference on Artificial Intelligence and Interactive Digital Entertainment (AIIDE-15), [online] pp.79-85. Available at: https://pdfs.semanticscholar.org/9801/b69ac1faaffafecfea250ec65a5ac33cd8af.pdf [Accessed 20 Feb. 2020].

Shopify. (2020). Start, grow, and scale your business - Shopify. [online] Available at: https://www.shopify.com/ [Accessed 25 Feb. 2020].

Stripe.com. (2020). Stripe Payments: A complete payments platform, engineered for growth. [online] Available at: https://stripe.com/en-my/payments [Accessed 17 Feb. 2020].

Taylor, M. (2019). 'The Most Exciting Tech Niche For 2020'. [online] Bloomberg. Available at: https://www.bloomberg.com/press-releases/2019-12-30/the-most-exciting-tech-niche-for-2020 [Accessed 20 Feb. 2020].

Wei, J., He, J., Chen, K., Zhou, Y., Tang, Z. (2017). Collaborative filtering and deep learning based recommendation system for cold start items. DOI: 10.1016/j.eswa.2016.09.040

Xudong, L., Meijiao, G., Kangqing, L. and Zhiwei, Q. (2016). Analyzing the influencing factors of mobile game consumption. 2016 13th International Conference on Service Systems and Service Management (ICSSSM), pp.1-6.

APPLICATIONS OF SARS-COV-2 SEQUENCING DATA

Cláudia Oliveira da Silva[1], Tatiana Donai Lopes[1] and Brígida Mónica Faria[1,2]
[1]*Escola Superior de Saúde - Politécnico do Porto (ESS-P.Porto), Portugal*
[2]*Laboratório de Inteligência Artificial e Ciência de Computadores (LIACC), Portugal*

ABSTRACT

Monitoring and understanding pathogen epidemiology and evolution is crucial, especially during an outbreak. COVID-19 pandemic, caused by the newly identified virus SARS-CoV-2, is one of the current major challenges that require the best scientific and technological means. Secondary to sequencing, one of the most basic steps in the study of the many virus strains is sequence alignment. In this work, the focus was on the search and selection of a Biopython algorithm of global pairwise sequence alignment, its implementation and analysis of effectiveness and complexity. To apply this algorithm, which provides the level of similarity between sequences, it was used SARS-CoV-2 genomic sequences of samples collected in 10 countries to analyse its similarity with the reference sequence (NC_045512). There were obtained very high similarities between all sequences and it was observed a decrease of similarity over time in most of the countries included in this study. These results are concordant with recent ones that are publicly shared. In this context, the algorithm performed effectively and its low complexity will not limit its application in a bigger volume of data.

KEYWORDS

SARS-CoV-2, Pairwise Alignment, Similarity, Biopython

1. INTRODUCTION

Declared as a global public health emergency, on 11th March 2020, by the World Health Organization, COVID-19 pandemic is one of the major human challenges of current time. This viral respiratory illness is caused by a new Coronavirus called SARS-CoV-2 (Phan 2020). Previously unknown, this is a Betacoronavirus discovered using sequencing in samples from patients with pneumonia. Phylogenetically, this novel virus forms a clade within the subgenus Sarbecovirus, Orthocoronavirinae subfamily and it is the seventh member of the family of coronaviruses that infect humans (Zhu, Zhang *et al.* 2020).

So far, epidemiological investigations have suggested that the outbreak is related to a seafood market in Wuhan, China (Wu, Zhao *et al.* 2020). The first virus genomes and associated data were publicly shared via GISAID© (https://www.gisaid.org/) on 10th January 2020. It is crucial to monitor and understand pathogen epidemiology and evolution, specially during an outbreak. Rapid methods that can aid in the analysis, interpretation and dissemination of results are fundamental as sequencing is becoming faster and its costs are continually dropping (Hadfield, Megill *et al.* 2018). Sequence alignment is essential to study protein structures, to establish phylogenetic relations and inference of molecular evolution. The computational tools are extremely necessary to achieve accurate and faster results. Pairwise sequence alignment is one of the fundamental means in bioinformatics to assess the degree of similarity as well as to find differences, that may indicate functional, structural or evolutionary relations between two biological sequences (Muhire, Varsani *et al.* 2014). This tool forms the basis of many database search programs, such as BLAST.

In what concerns global sequence alignments, solutions have been proposed in the past to find the optimal global alignment between two sequences (that comprehends the total length of the sequences) by applying the concept of dynamic programming – for global alignment, the original algorithm is defined as Needleman–Wunsch by the names of the authors who first proposed it: Needleman and Wunsch, 1970 (Baichoo and Ouzounis 2017). Many bioinformatic tools use Python language. Python is a high-level programming language and available in open source. The Biopython project is a mature international collaboration of volunteer developers, providing Python libraries for a wide range of bioinformatic problems. Biopython includes a set of tools written in Python, which are used for read and writing different sequence file formats and multiple sequence alignments, among other features. It is freely available for all the major operating systems with documentation and source code (https://biopython.org) under the Biopython license (Cock, Antao *et al.* 2009).

Concerning the similarity data, recent studies show equivalent results for the similarity between SARS-CoV-2 sequences. Wang *et al* obtained a similarity of 99,99% (99,91%-100%) at the nucleotide level, among viral strains from different countries (China, America, Australia, Thailand, The United Kingdom, Germany, France, Finland, Korea, Singapore and others). These sequences were retrieved until 14th February (Wang, Liu *et al.* 2020). Li *et al* studied the similarities between 194 COVID-19 strains from 21 countries had obtained an average similarity between any comparison of two sequences of 0.995561/0.995342. It was also determined the average percentage similarities between sequences of the viral strains across samples collected from different months, and although the overall similarity of the human strains was high, it was observed a reduction of similarity in later months, indicating that mutations within the human population are occurring. In December 2019, the similarity was on average 0.999054, corresponding to an average of 29,75 different nucleotides. In March 2020, this similarity had dropped to 0,988468, corresponding to an average of 348,33 different nucleotides. These differences show evolutional changes of the virus, which might imply attenuated or even more virulent strains (Li, Liu *et al.* 2020). The work of Randhawa *et al* also achieved over 99% sequence similarity within the virus sequences, validating their common lineage and source (Randhawa, Soltysiak *et al.* 2020).

This work consisted of the search and selection of a Biopython algorithm, its implementation and analysis of its effectiveness and complexity. It was chosen a pairwise sequence alignment algorithm which performs a global alignment. Applying the algorithm, forward described, provides the level of similarity between sequences, were used SARS-CoV-2 genomic sequences of samples collected in 10 countries to analyse its similarity with the reference sequence. The main goal of this study was to apply an alignment bioinformatic tool to check its effectiveness by comparing its results with the ones that are being achieved and publicly shared.

2. METHODS

2.1 Data

To obtain the sequences for alignment, DNA-seq data of SARS-CoV-2 was collected from GISAID (the sequences were downloaded in FASTA format). There were used 20 complete genome sequences from SARS-CoV-2 virus, 2 per each country. The sequences were chosen based on collection data, the first sequence representing the earliest sequencing of SARS-CoV-2 in each country, and the second constituting the last sequencing published at the time of the study (8th of June). The reference sequence (being a comparation method that will be explained later in the paper) was taken from NCBI (https://ncbi.nlm.nih.gov) (Table 1). Sequences that presented stretches of NNNs were excluded. There were included 10 countries in 6 continents: China, Thailand, India, Russia, Italy, Portugal, South Africa, United States of America, Brazil and Australia, represented by white squares in Figure 1. The choice of these countries is related to two inclusion criteria: having representation from all over the world, including at least one country for each continent, and the number of cases in these countries relatively high.

Table 1. Summary of the countries studied with Accession ID from GISAID and Collection Date

Country	Accession ID	Collection date	Country	Accession ID	Collection date
Portugal	1st- EPI_ISL_413647	01/03/2020	EUA	1st-EPI_ISL_404895	19/01/2020
	2nd-EPI_ISL_454272	02/05/2020		2nd-EPI_ISL_461476	30/05/2020
China	1st-EPI_ISL_402119	20/12/2019	India	1st-EPI_ISL_413522	27/01/2020
	2nd-EPI_ISL_444969	16/04/2020		2nd-EPI_ISL_461506	27/05/2020
South Africa	1st-EPI_ISL_417186	07/03/2020	Italy	1st-EPI_ISL_412974	29/01/2020
	2nd-EPI_ISL_455635	05/05/2020		2nd-EPI_ISL_436732	27/04/2020
Brazil	1st-EPI_ISL_413016	28/02/2020	Russia	1st-EPI_ISL_460096	02/03/2020
	2nd-EPI_ISL_458149	06/04/2020		2nd-EPI_ISL_450291	23/04/2020
Australia	1st-EPI_ISL_407893	24/01/2020	Thailand	1st-EPI_ISL_403962	08/01/2020
	2nd-EPI_ISL_456649	27/05/2020		2nd-EPI_ISL_447026	03/04/2020
Reference	**NC_045512**	**30/03/2020**			

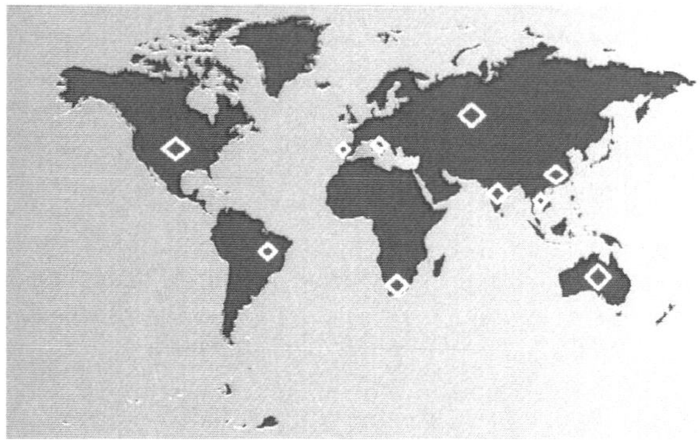

Figure 1. Representation of the geographic location of the countries of origin of the studied sequenced samples

The studied sequences were collected from patients diagnosed with COVID-19. Samples were taken from 20 patients, 8 women, 7 man and 5 unknowns, with a mean age of 48,6±21,74.

2.2 Sequence Alignment Algorithm

To align and compare the sequences of this study, an algorithm in Python was adapted from Nagesh Singh Chauhan (https://github.com/nageshsinghc4/COVID-19-coronavirus). The code was assembled based on the module defined as *pairwise2*. This module provides functions to get global and local alignments between two sequences, with the main goal of knowing the percentage of similarity between two sequences. The *Bio.SeqIO* module provides a simple interface for read and writing biological sequence files in various formats. Regardless of the file format, the information is held as *SeqRecord* objects (Cock, Antao et al. 2009).

In this study, the CPU time was measured in different points in the source code, with the aim of knowing how much CPU time was used to perform instructions. The computational equipment used was *HP Pavilion Laptop 15- cw0xx*. The implemented code is partially displayed in Figure 2, where it was named the *pairwise2* instruction as "*alghorithmSARS_COV*". The "first.seq" represents the first sequencing from each country, and "last.seq" the last sequencing.

```
alghoritmSARS_COV = pairwise2.align.globalxx(first.seq, last.seq, one_alignment_only=True,
score_only=True)
print('SARS/COV Similarity (%):', alghoritmSARS_COV / len(ref.seq) * 100)
```

Figure 2. Fragment of the implemented algorithm of the *pairwise2* module

This work was divided in two parts. In the first part, the last and first sequencing were compared to find the percentage of similarity between them; in the second part, the reference sequence was compared with the first and last sequencing from each country.

3. RESULTS AND DISCUSSION

In the first part of this work, the algorithm was executed for the two sequences from each country (first/last). The output of the code gave information about the percentage of similarity between the tested sequences. For all 10 countries the percentage of similarity was above 99%, as presented on Table 2.

Table 2. Summary data of the length and % of similarity of the first and last sequencing from each country

Country	Sequence length (nucleotides)	% of similarity	Country	Sequence length (nucleotides)	% of similarity
Portugal	1st- 29 903 2nd- 29 763	99,49%	EUA	1st- 29 882 2nd- 29 891	99,83%
China	1st- 29 891 2nd- 29 882	99,95%	India	1st- 29 854 2nd- 29 903	99,87%
South Africa	1st- 29 903 2nd- 29 903	99,55%	Italy	1st- 29 903 2nd- 29 874	99,78%
Brazil	1st- 29 890 2nd- 29 903	99,53%	Russia	1st- 29 543 2nd- 29 903	99,97%
Australia	1st- 29 782 2nd- 29 903	99,31%	Thailand	1st- 29 848 2nd- 29 782	99,01%

In the second part of the task, the compared sequences were the reference sequence from SARS-CoV-2 and the first (ref/first) and last (ref/last) sequence from each country. As seen on Table 3, all the similarity percentages presented values above 98%. The average percentage of similarity between the reference sequence and first sequencing from each country was 99,89% ±0,0016. The average percentage of similarity between the reference sequence and last sequencing from each country was 99,59% ±0,0039.

Table 3. Summary data of the % of similarity of the first/last sequencing from each country with the reference sequence

Country	% of similarity (ref/first)	% of similarity (ref/last)
Portugal	99,91%	99,49%
China	100,00%	99,91%
South Africa	99,90%	99,49%
Brazil	99,58%	99,95%
Australia	99,58%	98,98%
EUA	99,99%	99,84%
India	99,98%	99,74%
Italy	99,99%	99,79%
Russia	99,97%	99,90%
Thailand	100,00%	98,83%

Statistical differences were calculated for the means displayed above. According to Shapiro-Wilk test, the normality was assumed ($p > 0{,}05$). The t-student test for paired samples was performed. The differences between the mean of ref/first and ref/last were statistically significative ($p=0{,}044<0{,}05$), for the differences between the mean of first/last and ref/last, were not statistically significative ($p=0{,}557>0{,}05$), what can be justified by the fact that the first sequences from some countries were coincident or close in time to the reference sequence. Finally, the differences between the mean of ref/first and first/last, were statistically significative ($p=0{,}019<0{,}05$). Except for Brazil and Australia results, in general, the similarities decreased over time, between the first and last sequences analysed in this work. This decrease may imply that are occurring evolutional changes of the virus, as supported by recent publicly shared results (Li, Liu *et al.* 2020, Randhawa, Soltysiak *et al.* 2020, Wang, Liu *et al.* 2020). These results were expected, since all the similarities values are analogous to those that are being achieved by the previously referenced works, therefore the algorithm applied in this study was considered effective. For this paper, the CPU time was measured for the function of the alignment (pairwise2.align.globalxx). Ten trials were made in order to get an average (Table 4). The average CPU time for the mentioned function was 23,76±0,72.

Table 4. CPU times of each try

Trial	CPU time	Trial	CPU time
1	23,95	6	22,92
2	24,18	7	23,29
3	24,90	8	24,79
4	23,63	9	23,71
5	22,66	10	23,62

The algorithm performed with high efficiency, so its application in bigger volume of data will not be compromised.

4. CONCLUSION

In conclusion, with the time passing, the percentage of similarities between the studied sequences have been decreasing, however this was not verified in all the comparisons and countries. It can also be apprehended that SARS-CoV-2 is a virus with a relatively low mutation rate, being a great advantage for a therapeutic solution. Summing up, the pairwise alignment algorithm that was used in this project was effective and showed high efficiency, which indicates advantages in its application. Regardless of these features, in a pandemic context, the availability of even faster methodology, as machine learning methods can be very useful.

In future work, it would be valuable to extend the application of the algorithm to further collection dates and to other countries data, to verify if the sequence similarities would maintain equivalent to other published results. To implement and analyse another algorithm with this data, would also be interesting for comparison and eventually give some inputs to optimization and integration in programs that are already being applied.

ACKNOWLEDGEMENT

Authors would like to acknowledge Escola Superior de Saúde – P.Porto and LIACC. This research was partially supported by LIACC (FCT/UID/CEC/0027/2020).

REFERENCES

Baichoo, S. and C. A. Ouzounis (2017). *Computational complexity of algorithms for sequence comparison, short-read assembly and genome alignment.* Biosystems 156-157: 72-85.

Cock, P. J. A., T. Antao, J. T. Chang, B. A. Chapman, C. J. Cox, A. Dalke, I. Friedberg, T. Hamelryck, F. Kauff, B. Wilczynski and M. J. L. de Hoon (2009). *Biopython: freely available Python tools for computational molecular biology and bioinformatics.* Bioinformatics 25(11): 1422-1423.

Hadfield, J., C. Megill, S. M. Bell, J. Huddleston, B. Potter, C. Callender, P. Sagulenko, T. Bedford and R. A. Neher (2018). *Nextstrain: real-time tracking of pathogen evolution.* Bioinformatics 34(23): 4121-4123.

Li, Y., B. Liu, J. Cui, Z. Wang, Y. Shen, Y. Xu and K. Yao (2020). *Similarities and Evolutionary Relationships of COVID-19 and Related Viruses*. Available at: https://arxiv.org/abs/2003.05580

Muhire, B. M., A. Varsani and D. P. Martin (2014). *SDT: a virus classification tool based on pairwise sequence alignment and identity calculation.* PloS one 9(9): e108277-e108277.

Phan, T. (2020). *Genetic diversity and evolution of SARS-CoV-2.* Infection, genetics and evolution : journal of molecular epidemiology and evolutionary genetics in infectious diseases 81: 104260-104260.

Randhawa, G. S., M. P. M. Soltysiak, H. El Roz, C. P. E. de Souza, K. A. Hill and L. Kari (2020). *Machine learning using intrinsic genomic signatures for rapid classification of novel pathogens: COVID-19 case study.* PLoS One 15(4).

Wang, C., Z. Liu, Z. Chen, X. Huang, M. Xu, T. He and Z. Zhang (2020). *The establishment of reference sequence for SARS-CoV-2 and variation analysis.* J Med Virol.

Wu, F., S. Zhao, B. Yu, Y. Chen, W. Wang, Z.-G. Song, Y. Hu, Z.-W. Tao, J.-H. Tian, Y.-Y. Pei, M.-L. Yuan, Y.-L. Zhang, F.-H. Dai, Y. Liu, Q.-M. Wang, J.-J. Zheng, L. Xu, E. Holmes and Y.-Z. Zhang (2020). *A new coronavirus associated with human respiratory disease in China.* Nature 579: 1-8.

Zhu, N., D. Zhang, W. Wang, X. Li, B. Yang, J. Song, X. Zhao, B. Huang, W. Shi, R. Lu, P. Niu, F. Zhan, X. Ma, D. Wang, W. Xu, G. Wu, G. F. Gao and W. Tan (2020). *A Novel Coronavirus from Patients with Pneumonia in China, 2019.* N Engl J Med 382(8): 727-733.

THE INTELLIGENT SYSTEMS FOR LANGUAGE PHONETIC INTERFACES

Natalia Yanova
Altai State University, Lenina 61, Barnaul, Russia

ABSTRACT

The project aims to develop intelligent natural language analysis tools. The aim of the project is to formalize the interpretative approach in the study of perception and understanding of language interfaces. The project implements an expert system of psychophonetic analysis in the field of onomastics. The system is designed for psychological diagnostics of anthroponyms in the Russian language. The project offers a research technique for the psychophonetic study of naming in natural language. The project discusses the formalization of psychophonetic functions of the mental lexicon. The subject of the analysis is the psychological structure of phonosemantic decoding of nouns. A psychometric model is proposed for calculating the interpretation functions of the psychophonic meaning of names. The research solution includes mobile software application for IOS and Android (smart-test 'What's Name').

KEYWORDS

Natural Language Processing, Sentiment Analysis, Expert systems, Psychophonetics

1. INTRODUCTION

The development of natural language intellectual analysis systems sets the prospect of a convergence of the humanities, natural sciences and engineering. Calculation and modeling of Hidden Structure and Function in the Lexicon becomes a common subject of analysis of neurocomputer, neurocognitive and neurolinguistic approaches to language processing in living and artificial systems (Sharp at al. 2017). This is facilitated by methods of cognitive-mathematical modeling in the study of perception and understanding of a language on a computational basis. The goal is to formalize the principles and functions of interpretation in a language (Strauss at al. 2018). The measurement of interpretation functions (language comprehension / generation / ambiguity / predictability, attribution) is a prospect for semantic information processing methods. At the same time, the convergence of terms and theories in attempts to formalize the principle of interpretation is slower than methods and techniques (Suprun, Yanova & Nosov, 2015).

Cognitive and mental processes of language understanding find various technical implementations in large related areas: natural language processing (NLP), natural language understanding (NLU), knowledge representation, natural language generation (NLG). The problem of interpretation as the complexity of semantic decoding affects narrower areas of analysis: Discourse Integration (semantics of context), Pragmatic Analysis (pragmatics of experience and situation), Emotion Detection (recognition of emotions), Sentiment Analysis (analysis of text tonality), Opinion Mining (mental response), Text Mining (intellectual processing of text). The 'super-task' of such studies is to measure not so much the accuracy and errors of interpretation as the assessment of the human factor and psychology (Chen at al. 2018).

The evaluation functions of understanding and interpretation in the human language pose a challenge for finding new engineering solutions in Human Interaction and Emerging Technologies. This is evidenced by the rapid development of psychologically oriented technical tracks: Digital Human Modeling, Human-Centered Design, Emergent Properties of Human Behavior, Usability and User Experience, Ubiquitous & Affective Computing, Needs and Emotions for Intelligent Systems. Among the tools of language analysis with 'psychological calculations': test expert systems, semantic modeling systems, recognition and decoding systems, dialog systems. Modern smart-applications combine and expand their capabilities.

The engineering development of such systems takes into account human psychology (Andina et al. 2015). Increasingly, the question is being raised about modeling the emotional processes of cognition (intentional and evaluative). From word-based computing, we are moving to computing of perceptions, goals, intentions, emotions, attitudes. This is the area of 'language personality' psychodiagnostics. Psychodiagnostics and psychometrics in the cognitive digital revolution are becoming part of the information, cognitive and neurotechnologies. Intelligent systems in everyday life become mental assistants. Today they provide access not only to information (Data analysis) and knowledge (Data mining), but also to cognition (Opinion mining). Such expert systems developed on the basis of the Theory of Mind (Wellman & Liu, 2004) in psycholinguistics proves the differences between verbal and mental lexicon as they measure not only the external meanings of a word, but also internal ones (mental representation).

2. METHODOLOGY AND METHOD

This project presents an expert system for the psychological analysis of onomastics of the Russian language. The goal is to analyze the perception of sound nomination in natural language. The system implements the 'Opinion mining' data format with an extended class of tasks, 'Emotion Detection' and 'Sentiment analysis'.

The field of such research belongs to psychophonetics that connects the psychology of perception with the phonology and phonetics of language. The perceptual side of speech sounding is the essence of psychophonetic analysis. In this method, an attempt is made to combine phonemic and semantic features of the language implementation in speech. We study 'psychophonetic of language and 'phonosemantic of speech'. The method includes the diagnosis of the euphony of the phonemes and allophones sounding. If a phoneme is a language abstraction, then an allophone is a specific implementation of a phoneme. A native speaker can always determine a mentally significant set of allophones in the implementation of phonemes. We investigate the psychology of phoneme perception in allophone types (basic, combinatorial, positional) to predict the evaluation of the lexicon sounding in a particular mentality. The totality of all possible phoneme allophones in a language is called distribution, and their evaluation and interpretation is called attribution.

The search for stable sound combinations of phonemes is of great interest to linguists, starting with Charles Osgood and his method of semantic differential. His idea of psychophonetic meaning indicates a motivated connection between sound and semantics and explains the effects of sound image and sound symbolism of language in speech. The psychophonetics of the name has linguistic boundaries, since languages have different phonemic inventory and different phoneme distribution and attribution of allophones. For this reason, the psychology of naming makes sense only for the native language and is relevant with borrowed words. Our project explores the mental perception of proper names (both native and foreign) in Russian. The object of psychophonetic analysis in onomastics is the phonosemantic code of the name. The research question concerns the decoding function of psychophonic meaning. The structure of denotate, designate and connotate is considered. The objective of the study is to evaluate the psychology of sounding a name in a mental lexicon. The research method is psychodiagnostics of anthroponyms (proper names). The engineering solution is a mobile application (smart test). Let's consider the design of the test to evaluate the perception of the person's name in the Russian language.

3. TECHNOLOGY AND APPLICATION

Our application is based on computing with names and intended for the psychological analysis of the consonance of the name/patronymic/surname. The application combines both a test function and a decoder function for naming. The mobile application includes versions for IOS and Android (Tools SNY Research Group). Instruction manual for user is: 'Have you ever tried to come up with a name that chimes with your chosen audience?'Smart-test allows you to get the access code to the enigma of painting a picture with a name in your mind. Mobile application test any name to ascertain the perception of its sound in Russian choosing the right combination of first name-surname, first name-patronymic or surname-first name- patronymic, and thus create new forms of names and forms of address. This is usability of applied linguistics in everyday life. Takes a step from discovery into the science of puzzles – what to call a child, how to choose an iconic slogan, what form of address is preferable. You come up with the questions - the program comes up with the answers. Simply say or write down a name and obtain its unique underlying code and thus an insight into its frequency interpretation.

The result of test is a phonosemantic code for the name and a psychophonic profile for a specific variant of naming. The test provides a quantitative and qualitative assessment of the interpretation of the name, taking into account socio-cultural and mental stereotypes. Assessing the likely perception of the sound of the name includes the computational indices of the emotional and mental code. Integral assessment of naming is a condition of "acceptance-rejection" of a name for native speakers.

The calculation model is obtained from research on the assessment of psychophonetic equipment by native speakers of the Russian language. Phonemic inventory includes 46 phonemes, 33 letters, 56 stable "stressed/unstressed" combinations, 260 stable "soft/hard" combinations on 30 bipolar scales. An experimental study included testing native Russian speakers (1000 people) for the perception of allophones (basic, combinatorial, positional) on 30 scales. As a prototype, we used the Zhuravlev approach (Zhuravlev, 1981). Taking into account the frequency of sound in a language and a word, the place of sound and its stress, its method offers a formula for calculating the phonetic significance of a word:

$$F = \frac{\sum_i f_i k_i l_i \frac{P_{\max i}}{P_i}}{\sum_i k_i l_i} \qquad (1)$$

$P_{\max i}$ - maximum frequency of the sound in a given word, P_i - frequency of the sound in a word, f_i - the value of the semantic differential of the phoneme on the each l_i scale, k_i - the value of the place of sound (the first/ not the first phoneme in the word) and its stress (the stressed/ unstressed phoneme in the word).
We use this formula for Russian letters, except for the calculation f_i. In our case, instead of Osgood's semantic differential method on a linear scale, the method of semantic analysis on a relativistic scale is used. The relativistic scaling method takes into account not only the intensity, but also the rigidity of the assessment in mentality. The value of function f_i has not linear, but angular coordinates. The measurement method for f_i in the relativistic scale is described in the author's publication (Yanova, 2016).

The computational algorithm of phonetic code indexes:

- Calculation f_i for i - scale, N_i
- Selection scales with $f_i > 0{,}5$, N_j
- Volume Index $V = N_j / N_i * 100\%$ (2)
- Determination of the reference and experimental valence of the sign for the i - scale, K_i (number of theoretical matches/key to the test) and K_j (number of experimental matches/ key to the test).
- Consonance Index $C = K_j / K_i * 100\%$ (3)
- Sound Index $S = \sum_{j=1}^{Kj} f_j / \sum_{i=1}^{Ki} f_i * 100\%$ (4)

The calculation of mental code indexes is based on regression models (stepwise regression) from a list of 30 scales as independent variables for each dependent variable (mental code index).

4. RESULTS

Computing parameters of smart-test describe the phonetic and mental interpretation for a variant of nomination. Phonetic interpretation includes indexes of the phonetic code and reliable scales of the psychophonetic profile. Mental interpretation includes indexes of mental stereotypes of sound perception. Consider an experimental analysis example for a native and foreign name (Table 1, Figure 1).

Table 1. Consonance of first and last foreign name in Russian

'Donald Trump'	$f_i k$	*'Emmanuel Macron'*	$f_i k$
heavenly- *earthly*	9,65	*calm*-anxious	-6,83
feminine-*masculine*	9,16	cheap-*expensive*	5,21
light -*heavy*	7,86	cowardly-*brave*	5,15
cowardly-*brave*	7,60	add-on (*free*)	5,08
frivolous-*serious*	7,50	*clean*-dirty	-4,66
child-*adult*	6,43	feminine-*masculine*	4,29
stable-volatile	-6,98	*stable*-volatile	-4,30
obedient-moody	-5,28	heavenly-*earthly*	4,14
calm-anxious	-5,05	*aristocratic*-democratic	-3,84
sick-*healthy*	4,58	*obedient*-moody	-3,79
light-*dark*	4,48	*safe*-scary	-3,60
gentle-*coarse*	4,31	frivolous-*serious*	3,49
strict-free	-4,88	ugly-*beautiful*	3,37
cheap-*expensive*	3,78	sick-*healthy*	2,96
Volume Index	36,70	Volume Index	23,30
Consonance Index	70,00	Consonance Index	63,30
Sound Index	65,20	Sound Index	80,40
Gender Code	male	Gender Code	male
Sex Code	sexual	Sex Code	sexual
Adult Code	adult	Adult Code	adult
Native Code	uncertain	Native Code	uncertain
Connotation Code	neutral	Connotation Code	neutral

Computing parameters for phonetic code (%):

Volume Index (volume of the name) - index of the name recognition in Russian. This index characterizes the speed and ease of name recognition in the mentality. Volume index defines the name recognition code in the language of native speakers. It calculates the denotative value of the name (states of attributes by the denotation function).

Consonance Index (consonance of the name) - index of the name euphony in Russian. This index shows how expressive the name sounds to native speakers. It calculates the connotative value of the name. The index is determined by the number of matches of name positive attributions with the phonetic norm.

Sound Index (power of the name sounding) - index of the cultural influence. This index expresses the strength and stability of the name interpretation in Russian. It reveals the correspondence between the sound form and the lexical content of the name meaning. The index calculates the designative value of the name. Computing parameters for mental code (%):

Gender Code - compliance with gender stereotype of the name perception (masculine/female/ androgynous - no gender stereotype of sounding). Sex Code - sexual appeal in the sound of the name.

Adult Code – age stereotype of the name sounding: perceived as an adult, carries an assessment of respectful treatment, suggests distance in communication; perceived as childish, has an assessment of ease and informality in communication, assumes personal, not official distance in communication.

The specified code parameters are calculated on the basis of correlations with the corresponding scales (male, female, adult, childish, sexual). Name calculation integral parameters:

Native Code - matching the sound of the name to the mentality of the native language: native/foreign (identification/ no identification with the Russian mentality). This parameter defines the Russian language phonosemantic in the sound of the name. It is calculated as a correlation with the " "own or other" scale. Connotation Code - valiancy of the name sounding in Russian (positive, negative, neutral). The parameter is calculated by correlating the integral characteristics with the positive pole of the scales in the phonetic norm.

An experimental example of a computational model for native name in Russian:

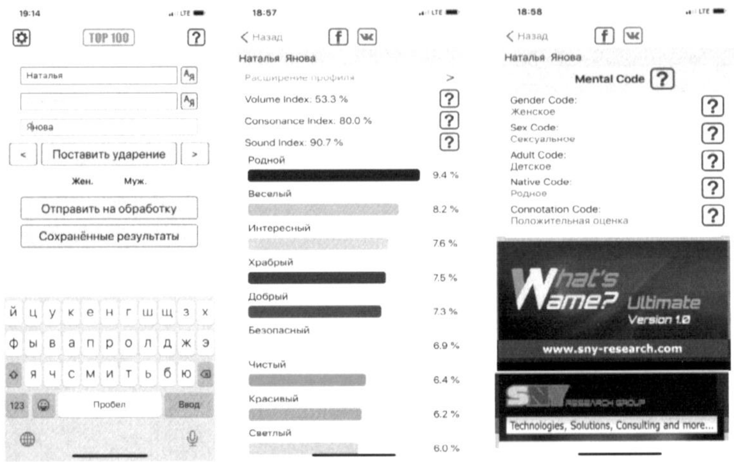

Figure 1. Mobile application: experimental example

5. CONCLUSION

The method for computing the perception and interpretation of names in Russian language allows explaining the hidden structure between lexicology and phonetics, to discover the semantic nature of language gaps associated with psychological function of voice information encoding. The computational model is carried out according to the sign structure that allows calculating such functions of name interpretation as recognition, euphony and influence. Checking the correspondence of the name to the basic mental stereotypes allows finding out the attitude to the name of a native Russian speaker. The significance of the work is connected with the theoretical and practical issues of onomastics, and is of particular significance for intercultural communication. The study helps to reveal for psychological differences between the nomination in different languages and cultures. It proposes not only the psychophonetic profile but also the structure of the psychophonetic meaning of the name. The user can independently assess the degree of congruence of perception and understanding of any name in Russian language. The know-how of the expert system consists of analyzing not only phonemes but also allophones. The system allows us to analyze of various options for nominations and choose among them the most successful one. Serious scientific theories and computational methods are becoming in demand for solving everyday problems.

REFERENCES

Andina, G. et al, 2015. Phonology and arithmetic in the language–calculation network. *In Brain and Language*, Vol. 143. pp. 97-105.

Chen, A. at al, 2018. Are lexical tones musical? Native language's influence on neural response to pitch in different domains. *In Brain and Language.* Vol. 180–182, pp. 31-41.

Sharp, B., Sedes, F., Lubaszewski,W., 2017. *Cognitive Approach to Natural Language Processing*. ISTE Press, Elsevier, London/Oxford, United Kingdom.

Strauss G.P., Allen D. N., 2008. Emotional intensity and categorization ratings for emotional and nonemotional words. *In Cognition and Emotion*, Vol.22, No.1, pp.114-133.

Suprun, A., Yanova, N., Nosov, K. 2015. Semantic Analysis of Meanings in Psycholinguistics. *In Journal of Russian and East European Psychology*, Vol.51, No.5, pp.170-172.

Tools SNY. Available at: http://www.sny-research.com/ (Accessed: 20 June 2020).

Wellman H.M., Liu D., 2004. Scaling of theory-of-mind tasks. *In Child Development*. Vol. 75, No.2, pp.523–541.

Yanova, N., 2016. Relativistic psychometrics in subjective scaling. *In Elsevier Procedia Computer Science*, V.102, pp. 82-89.

Zhuravlev A.P., 1981. *Phonetic meaning*. Publishing house of Leningrad State University, Leningrad, Russia.

AUTHOR INDEX

International Association for Development of the Information Society (IADIS)
Rua Sao Sebastiao Da Pedreira
No. 100, 30, 1050-209
Lisbon, Portugal

ISBN 978-1-7138-2273-8
9 781713 822738

CURRAN ASSOCIATES INC.
proceedings.com

International Conference on Computer Graphics, Visualization, Computer Vision and Image Processing (CGVCVIP2022); Connected Smart Cities (CSC2022); Big Data Analytics, Data Mining and Computational Intelligence (BIGDACI2021); Theory and Practice in Modern Computing (TPMC 2022)

Held at the 16th Multi-Conference on Computer Science and Information Systems (MCCSIS 2022)

Lisbon, Portugal
19-22 July 2022

iadis